The Study of F.......y
Education: A Source Book

The Study of Primary Education: A Source Book

VOLUME 1

Compiled by

Colin Richards

with

Rosemary Clayfield
Brenda Lofthouse

The Falmer Press

(A member of the Taylor & Francis Group)

London and Philadelphia

UK   The Falmer Press, Falmer House, Barcombe, Lewes, East Sussex, BN8 5DL

USA   The Falmer Press, Taylor & Francis Inc., 242 Cherry Street, Philadelphia, PA 19106-1906

First published in 1984

Library of Congress Cataloging in Publication Data

Main entry under title:

The Study of primary education.

  Includes bibliographies and indexes.
  1. Education, Elementary. 2. Education, Elementary—
Great Britain. I. Richards, Colin. II. Clayfield,
Rosemary. III. Lofthouse, Brenda.
LB1555.S887 1984 372 84-13825
ISBN 0-905273-64-8 (v. 1)
ISBN 0-905273-63-X (pbk. : v. 1)

Jacket design by Leonard Williams

Typeset in 11/13 Plantin
by Imago Publishing Ltd., Thame, Oxon.

Printed in Great Britain by Taylor & Francis (Printers) Ltd, Basingstoke

Contents

Contents

Contents

General Introduction

The nature of primary school teaching is difficult to appreciate for those who have no experience of it, except as a pupil. From a child's view, it seems straightforward enough. In reality, the task of the teacher is a complex and demanding one, requiring a wide range of skills and personal qualities, as well as extensive knowledge. Volumes 1 and 2 of these source books have been compiled to help in the professional development of primary school teachers, but the nature of the help they can give needs to be appreciated by potential readers.

In a recent report (*Postgraduate Certificate in Education Courses for Teachers in Primary and Middle Schools: A Further Consultative Report*), the Universities Council for the Education of Teachers spelt out five elements in the professional 'equipment' of teachers of younger children: (1) technique, (2) curricular knowledge, (3) professional knowledge, (4) personal and interpersonal skills and qualities, and (5) constructive revaluation. The compilers of these source books acknowledge the importance of all five elements but do not believe that any book can do justice to all of them. The source books focus on two: they contribute both to primary teachers' professional knowledge and to the development of their ability to re-evaluate their own experience and the enterprise of primary education itself. They do this by introducing readers to extracts from 'official' publications and from academic material which put primary education in context and which introduce readers to many of the important theoretical, yet professional, issues that need to be considered by practitioners. Most of the extracts focus directly on primary education or on primary-aged children; this was a major criterion used in selecting material for inclusion in the source books. The volumes are not intended to provide a complete course of study; they need to be supplemented, where possible, by students' general reading in educational and professional studies: psychology, sociology, history, philosophy, curriculum studies and management studies. However, though not intended as a substitute for students' reading of a wide range of original material, the source books acknowledge the constraints of time and of availability of such material, under which students have to study.

The books are intended to be used by students taking BEd or PGCE courses and by teachers in service, taking diploma courses in primary education. The material extracted can be used by tutors as a focus for seminars or as reading to back up lectures, and by students as a source for essays or as a starting point for further reading. The books are not intended to be read straight through from cover to cover but can be used selectively and flexibly at various stages in the course. For convenience, the extracts have been organized into a number of sections. The nature of these sections does not necessarily indicate how the compilers believe that professional knowledge should be taught. The books, in fact, presuppose no one way of providing students with the necessary professional knowledge and understanding.

Volume 1 comprises extracts which examine primary education from historical, ideological, philosophical, sociological and psychological perspectives. Volume 2 deals with teaching studies, curriculum studies, and roles and relationships. Beacuse of limitations of space, primary education has been confined to the education of children aged 5 to 11, though the compilers acknowledge that in so doing they may offend teachers in nursery or middle schools who regard themselves, justifiably, as primary practitioners.

The compilers would like to thank the following for their help in suggesting extracts for inclusion: Peter Moran, Neville West, Jim Campbell, Iain Rodger, Bill Percival, Phil Hegarty, Cedric Cullingford, Alan Blyth, Paul Harling, Maurice Craft and Alan Coulson. Users of the source books are invited to send in further suggestions for additions to, or deletions from, the extracts included.

The contents of these source books indicate the demands made on primary teachers in just two of the five elements outlined above. They also illustrate that the professional development of teachers is almost as complex and demanding a task as primary teaching itself.

Colin Richards
Rosemary Clayfield
Brenda Lofthouse
January 1984

Compilers' Notes

In each of the sections of Volume 1 except the last, the extracts have been chosen and the editorial material written by Colin Richards. Rosemary Clayfield has chosen and edited most of the material in the last section of the book. Brenda Lofthouse has been responsible for the general administration involved in the compilation and for some of the detailed copy-editing.

In editing the material the compilers have:

(1) provided their own title for each extract;
(2) standardized the format of the references;
(3) deleted all cross-references in the original text;
(4) placed editorial insertions in squared brackets within the extract itself.

The source of the material is given in detail immediately beneath the heading of each extract. The page numbers in the detailed reference refer to each of the pages in the original text, from which passages making up the extract have been taken. For example, if the reference refers to pages 2, 2–3, and 3, then one of the passages making up the extract has been taken from page 2 of the original text, one passage has been taken from a piece beginning on page 2 and running on to page 3, and a third passage has been taken from elsewhere on page 3.

In the editorial material introducing each section and each extract, all the page numbers in brackets within the text refer to other pages within the source book, so as to aid cross-referencing. Any quotation used in the editorial material, unless otherwise referenced, can be found in the text from which the extract has been taken.

Acknowledgements

The publishers are grateful to the following for permission to reproduce copyright material:

George Allen and Unwin for GRETTON, J. and JACKSON, M. (1976) *William Tyndale*; NEWSOME, J. and E. (1977) *Perspectives on School at Seven Years Old*; BRUNER, J. (1974) *Beyond the Information Given*.

The family of C. Schiller for SCHILLER, C. (1979) *In His Own Words*, in GRIFFEN-BEALE, C. (Ed.), A.C. Black.

The editor and publishers of the *British Educational Research Journal* for HARTLEY, D. (1978) 'Sex and social class: A case-study of an infant school', 4, 2, Carfax.

Cambridge University Press for MARSHALL, S. (1963) *An Experiment in Education*.

Critical Quarterly Society for COX, C. and DYSON, A. (1968) 'Fight for education'; COX, C. and DYSON, A. (1969) *Black Paper Three*.

J.M. Dent and Sons Ltd. for Cox, C. and BOYSON, R. (1975) *Black Paper 1975*.

The editor and publishers of *Education 3–13* for BREARLEY, M. (1974) 'Open schooling: An introduction', 2, 2; FROOME, S. (1974) 'Back on the right track', 2, 1; WILSON, P. (1974) 'Plowden aims', 2, 1.

Falmer Press/The Open University Press for DALE, R. (1981) 'Control, accountability and William Tyndale', in DALE, R. *et al.* (1981) *Politics, Patriarchy and Practice*, Vol. 2.

Fontana Paperbacks for DONALDSON, M. (1978) *Children's Minds*; RUBIN, Z. (1980) *Children's Friendships*, William Collins.

Granada Publishing for SCHEFFER, H. (1968) 'Identification', in LUNZER, E. and MORRIS, J., *Development in Human Learning*.

Heinemann for EDWARDS, A. (1976) *Language in Culture and Class*; FLOUD, J.; HALSEY, A., and MARTIN, F. (1956) *Social Class and Education Opportunity*, *Heinemann Educational Books*.

The Controller of Her Majesty's Stationery Office for extracts from BOARD OF EDUCATION (1926) *The Education of the Adolesecent*; BOARD OF EDUCATION (1931) *The Primary School*; BOARD OF EDUCATION (1933) *Infant and Nursery Schools*; BOARD OF EDUCATION (1937) *A Handbook of Suggestions for Teachers*; CENTRAL ADVISORY COMMITTEE (1967) *Children and their Primary Schools*; EDUCATION ACT (1944); *Education in Schools: A Consultative Document* (1977); HALSEY, A. (Ed.)

(1972) *Educational Priority*, Vol. 1; *A Language for Life* (1975); *Mathematics 5-11: A Handbook of Suggestions* (1979); *Primary Education in England: A Survey by HM Inspectors of Schools* (1978).

Holt, Rinehart and Winston for AUSUBEL, D.; NOVAK, J.; and HANESIAN, H. (1978) *Educational Psychology: A Cognitive View*, 2nd ed., CBS College Publishing.

Longman for DAVIE, R. *et al.* (1972) *From Birth to Seven*, Longman Group Limited.

MIT for VIGOTSKY (1962) *Thought and Language*, MIT Press.

NFER for GOODACRE, E. (1968) *Teachers and Their Pupils' Home Backgrounds*, NFER-Nelson.

The editor and publishers of Paedagogica Europaea for TAMBURINNI, J. *Play and Intellectual Development*, 9, 1.

Penguin Books Ltd. for MIDWINTER, E. (1972) *Priority Education*; WOLFF, S. (1981) *Children under Stress*; WRIGHT, D. (1971) *The Psychology of Moral Behaviour*.

Martin Robinson for BANTOCK, G. (1980) *Dilemmas of the Curriculum*.

Routledge and Kegan Paul for BERNSTEIN, B. (1971) *Class Codes and Control*, Vol. 1; BERNSTEIN, B. (1975) *Class, Codes and Control*, Vol. 3, Towards a Theory of Educational Transmission, 2nd ed.; BLYTH, W.A.L. (1965) *English Primary Education*; DEARDEN, R. (1968) *The Philosophy of Primary Education*; DEARDEN, R. (1969) *The Aims of Primary Education*, from PETERS, R. (Ed.) *Perspectives on Plowden*; DEARDEN, R. (1976) *Problems in Primary Education*; GALTON, M. *et al.* (1980) *Inside the Primary Classroom*; NASH, R. (1973) *Classrooms Observed*; PETERS, R. (1969) *A Recognisable Philosophy of Education*, from PETERS, R. (Ed.) *Perspectives on Plowden*; ROBINSON, P. (1981) *Perspectives on the Sociology of Education*; SHARP, R. and GREEN, R. (1975) *Education and Social Control*; WHITE, J. (1982) *The Aims of Education Restated*; WILSON, P. (1971) *Interest and Discipline in Education*.

Ward Lock for ISAACS, N. (1961) *The Growth and Understanding in the Young Child*, Ward Lock Educational.

Wiley for KING, R. (1978) *All Things Bright and Beautiful?* John Wiley and Sons.

Writers and Readers for KITWOOD, T. and MACEY, M. (1977) *Mind that Child*, Writers and Readers Publishing Cooperative Society.

1 *Primary Education: Historical Perspectives*

Introduction

For most of those who teach in them and for all those who learn in them, the place of primary schools within the educational system and within society more generally is rarely, if ever, seriously questioned. Teachers view them as the institutional expression of the state's concern to educate the young up to the age of 11; children see them as part of the 'natural' order of things. Yet primary, as opposed to elementary, education and schools to foster this kind of education are comparatively recent developments within the educational system of England and Wales. As a stage of education, primary education was formally established by the 1944 Education Act (pp. 34–36), though it had been government policy since 1928 to establish schools specifically for children of this age-group. During its short history, primary education has had to contend with a number of formidable problems in its attempts to create a distinct identity, as the second paper in this section documents. These included the legacy of the elementary school tradition with its relatively narrow, instrumental emphasis on the three Rs; the selective role assigned to primary schools and symbolized by the '11+' examination; the vast expansion followed by spectacular contraction in the number of children of primary school age; and the inability of the sector to attract resources on a scale comparable to secondary and higher education. Despite these difficulties it has established itself as a distinct, and in some ways distinctive, sector, though with very considerable internal variations in 'philosophy' and practice, as the papers in the second section of the reader reveal.

The material in this section has been chosen to illustrate developments and landmarks within primary education, not within elementary education (in relation to which there is a more extensive historical literature). For a short overall view of the 'pre-history' of primary education, readers are referred to Blyth's (1965) essay, 'Three traditions in English primary education' (in *English Primary Education*, Vol. 2, Routledge and Kegan Paul), from which the first extract in this section is taken. The second extract, Simon's essay on the 'Evolution of the primary school', is an important analysis — to date, the only published account of the development of primary education since it was first proposed as a separate stage in education by the Hadow Report of 1926 (pp. 22–23). Many of the remaining extracts are from government publications documenting the establishment of, and the official thinking behind, these new institutions. Prominent among these documents were the Hadow Reports of 1931 and 1933 (pp. 24–27 and 28–29) which did much to shape the development of primary education immediately before and after the Second World War, and the Plowden Report of 1967 (pp. 37–39) which provided more up-to-date 'footnotes' to Hadow, almost forty years on. This section also contains three extracts from the Black Papers outlining the kind of criticisms levelled against primary schools post-Plowden, and two pieces from official publications attempting a more balanced appraisal of the strengths and weaknesses of primary education. Simon's essay makes brief reference to the notorious William Tyndale 'affair' which helped fuel the public disquiet; some of the main issues associated with that cause célèbre are discussed by Gretton and Jackson (pp. 45–50). The section concludes with a brief analysis (based on the findings of the HMI Primary Survey of 1978 of what changes have characterized primary schools during the last two decades — a theme also taken up by Simon in his (1981) essay, 'The primary school revolution: Myth or reality?' (in *Research and Practice in the Primary Classroom*, Simon, B. and Willcocks, J. (Eds), London, Routledge and Kegan Paul).

Three Traditions in English Primary Education

(From Blyth, W., 1965, *English Primary Education*, Vol. 2, London, Routledge and Kegan Paul, pp. 20, 20–1, 30, 34–5, 35, 40–1, 41, 42, 43.)

This first extract has been included for two main reasons. Firstly, it serves to remind readers that primary education was not created from nothing by either the 1944 Education Act or the Hadow Reports of 1926, 1931 and 1933. Schools catering for children of primary school age had a long history, though state provision for this age group dates back only to the nineteenth century. As Blyth argues, primary schools grew 'mainly, if tardily' out of elementary schools, though other formative influences are distinguished in his analysis. Secondly, the extract indicates that competing views of primary education (such as those featured in the next section) have a history and are not simply the result of contemporary or near-contemporary circumstances and thinking. The author's historical analysis neatly complements the ideological analysis presented later in this book. A particularly valuable feature is the delineation of the 'preparatory' tradition — a tradition neglected elsewhere in this reader and in most contemporary discussion of primary education.

English society was not built round its schools. Whatever may have been true of newer nations such as the United States, whose social evolution has been mainly confined to the age of widespread education, in England social development has in general been concurrent with, or prior to, educational development. Consequently, primary education has taken institutional shape within English society, and it has done so in three interacting but distinguishable traditions. These bear some comparison with the developments in other Western European countries, but also display features peculiar to England. The first two of these traditions are much older than the third. They may be termed respectively *elementary* and *preparatory*. The third tradition is comparatively recent in origin but differs from the other two in that primary education is regarded as something for its own sake, a common right of all children in the Midlands of childhood. This will be referred to as the *developmental* tradition....

[The author begins by considering the elementary tradition.]

...Occasionally, one still hears the term 'elementary' used as though it were currently valid, often by those who never frequented elementary schools when it was in fact valid. Legally, it was intentionally drummed out by the Education Act, 1944, and its passing was acclaimed most joyfully by those who had been most closely associated with it. It had to go, if there was to be any true primary education in the modern sense. One can — we did — have both elementary schools and secondary schools, but one cannot have both elementary schools and primary schools. For elementary schools are a whole educational process in themselves and one which is by definition limited and by implication inferior; a low plateau, rather than the foothills of a complete education.

Yet English primary education grew mainly, if tardily, out of English elementary education with its characteristic emphasis on the basic skills, and in some ways it still bears the marks of its ancestry....
[Alan Blyth goes on to discuss the development of the elementary tradition beginning with the song schools of the middle ages, through the elementary schools of the sixteenth century, and the 'whole complex of dame schools, parochial schools and private schools' of the seventeenth and eighteenth centuries, to the widespread provision of elementary schools in the nineteenth century.]
...The term 'elementary' is legally defunct but it still has a social meaning. The term 'preparatory' was never legally established; but it too, has been invested by tradition with a very precise and important meaning which is still current and influential. In one sense indeed it is nearer to the developmental than to the elementary tradition, for it does at least take some account of sequence rather than of social status as a principle of differentiation. But at the same time it implies in name what 'junior elementary' often implied in fact, that the education of younger children is mainly to be conceived in terms of preparation for the later stages of education rather than as a stage in its own right. In practice, the preparatory tradition has struck an uneasy compromise between the two meanings emphasising both the developmental and the strictly preparatory function....
[He sketches the history of the preparatory tradition and suggests that its growth in the nineteenth century was related to two major developments in secondary education: the reform and growth of the public boarding schools for boys, and the revival and extension of day grammar schools both for boys and for girls. By the early twentieth century...]
...the preparatory tradition had become embedded in the upper and middle sections of English society while a few lower-middle and occasionally even prosperous working-class families also adhered to it. Whatever its diversity, it had one element in common, namely the assumption that post-preparatory education (if that phrase may be pardoned) was a normal expectation of childhood within higher socio-economic groups and that the education of younger children up to the age of ten in the preparatory departments of the girls' grammar schools, eleven in the private schools, or (exceeding the Midlands range) twelve or thirteen in the boys' preparatory

schools, should be geared to what was to follow. For prep-school boys indeed, the next phase in the life cycle was often regarded as its zenith, with regrettable results. For girls, with the battle for equality still before them, the status of educated adulthood, married or not, probably exercised a greater appeal. But for them all, there was the incentive to look at least one step ahead with a justified expectation of educational and other advantage. In the preparatory tradition, real education was beginning at just the same age as, in the elementary tradition, full-time education was assumed to be ending.

The twentieth century has seen a complex interaction between these two traditions but this has in its turn been overshadowed by the impact on both of the third, or developmental, approach. . . .

Alongside the two existing traditions, there has emerged in England a third which is bound neither by the limitations of an education felt or intended to be cheap and inferior, nor by the demands imposed by its own sequel. This may be referred to as the *developmental* tradition, because its principles are based on those of child development. Its origins cannot be sought earlier than the eighteenth century, for that was when education itself began to acquire some form of autonomy. On the whole, the developmental tradition has worked its way into the matrix of English social life from the periphery as is customary in many instances of social change. Indeed, much of its motivation has come from overseas, but it has been built into English institutions through a long period of individual endeavour, culminating in activity sponsored more directly from the centre. . . .

[A number of formative influences on this tradition are traced during the nineteenth and the early twentieth centuries. The author distinguishes five factors which gave impetus to the developmental tradition during the first half of this century.]

. . . The first of these was the growth of psychology which was becoming established as part of the general intellectual climate of the age. It was related both to the over-confident extension of mental testing, itself largely conducted within the elementary schools, but also to the new horizons in hormic and developmental psychology. At the same time, there developed a further facet of the teachings of Dewey, namely his emphasis on the curricular importance of collective preparation for change, and on liberation from the traditional thought-patterns which could be regarded as undemocratic whether in the home, the school or society at large. Third, and linked with the previous came the great wave of emancipation that characterised the years after 1918. Children were to be given the chance to be themselves at any age and in concert with their peers of both sexes. This trend, often associated with experimental schools, emphasised the positive support which the developmental tradition gave to co-education. A fourth factor which probably influenced the changing conception of primary education was the growth of what is now rather loosely described as the 'Welfare State.' The fifth factor is an extension of a process already mentioned. The rapid growth of the concept of 'secondary education for all', officially enunciated for the Labour Party by Tawney (1923) and soon afterwards to some extent by all parties led to a concurrent definition of primary education as the preceding stage. In one sense, it was thus 'preparatory'. . . .

[Schools catering for children of junior age became the battleground for a number of forces, especially those of child development and those of the 'scholarship' examination. The developmental tradition was given a great boost when . . .] the Consultative Committee of the Board of Education prepared the report on *The Primary School* (1931). It was a consistent and radical-flavoured document which took its stand squarely on the developmental tradition and recognised the significance of the changes which were taking place. It paid due, though not excessive, regard to the philosophy of Dewey and his followers. . . it espoused and reinforced unhesitatingly the nascent belief that children aged seven to eleven should be educated in a social institution with an autonomous quality of its own. Thus it firmly annexed the education of children throughout the Midlands years to the developmental rather than the elementary or preparatory tradition. This Report was followed two years later by its counterpart on *Infant and Nursery Schools*, but this, though equally forthright, was less of an innovation because it dealt with the heartland of the developmental tradition rather than its advancing frontier.

From this point onwards, the basis of a separate developmental tradition in primary education has been incontrovertibly laid.

[Writing at about the time when the Plowden Committee was set up (1964–5), the author concludes:]

. . . Recent developments have thus shown that the developmental tradition continues to gain ground, not only because of changes within the schools but also on account of social change in English society itself. Meanwhile, it must be remembered that the preparatory tradition continues to flourish modified only in part, with a clientèle that is numerically insignificant but socially preponderant, while the divisions within the teaching force, which cannot yet be confidently termed a profession, still run socially deep. The elementary tradition, too, lurks in many corners of the public educational system and is perpetuated by many instances of social inertia. Thus the developmental tradition is still far from unchallenged and the common primary school, for both sexes and all abilities and classes, is in practice a chimera. Any study of contemporary primary education which overlooked the continuing influences of the older traditions would present an oversimplified and distorted picture. On the other hand, any study which belittled the new and in a quite genuine sense revolutionary quality of the developmental tradition would ignore one of the greatest potentialities for wholesome growth which exists in English society today.

Reference

TAWNEY, R. (1923) *Secondary Education for All: A Policy for Labour*, London, Allen and Unwin.

The Evolution of the Primary School

(From Galton, M.; Simon, B.; and Croll, P., 1980, *Inside the Primary Classroom*, London, Routledge and Kegan Paul, pp. 29–42.)

The chapter which forms this extract clearly and succinctly puts contemporary primary education in context by providing an outline of its development in four stages, and by drawing attention to the forces, legislation and events which have shaped its character. It traces the roots of primary education in the elementary school, acknowledges the longstanding provision of separate infant schools or departments in some areas, and documents how primary schools arose out of a concern for the needs of *older* children. It discusses a number of important influences on the primary school:

1 the weight of the elementary school tradition with its concern for literacy, numeracy, conformity and obedience;
2 the scholarship examination, later to be called the 11+ examination, for which the primary school prepared so many of its pupils;
3 the views of psychologists such as Burt which justified streaming and selection at 11;
4 the perspectives of Froebel, Montessori and the New Education Fellowship which permeated training colleges and promoted a liberal romantic view of primary education; and
5 the abolition of selection at eleven in many local education authorities leading to a liberalization of primary education.

The chapter clearly demonstrates its thesis that 'primary education, very much the poor relation in the educational system, has been in a state of almost continuous transition throughout its short history, the result both of changes at the secondary level and of changing approaches to the education of young children'. With its overview, this extract forms a good introduction to each of the remaining extracts in this section of the reader.

Although several million children are now educated in separate primary schools of one kind or another, these have a comparatively recent and certainly a short history. This form of schooling was first accepted as official policy only some fifty years ago, in 1928. It then took some forty years to implement. Not until the mid-1960s were *all* children between the ages of five and eleven educated in separate 'primary' schools. No sooner was this achieved than new changes were brought about by new thinking and legislation. The Education Act of 1964 made possible the establishment of 'middle' schools covering the ages of nine to thirteen. To complicate matters further, only three years later, the Central Advisory Councils for Education for both England and Wales recommended that 'middle' schools for children aged eight to twelve should be the norm. Both these options have been taken up by a number of local authorities, with the approval of the Department of Education and Science, largely to facilitate comprehensive secondary reorganization.

'Primary' education today, therefore, in spite of its relatively recent establishment, is already again in a state of flux. What had become the norm (infant schools or departments for children aged five to seven followed by a junior school to eleven) has already been phased out in some parts of the country, to be replaced by one of two alternative systems, (i) 'first', sometimes called 'lower', schools for children aged five to nine, followed by 'middle' (nine to thirteen) and 'upper' schools (thirteen to eighteen), or (ii) first schools for children aged five to eight, followed by 'middle' (eight to twelve) and upper schools for the twelve to eighteens (or sometimes twelve to sixteen and sixteen to eighteen). These three systems now exist in parallel in different parts of the country.... It is essential, if we are to place existing schools and their practices in context, to gain some understanding of their development, of the forces that have shaped their character and procedures. Only historical analysis can throw light on the changing forms of primary education, explicate the reasons for the emergence of this particular institutional form, and illuminate its evolution both in terms of practice and of theory....

Origin of the Junior School (1870–1926)

The concept that education below eleven should be defined as 'primary', and that above as 'post-primary' (or 'secondary') first appeared in an official document in the Report of the Consultative Committee to the Board of Education, known after its chairman, as the 'Hadow Report' (Hadow, 1926). The proposal was adopted as national policy in 1928. Even at that stage, however, the discussion was largely conceptual. Only with the Education Act of 1944 was a public system of education finally brought into being in England and Wales which established, in statutory terms at least, the reality of two stages of education, primary and secondary. It is in this sense that the 'primary' school in this country has a short history, and, as we have seen, the concept of 'primary' education is already somewhat confused only some thirty to forty years later.

Before 1944 the great majority of children of the present primary age range (five to eleven) were in *elementary* schools; they were educated together with older children in 'all-age' schools within the elementary system. This system was established, specifically and deliberately, for one section of society only — that is, for the working class. The original objectives of universal, compulsory education, established by 1880, were then still defined in terms of the 'standard' system brought in by 'payment by results' in 1862, though this system began to be modified after 1870. Payment by results focused the teacher's attention very specifically on the three R's; the objective was the achievement of an elementary level of literacy and numeracy by the working-class population. Clearly there were other objectives as well, though not so overtly defined; specifically those which might be described as social-disciplinary, the achievement of which was sought through what is now referred to as the 'hidden curriculum' rather than through the content of instruction (acceptance of the teacher's authority, of the need for punctuality, obedience, conformity, and so on). It is worth noting that the system of payment by results was modified in the 1880s to put greater emphasis on this latter aspect, as compared with the three R's.

The elementary system, in its origins and indeed up to the mid-1920s, did not include any special provision for younger children below the age of eleven, with the exception of infant schools and departments covering the age range five to seven in some areas. These, which constituted a unique feature of the English educational system, were connected with the early start of compulsory education. At the age of five it was, in 1870, and is still, below the compulsory age in other advanced industrial countries (in France, Germany, Sweden, the age is six, in the USSR it is seven). This early age of entry was partly a product of the establishment, from 1870 and even earlier, as an accepted and essential part of the system of infant schools and departments catering for children below the age of six or seven and including many children aged three and four.

This tradition is normally said to owe its origin to Robert Owen's famous 'infant school' at New Lanark in the early 1820s and the subsequent development of such schools by Wilderspin and others in the 1820s to 1840s. But, by the 1860s and 1870s the main objective in separating out the infants, it appears, was to ensure that the teaching of the older children should not be unduly disturbed by what Matthew Arnold (and others) referred to as the 'babies'. Originally the infant school or department passed on its children to the elementary school at six, since the first 'standard' examination (standard I), brought in in 1862 under payment by results, was designed for children aged six to seven, but the code of regulations issued in 1871 created an infant stage below standard I for the five to seven age range. Thus the age of seven became the age of transfer from the infant school (or department) to the elementary school as a whole (Whitbread, 1972, p. 41). In the evolution of the concept of the junior school, the separate existence of infant schools or departments, defining the age of entry, is clearly important. However it must not be assumed that infant schools or departments were ubiquitous; in 1930 they accounted for approximately half the children aged five to seven, the rest were still in all-age elementary schools catering for children aged five (and below) to fourteen.

If the existence of infant schools and departments cut off the younger children, developments in the education system, particularly around and after the turn of the century, began to demarcate an upper limit of eleven or twelve, or at least to indicate that such a demarcation might, given the conditions, become a practical possibility. There were a number of reasons for this, all relating to the growth of new forms of 'secondary' schools following the 1902 Education Act. The scholarship and free place system, established in 1907 (but existing earlier), created a link between the elementary and secondary systems by which the latter recruited pupils from the elementary schools at around the age of ten to twelve. The same was the case with the new selective 'central' schools within the elementary system, established in London, Manchester and elsewhere from about 1910. So the age of around eleven was becoming accepted as the age of transfer to secondary and other schools already before the First World War. An impetus was given to this by the Education Act of 1918 which stated that special provision should be made for 'the older or more intelligent children' in elementary schools by means of central schools, extended courses, and the like, and by the actions taken (or proposed) by local authorities under the Act in the early 1920s. This set the scene for the proposals of the Hadow Report in 1926 for the division of the elementary school system into two stages, junior and senior, with a break at eleven for all. Here was the real origin of the junior school, or of the division between primary and post-primary education.

It is worth noting at this point that the motivation for this fundamental change did not arise from any serious consideration of the needs and character of children aged seven to eleven (or five to eleven). It arose solely from a consideration of the needs of the older (senior) children; and indeed it is symptomatic that the crucial report on which action was taken, setting up separate junior or primary schools, was entitled *The Education of the Adolescent* (1926). The origins and significance of this report have been analysed elsewhere (Simon, 1974) so will not be gone into here; particularly since the establishment of the junior school as a separate institution was very much a by-product of the report, and little of any significance is said there on the topic. However, it is worth noting that, although in some of the large urban areas junior departments (so called) of all-age schools had already been established as a consequence of the developments mentioned above, by the mid-1920s, when the Consultative Committee reported, only some 6 per cent of children aged seven to eleven were in such departments. All the rest, the great bulk of the children in those age groups, were still organized as they had been since 1870, in all-age schools catering for children aged five or seven to fourteen. These normally were organized as separate boys' and girls' departments, usually with a mixed infants' school as the base. In large urban schools of the kind built by the School Boards following the Education Act of 1870, the infants' school was on the ground floor, the boys' and girls' departments on the floors above. In rural areas there would usually be a separate infants' class with one, two or more other classes according to the size of the school taking children up to fourteen.

Developments Following the Hadow Report

This, then, marks the beginning of the separate junior school as national policy; emerging, as it were, unforeseen and as a by-product, from the womb of the elementary system, and bearing, at least in its origin, all the marks of that system in terms of cheapness, economy, large classes, obsolete, ancient and inadequate buildings, and so on. With reorganization after 1928 (when the Hadow Report's recommendations were accepted by the government) the usual practice was to provide new buildings, where possible, for the older pupils in the new senior elementary schools, since these needed facilities for specialist teaching, for the first time including laboratories, craft rooms, gymnasia, art rooms and so on. So reorganization went ahead, though very unevenly in different parts of the country. Over-all, 48 per cent of children aged seven to eleven were in separate junior schools (or departments) by 1938.

Only in 1931 was attention focused specifically for the first time on 'The Primary School' with the publication of a report by the Consultative Committee with that title. Yet even here it is interesting to note the terms of the reference to that Committee. This was simply 'to enquire and report as to the courses of study suitable for children (other than children in infants departments) up to the age of eleven *in elementary schools* with special reference to the needs of children in rural areas' (our italics).

Reference has already been made to the original, narrow objectives embodied in the elementary school tradition; the strictly instrumental approach relating to literacy and numeracy and to its social disciplinary aspects. All this is well known and is explicable in terms of the original social function of this school system. Nevertheless, what might be called peripheral, or external theoretical influences were beginning to make some impact on the system from the turn of the century, or even before. There was, first, the kindergarten movement, based on Froebel's theory and practice, which began to penetrate the schools from the 1890s, involving the concepts of 'natural development', 'spontaneity', and so on; even if contemporary analysis, for instance, an investigation carried through by a group of women HMIs in 1905 (Board of Education, 1905), indicated that Froebel's system was applied in an extremely mechanistic manner; that is, was adapted to Board school drill practice, so losing its educative significance. Nevertheless the ideas were there, and the movement institutionalized with the foundation of the Froebel Institute and other colleges for the training of teachers on Froebelian principles, often financed by wealthy philanthropists interested in transforming middle-class educational practice for young children.

This was followed, after the turn of the century, by the considerable impact made by Dr Maria Montessori, with her emphasis on structured learning, sense training and individualization. Both influences were more strongly felt in the infant schools than in other sections of the elementary system (their main impact was probably felt in middle-class private schools). Perhaps more immediately relevant to the maintained school system was the work of Margaret McMillan, with her emphasis on improving hygienic conditions, overcoming children's physical defects, and providing an 'appropriate' environment for young children. This work and that of her sister, Rachel, was certainly influential in bringing new concepts concerning activity and creativity again largely to the infant school but nevertheless affecting teachers and others in the elementary school system as a whole. Finally, given this brief survey, the year 1911 saw the publication of *What Is and What Might Be* by Edmond Holmes, ex-Chief Inspector of Elementary Schools; the first striking manifesto of the 'progressives' in its total condemnation of the arid drill methods of the contemporary elementary school, and its espousal of the enlightened, all-sided, humanist approach of the model village school-teacher Egeria (who is said actually to have existed). The publication of this book marks the start of the 'new' education; ideas to be crystallized and institutionalized with the foundation of the New Education Fellowship shortly after the First World War (Selleck, 1972).

In the immediate post-war period ideas of this kind were strongly represented in theoretical discussion on the education of young children; and partially implemented in the practice of those schools which turned towards group work and individualization. This was a central feature of the so-called Sub Dalton Plan embodying some, at least, of John Dewey's ideas which, paradoxically, although emanating from the USA, was implemented to a far greater extent in British primary schools (Kimmins and Rennie, 1932, pp. 82–4). Another potent new influence from the early 1930s was Susan Isaacs, whose two books, on the intellectual and social development of young children, were published at this stage (Isaacs, 1930, 1933).

It was these aspects that were stressed in the Consultative Committee's report on *The Primary School* (1931). This emphasized the need for a completely new approach to primary education which, it was argued, was now made possible with the break at eleven. To give a sense of this report it is best to quote directly from the section on the curriculum for the primary stage of education (pp. 139–40). The report stresses the need 'to supply the pupils with what is essential to their healthy growth, physical, intellectual and moral', adding the much-quoted view that 'the curriculum of the primary school is to be thought of in terms of activity and experience, rather than of knowledge to be acquired and facts to be stored'. The importance of physical training, including training in 'good carriage and graceful movement' is emphasized, as is the fundamental importance of language training, with 'systematic training in oral expression'. Aesthetic sensibility must be cultivated through drawing, craft work and music, together with the development of manual skills. The traditional practice of dividing the matter of primary instruction into separate 'subjects', taught in distinct lessons 'should be re-considered' — central topics may be a useful alternative. Although the report emphasizes that provision should be made 'for an adequate amount of "drill" in reading, writing and arithmetic', over-all emphasis clearly reflects the new approaches; especially in the broader aims and objectives now conceived as relevant to primary education.

The 1931 report, though favourably received, made little impact at the time. Of course, very few separate 'junior' schools, as such, had by then been brought into being, while as M.L. Jacks put it, 'the conditions necessary for its implementation were almost wholly lacking' (Ross, 1960, p. 33). In 1932, for instance, well over 50 per cent of children of primary school age were in classes with over forty pupils. However this report, in general, certainly reflected the outlook of the 'new', child-centred, 'progressive' approach to education even if, as we shall see, it strongly recommended the introduction of streaming into the new junior schools. R.J.W. Selleck argues, in *English Primary Education and the Progressives, 1914 to 1939*, that the approach of the 'new' educationalists, somewhat watered down from its wilder manifestations in the early 1920s, had, by 1939, become the official orthodoxy; propagated in training colleges, Board of Education in-service courses, by local authority inspectors, and the like. How far it affected actual *practice* in the schools is, however, another matter.

The Selective Function of the Junior School

The primary school, though now envisaged in the sense outlined above, was, however, subject to sharply contradictory influences. While the 1931 report developed the idea of universal popular education of a new, broader, child-centred, activity type, the actual emergence of the junior school on a mass scale, which only took place *after* the Second World War, coincided precisely with the crystallization of the school system as primarily a sorting, classifying, selective mechanism; a function in which the junior school played a central role and one which reached its height, in this form, as late as the mid-1950s, just at the time when 'Hadow reorganization' was rapidly being completed throughout the country. The 1931 report, basing itself on the psychology of individual differences, and fully accepting the advice of psychometrists who at that time asserted the *absolute* determination of 'intelligence' by hereditary or genetic factors (Cyril Burt and Percy Nunn were both co-opted on the drafting committee) strongly advocated the necessity of streaming as the basic form of internal school organization for all primary schools large enough to form parallel classes in each age group. New schools, where possible, were to be designed on the basis of a 'treble track' system.

With the completion of reorganization following the Second World War, and the greatly increased competition for grammar school places which the 1944 Act, in spite of providing 'secondary education for all', did nothing to alleviate, streaming spread, in Brian Jackson's words 'with barely credible rapidity throughout the country' (Jackson, 1964, p. 150). Since the selection examination consisted normally of 'objective' tests in the three R's plus 'Intelligence', this inevitably provided the main objective for primary school education *as a whole* (*all* children were now entered for this examination, whatever their stream or educational level; this was regarded as essential to allow 'equality of opportunity'). So, in spite of the call for freedom and quite new approaches in the 1931 report, and in spite of a move in this direction in the late 1940s and some modification of practice in different parts of the country, in general the old elementary school syndrome which that report had regarded as quite out-moded, inevitably persisted, if in a somewhat modernized guise. The basic class teaching approach, with the main emphasis on numeracy and literacy, continued in the new junior schools after the Second World War; in fact the tradition derived from 1870 was still dominant. The continued existence of large classes through the late 1940s and 1950s reinforced this method of school organization with its related pedagogy.

From its inception, the junior school has always had a dual role in the sense that before the Second World War a few of its pupils (about 10 per cent) were selected for the secondary school, while the majority remained in the elementary system either in the same school (where it was 'all-age') or in the senior school. This remained the case in the new dispensation following the 1944 Education Act, the senior schools being re-named 'secondary modern'. The tripartite system then established (including secondary technical schools) gave enhanced importance to the 11-plus examination, and reinforced the system of streaming which had success in this examination (in terms of gaining places in grammar schools) as one of its objectives.

It may be thought that the concepts underlying the 'child-centred' approach, and those underlying streaming are contradictory, yet both were accepted by the Consultative Committee in the report on *The Primary School* (1931) (as in other reports in the inter-war years). However this is not necessarily the case. Child-centred approaches, particularly Froebelian, were based fundamentally on the notion that the child's inborn characteristics must be allowed to flower; that the school's function is, in Froebel's words, 'to make the inner outer' (Bowen, 1903, p. 98). Hence the emphasis on natural, spontaneous development. The school's role is to provide optimum conditions for such development. This ties in closely with the views of the dominant school of psychology in the inter-war years (psychometry) whose main tenet, as mentioned above, was that the child's most important mental characteristic, defined as 'Intelligence' (seen as a measure of intellectual potential) was *wholly* fixed and inborn, and was not subject to change as a result of educational or any other experiences. What was necessary was to provide an education appropriate to the child's inborn, and measurable, intelligence level. Thus Susan Isaacs, an influential proponent of 'activity methods', as they were called, strongly insisted on the necessity for differentiation of young children through streaming based on 'Intelligence' (Isaacs, 1932). It was, therefore, possible to reconcile child-centred approaches with hierarchic organization (streaming) within the junior school. Nevertheless it is evident that a tension developed between the two approaches in the years following the Second World War, the selective function of the junior school imposing clear restraints on the teachers, whose outlook was inevitably affected by the need to get good results in the 11-plus examination, in the interests both of the pupils and of the school.

It is difficult now to reconstruct the intense pressure on schools and teachers that built up in the 1940s and 1950s relating to the selection examination; the league tables that parents drew up for local schools, the telephoning round to find out who had done well and the sense of failure that some teachers experienced when their pupils won fewer places than others, or than expected; not to speak of the effects on the children. This was the reality that teachers had to face, arising from the context of the junior school within the tripartite (or selective) system; and this clearly was a dominant influence relating both to teachers' objectives and, therefore, to the teacher's style and forms of organization within the classroom. . . . Once again the fate of the junior school and its educational role depended on developments at the upper levels.

Comprehensive Reorganization: The Abolition of the 11-plus

But, with the transition to comprehensive secondary education, this dependence showed itself in an opposite sense. Comprehensive reorganization can be said to have got under way, in terms of entire local authority systems, from the mid-1960s, when the junior schools — or those in reorganized areas — found themselves to a large extent freed from the direct pressures and constraints just mentioned.

The abolition of the 11-plus, which was the concomitant of this reorganization (and to a large extent its motive force) now quite suddenly, and somewhat unexpectedly, created a new situation, and, in a real sense, the schools found new options open. Ironically, as we have seen, this transformation brought with it the demise of the seven to eleven junior schools as *national* policy although this system still predominates in the country as a whole alongside the new forms of age grouping defined earlier.

One striking feature of recent developments is the rapidity of change the schools have experienced. This may link with the contradiction between theory and practice which clearly developed after 1931; between the theory of the 'progressives' as crystallized in the 1931 report, and the actual practice of the junior schools as this persisted under the mounting constraints of the 11-plus. During this period, the focus of 'progressive' developments in practice was the infant school, which, although certainly affected by the increasingly competitive nature of the 11-plus (it was not uncommon to introduce streaming for six-year-olds), was relatively free to develop autonomously forms of organization and activities which were held to be educationally appropriate for five- to seven-year-olds. Practice here was certainly affected from the mid-1930s by the highly 'progressive' report of the Consultative Committee on *Infant and Nursery Schools*, published in 1933, clearly influenced by the work of Susan Isaacs, as also by the ideas of Froebel, Montessori and Dewey. There is evidence that 'progressive' infant school practices spread into the lower forms (and streams) of junior schools following the Second World War, particularly during the 1950s and especially in certain specific local authority areas. It is perhaps symptomatic that when Lilien Weber came from New York to study advanced school practice in England in the mid-1960s it was to the infant school that she devoted her attention. There is very little on junior schools in her book subsequently published under the title *The English Infant School and Informal Education* (Weber, 1971).

But the ideas of 'progressive' educators, using this term in its broadest (and most positive) sense, suffered a continuous frustration as regards *practice* in the junior school both before and after the Second World War, even if pioneering books like M.V. Daniels's *Activity in the Junior School* did appear (and were influential) in the late 1940s when 'activity' methods spread quite widely and had a certain vogue. A kind of backlog of progressive ideas and practices built up almost since 1911 (Holmes) (reinforced by war-time evacuation experiences, when teachers were driven back on to their own resources and began to act both more autonomously and more flexibly than before), was liberated in those areas where the 11-plus was early abolished or profoundly modified. These were particularly Leicestershire, the West Riding of Yorkshire, Oxfordshire, Bristol and London. Here were the nests of the new breakout. It was in these areas, also, that the system of streaming, which reinforced the methodology of class teaching, was most rapidly discarded. The swing from streaming in the junior schools in these and other areas, which started very slowly in the mid-1950s, meeting strong opposition, suddenly took off with extraordinary rapidity in the mid- to late 1960s, gaining influential support from the Plowden Report of 1967.

The 1960s

Educational developments in the 1960s were so rapid, all-embracing, and, in retrospect, perhaps surprising, that it is worth spending a little time on that decade, particularly because some of the problems facing primary education today clearly have their roots in this period and the apparent subsequent reaction from ideas and practices then regarded as positive. The 1960s saw not only the swing to comprehensive secondary education — one important condition for freeing the primary schools from earlier constraints — they also saw the acceptance *in toto* of the targets for a massive expansion of higher education as proposed in the Robbins Report, *Higher Education* (Robbins, 1963), and of the perspectives outlined (if somewhat ambiguously) in the Newsom Report, *Half Our Future* (Newsom, 1963). Of major importance to the subject of this book was the publication of the Plowden Report, *Children and Their Primary Schools* (1967), which, if also ambiguous in parts (particularly as concerns the curriculum), clearly and definitely espoused child-centred approaches in general, the concept of 'informal' education, flexibility of internal organization and non-streaming in a general humanist approach — stressing particularly the uniqueness of each individual and the paramount need for individualization of the teaching...learning process. There is little doubt that, when it appeared, the Plowden Report effectively crystallized a growing consensus as to the ideal nature of primary education; it built on, but took further, concepts initially propagated in the Consultative Committee's reports on *The Primary School* (1931) and *Infant and Nursery Schools* (1933).

But there were other factors affecting school practice at that time. One of these was the development of what is called the 'permissive society', and particularly the tendency to place fewer restraints on children and young people by parents and those in authority generally; combined on the other hand with a new consciousness on the part of young people as to their role in society, no doubt the result of higher earning powers in conditions of full employment, relative affluence, and so increased independence and autonomy. While it is difficult to evaluate such a tendency, there is little doubt that this affected pupil behaviour and attitudes in schools — perhaps even those of young children in primary schools. But there were other factors operating as well. Over this period there was a strong tendency, not only for local authorities specifically to encourage innovation and change in primary schools, but also for the head teachers themselves to allow a high degree of autonomy in classroom practice to class teachers; a result, perhaps, not only of the increased tendency towards the questioning of authority but also of the increasing professionalization of the primary school teacher, linked to the extension of training to three years in 1963. All this enhanced the variation of practice in the classroom. Schools tended no longer to operate as a single unit with common objectives using similar methods throughout the school; instead, different approaches could be found, and were tolerated, in different classrooms within the same school (Taylor, 1974).

In addition, the 1960s saw a decline in the inspectorial role both of HMIs and, in particular perhaps, of local authority inspectors who traditionally (especially in urban areas with their School Board traditions of administration) kept the primary schools on a tight rein. The former almost entirely ceased to carry out full inspections; in the case of local inspectors the tendency was to take on an advisory rather than an inspectorial function with the diminution of authority that this implies. This does not necessarily mean a decline in influence, since an effective adviser may have very considerable impact on the schools, and, through organizing activities such as the annual Leicestershire Teachers Primary Residential Workshops, profoundly affect school practice. Nevertheless, under this system, such influence has been exerted rather through the free concurrence of heads and teachers than through reliance on the authority of inspectors.

Finally, the 1960s saw the erection of new schools on the open plan principle, or the modification of old buildings on these lines. This created a new situation which inevitably affected classroom organization and methodology.

The Situation Today

It is in the light of these factors, many of them generally regarded at the time as educationally positive, that contemporary attitudes to and criticisms of the schools need to be evaluated. Here it is relevant to refer to the general disenchantment with education as a palliative of society's ills, which first found expression in the USA following the supposed (and some hold premature) evaluation of the Headstart programmes as a failure. This view, embodied in the Coleman (1966) and Jencks (1972) reports coincided with the beginning of a world economic recession (late 1960s), providing a rationale for economic cutbacks in education not only in England but in most advanced western industrial countries. If schools 'make no difference', why support them? The economic climate that developed also provided the context for the views presented in the series of Black Papers ... [of which] the first, published in 1969, specifically focused on new developments in the *primary* schools as a main cause not only of student unrest in the universities but of other unwelcome tendencies or phenomena (Cox and Dyson, 1969). It is in this context also that, in 1975, the events surrounding the Tyndale school dispute unfolded in London (concerning the implementation of an extreme version of 'progressive' methods in a primary school), followed in May 1976 by the massive publicity given by the media to Bennett's study (1976) represented as a condemnation of so-called 'informal' methods in the primary school. All this formed the background to Prime Minister Callaghan's speech (autumn 1976) warning against certain current tendencies in education, and the events which have followed: 'The Great Debate', DES and HMI initiatives relating to the curriculum, the establishment of the Assessment of Performance Unit, the beginning of mass testing by local authorities, and so on. The climate in which schools now function has certainly changed, affecting directly their mode of operation and perhaps also their objectives. . . .

Summary

It appears that the history of the primary school may be divided into four phases. First, its pre-history up to 1928, when the junior school as such had no independent existence, though embryonic forms were embodied within the elementary school system including infant schools and departments. Practices, approaches, attitudes and buildings derived from this phase are still to be found. Second, the period from 1928 to 1944 when junior schools, as such, began to come into being within the system of *elementary* education, and when a specific theoretical approach to primary education began to be formulated and receive official support (for short 'progressive', or 'child-centred'). Third, from 1944 to about 1970, a period which saw the universal provision of primary schooling (in its various forms) covering the age range five to eleven; a period when the specific theoretical approach developed earlier began to be implemented on a reasonably wide scale, culminating in the Plowden Report. Fourth, the present period, from about 1970 or shortly after to today and projecting into the future; a period marked by economic difficulties, controversy over means and ends, new restraints on the teacher, and by the demise of 'primary schooling' in the sense previously established with the development of new organizational (or institutional) forms. One thing seems clear; primary education, very much the poor relation in the educational system, has been in a state of almost continuous transition throughout its short history, the result both of changes at the secondary level and of changing approaches to the education of young children. Evaluation of contemporary practice must take this into account.

References

BENNETT, N. (1976) *Teaching Styles and Pupil Progress*, Open Books.

BOARD OF EDUCATION (1905) *Reports on Children under Fives Years of Age in Public Elementary Schools, by Women Inspectors*, London, HMSO, Cd 2726.

BOWEN, H. (1903) *Froebel and Education by Self Activity*, Heinemann.

COLEMAN, J. (1966) *Equality of Educational Opportunity*, US Department of Health, Education and Welfare.

COX, C. and DYSON, A. (Eds) (1969) *Fight for Education: A Black Paper*, Critical Quarterly Society.

HADOW REPORT (1926) *The Education of the Adolescent*, Report of the Consultative Committee, London, HMSO.

HADOW REPORT (1931) *Report of the Consultative Committee on the Primary School*, London, HMSO.

ISAACS, S. (1930) *Intellectual Growth in Young Children*, London, Routledge and Kegan Paul.

ISAACS, S. (1932) *The Children We Teach: Seven to Eleven Years*, University of London Press.

ISAACS, S. (1933) *Social Development in Young Children: A Study of Beginnings*, London, Routledge and Kegan Paul.

JACKSON, B. (1964) *Streaming: An Education System in Miniature*, London, Routledge and Kegan Paul.

JENCKS, C. (1972) *Inequality: A Reassessment of the Effects of Family and Schooling in America*, Basic Books.

KIMMINS, C. and RENNIE, B. (1932) *The Triumph of the Dalton Plan*, Nicholson and Watson.

NEWSOM REPORT (1963) *Half Our Future*, Report of the Central Advisory Council for Education (England), London, HMSO.

PLOWDEN REPORT (1967) *Children and Their Primary Schools*, Report of the Central Advisory Council for Education (England), London, HMSO.

ROBBINS REPORT (1963) *Higher Education*, Report of the Committee on Higher Education, London, HMSO.

ROSS, A. (1960) *The Education of Childhood*, Harrap.

SELLECK, R. (1972) *English Primary Education and the Progressives 1914–1939*, London, Routledge and Kegan Paul.

SIMON, B. (1974) *The Politics of Education Reform 1920–1940*, Lawrence and Wishart.

TAYLOR, P. *et al.* (1974) *Purpose, Power and Constraint in the Primary School Curriculum*, Macmillan.

WEBER, L. (1971) *The English Infant School and Informal Education*, Prentice-Hall.

WHITBREAD, N. (1972) *The Evolution of the Nursery-Infant School: A History of Infant and Nursery Education in Britain, 1800–1970*, London, Routledge and Kegan Paul.

A Proposal to Establish Primary and Post-Primary Education

(From The Hadow Report, 1926, *The Education of the Adolescent*, Report of the Consultative Committee, London, HMSO pp. xix, 70–2, 139.)

This short piece summarizes the Hadow Committee's conclusions for the reorganization of elementary education into two successive stages: primary education and post-primary education. The reorganization was proposed, not mainly for the benefit of primary-aged children, but in order to cater more appropriately for the 'tide' of adolescence. Eleven was chosen as the age marking the end of primary and the beginning of post-primary education. The last part of the extract discusses the kind of examination to be given children of 11 to 'discover in each case the type [of school] most suitable to a child's abilities and interests'. This '11+' examination was to have a dominating, and largely restrictive, influence on the upper primary curriculum for many decades post-Hadow, and still exercises such an influence in some parts of the country.

There is a tide which begins to rise in the veins of youth at the age of eleven or twelve. It is called by the name of adolescence. If that tide can be taken at the flood, and a new voyage begun in the strength and along the flow of its current, we think that it will 'move on the fortune.' We therefore propose that all children should be transferred, at the age of eleven or twelve, from the junior or primary school either to schools of the type now called secondary, or to schools (whether selective or non-selective) of the type which is now called central, or to senior and separate departments of existing elementary schools....

The first main conclusion which we have reached is concerned with the successive stages in education and with the relations which should exist between them. It is as follows: *Primary education should be regarded as ending at about the age of 11+. At that age a second stage, which for the moment may be given the colourless name 'post-primary', should begin; and this stage which, for many pupils would end at 16+, for some at 18 or 19, but for the majority at 14+ or 15+, should be envisaged so far as possible as a single whole, within which there will be a variety in the types of education supplied, but which will be marked by the common characteristic that its aim is to provide for the needs of children who are entering and passing through the stage of adolescence.*

Such a conception of the relations between primary and post-primary education obviously presents some points of contrast with the arrangement which has hitherto obtained in England, under which, until recent years, approximately 90 per cent of children have received elementary education up to the age of 13 or 14, and a small minority have been transferred to secondary education, or to that given in central schools, at about the age of 11;... It appears, however, to correspond to the views held by a large and influential section of educational opinion, and it has already received partial recognition both in administrative action taken by the Board and in a recent resolution on educational policy of the House of Commons. There was, indeed, something like unanimity among our witnesses as to the desirability of treating the age of 11 to 12 as the beginning of a new phase in education, presenting distinctive problems of its own, and requiring a fresh departure in educational methods and organisation in order to solve them.... *While we think all children should enter some type of post-primary school at the age of 11+, it will be necessary to discover in each case the type most suitable to a child's abilities and interests, and for this purpose a written examination should be held, and also, wherever possible, an oral examination. A written psychological test might also be specially employed in dealing with border line cases, or where a discrepancy between the result of the written examination and the teacher's estimate of proficiency has been observed. Where Local Education Authorities so determine, a preliminary examination might be held in order to discover candidates who should be encouraged to go forward to the free place examination proper.*

Arrangements for organising and conducting examinations for admission to schools of different types should be left to the Local Education Authorities.

Primary Education: A New Vision

(From The Hadow Report, 1931, *Report of the Consultative Committee on the Primary School*, London, HMSO, pp. 133, xv–xvi, xviii–xix, xxviii–xxix, 92–3.)

This extract and the report from which it is taken provide a classic statement embodying a conception of primary education which has served as an educational ideal for over half a century. The Hadow Report of 1931 provided a rationale for the primary stage of education, first proposed officially by the same Consultative Committee in its 1926 report (pp. 22–23). The Committee in its later report put forward a powerful vision of what primary education should be: a stage of education with 'its own standards of achievement and excellence' and with an aim of awakening children to 'the basic interests of civilised existence'. It envisaged an expanded role for the school: 'The schools whose first intention was to teach children how to read have ... been compelled to broaden their aims until it might now be said that they have to teach children how to live.' Its expressed concern was for all children: 'What a wise and good parent would desire for his own children, that a nation must desire for all children.' It stressed the importance of 'activity and experience', but not, on closer reading, at the expense of 'knowledge to be acquired and facts to be stored'. The whole report is a remarkably optimistic, forward-looking statement, all the more remarkable for being issued at a time of economic recession. Other reports or commentaries on primary education are but pale reflection (some might say 'distortions') of its vision.

In the evolution of educational theory and practice in England and Wales since the beginning of the last century the conception of the primary school for children between the ages of five and eleven, with a separate organisation, where possible, for those between the ages of seven and eleven, marks a new departure and brings with it new problems. To-day primary education is recognised as ending at about the age of eleven; secondary education of various types is that which follows; and the importance of considering the education of children in primary schools as something which must have a character of its own, arises from these facts ... clarification of the purpose of the primary school is the necessary pre-requisite of an improvement in its quality. It becomes possible to concentrate attention on the task of making provision for a relatively homogeneous group. If the successful development of secondary education depends on treating the years after eleven as a definite phase in child-life, with distinctive educational requirements and with problems of its own, the necessity for a similar realisation of the special province and role of primary education is not less imperative. The primary school is not a mere interlude between the infant school and the later stages of education, nor is its quality to be judged by its success in preparing children to proceed to the latter. It is continuous with both, because life is continuous, and it must be careful, accordingly, to preserve close contact with both. But just as each phase of life has its special characteristics, so the primary school has its special opportunities, problems, and difficulties; and these it must encounter by developing its own methods, perfecting its own technique and establishing more firmly its own standards of achievement and excellence. Its criterion must above all be the requirements of its pupils during the years when they are in its charge, not the exigencies of examinations or the demands of the schools and occupations which they will eventually enter. It will best serve their future by a single-minded devotion to their needs in the present, and the question which most concerns it is not what children should be — a point on which unanimity has hardly yet, perhaps, been reached — but what, in actual fact, children are. Its primary aim must be to aid children, while they are children, to be healthy and, so far as is possible, happy children, vigorous in body and lively in mind, in order that later, as with widening experience they grow towards maturity, the knowledge which life demands may more easily be mastered and the necessary accomplishments more readily acquired.... During the last forty years, and with increasing rapidity in the twelve years since 1918, the outlook of the primary school has been broadened and humanised. To-day it includes care, through the school medical service, for the physical welfare of children, offers larger, if still inadequate, opportunities for practical activity, and handles the curriculum, not only as consisting of lessons to be mastered, but as providing fields of new and interesting experience to be explored; it appeals less to passive obedience and more to the sympathy, social spirit and imagination of the children, relies less on mass instruction and more on the encouragement of individual and group work, and treats the school, in short, not as the antithesis of life, but as its complement and commentary.

What is needed now is not to devise any new system or method, but to broaden the area within which these tendencies are at work. It is not primarily a question of so planning the curriculum as to convey a minimum standard of knowledge, indispensable though knowledge is, and necessary as is the disciplined application by which alone knowledge can be acquired. The essential point is that any curriculum, if it is not to be purely arbitrary and artificial, must make use of certain elements of experience, because they are part of the common life of mankind. The aim of the school is to introduce its pupils to such experiences in an orderly and intelligent manner, so as to develop their innate powers and to awaken them to the basic interests of civilised existence. If the school succeeds in achieving that aim, knowledge will be acquired in the process, not, indeed, without effort, but by an effort whose value will be enhanced by the fact that its purpose and significance can be appreciated, at least in part, by the children themselves.... Few features in the history of the last thirty years are more striking or more inspiring than the improvement in the health, the manners, the level of intellectual attainment, the vitality and happiness of the rising generation. In that improvement the schools have played no unimportant part. The primary school is on the way to become what it should be, the common school of the whole population, so excellent and so generally esteemed that all parents will desire their children to attend it. It is in the light of that ideal that we should wish our report to be read. We do not pretend to have made startling discoveries or to have enunciated novel truths. The root of the matter is, after all, simple. What a wise and good parent would desire for his own children, that a nation must desire for all children ... the special task of the schools which are concerned with the later years of primary education will be to provide for the educational needs of childhood, just as it is the function of the nursery and infant schools to deal with the needs of infancy, and of the post-primary schools to deal with the needs of adolescence. In framing the curriculum for the primary school, we must necessarily build upon the foundations laid in the infant school and must keep in view the importance of continuity with the work of the secondary school, but our main care must be to supply children between the ages of seven and eleven with what is essential to their healthy growth — physical, intellectual, and moral — during that particular stage of their development. The principle which is here implied will be challenged by no one who has grasped the idea that life is a process of growth in which there are successive stages, each with its own specific character and needs. It can, however, hardly be denied that there are places in our educational system where the curriculum is distorted and the teaching warped from its proper character by the supposed need of meeting the requirements of a later educational stage. So long as this is the case, it must remain important to emphasise the principle that no good can come from teaching children things that have no immediate value for them, however highly their potential or prospective value may be estimated. To put the point in a more concrete way, we must recognise the uselessness and the danger of seeking to inculcate what Professor A.N. Whitehead calls inert ideas — that is, ideas which at the time when they are imparted have no bearing upon a child's natural activities of body or mind and do nothing to illuminate or guide his experience.

There are doubtless several reasons why a principle so obviously sane should in practice be so often neglected. Perhaps the reason most relevant to our inquiry is that in the earliest days of popular education children went to school to learn specific things which could not well be taught at home — reading writing and cyphering. The real business of life was picked up by a child in unregulated play, in casual intercourse with contemporaries and elders, and by a gradual apprenticeship to the discipline of the house, the farm, the workshop. But as industrialisation has transformed the bases of social life and an organisation — at once vast in its scope and minute in its efficiency — has gripped the life of the people, discipline associated with the old forms of industrial training has become increasingly difficult outside the walls of the school. The schools whose first intention was to teach children how to read have thus been compelled to broaden their aims until it might now be said that they have to teach children how to live. This profound change in purpose has been accepted with a certain unconscious reluctance, and a consequent slowness of adaptation. The schools, feeling that what they can do best is the old familiar business of imparting knowledge, have reached a high level of technique in that part of their functions, but have not clearly grasped its proper relation to the whole. In short, while there is plenty of teaching which is good in the abstract, there is too little which helps children directly to strengthen and enlarge their instinctive hold on the conditions of life by enriching, illuminating and giving point to their growing experience.

Applying these considerations to the problem before us, we see that the curriculum is to be thought of in terms of activity and experience rather than of knowledge to be acquired and facts to be stored. Its aim should be to develop in a child the fundamental human powers and to awaken him to the fundamental interests of civilised life so far as these powers and interests lie within the compass of childhood, to encourage him to attain gradually to that control and orderly management of his energies, impulses and emotions, which is the essence of moral and intellectual discipline, to help him to discover the idea of duty and to ensue it, and to open out his imagination and his sympathies in such a way that he may be prepared to understand and to follow in later years the highest examples of excellence in life and conduct. . . .

Infant Education: The Orthodox View Repeated

(From The Hadow Report 1933, *Report of the Consultative Committee on Infant and Nursery Schools*, London, HMSO, pp. 121–2, 122–3.)

This is an extract from a third report issued by the Consultative Committee of the Board of Education. The text is taken from the Committee's discussion of the infant school, described in Simon's essay as 'a unique feature of the English educational system' (p. 10). Liberal romanticism has always flourished in infant education to a greater extent than elsewhere; its influence can be clearly discerned in the text: 'It is the *special* function of the infant school to provide for the educational *needs* of the years of transition that separate babyhood from childhood.' 'Our main concern must be to supply children between the ages of five and seven plus with what is essential for their *healthy growth*.' 'It is through opportunities for further *experience* and *experiment* that *growth* will be best be fostered in the infant school.' The 1933 Report did much to confirm liberal romanticism as the accepted orthodoxy of English infant education.

At the age of five the child enters the primary school. In this country it has been the custom to deal with the earlier years (five to seven *plus*) in separate schools or divisions and since these are part of the primary school, it follows that the fundamental principle governing the curriculum which we enunciated in chapter VII (pages 91 to 106) of our *Report on the Primary School* applies broadly to the infant school also. *It is the special function of the infant school to provide for the educational needs of the years of transition that separate babyhood from childhood.* Our main concern must be to supply children between the ages of five and seven *plus* with what is essential for their healthy growth, physical, intellectual, spiritual and moral, during this particular stage of development. This does not mean that this stage is to be, or indeed can be dealt with in isolation from what has preceded it or from what is to follow it. It is essential to keep in mind the importance of continuity with the work of the later years of the primary stage, but no one who has grasped the idea that life is a process of growth in which there are successive stages, each with its own specific character and needs, will dispute the conclusion that the best preparation for a later stage is to base the training during the particular stage on the immediate needs of that stage. In the words of our previous Report (page 92), 'no good can come from teaching children things that have no immediate value for them, however highly their potential or prospective value may be estimated.'

We therefore adopt as the guiding principle determining the training and teaching of the infant school the same principle that we laid down for the primary school as a whole: '*the curriculum is to be thought of in terms of activity and experience rather than of knowledge to be acquired and facts to be stored.*' . . .

This general principle requires the whole span of the primary stage for its full development and its application to the infant school will be more pervasive than direct. It would be entirely inappropriate for instance to attempt to translate it into any rigid or logically ordered curriculum for the infant school. Indeed to apply the term 'curriculum' at all to the training and teaching carried on before the age of seven *plus* is dangerous as suggesting a systematic procedure which is opposed to the unordered way in which the child has hitherto developed his powers. The child, even if he has unhappily missed the advantages of a good home, or a good nursery school or class, has already learnt to use his native powers over a wide field of activities and interests. He has acquired mastery of the simpler muscular movements and has begun to coordinate them. He has learnt to speak, and begun to build up a working vocabulary by which to express his needs. He has a general, and in some directions an intimate knowledge of his surroundings from which he has gained simple ideas about many things. All this he has acquired through personal experience and experiment in the natural course of growth, but always without plan or ulterior motive. It is through opportunities for further experience and experiment that growth will best be fostered in the infant school.

This does not meant that the school has to stand aside and leave the child to follow the wind's way all the time. In recent years, both in this country and in America, there has been a tendency to exaggerate the childishness of the child, and to deprecate any procedure, especially in the training of the mind, which will interfere with it. The free urge of the child is not sufficient to secure his full development; the best way of doing things is not always that which occurs to the unaided mind. The school, in providing opportunities for new experiences must deal with the child as a growing person and not merely as a child. It is hardly yet realised that after infancy is over intellectual growth is in many respects quantitative, rather than qualitative, and shows itself not by the sudden appearance of the power to carry out a particular intellectual function, but by a gradual extension of the time during which that function is carried out continuously. The healthy child attaches no value to his childishness; all his instincts prompt him to savour the experiences of those older than himself, and the school which would confine him entirely to childish things because it thinks them most appropriate to his years, does him a grave disservice. In the provision of opportunities for further experience and experiment the school must make a delicate compromise between the immediate powers and needs of the child and his future needs as a potential adult.

A Rationale for Infant and Junior Education

(From Board of Education 1937, *Handbook of Suggestions for Teachers*,London, HMSO, pp. 98–9, 100–3.)

This extract, comprising two passages from the 1937 *Handbook of Suggestions*, summarizes the rationale for infant and junior school education which was part of 'official' thinking immediately prior to the Second World War and which was a major influence on the development of primary education following the 1944 Education Act (pp. 34–36). The passage on the infant school has a confident buoyant tone; the one on the junior school is rather more tentative, though still optimistic and forward-looking. The extract neatly embodies many of the tensions (some would say 'contradictions') which have characterized primary education (especially at the junior stage) since its inception: the tensions between what children are interested in and what adults judge to be of 'permanent value', between education for the here-and-now and 'preparation for the years beyond', between 'freedom' and 'discipline', and between teachers taking advantage of children's 'dominant interests' and 'planning a systematic course of activity' for their pupils. The attempted resolution of such tensions (or contradictions) has had, and continues to have, both positive and negative consequences; it has contributed to both the fascination and the frustration involved in educating children in primary schools.

An Infant School that is animated by the principles indicated in this chapter will be a place where life has all the freshness and vividness of early childhood, and where activities are pursued in a spirit of lively adventure. It will have provided the children with many new interests; and it will have given them in a measure suited to their age and maturity both the freedom and the discipline, through which their awakening sense of group membership may best be developed. Its product should be a child who, in comparison with the child of five, is self-possessed, responsible, independent, and capable of devoting himself to a straightforward task with a remarkable intensity of purpose and a high regard for the proper way of performing it.

Similarities and Differences between Children in Their Development. So far as the simple physical and social habits are concerned development is largely a matter of age and training and should not differ greatly as between one child and another at the end of the school course; but where activities are concerned which are not matters of routine, there will be marked variation in achievement. Hence it is undesirable in this field to lay down any fixed standard which all Infants may be expected to reach. Where conditions are normal, however, it is probable that the great majority of the children will have acquired considerable facility in speech, and in reading, writing, and number.. . .

Differences in attainment, and indeed in most other respects, are natural and inevitable among children at the end of their course in the Infant School, but what has been said in this chapter will show that behind these differences lies a common training with a common purpose. Expressed briefly, this purpose is to give the children experiences that will help them both now and later to adjust themselves to life in a civilised community.

1   The Junior School As a New Form of Organisation.   The Junior School, which is the final stage of primary education, is intended for children between the ages of 7 and 11, though in practice both the lower and the upper age-levels are found to vary considerably. It did not come into being because children of this particular age-range were known to have special needs and to present special problems. It arose through the successive splitting off of the Infant and the Senior School from the original type of Public Elementary school for children of all ages. As yet the Junior School is young, its traditions are still in the making, and its full potentialities unrealised, but already it has shown a surprising vitality and has opened up new vistas of educational progress that promise well for its future. Separation from the other types of school has given an impetus to the study of the characteristics of children between the ages of seven and eleven, but it has also brought difficulties inseparable from introducing yet another division into what after all is a single process of continuous organic growth. The transfer from stage to stage almost inevitably entails a temporary check in progress and only by the closest co-operation between Infant, Junior, and Senior Schools can the loss be reduced to a minimum.

2   The Junior Stage No Longer Regarded As One of Mere Passive Preparation.   For a long time the work of Standards I to IV, the counterpart of the modern Junior School, was based upon the idea that the period of childhood which they covered was pre-eminently a time for a narrow and rigorous treatment of the 'Three Rs'. It was a common belief that the rote-memory of the child was then at its best, and his nature so plastic as to retain almost indelibly the impressions of any lesson learnt. Particularly did the notion prevail that the mind of the child at this age was a tool to be fashioned and sharpened for the more serious work of the later stages of education.

The danger in this view is, of course that the minds of children may be regarded merely as passive instruments in the hands of the teacher. But as Professor Whitehead has said. 'The mind is never passive.... You cannot postpone its life until you have sharpened it. Whatever interest attaches to your subject-matter must be evoked here and now; whatever powers you are strengthening in the pupil, must be exercised here and now.'

3 *The Modern View: A Systematic Course Based on Children's Natural Interests.* One of the main concerns of the Junior School will be to discover those activities of child life which promise the best combination of immediate interest and permanent value. The work of exploration demands close observation of the spontaneous behaviour of children and systematic study of their development. We must take note of the things which seem to them to be most significant in the life of the world about them, and find out in what sort of terms they explain to themselves the events that make up their life. We must study the growth of their language and familiarise ourselves with the words, phrases, and modes of expression, that pass into currency at this stage, and with the forms of literature that have the strongest attraction. We must discover their compelling motives and modes of activity and be able to say what things make the deepest appeal to their feelings. In all these things the Junior School child differs in greater or lesser degree from younger and older children, and only upon an understanding of his particular qualities and immediate needs can his education be rightly conducted.

But to take advantage of dominant interests as they arise does not mean that the course which the school provides should be wholly opportunist or unorganised. Inherent in each stage of growth are the resources of the earlier stages and the potentialities of the later ones, and it would be folly to ignore at any moment either the experiences which the child has hitherto had or the qualities which the school aims at developing. The school cannot evade the duty of planning a systematic course of activity for its pupils; nor can it escape its responsibility to the public for maintaining proper standards of achievement in the fundamental subjects.

II The Aim of the Junior School

4 *A full and active life not dominated by external standards.* There is every reason why the aim of the Junior School should be set out in terms of the nature of its pupils rather than exclusively in terms of subjects and standards of achievement. It would, indeed, be anomalous if on the one hand Infant School teachers were to be encouraged to plan a life of free activity for little children, and on the other hand the teachers of Senior School children were to be asked to arrange courses of work suited to the

varying capacities and interests of their pupils, while at the same time the Junior School child had still to do nothing but follow the traditional track with an imposed curriculum and an external standard of achievement. If it is wrong in the Infant and Senior Schools to ignore the capacities and interests of children it must be equally wrong in the Junior School. But it by no means follows that children should decide entirely for themselves exactly what and how much they should do or learn, irrespective of the requirements of the society in which they find themselves. The course of instruction for children which will appear reasonable to most teachers will be one which can be followed with due regard both for the welfare of the child and for that of the community of which he is a member.

It is not to be expected that Junior School teachers will be able to free themselves at short notice from the external standards to which they have so long been accustomed. Indeed, it may be some time before they can win the same measure of freedom as is commonly conceded to their colleagues in other departments. Already, however, many Junior Schools have profited by adopting the more generous ideas set out in the Hadow report on *The Primary School*, and the movement thus started will no doubt gather momentum as the years go by.

It will be the aim, then, of the Junior School to provide an education which is suited to the nature of children between the ages of seven and eleven as well as to give a satisfactory form of preparation for the years beyond.

The Formal Establishment of Primary Education

(From the Education Act, 1944, extracts from Parts I, II and IV.)

The 1944 Education Act formally established primary education as the first of 'three progressive stages' into which the statutory system of public education in England and Wales was to be organized. This organization still remains, albeit with some minor modifications, such as those resulting from the creation of middle schools which straddle the primary and secondary stages. Under the 1944 Act, the Minister of Education was made responsible for the education of the people of England and Wales, and the local education authorities were made responsible, 'under his control and direction', for providing 'efficient education' throughout the three stages of primary education, secondary education, and further education. The extract also includes the clauses on the act of worship and religious instruction and the clause outlining the duty of each parent to 'cause' his child 'to receive efficient full-time education suitable to his age, ability and aptitude, either by regular attendance at school or otherwise'.

THE EDUCATION ACT · 1944

Part I

I. It shall be lawful for His Majesty to appoint a Minister (hereinafter referred to as 'the Minister') whose duty it shall be to promote the education of the people of England and Wales and the progressive development of institutions devoted to that purpose, and to secure the effective execution by local authorities, under his control and direction, of the national policy for providing a varied and comprehensive educational service in every area.

THE STATUTORY SYSTEM OF EDUCATION. LOCAL ADMINISTRATION

Part II.6

Subject to the provisions of Part I of the First Schedule to this Act, the local education authority for each county shall be the council of the county, and the local education authority for each county borough shall be the council of the county borough.

THE THREE STAGES OF THE SYSTEM

Part II.7

The statutory system of public education shall be organized in three progressive stages to be known as primary education, secondary education, and further education; and it shall be the duty of the local education authority for every area, so far as their powers extend, to contribute towards the spiritual, moral, mental, and physical development of the community by securing that efficient education throughout those stages shall be available to meet the needs of the population of their area.

Part II.25

(1) Subject to the provision of this section, the school day in every county school and in every voluntary school shall begin with collective worship on the part of all pupils in attendance at the school, and the arrangements made therefore shall provide for a single act of worship attended by all such pupils unless, in the opinion of the local education authority or, in the case of a voluntary school, of the managers or governors thereof, the school premises are such as to make it impracticable to assemble them for that purpose.

(2) Subject to the provisions of this section, religious instruction shall be given in every county school and in every voluntary school.

(3) It shall not be required, as a condition of any pupil attending any county school or any voluntary school, that he shall attend or abstain from attending any Sunday school or any place of religious worship.

(4) If the parent of any pupil in attendance at any county school or any voluntary school requests that he be wholly or partly excused from attendance at religious worship in the school, or from attendance at religious instruction in the school, or from attendance at both religious worship and religious instruction in the school, then, until the request is withdrawn, the pupil shall be excused from such attendance accordingly.

Part II.35

In this Act the expression 'compulsory school age' means any age between five years and fifteen years, and accordingly a person shall be deemed to be over compulsory school age as soon as he has attained the age of fifteen years:

Provided that as soon as the Minister is satisfied that it has become practicable to raise to sixteen the upper limit of the compulsory school age, he shall lay before Parliament the draft of an Order in Council directing that the foregoing provisions of this section shall have effect as if for

references therein to the age of fifteen years there were substituted
references to the age of sixteen years....

Part II.36

It shall be the duty of the parent of every child of compulsory school age
to cause him to receive efficient full-time education suitable to his age,
ability, and aptitude, either by regular attendance at school or otherwise.

Part II.68

If the Minister is satisfied, either on complaint by any person or otherwise,
that any local education authority or the managers or governors of any
county or voluntary school have acted or are proposing to act unreasonably
with respect to the exercise of any power conferred or the performance of
any duty imposed by or under this Act, he may, notwithstanding any
enactment rendering the exercise of the power or the performance of the
duty contingent upon the opinion of the authority or of the managers or
governors, give such directions as to the exercise of the power or the
performance of the duty as appear to him to be expedient.

Part IV.76

In the exercise and performance of all powers and duties conferred and
imposed on them by this Act the Minister and local education authorities
shall have regard to the general principle that, so far as is compatible with
the provision of efficient instruction and training and the avoidance of
unreasonable public expenditure, pupils are to be educated in accordance
with the wishes of their parents.

A Report of Progress

(From Central Advisory Council for Education (England), 1967, *Children and Their Primary Schools*, Vol. 1, London, HMSO, pp. 460–1, 463.)

As a landmark in the development of English primary education, *Children and Their Primary Schools* (the Plowden Report) features in several places in this volume. Pages 71–72 discuss the 'recognisable philosophy of education' with which the report has been associated; pages 179–183 refer to the importance the report attached to the home and, in particular, to parental attitudes, pages 184–186 feature its proposals for educational priority areas; and pages 324–326 summarize its views on children's learning. Here, there is a brief extract from the report's concluding chapter, the first section of which attempts a review of developments since the Second World War. The report is emphatic about the degree of progress which has been achieved: 'Our review is a report of progress and a spur to more . . . in the report we have for the most part described English primary education at its best. That in our belief is very good indeed. Only rarely is it very bad. The average is good.' Though making passing reference to the 'more dismal corners of primary education', the report is optimistic and confident — so much so that a questionable assertion is paraded as unchallengeable truth: ' "Finding out" has proved to be better for children than "being told".' The publication of the Plowden Report represented the high water mark in the fortunes of primary education post-Hadow. Neither before nor since have primary schools and, in particular, primary teachers received so much support and approval for their policies and practices.

1229. Our terms of reference, 'primary education in all its aspects and the transition to secondary education' were wide ranging. Our interpretation has been correspondingly wide. We conceived it as our duty to see the primary school not only in its strictly educational context but also as a part of society and of the economy. . . .

Since the war there has been a great increase in secondary education and in further and higher education. These developments were necessary if we were to hold our own with other advanced industrial countries. We are certainly not leading an advance party. This progress, however, has been in part at the expense of primary education. We think that a higher priority in the total educational budget ought now to be given to primary education. It is desirable in its own right: nobody ought to be satisfied with the conditions under which many of the four million primary school children are educated. It is also desirable in the interests of secondary and further education. A good deal of the money spent on older children will be wasted if more is not spent on them during their primary school years. Yet not everything costs money. Some of our recommendations call mainly for changes of attitude, understanding and knowledge in individual teachers.... We found that the Hadow reports understated rather than over estimated the differences between children. They are too great for children to be tidily assigned to streams or types of schools. Children are unequal in their endowment and in their rates of development. Their achievements are the result of the interaction of nature and of nurture. We conclude that the Hadow emphasis on the individual was right though we would wish to take it further. Whatever form of organisation is adopted, teachers will have to adapt their methods to individuals within a class or school. Only in this way can the needs of gifted and slow learning children and all those between the extremes be met.

1233. The appraisal we have made of the curriculum, and of the methods which have proved to be the most fruitful, confirm many or most of the suggestions that our predecessors made. Their insights have been justified and refined by experience. 'Finding out' has proved to be better for children than 'being told'. Children's capacity to create in words, pictorially and through many other forms of expression, is astonishing. The third of the three R's is no longer mere mechanical arithmetic, French has made its way into the primary school, nature study is becoming science. There has been dramatic and continuing advance in standards of reading. The gloomy forebodings of the decline of knowledge which would follow progressive methods have been discredited. Our review is a report of progress and a spur to more.

1234. This may sound complacent. We are not. The more dismal corners of primary education produce plenty of evidence of parochialism, lack of understanding of the needs of children and of the differing homes from which they come, lack of continued training of teachers and lack of opportunities for professional contact. Had we ignored these facts, we should have ignored what is well known to teachers and, increasingly, to parents. If all or most teachers are to approach the standards of the best, far more effort must be put into their in-service training.

There may be a good school without good buildings, though this is no excuse for the deplorable conditions in which many children are educated. There cannot be a good school without good teachers. Even one or two can leaven a whole staff. But there are staffs without leaven. We set these facts down here lest we should be accused of wilful ignorance because in the Report we have for the most part described English primary education at its best. That in our belief is very good indeed. Only rarely is it very bad. The average is good. . . .

The favourable judgment we have formed of English primary education as a whole, and the confidence with which we have made far reaching recommendations for its development reflect the devoted and perceptive service of the vast majority of the 140,000 primary school teachers. Most of what is best in English schools has come straight from individual teachers. We could wish no child a happier fate than to encounter as many do, a good teacher.

Progress Refuted: The Black Papers

(From Cox, C. and Dyson, A. (Eds), 1970, *Black Paper Three*, Critical Quarterly Society, p. 8; Cox, C. and Dyson, A. (Eds), 1969, *Fight for Education*, Critical Quarterly Society, pp. 5–6; Cox, C. and Dyson, A. (Eds), 1969, *Fight for Education*, Critical Quarterly Society, pp. 48–50.)

The accolade given primary education by the Plowden Report (pp. 37–39) was swiftly followed by virulent criticisms from those described in the second section of the source book as 'educational conservatives' (pp. 78–86). Through a series of 'Black Papers', the first of which was published in 1969, they attacked what they saw as 'permissive education' in primary schools and in comprehensive secondary schools. These three extracts capture the vehemence and insidiousness of their criticisms.

The first extract provides a simplistic but powerful caricature of what progressivism (or liberal romanticism) implies, that is, 'the belief that children must find out everything for themselves, must never be told, never be made to do anything, that they are naturally good, must be free of all constraints of authority.' Progressive education, and with it primary education, are then implicated in 'the growth of anarchy' and in 'the worst features of the pop and drug world'. The direct association of primary education with the 'roots of anarchy' is asserted in the second extract, published in 1969 at the climax of student unrest which had included the affair of Hornsey College of Art where the art students had taken control of their own education for several months. The 'revolution' in primary education (note the political overtones in the word) is directly linked with student protest and unrest. The third extract has been included partly as an example of the hearsay evidence on which many Black Paper assertions were based. It was written by a secondary school headteacher whose knowledge of primary schools was gleaned from some of his 'friends in junior schools'. Here again, changes in primary education are held partly responsible for changes in the wider society, such as the growth in the numbers of mentally-disturbed people, the increase in crime and the trend towards greater truancy at the secondary school stage. Although the absurdity of the most extreme Black Paper criticisms could easily be demonstrated, and although the validity of many of their less extreme assertions could be questioned, the Papers did have a considerable influence on political and public opinion. Why was this? Could it be that there was *some* substance in the disquiet so vociferously expressed by these writers?

[Basic Progressive Fallacies]

Just as the comprehensive factions are now split between traditionalists and non-streamers, so 'progressive' educationists are split in their attitudes to child-learning. Intelligent progressives rightly believe in the value of discovery methods, creative activity, new techniques of learning. So do we, when these methods are applied with common sense. But intelligent concern for new methods shades off quickly into the belief that children must find out everything for themselves, must never be told, never be made to do anything, that they are naturally good, must be free of all constraints of authority. Parents know how often the teachers in a progressive school do not properly understand the sophisticated techniques of 'progressivism,' and slip into easy acceptance of this permissive ethos. A teacher is an authority, a person specially trained to develop the potentiality of his pupils and in the disciplines of study. It is his duty to pass on skills and wisdom to children, and to ensure that they are trained in civilised manners and ways of thought. If he abdicates these reponsibilities he is guilty of the most serious neglect. This training must include helping children to evaluate the teacher's own opinions critically, to look objectively at all dogmas. But the duty of parents and teachers is *to direct*, not to remain passive and uncommitted to high standards of behaviour and learning.

The results of permissive education can be seen all round us, in the growth of anarchy. For if adults withdraw and allow children to find their own 'true' personality, the result is a vacuum into which all the worst features of the pop and drug world can enter.

[The Roots of Anarchy]

What are the roots of anarchy? In a recent article in the *Evening Standard* (15th October 1968) Timothy Raison suggested that a common malaise runs right through our present education; the roots of student unrest are to be found as early as the primary school:

> Nevertheless, the art students often embody the innocence, the passionate belief that if you would only leave people alone their best would come out, that is the attractive element in true, non-violent anarchism.... And this romantic view is widespread, not merely among art students, but many others who are likely to be marching....
>
> I sometimes wonder whether this philosophy — which I am sure many of the protest marchers feel, however inarticulately —

does not owe at least something to the revolution in our primary schools.

Influenced by a variety of psychologists from Freud to Piaget, as well as by educational pioneers from Froebel onwards, these schools have increasingly swung away from the notion (which characterises secondary education) that education exists to fit certain sorts of people for certain sorts of jobs, qualifications and economic roles, to the idea that people should develop in their own way at their own pace.

Competition has given way to self-expression. And now this has worked its way up to the student generation. They don't want to be chivvied through exams on to a career ladder: they want to be (what they conceive to be) themselves: and if the system stands in the way of this, marching about Vietnam in some indefinable way enables them to make a protest against the system and in favour of something better. At times one can imagine them, like infants' school children on television singing: 'There is a happy land, far far away'....

[Some of My Friends in Junior Schools Tell Me....]

No one would wish to return to the days when junior school children were rigidly confined to their rows of desks and learnt long lists of largely unrelated facts. But what is happening now? The restrictions of the old 11+ have almost disappeared, but the resulting freedom has been used in a multiplicity of ways. The children moving on to secondary schools present a bewildering problem even among the brightest groups.

Some at eleven can write fluently and imaginatively paying due attention to paragraphing, punctuation and spelling with none of their enthusiasm dampened. Others, of comparable intelligence, write illegibly, have no idea of arrangement of work and are thoroughly frustrated. Unfortunately the numbers in the latter category increase year by year.

These observations lead one to study methods in junior schools to try to see what is the effect not only on their progress mentally, but on their attitude and behaviour.

According to some present day psychologists, all teaching of young children must be child-centred: the teaching must grow from the child's interests and not be limited by any time-table divisions. Freedom of expression is all important and the method of conveying it is relatively unimportant. So far so good, but at what point should the child learn that correctness and accuracy have their place? All may be well at the junior school stage, but the freedom of the look and say method of reading, of the outpouring of ideas without arrangement or plan has disastrous results at a later stage. For instance, when learning a foreign language, one incorrect letter may well alter the whole meaning of a sentence.

Some of my friends in junior schools tell me that marking and correcting is a thing of the past as it may bring a sense of failure to a child. So one sees mistakes becoming firmly implanted in the child's mind. Many schools arrange projects for their children and some begin through this to learn the excitement of independent research and the joy of exploring in the library. Others undertake the work but do little more than copy passages from the encyclopaedia and stick cut out pictures in their books.

It is interesting to find that the children who, by the age of eleven, have mastered the skills of the three R's have gained a freedom which enables them to extend their horizons without the frustrations felt by those who at this stage realise the limitations imposed on them by the lack of disciplined thought.

To go back a stage further: at nursery level, the matron of a baby's home, is told by the visiting inspector that her nursery is too tidy because she trains her under fives to put away their toys at the end of each day. In a nursery class another inspector says it is wrong to forbid children to take home toys which do not belong to them.

All these children are growing up in a welfare state where it appears to them that everything in school is free; it is a world where they follow their own inclinations and where things are not right or wrong but merely a matter of opinion and where there are virtually no rules.

Does this produce a happy, well-balanced child? Statistics show the opposite to be true. Never before have there been so many people mentally disturbed, and the official criminal statistics, issued by the Home Office, show that the greatest number of indictable offences recorded for males occurs in the 14 and under 17 age group, 3,242 per 100,000 of the population in that age group.

Attitudes and behaviour in the country as a whole, of course, exert great pressure on our young people, but the schools must take a share of the blame. At the very heart of the problem is the need for self-discipline, for freedom within certain defined limits, for the security resulting from a realisation of cause and effect, from having certain decisions imposed and being able to enjoy the peace and security that comes from an ordered life.

The world is a noisy, chaotic and restless place, yet in schools we see the same lack of quiet encouraged. It is putting a great strain on young children to leave them constantly to make decisions with rarely any time in the day when they are quiet and listening. This feeling was expressed in a delightfully naive manner by a little 11 year old, beginning life in an ordered secondary school, who said she liked her new school because discipline was allowed.

A child who has always followed his own inclination finds it hard to sit down and learn his French and Latin verbs or his tables and yet, this knowledge acquired, he has the freedom to make rapid progress towards the exciting discoveries awaiting him at a more advanced stage. How comforting it is to know that, whatever distress there may be among the nations, two and two still make four.

The child who has been free to wander in his junior school much as he pleases, fails to see at a later stage, why he should not wander further afield. Many children who come before juvenile courts have committed their offences during school hours, although the truancy is rarely known at the school. The boy has been present for registration and then has disappeared.

The lack of restraint at junior school level does not have such serious results as when the children are older. There are few restrictions and adolescents are nearly all to some extent rebellious, but they find there are no brick walls available against which they can bang their heads, so they vent their pent-up feelings on railway carriages and on rival youth groups. How much better it is for them to find an outlet for their feelings by breaking some school rule which will not do much harm to anyone! Does not the child centred training produce the selfish and self-centred adolescent who cares little for any one but himself?

Many of my colleagues who are working in secondary schools would agree that the children who are the most well-balanced and who make the steadiest progress, are those who come from the junior schools where the children have had plenty of opportunity for independent, free study, but who have learnt the importance of listening and concentrating and who have found the satisfaction which comes from doing something, at whatever standard, really well.

The William Tyndale Affair: A Cause Célèbre

(From Gretton, J. and Jackson, M., 1976, *William Tyndale: Collapse of a School or a System?*, Allen and Unwin, pp. 5, 121–6.)

Following the publication of the first Black Papers at the end of the sixties, criticisms of state education continued to grow, fuelled by the writings and public statements of 'educational conservatives', by disquiet over reading standards and the teaching of English, and by growing political disillusionment with the effects of public expenditure on education. In the mid-seventies criticism of primary education reached a peak, partly as a result of the notorious William Tyndale affair. William Tyndale was a junior school in north London where in 1974 some of the staff, especially Messrs Ellis, Haddow and Austin, introduced radical changes, associated with an extreme form of liberal romanticism (though it needs to be said that many adherents of liberal romanticism did not wish to associate themselves with some of the changes introduced or with the manner of their introduction). The result was a violent dispute within the staff of the junior school, and between a segment of the staff and the school managers, which then involved leading local government politicians, the local inspectorate and, eventually, in 1975–6, a public inquiry conducted by Robin Auld QC into the teaching, organization and management of the junior school and its neighbouring infant school.

The affair was important in bringing out into the open and to the forefront of discussion a number of major educational problems requiring clarification and resolution. These issues included the control of the school curriculum, the responsibilities of local education authorities, the accountability of teachers, and the assessment of effectiveness in education. These problems have been the subject of much discussion and considerable action since 1976, as other papers in this source book and its accompanying volume testify. No attempt is made here to do justice to the complexity of the William Tyndale affair, especially to the differing interpretations of both events within the school and their wider significance. This extract provides *one* summary interpretation, written by two educational journalists. For other interpretations, readers are referred to Ellis, T. *et al.* (1976) *William Tyndale: The Teachers' Story*, Readers and Writers Publishing Cooperative; Dale, R. (1981), 'Control, accountability and William Tyndale', in Dale, R. (Ed.), *Politics, Patriarchy and Practice*, Lewes, Falmer Press, pp. 209–219; and Auld, R. (1976), *William Tyndale Junior and Infant Schools Public Inquiry*, London, ILEA.

In the autumn of 1973 William Tyndale was an ordinary enough junior school in a rundown area of north London; within just two years the school had fallen apart and striking teachers, angry parents and helpless politicians were confronting one another through the headlines of the national press and the current affairs programmes of television. It took a further year, which must have seemed to many of those directly concerned to have lasted as long as the previous two, for the inquiry to be completed and its report published and, in a further blaze of publicity, for the leading politicians and the more active of the school's managers to resign while the headteacher and five of his colleagues prepared to face disciplinary proceedings....

The main ingredients of William Tyndale could be found all over the country: a staff with strong radical convictions, a weak headteacher, a dithering inspectorate, worried parents and a local education authority that did not know what it wanted of its primary schools. The mixture was common enough, but previously it had not been throught of as dangerously explosive. The *Zeitgeist*, however, had changed. Gone were the heady, spendthrift days of the 1960s when education and all the social services boomed, and books like Anthony Crosland's *The Future of Socialism* (actually published in 1956) could paint a rosy picture of a future full of beautiful people all happily caring for one another. In their place was the pessimism of the seventies, with their rapidly deteriorating cities and their visions of permanent economic decline inducing a desire to hang on to what was known and tangible, however irrational that might be. ('Catch a falling £ and put it in your pocket, Save it for a rainy day.') Combined with the fact that people's expectations of the welfare state had outrun their willingness to pay the consequent texes, this meant, in education, a decline in the power of the teacher (the labour market was no longer running in his favour) and a concern for minimum standards. At its best, this could mean a concern for minimum standards for all children; at worst, it tended to be more selfishly inspired.

Attainment. Mr Ellis, Mr Haddow and Mr Austin, if not all their followers, had a fairly clear idea of what they expected schools to do. Schools, for them, had a profound effect on children; the point was how to use that effect ... their main preoccupation was with the (largely false) dilemma of whether they, and schools, should be agents of social change or agents of social control. They wanted change and that was a perfectly respectable position. That sort of thinking had not only inspired much of the Plowden Report on primary education, it had been responsible for the millions of pounds invested in Western-type education in the newly independent countries of the Third World. Thousands of teachers, too, who were not necessarily as extreme in their methods, were concerned that schools should exist to serve not just the average and above-average, but also, and perhaps especially, the below average. Interestingly, by the time they came to give evidence at the inquiry, both Mr Ellis and Mr Haddow had adopted the position which has come to be associated with Christopher Jenks, following the publication in 1974 of his book *Inequality* — namely, that as agents of social change, schools and education were non-starters. However many resources were poured into them, schools just did not make that much difference to the life chances of the disadvantaged children. Whatever the rights and wrongs of that controversy, few people, whether parents, teachers or educationists, have ever behaved as though schools did not affect society. Most people, though, being naturally conservative, wanted them to buttress the society they knew rather than change it into something they did not; if change was to come, they wanted it brought about by mature minds which had been educated to be critical while at school — a very different proposition from the radical one.

Another view was that schools existed not to change society, but to prepare for change. The world was changing very much faster than in previous generations, and it was a reasonable prediction that the rate of change would go on accelerating. Technology that was taught in schools today would be out of date tomorrow, and would in any case be too much for any one individual to master. The world of tomorrow was bound to be a world of group activity and co-operative projects and it was important that children be prepared for a world of continuous adaptation. All questions of social reform apart, co-operative informal teaching methods would be more suitable for that purpose than formal, traditional ones.

Either of these approaches — changing society or preparing society for change — was bound to make exceptionally heavy demands on the teachers. The great innovators in education were all exceptionally gifted pedagogues. At William Tyndale, there were a few good teachers but that was not enough, even if it had been supplemented by the diligence and enthusiasm which many teachers show, on which to build the ambitious programme the staff had in mind. Teacher training, too often thought of as a panacea, could make little difference, as colleges of education were limited both by the quality of the students they received (Mr Ellis was one of the very few graduates in primary teaching) and by the intrinsic difficulty of teaching people how to teach. All they could do was to provide their students with a minimum of further education, a few good ideas for progressive teaching and one or two basic techniques of classroom control which it was hoped would act as a safety net.

What was left, then, as an aim of primary education? Once the 11-plus had gone, there was no measure of achievement at all, however unsatisfactory. Children moved on up into secondary schools when they were 11 or 12, whether or not they had learnt how to read or write; there was no question of keeping anyone back. The notion, popular among parents, that children should be taught the 'basics' while at primary school was the only hint of a minimum standard. Even that, though, if it were to be formalised, would require some form of attainment testing, and since the abolition of the 11-plus it had become impossible for educationists to reach agreement among themselves on a value-free objective test — or even on the merits of testing at all.

Assessment.   It is difficult to talk of assessing the performance of teachers when there is no agreement on what teachers are supposed to be doing. In the absence of any agreed criteria all that is possible is for professional experts to go into a school, look at what the teachers were doing, talk to the teachers themselves about it, and then make their own assessment. That is what a full inspection was all about. But there was no basis on which one school could be compared with another — except the subjective impressions of the inspectors, a group of men or women whose sole qualification for the job was that they had once been good teachers. Moreover, the touchiness of many teachers and their unions, concerned with their status as qualified professionals and therefore not subject to outside control . . . contributed to the general unwillingness of the inspectors to force their opinions down anybody's throat.

Another factor at work here was what one might term the unacceptable face of authority. Research evidence suggests that both parents and children like teachers to be tough, authoritarian figures but, like social workers, teachers had come increasingly to think of themselves — and be thought of by others — as one of the 'caring professions'. That meant, in this context, that they did not make 'judgments' about their 'clients', whether they were incontinent old men, dangerous juvenile delinquents or backward schoolchildren; all they did was make the non-moral assessments that were necessary for them to do their job. But what was true for their clients had also become true for themselves. Together with the fashion for participation and democratic decision making in everything (and not just politics), that meant that it had become virtually impossible for anybody who had a position of responsibility in the hierarchy to say: you are doing your job badly — do it better or get out. Soft-centred liberals should remember that more revolutions have failed through inefficiency than for any other single cause.

Inspectors, therefore, preferred the role of adviser. In fact, rather than see themselves as the shock troops who could be sent in at the slightest hint of trouble, they preferred the image of staff officers, helping, advising, prodding the troops in the front line, but rarely taking the field themselves. They saw themselves rather as a teaching elite; knowing that there were not enough of them to go round every school, they tried to spread their qualities as wide as possible by working at one remove through the classroom teachers. There was certainly a case for that, just as there was a case for fewer, better-trained teachers and more untrained (and less expensive) teacher aides.

But if inspectors abandoned their role of assessors, who was to make judgments about how well or badly teachers might be doing their job? The teachers themselves? The ILEA inspectorate, at least, would like to evolve some formula for teacher self-assessment. Curiously, however, that is something teachers themselves have not pressed for. Despite their oft-repeated concern for their professional status, they have been strangely unpreoccupied with some of the things that would give meaning to that status, such as control of the qualifications for entry into the profession, or the sort of freedom from the judgement of outsiders that is enjoyed by doctors and lawyers. Both these professions have some sort of council which hears and judges claims of professional misconduct. The teachers have never pressed for a general teaching council along the same lines.

Indeed, one of the points to emerge most strongly from any discussion of the issues raised by William Tyndale was the ambiguous nature of teachers' claims to professional status. Certainly, there were ways in which teachers could justifiably claim that they adopted a professional attitude to their work, but the fact that in other respects society was not prepared to grant them that status was symptomatic of something very important. A doctor's clinical judgement is just that: a judgement of fact and diagnosis about clinical matters. A teacher's judgements are made about values, and very fundamental ones at that. Those sort of judgements were thought to be too important to be left to teachers alone.

Accountability. But by the same token as the story of William Tyndale amply illustrated, nobody else was willing to take on the responsibility for the judgements — and performance — of teachers. If nothing was done about it, sooner or later market forces would begin to take a hand, as in a sense they did at William Tyndale when parents began to vote with their feet by taking their children away. There were already pressures, by those involved in educational politics on the extreme left as well as the extreme right, for this sort of parental assessment to be institutionalised — say, through a voucher system, under which parents would be given an educational ticket for each of their children which they could cash at the school of their choice. Schools would then be competing with one another for clients, just as they do already in the private sector. But that would have several disadvantages, the major one of which is common to all solutions that involve the undifferentiated voice of parents or the community. Everybody has been to school, but nobody has ever learnt anything about education there. If it was wrong, as it surely was, to leave teachers free to exercise their uncontrolled will on children, then it was also wrong to leave decisions about the type of education children should receive to parents. . . .

That left some sort of representative community control — which of course had been the thinking behind the institution of managers and governors in the first place. However, . . . under that system managers left a lot to be desired, in terms of both their appointment and their competence. One solution might have been for them to be directly elected at the same time as local councillors. But however they might be appointed, they had to know something about education and educational issues so that, if teachers or the headteacher wanted to introduce new policies into the school, they would have to justify them to the managers — but to managers who would be reasonably well informed.

All these issues we have mentioned — the powers and responsibilities of local authorities, the control of the curriculum, the criteria for assessing a school's efficiency, the aims of primary education, the need for testing, the role of the inspectorate, the function of managers and the professionalism and accountability of teachers — are proper subjects for consideration by the Secretary of State for Education. Only he can see that the lessons of William Tyndale are, where appropriate, applied nationally and only he is in a position to assess the implications for bodies such as the Schools Council. But above all, only the Secretary of State can take an overview of the issue which underlies every other: the proper balance to be struck between politicians and the community on the one hand, and teachers and the other professionals on the other. After William Tyndale, the Secretary of State can no longer pretend, as he and his predecessors have so often tended to do, that it is all happening somewhere else.

Public Debate and Official Response

(From Department of Education and Science, 1977, *Education in Schools: A Consultative Document*, London, HMSO, pp. 2–3, 8–9.)

Criticism of the state educational system led to James Callaghan's Ruskin College speech in the autumn of 1976 and to the resulting 'Great Debate', discussed in paragraph 1.5 of this extract. The extract is taken from the 'Green Paper' of 1977, published by the Department of Education and Science at the end of the 'Debate'. The first of the two passages reproduced here attempts a balanced appraisal of the criticisms made about the educational system in general. It acknowledges that 'there is legitimate ground for criticism and concern' but refutes the major claim of critics: 'It is simply untrue that there has been a general decline in educational standards.' The second passage discusses primary education and argues that 'child-centred' developments have been influential but only partially successful in the schools. It provides a heavily qualified endorsement of developments in primary education. In particular, liberal romanticism is believed to have been successful only 'in the right hands'. The Department stresses the centrality of numeracy and literacy and the importance of progression within the curriculum, of continuity between schools and of consistency across schools 'in kind if not in detail'. The 1977 Green Paper was the first Departmental criticism of the effects of developments in primary education, since these were set in train by the Hadow Report of 1931 (pp. 24–37). The period since 1977 has been considerable efforts being made by the Department, through the Inspectorate, to help schools 'restore the rigour without damaging the real benefits of the child-centred developments'.

Introduction

1.1   In his speech at Ruskin College, Oxford on 18 October 1976 the Prime Minister called for a public debate on education. The debate was not to be confined to those professionally concerned with education, but was to give full opportunity for employers and trades unions, and parents, as well as teachers and administrators, to make their views known.

1.2   The speech was made against a background of strongly critical comment in the Press and elsewhere on education and educational standards. Children's standards of performance in their school work were said to have declined. The curriculum, it was argued, paid too little attention to the basic skills of reading, writing, and arithmetic, and was overloaded with fringe subjects. Teachers lacked adequate professional skills, and did not know how to discipline children or to instil in them concern for hard work or good manners. Underlying all this was the feeling that the educational system was out of touch with the fundamental need for Britain to survive economically in a highly competitive world through the efficiency of its industry and commerce.

1.3   Some of these criticisms are fair. There is a wide gap between the world of education and the world of work. Boys and girls are not sufficiently aware of the importance of industry to our society, and they are not taught much about it. In some schools the curriculum has been overloaded, so that the basic skills of literacy and numeracy, the building blocks of education, have been neglected. A small minority of schools has simply failed to provide an adequate education by modern standards. More frequently, schools have been over-ambitious, introducing modern languages without sufficient staff to meet the needs of a much wider range of pupils, or embarking on new methods of teaching mathematics without making sure the teachers understood what they were teaching, or whether it was appropriate to the pupils' capacities or the needs of their future employers.

1.4   Other criticisms are misplaced. It is simply untrue that there has been a general decline in educational standards. Critics who argue on these lines often make false comparisons, for instance with some non-existent educational Golden Age, or matching today's school leavers against those of a generation ago without allowing for the fact that a far larger proportion of boys and girls now stay on into the sixth form. Recent studies have shown clearly that today's schoolchildren read better than those of thirty years ago. Far more children, over a wider range of ability, study a modern language or science than did a generation ago. Many more take, and pass, public examinations. Many more go on to full-time higher education.

1.5   The picture, then, is far from clear. Much has been achieved: but there is legitimate ground for criticism and concern. Education, like any other public service, is answerable to the society which it serves and which pays for it, so these criticisms must be given a fair hearing. In response to the Prime Minister's initiative the Ministers concerned held a series of meetings with national organisations representing a wide range of people having a special interest in education. These meetings set the scene for a series of regional conferences held in the opening months of this year with invitations issued to local authorities in each region, to teachers, employers, trades unions, the churches, parents and students. In this setting many valuable ideas were put forward, both at the conferences themselves and in written documents. The conferences were followed by a further round of meetings with those consulted the previous autumn. This combination of meetings and conferences — in many ways a unique form of consultation for this country — identified a substantial measure of agreement on what needed to be done to improve our schools. . . .

Primary Schools

2.1   Primary schools have been transformed in recent years by two things: a much wider curriculum than used to be considered sufficient for elementary education, and the rapid growth of the so-called 'child-centred' approach. The primary curriculum has been enriched by a feeling for colour, design and music, and by the introduction of simple scientific ideas. Children engage in work designed to increase their control over themselves physically and mentally, to capture their imagination and to widen their knowledge and understanding of the world about them. The child-centred approach takes advantage of the child's individual stage of development and of his or her interests: it complements the wider curriculum by harnessing the natural enthusiasm of young children for learning things by their own efforts instead of merely being fed with information. In the right hands, this approach has produced confident, happy and relaxed children, without any sacrifice of the 3Rs or other accomplishments — indeed, with steady improvement in standards. Visitors have come from all over the world to see, and to admire, the English and Welsh 'primary school revolution'.

2.2   Unfortunately, however, the work has not always been in the hands of experienced and able teachers. While only a tiny minority of schools adopted the child-centred approach to the exclusion of other teaching methods, its influence has been widespread. It has proved to be a trap for some less able or less experienced teachers who applied the freer methods uncritically or failed to recognise that they require careful planning of the opportunities offered to children and systematic monitoring of the progress of individuals. While the majority of primary teachers, whatever approach they use, recognise the importance of performance in basic skills such as reading, spelling and arithmetic, some have failed to achieve satisfactory results in them. In some classes, or even some schools, the use of the child-centred approach has deteriorated into lack of order and application.

2.3   The challenge now is to restore the rigour without damaging the real benefits of the child-centred developments. This does not imply any great change in the range of what is taught, but the following features, already recognised by the most effective schools, need to be accepted throughout the system:

(i)   in all schools teachers need to be quite clear about the ways in which children make and show progress in the various aspects of their learning. They can then more easily choose the best approach for their pupils.

(ii)   Teachers should be able to identify with some precision the levels of achievement represented by a pupil's work. In parts of the curriculum such as arithmetic, it is relatively easy to organise a series of targets for the pupils according to a logical sequence of difficulty. In other parts of the curriculum where teachers are planning to develop their pupils' imagination and social awareness, it may not be possible to be so precise. Teachers can nonetheless plan a progression in these parts of the curriculum and so ensure that they make their proper contribution to the child's education.

(iii)   Teachers in successive classes or schools need to agree about what is to be learned. They should as a matter of professional habit pass on clear information about work done and levels of achievement.

(iv)   Even allowing for local and individual needs, children throughout England and Wales have many educational requirements in common. It is therefore reasonable to expect that children moving from a primary school in one part of the country to another elsewhere will find much that is familiar in kind if not in detail.

(v)   There are some skills for which the primary schools have a central, and indeed over-riding, responsibility. Literacy and numeracy are the most important of these: no other curricular aims should deflect teachers from them. By definition they must form part of the core of learning, the protected area of the curriculum.

A Brief Professional Appraisal

(From Department of Education and Science, 1978, *Primary Education in England: A Survey by HM Inspectors of Schools*, London, HMSO, pp. vii–viii)

This short piece is included as a complement to the paragraphs from the 1977 Green Paper (see pp. 51–54). It is reproduced from the foreword to the report of the national primary survey, which involved HM Inspectors of Schools in visiting a representative sample of English primary schools and in inspecting the work of over a thousand classes. The passage provides a very brief summary of the state of English primary education in the mid-seventies, as seen by the Inspectorate. It records the concern of primary teachers that children should be well-behaved, literate and numerate; it refers to 'encouraging results' in reading; but it also acknowledges that 'in some aspects of the work the results overall are sometimes disappointing'. The report to which it was a foreword presented a description and analysis of primary education based on professional observation and evaluation rather than on hearsay or on wishful thinking. Its significance is discussed in the next extract in this section; many of its most important passages are reproduced in Volume 2 of the source book.

This report is an account of some aspects of the work of 7, 9 and 11 year old children in 1,127 classes in 542 schools so chosen as to be representative of primary schools in England. It gives information about the organisation of schools, the range of work done by the children, and the extent to which the work is matched to their abilities. It also includes an analysis of the scores obtained by children in objective tests administered by the National Foundation for Educational Research.

It is based on the direct observation of children's work by HM Inspectors experienced in primary education. The suggestions for the further development of that work reflect what was already successfully practised in a substantial number of classes and schools. . . .

What emerges from the report is that teachers in primary schools work hard to make pupils well behaved, literate and numerate. They are concerned for individual children, and especially for those who find it difficult to learn. If the schools are considered as a whole, it is clear that children are introduced to a wide range of knowledge and skills.

The efforts of children and teachers have produced encouraging results in the reading test for 11 year olds, where objective comparisons can be made with the past; there is no comparable objective evidence of past standards in other parts of the curriculum. In some aspects of the work the results overall are sometimes disappointing. The reasons for this vary, and rarely stem from inattention or poor effort. In some cases, the evidence clearly suggests that difficulty arises because individual teachers are trying to cover too much unaided. Some fairly modest re-adjustment of teacher' roles would allow those with special interests and gifts to use them more widely, as is shown in some classes where particularly successful work is done.

'Demythologising' Primary Education

(From Richards, C., 1980, 'Demythologising primary education', *Journal of Curriculum Studies*, 12, 1, pp. 77–8.)

The HMI primary survey, featured in the previous extract, was the first publicly accessible, rigorous professional appraisal of developments in primary education since the changes set in train by the Hadow Report of 1931 (see pp. 24–27). As this extract argues, the survey did much to strip primary education of its myths, both favourable and unfavourable. The picture it painted was one of organizational rather than curricular or pedagogic change: a perspective very different from the views of either primary education's detractors or sympathizers. Many of the previous papers in this section dealt in visions, in prescriptions, or in criticisms (often based on very partial evidence). The survey provided much needed information to correct utopian or simplistic perspectives. It provided an agenda for professional discussion and renewal, based on closer knowledge of primary policy and practice.

When the history of English primary education in the 20th century comes to be written, three dates are likely to be seen as particularly significant: 1931, when the notion of the 'primary school' received official recognition in the Hadow Report; 1967, when 'child-centred education' (however loosely defined) was accepted as the official orthodoxy of English primary education; and 1978, when the publication of *Primary Education in England: A Survey by HM Inspectors of Schools* provided the first publicly accessible, rigorous overall appraisal since Hadow. (The appraisal conducted by the Inspectors of the Plowden Committee in the 60s did not, in my view, meet these criteria.) The survey published in 1978 counters very effectively the wild assertions and scare-mongering rife following Tyndale and Bennett in 1976, a year when the fortunes of primary education reached their nadir. However, it provides cold comfort for curriculum developers and for both the advocates and the critics of 'child-centred education'. To my mind, with the major exception of its very simplistic treatment of teaching approaches the survey does justice to many of the complexities, successes, shortcomings and subtleties of primary practice.

The survey's findings and recommendations do not rest on carefully conducted classroom observational research: it cannot be criticized by the canons of OSCAR, PROSE, STOS, ORACLE or whatever. It is an evaluation report in a very important but (for curriculum workers) much neglected tradition which has its own repertoire of techniques, its own standards of appraisal and its own code of professional conduct — a tradition stemming from the 'craft' of school inspection. However, the confidential, almost apostolic nature of the transmission of this craft (itself predating curriculum evaluation as we know it by almost a century) makes it impossible for outsiders to provide (in its own terms) methodological critiques of the national inspection reported in the survey. Perhaps publication of this and other recent DES appraisals of practice might encourage curriculum scholars interested in evaluation to explore more thoroughly the problems and issues raised by the evaluative aspects of inspection.

Most importantly, the survey underlines the centrality of the curriculum in primary education. Its concern for intellectual development through appropriately designed curricula represents a significant readjustment of emphasis compared with Plowden; though important, organization, pupil grouping, teaching approaches, staffing and resource allocation have for too long preoccupied decision-makers in primary schools and deflected them from the still more central tasks of deciding what particular skills, concepts, knowledge and attitudes primary children should acquire and of incorporating these into planned (and evaluated) teaching/learning sequences. The report focuses on these problems, draws up a valuable, though incomplete, agenda for professional discussion (which cannot be reviewed in detail here) and provides opportunities for work in curriculum studies to make a contribution to reviewing, refining and enhancing the rather impoverished primary curriculum.

Curriculum studies in the British tradition has been largely ameliorative in orientation, with the problems of secondary education being predominant among its concerns. In comparison, the primary curriculum has been relatively neglected, partly at least because those working in curriculum have appeared to accept the mythology of primary education current over the last decade or so. The survey does much to 'demythologize' primary education. Judging from the practices revealed in the survey, the 'quickening trend' towards 'child-centred education' detected by the Plowden Committee has not materialized on a substantial scale in top infant and junior classes; 'the primary school revolution' has not been tried and found wanting but never been tried and found wanting but never been tried at all except in a small number of schools; most primary school teachers have not responded in the 'open', flexible, imaginative way curriculum developers naïvely assumed they would. In particular, most proposals for curriculum change made in the 60s and early 70s have been based on assumptions about teaching, learning, knowledge and children which do not appear to inform the practice of the majority of teachers. The current curriculum is revealed as scarcely more than a revamped elementary school curriculum with the same major utilitarian emphases.

These findings raise a number of interesting questions. How and why did the myth of 'the primary school revolution' arise? How was it sustained for such a long period? In whose interests was it perpetuated? What part was played in this by the media (and those with ready access to the media) and by individuals like Christian Schiller who seems to have exercised an unpublicized but tremendous influence on many who later became important opinion-leaders? During the period 1960–1975 what was the nature of the 'political' interplay among various interest groups within primary education? The major changes that the survey notes are organizational rather than curricular — in particular the remarkable spread of non-streaming and the introduction of vertical grouping in a substantial number of infant and junior classrooms. How did the non-streaming movement develop, by whom was it fostered and for what reasons? Were the practices associated with the supposed 'revolution' simply teachers' pragmatic, relatively superficial responses to the need to cope with unstreamed or vertically grouped classes? Has organizational rather than curricular or pedagogic change been the major distinguishing feature of primary education during the last 20 years?

In this way, the publication of the national survey raises many important issues for students of the primary curriculum, some concerned with the recent history of primary education, and others with future curriculum policy-making (though the latter need the perspective provided by the former). The survey should be read as both an educational and a political document — political in the sense that it reflects and influences the distribution and exercise of power over the primary curriculum. If it appears to read awkwardly at times, this is not usually because it is hiding a lack of substance behind convoluted, constipated civil-service prose. This is because it is deliberately conveying different messages at different levels to a variety of interest groups within and outside primary education. *Primary Education in England* is often very subtle and not always clear, but so is the process of primary education itself.

2   *Primary Education: Contrasting Views*

Introduction

At its simplest, primary education can be regarded as an administrative stage, set up as a result of the 1944 Education Act: 'The statutory system of public education shall be organised in three progressive stages to be known as primary education, secondary education and further education' (see p. 35). Even that seemingly straightforward view has its problems forty years on. Should pre-school education be regarded as part of primary education or separate from it? Are middle schools of all types included, or only some variants, or none?

Primary education, however, is much more than an administrative entity. It is something experienced by millions of children over a number of years and conveyed through the intentions and actions of many thousands of teachers. It is not at all easy to characterize faithfully, but very easy to simplify, as extracts from the Black Papers (see pp. 40–44) illustrate. Primary education comprises beliefs and practices thought appropriate for children in a particular age-range (variously defined, but for our purposes the 5–11 age-group). Primary education does not refer to a clearly specified set of beliefs and associated practices held by *all* teachers and influencing *all* primary-aged children, but to a dynamic variety of competing views as to what the enterprise is all about and how it might be conducted. Though seldom stated explicitly and often taken for granted, these differing views influence the patterns of relationships established between teacher and children, the form of the curriculum undertaken, and the way schools or classes are organized. Except in an administrative sense, there is no single entity called primary education, but a set of competing beliefs (or ideologies) and their associated practices. This section of the book seeks to introduce readers to the most important of these competing ideologies. (For a general introductory perspective on ideologies see Skilbeck, M., 1976, *Ideologies and Values*, E203 Curriculum Design and Development, Open University Press).

Educational ideologies comprise different clusters of beliefs, values, principles, sentiments and understandings; they attempt to give meaning, and direction to the complex and diverse practical enterprise of teaching. They employ their own combinations of ideas and metaphors which give their adherents a sense of what is 'right' for children in schools. Most have their 'gurus', their 'sacred books' and their 'texts'. At least three writers have attempted to examine primary education from this general perspective, though the first of these did not use the term 'ideology' as such. Twenty years ago Blyth (1965) distinguished three 'traditions' (elementary, preparatory and developmental) in the development of English primary education; extracts from his analysis appear as the first paper in section 1 of the reader. More recently, Golby (1982) has examined three 'traditions' in the primary field — the *progressive, elementary* and *technological* traditions (see the last paper in this section). These writers provide alternative frameworks to the one employed here to characterize contrasting views of primary education. Here, four main ideologies are identified (Richards, 1979, 1982):

1 *liberal romanticism* — which starts from, and constantly refers back to, the individual child when developing educational principles. Compared with other ideologies it advocates a more equal partnership of teacher and taught, with teachers learning 'alongside' children, and it offers children a relatively high degree of choice in the type, content and duration of activities;

2 *educational conservatism* — which stresses the importance of continuity with the past and views the curriculum as a repository of worthwhile activities and values into which learners need to be initiated in an orderly systematic way;

3 *liberal pragmatism* — which argues that schools need to be equally responsive to the demands of the wider society as to the 'needs' of the individual. School is seen as providing a set of learning experiences, largely but not entirely structured and directed by the teacher, but respecting, to some degree, both the individuality of the child and the importance of continuity with the past;

4 *social democracy* — which views education as one means towards realizing social justice. School is seen as an agency concerned, not so much with enhancing the individuality of each child, but with helping to create social beings who can work cooperatively to bring about change both in the immediate environment and in society generally.

With the exception of the last extract, the extracts forming this section have been chosen to illustrate each of these ideologies. They demonstrate clearly that primary education is far from being a simple uncontentious matter.

Reference

GOLBY, M., (1982) 'Microcomputers in the primary curriculum' in GARLAND, R. (Ed.), *Microcomputers and Children in the Primary School*, Lewes, Falmer Press.
RICHARDS, C., (1982) *'Primary Education 1974–80'* in RICHARDS, C. (Ed.), *New Directions in Primary Education*, Lewes, Falmer Press.

A *Liberal Romanticism*

Basic Assumptions

(From Brearley, M., 1974, 'Open schooling', *Education 3–13*, 2, 2, pp. 85–7.)

One of the problems for students of primary education is the looseness of many of the terms used in educational literature. Terms such as 'child-centred', 'open' or 'informal', for example, have a range of meanings. Too often, authors do not clarify what they mean by particular terms in particular contexts. In this extract, Molly Brearley, a former principal of a college of education and a member of the Plowden Committee, does make clear what she means by 'open schooling'. She gets to the heart of a liberal romantic view of primary education by uncovering a number of basic beliefs or assumptions about why and how children learn and about the role of teachers in facilitating such learning. Such beliefs are deeply held but, often, not made explicit by teachers subscribing to this view of primary education. They underlie the criteria for a 'good' school put forward in the second extract, the 'philosophy of education' discussed in the third, and the approach advocated in the fourth. For a more detailed, elaboration of one person's liberal romantic view of education, readers are referred to Armstrong's summary of Hawkins' 'Informed vision' (pp. 146–153); for a critical analysis Dearden's analysis of 'Child-centred education' (pp. 127–133) should be read.

The idea of 'Open-Schooling' has developed into something of a mystique. There is a suggestion that 'open' schools have a distinctive set of procedures and activities by which they can be recognised at once and that if these were adopted schools would immediately be 'open'. This would be seen as desirable by some people and undesirable by others.

We all know how easy it is to 'colour' words like open. This can be seen most clearly in the alternatives we choose. For most people 'open', by itself, is a good word but we define it very differently by our choice of opposites: closed, shut, planned, structural, formal, to name but a very few! The heart of the matter, however, lies much deeper. It is not a matter of semantics but of the basic *assumptions* on which the school is run. It is of the essence of this approach that the schools which result will be different from one another, as well as from other school regimes based on other assumptions, because the individual interpretations must be geared to the specific circumstances of the school. It is possible to go even farther and say that two schools which superficially look alike, with much the same equipment and activities going on might be based on quite different assumptions. These would reveal themselves pretty quickly to professionals but might not be equally clear to the layman.

A personal list of main assumptions (surrounded by many subsidiary ones) on which the idea of 'open-schooling' rests is outlined here.

Assumption 1

That man is a learning animal and young children are supplied with a fund of curiosity which will lead to learning if, in the first place, we don't prevent it and, in the second, we provide ample and appropriate material for learning the work on. Any teacher meeting a child at five years old (or three) who has lost this thrust for learning is dealing with a remedial problem (much more important than the curiously named 'remedial reading') and must put attention to this before anything else.

The great mass of children, fortunately, when they come to school at three or four or five are still 'open' to learning and our responsibility for keeping that openness is very great. The task of a first school is to feed the interests already there and to create new ones by the really active use of the environment and all that the teachers know about it. The belief in man as an essentially 'learning' organism implies that interest will bring effort and mastery rather than that externally demanded response is a necessary condition of learning. Needless to say, this is no exact polarisation: interest can be dissipated for lack of nourishment or may in itself be fleeting or indeed, may well be roused by some external stimulus. The point is, that unless the energy of interest is called on *at some point* the learning suffers and may well be very temporary. The problem group of truants and drop-outs have had plenty of teaching but clearly their interests have not been involved or they would not reject school.

Assumption 2

That one of the school's most important tasks is to retain and put on a sound footing the confidence in their power to learn that is present in young children. Probably every child goes to school with the belief that he can learn to read etc. And so he can, if he is not grossly defective (and even then there are many things he *can* learn). We can only retain this confidence if in fact what is demanded of him is within his powers. Comparison and competition between children, certainly in the early stages, is nonproductive. True, a child may be the only one in the class who cannot master a particular point. He will not be less so, if this is continually pointed out. He will, however, lose his confidence in his own powers. (This is not to argue against a proper understanding of our own limitations. In the first place, however, in the early years in school we have few reliable methods of knowing what these are and can easily be led into error by self fulfilling prophecies, and in the second place, life fully experienced will teach us that soon enough. It should not rest on the teacher's word.)

The role of confidence in learning and efficiency is far from being fully understood. This manifests itself clearly in competitive sport. It is only the competitor of exceptional self confidence who is not daunted by initial setback. Indeed the end result often seems to be determined by the amount of nerve that can be called on.

We can help a child to retain this confidence by aiding the building up of skills and abilities which prove to him that his confidence is well founded. This cannot be arbitrarily imposed on a whole class or group because the failure rate is too great to retain the confidence of all the learners. We must work from a basis of what he can do and has achieved. The idea of some 'average' standard to be reached at a given age can have no meaning for a child and, by definition, can fit only a proportion of the group, thereby damaging (if not equally) each end of the spectrum.

Assumption 3

That children, like the rest of us, must learn *first* through concrete experiences. The adult's part is to help in the formulation and abstraction of these. Experience alone teaches something, but, unless a child has sensitive and knowledgeable adults around who will help him knit his experiences together by analysis, synthesis and definition, the learning will remain fragmented and perhaps unusable. There may indeed be children of exceptional ability who do this without adult help but it is for most children the very heart of what they get from school. Knowledge and skills are not the ends but the means of education.

It is sad to find so many children still pitifully short of experience. The growth of vocabulary and use of language which everybody would regard as a concern of the school is often stunted for lack of the simplest day to day experience to feed it. I went into a school, in 1974, where not one child in a class of forty seven-year-olds had been the ten minute bus ride to the nearest park, not one had been the ten minute ride to the public library with a good children's section or the fifteen minutes ride to the next township which contains many interesting historical buildings, yet they were 'doing' the coming of the Normans (a race dressed entirely, it seems, in silver paper). The school is in the centre of a large run-down outer city housing estate. The building itself was well kept and bright with interesting pictures and objects within it but it was *not* based on first-hand experience and was not absorbing the children in spite of the sincere efforts of the staff whose concern was to make up for the drabness of the district. This is an example of the contrast that can exist between the actual appearance and activities in the school and the basic assumptions on which it is being run. In spite of much that was being done for the children it remained a closed system because abstractions were being *substituted* for the experiences from which they are made. It is far from easy to define or decide on the amount of first-hand experience which should precede the later more organised learning. A day's outing might provide experience for weeks of further work including other first-hand experiences arising from it. There is a conscientious feeling on the part of many teachers that time is short and that if they do not get in a certain amount of teaching and practice the children will be penalised. The amount of time spent on an activity however has little necessary correlation with the amount learnt as we all know if we examine our own experience. We know that a course or a 'craze' or a meeting with an expert may spark off a deeper level of thinking and experiencing than many previous months or years of routine learning.

We need to devise an education that bridges the gap between concrete experience and abstract language, for everybody. This is as important for the academically able child as for the less able.

The whole controversy of structured v. unstructured education has gone astray on the fundamental misunderstanding as to *where* the structuring must take place. The actual building of a mental structure is an activity that can only take place within the learner. No one can build without some kind of 'bricks' let alone straw, but equally, few people collect bricks or straw without some purpose in mind. We have to see that the source material and the stimuli for such mental structures are there but it is even more important that the teacher understands the nature of the building process and how it can be brought about. This is too large a subject to be expanded here but what could be called the 'template' view of structured learning gets one no further than the frieze of identical Father Christmases, though they might look pretty on the wall.

Assumption 4

That teachers are professionally able to evaluate their work. The battery of tests etc. that purport to do this have little (not 'no') proven value. Observation of children, the study of their work, their confidence, their attitudes to error and experiment must be known to the teacher. Those aspects that can be carefully (for many reasons I will not say accurately) measured are not necessarily the most important or predictive. The teacher must be professionally capable of judging when a child is ready (an active, cultivated, as well as a maturational, state) for further, more ordered, work. The books, the outside experts, visits etc. that will further their learning must be sought and the children encouraged to stretch themselves (not to be stretched) to master the material which alone will give them intellectual power. Of course the teachers suggest, encourage and support but the real and lasting motivation lies in the satisfaction the children find in this mastery.

Assumption 5

That being open to the world around includes being open to parents. This again is too big a subject to explore at this point. There is no part of the work in which one school is more likely to differ from another than this. There can be no uniformity: the circumstances of the school, the staff and the parents must make the procedures quite idiosyncratic. Since for good or ill we learn our basic lessons from our homes we have everything to gain by making education a joint task for home and school. The levels at which this cooperation can take place are poles apart and may indeed include times when children, parents and teachers need a rest from one another, but the principle remains that teachers and parents must cooperate if they wish their children to thrive.

Assumption 6

That 'living is now'. If school life is satisfying, stimulating, cooperative and, sometimes at best, exciting, commonsense tells us that this is likely to build a population concerned to live full and interesting lives with a real concern for the welfare of others not solely linked to material values. Who would not wish to live in such a society? We have too long believed in a magic open-Sesame kind of education. Perhaps 'open-schooling' could bring into being a more effective and realistic approach.

Criteria of a Good Primary School

(From 'What are the criteria of a good junior school?', Junior School Sub-Panel, Ministry of Education, May 1946, reprinted in Griffin-Beale, C. (Ed.), 1979, *Christian Schiller — in His Own Words*, A. and C. Black, pp. 1–2.)

As the text indicates, this paper was originally concerned with the junior school, an institution only recently established when the paper was first written. It is included here because it applies equally well to the primary school or, with the possible omission of the last point, to the infant or first school. The document was written by Christian Schiller, the first Staff Inspector of Junior Education, and a very powerful, though almost unacknowledged influence, on the development of post-war primary education. Concisely and clearly, it embodies many of the ideas and metaphors associated with liberal romanticism. It refers to stages of development, to phases of growth, and to children's powers of expression. It emphasizes the importance of language, observation, movement and the arts — all themes later elaborated by theorists and practitioners of like persuasion. It talks of children's happiness, self-confidence, interests and 'that pecular absorption which comes when activities exactly meet children's immediate needs' (see p. 147). It is a beautifully written and deceptively simple distillation of a very powerful view of primary education — a view which was to have a great influence on the Central Advisory Council for Education, the Plowden Committee, when it produced its report, *Children and Their Primary Schools*, published in 1967.

What Are the Criteria of a Good Junior School?
Junior School Sub-Panel, Ministry of Education

These notes try to suggest an outline to one answer to this question. But even the outline of an answer can only be drawn in words, and in this case in words which describe new ideas. New ideas should be spread out and all their meanings noted before being packed in a phrase, and this is a task which we might well undertake. But it will take time. Meanwhile it may be useful to launch out hopefully into language and see where we can get. What we might look for first in a junior school is its purpose; what it is attempting to do. In a good junior school we might expect to find:

— that the school conceives of primary education, not as a preparation for something to follow, but as a fulfilment of a stage of development;

— that the school seeks to achieve this fulfilment, not by securing certain standards of attainment, but by providing in abundance such experience and activities as will enable all the children to develop to the full at each phase of growth.

Next we might look to see in what ways this purpose is being carried out. In a good junior school we might expect to find:

— that the children are expressing their powers in language, in movement, in music, in painting, and in making things — that is to say, as artists;

— that the children are developing their powers in language, in observation, in counting, and in the use of the body — that is to say, as workmen;

— that the children are learning to live together to the best advantage.

Then we might look to see how effective is the organisation of the experience and activities provided. In a good junior school we might expect to find:

— that all the children in every class, from the very slow or backward to the very bright and forward, can be usefully occupied within the range of experience and activities normally provided;

— that the children's need for movement and for rest determine the arrangement of experience and activities, and how much the children get out of an experience or activity determines the amount of time given to it;

— that the children's experience and activities take full advantage of all the facilities available, and especially outdoors.

Lastly, we might look to see how far the school's purpose has been accomplished by noting what the children are and what they can do. In a good junior school we might expect to find:

— that the children are happy, self-confident, and are able to live agreeably with others;

— that the children are not only interested, but show that peculiar absorption which comes when activities exactly meet their immediate needs;

— that the children can talk freely and with understanding about the town or country around their home, and about what it contains;

— that the children's power of self-expression in at least one of the arts has developed sufficiently to satisfy their power of criticism;

— that in the oldest class there are only odd children who cannot read, write or count a little; and that in this class there are many children who can read fluently and with understanding, write quickly and legibly, and calculate easily by the four rules with numbers, and simple measures, up to 100 in size.

'A Recognisable Philosophy of Education'

(From Central Advisory Council for Education (England), 1967, *Children and Their Primary Schools*, Vol. 1, London, HMSO, pp. 187–8.)

Liberal romanticism received official endorsement in the report issued by the Central Advisory Council for Education (England) under the chairmanship of Lady Plowden. Thereafter, it became the orthodoxy of English primary education for almost a decade, at least as perceived by many policy-makers, commentators and educationists. The three paragraphs reproduced here capture the essence of that 'recognisable philosophy of education' which the Plowden Committee believed, mistakenly as it turned out, to be 'a general and quickening trend'. In particular, paragraph 505 is a memorable encapsulation of the liberal romantic view, standing along with paragraph 75 of the Hadow Report of 1931 (see p. 27) as the embodiment of a view of primary education which many have found very inspiring and many others have found sententious, sentimental and verging on the anti-intellectual. These paragraphs are superb examples of educational rhetoric, unsurpassed in style by the rhetoric of Plowden's opponents, as scrutiny of other papers in this source book will reveal. For a critique of this ideology, see the paper by Peters (pp. 117–122).

504.   If these methods were applied to all primary schools it would be apparent that the trend of their practices and outlook corresponds to a recognisable philosophy of education, and to a view of society, which may be summarised as follows.

505.   A school is not merely a teaching shop, it [transmits] values and attitudes. It is a community in which children learn to live first and foremost as children and not as future adults. In family life children learn to live with people of all ages. The school sets out deliberately to devise the right environment for children, to allow them to be themselves and to develop in the way and at the pace appropriate to them. It tries to equalise opportunities and to compensate for handicaps. It lays special stress on individual discovery, on first hand experience and on opportunities for creative work. It insists that knowledge does not fall into neatly separate compartments and that work and play are not opposite but complementary. A child brought up in such an atmosphere at all stages of his education has some hope of becoming a balanced and mature adult and of being able to live in, to contribute to, and to look critically at the society of which he

forms a part. Not all primary schools correspond to this picture, but it does represent a general and quickening trend.

506.   Some people, while conceding that children are happier under the modern regime and perhaps more versatile, question whether they are being fitted to grapple with the world which they will enter when they leave school. This view is worth examining because it is quite widely held, but we think it rests on a misconception. It isolates the long term objective, that of living in and serving society, and regards education as being at all stages recognisably and specifically a preparation for this. It fails to understand that the best preparation for being a happy and useful man or woman is to live fully as a child. Finally, it assumes, quite wrongly, that the older virtues, as they are usually called, of neatness, accuracy, care and persever- ance, and the sheer knowledge which is an essential of being educated, will decline. These are genuine virtues and an education which does not foster them is faulty.

507.   Society is right to expect that importance will be attached to these virtues in all schools. Children need them and need knowledge, if they are to gain satisfaction from their education. What we repudiate is the view that they were automatically fostered by the old kind of elementary education. Patently they were not, for enormous numbers of the products of that education do not possess them. Still more we repudiate the fear that the modern primary approach leads to their neglect. On the contrary it can, and, when properly understood, does lay a much firmer foundation for their development and it is more in the interests of the children. But those interests are complex. Children need to be themselves, to live with other children and with grown ups, to learn from their environment, to enjoy the present, to get ready for the future, to create and to love, to learn to face adversity, to behave responsibly, in a word, to be human beings. Decisions about the influences and situations that ought to be contrived to these ends must be left to individual schools, teachers and parents. What must be ensured is that the decisions taken in schools spring from the best available knowledge and are not simply dictated by habit or convention.

Teaching through the Arts

(From Marshall, S., 1963, *An Experiment in Education*, Cambridge University Press, pp. 170–3, 106–8.)

An educational ideology such as liberal romanticism is not a tightly argued creed codified in words and ritualized in practice. It admits of a variety of interpretations. English primary education has witnessed a number of variants of liberal romanticism, in some cases associated with geographical regions such as Oxfordshire or Leicestershire or the former West Riding of Yorkshire, and in some cases associated with individuals such as Robin Tanner or Sybil Marshall. This fourth extract is from the latter's aptly named 'experiment' in education and describes an approach through art, a theme underlying other variants, but idiosyncratically and powerfully rendered by Marshall in her village school in the fifties. The extract is in two parts. Part I describes her 'symphonic method' around which she based so much of her work and from which her children produced such 'vital, vigorous, felt English' and superb art work. Though concerned with art teaching in particular, Part II addresses a more general and perplexing question for the liberal romantic: What is the role of the teacher? How, in Plowden's words, is the teacher 'to select an environment which will encourage curiosity, to focus attention on enquiries which will lead to useful discovery, to collaborate with children, to lead from behind' (para. 875). How, in particular, is the teacher to assess children's work? [The extract begins with Marshall considering how her approach to education through art evolved, that is:]

... From a starting point which was nothing but an intuition that 'art' (meaning drawing) was a good thing, to the realisation that it was an education in itself; to the widening of the field by using art as a means towards a better, fresher view of the social subjects, history, geography, nature study; to the comprehension of its astounding significance in encouraging vital, vigorous, *felt* English, in direct contact with life being lived and to be lived. To bring the wheel full circle, one more turn was necessary. Education must have an end in view, for it is not an end in itself. The end can only be the knowledge of what it means really to live, and the wisdom to accept and make the most of what life offers each individual person. Such knowledge and such wisdom cannot be found within the limits of one's own age, ability and aptitude, nor by heredity, environment, nor instruction. It cannot even be bounded by time itself, for it would be an impercipient spirit who could not 'place' his own inevitable suffering a little better for having read and heard The Book of Job, *King Lear*, or Mozart's G Minor Symphony, and an even poorer one who could not be uplifted by some work of art which for him had special significance.

To believe in their own potentiality for creativity was for the children the first half of their journey towards being educated beings. The other half could be completed only when they could see their own lives surrounded, sustained, and indeed explained by the general experience of all humanity. This part of the journey will take them all the rest of their lives, but to know this is the greatest wisdom they can learn at school. To be able to approach the classic works of art without fear, and with pleasure, interest, understanding and love is to be able to tap the inexhaustible well of past human experience. It was a tentative search for the path leading to the second half of the journey, for a track of some kind that they could in future follow to the world of strength and delight they could find in the arts, that made me recognise the opening when yet another lucky chance delivered the chart right into my hands.

John had been a pupil of the school since he was four, but now he was seven, and about to be transferred to a preparatory school in Cambridge. On the evening of the day he left us, his mother rang me on the telephone, saying that John would like to give a school a present, and could come down to deliver it. Naturally, I was pleased with this mark of appreciation, and as these parents were of the very nicest kind and could be relied upon to choose wisely, I anticipated something in the nature of some really good books for the school library, or something similar. But when John and his mother arrived, I was overwhelmed. The gift was a Pye 'Black Box' record-player!

School had already closed for the Easter holiday, so I kept the precious thing in my house until we opened again for the summer term. On the first morning back I carried it round to school and presented it to the astonished class. After the first dumbfounded moment — I remember only one other like it, when surprise and delight robbed everybody of speech; that was when I announced to them that we had been given the prize for the best co-operative frieze in the 1957 *Sunday Pictorial* Exhibition — the first child to find a voice said, 'Play us something on it'.

I had no suitable records in school, so I dashed round the corner to my house and began to turn over records in frantic haste to find one I thought the children might enjoy. The first one to come to hand was Beethoven's Pastoral Symphony. I rushed back to school and set the disc spinning — no prayers, no register, no dinner money collection, no formal beginning to the day or the term; just twenty-six children, one adult, and Beethoven. At the end of the second movement, Derek said ecstatically 'Isn't it SMASHING!' I felt that it was indeed an extra-special moment, for while they had listened I had found the answer to the problem I had been trying to work out. We were going to base our whole term's work on 'The Pastoral', and see what came of it. The work in the last section of this book is the result.

It was only the first term of several that work was pushed off from some chosen work of art. I called my new method, in fun, 'the symphonic method', but the more I thought about it, the more I realised how apt a title I had hit upon. In this method the separate subjects are analogous to the different sections of an orchestra, playing in concert for full effect every now and then, but in between these moments, first one and then the other taking up the theme. This theme occurs and recurs, but the entire symphony is not one endless repetition of the melody. Though all the work is in some way related to the theme, it is not tied to it nor limited by it, as it is in the so-called 'project method'; nor does it employ one group of instruments only, as in the 'centre of interest' method. My objection to both those otherwise good ideas has been that the various subjects have been made to fit into the chosen theme, whether they would or not, or else neglected entirely because they were too far away to be tied to it, however clumsily. The 'symphonic method' allows for second subjects, bridge passages, variations, differences of tempo and indeed, wholly separate movements; yet the term's work, like a symphony, is only completely satisfactory as an entire whole.

This method is obviously not for everybody, any more than a violin is every musician's instrument; there are many who could get a better tune out of a mouth organ than they ever could out of a violin, and if they know that, they will be wise to leave the violin alone. But have they ever tried anything but a mouth organ? Until they have, they must not be too sure. Then again, for all I know, the sciences, in the hands of an expert teacher, might produce the same amount of interest and the same fresh English. Because I am by nature incapable, it seems, of working up much enthusiasm in myself about scientific matters, I doubt my own ability to teach through the sciences — but I think it could be done, and I expect the results in mathematics by that method would parallel the results I claim for English in my own method through the arts. The real secret of any method is the teacher's devotion and enthusiasm; one string and Paganini makes better music than a bored orchestra and a befuddled conductor. So, if anybody at all in the educational world has enjoyed this description of my experiments enough to start experimenting on his own behalf, I shall be well paid.

[What Is the Role of the Teacher?]

The new conception of child art simply takes into account that children are not solely adults in the making, but creatures in their own right, as tadpoles differ from mature frogs, or caterpillars from butterflies. They have their own set of emotions, abilities, and techniques. What is expected of them is child-like, not pre-adult work. All that is asked is that they should do what comes naturally to them, within the bounds of reason and common sense.

This never has meant that 'just anything' will do in art, any more than a set of figures printed upside down and back-to-front would be called a sum and accepted as such for very long, in the arithmetic lesson, though many children write their number symbols the wrong way round at first. In the early stages of number, as long as they understand the threeness of three, so to speak, the printing of the symbol backwards is of small moment, but the teacher usually tries her hardest to persuade a child that there is a right way round before he leaves the infant school. Similarly, in art, the figure with the arms coming out directly from the side of the head would be completely acceptable from a four-year-old, because of the moment of vision behind the attempt to portray a man: but to allow a normal child of eleven to draw a man like this on the grounds that it was 'child art' would be a piece of conscious naïveté that would turn the stomach of a sincere artist or teacher. So while we do not now impose adult standards, we work towards them as the child grows towards adulthood, which really means that all children go on developing naturally, and that the development should show in the work they produce.

It is therefore absolutely imperative for any teacher that he possess criteria of his own, and that because they can trust his judgement, his pupils can learn to form their own. He must have standards, and they must be high. In applying them he is bound to be critical, and fails in his duty if he is not. The teacher who smiles encouragingly at every unrecognisable daub and tells the perpetrator that it is good, just to encourage him, must expect nothing better, for as Dr Johnson so rightly said, he who praises everybody praises nobody. In fact, this teacher may often expect worse, especially from an intelligent class, for I would not put it beyond any boy I had in my recent class, under such influence, to put his tongue into his cheek and try deliberately to see just how far he could go. Most children instinctively mistrust this kind of fulsome flattery, and know, as country people say of a frozen potato, that it is 'oversweet to be wholesome'.

Nor are children averse to candid criticism provided that it is honest, fair and constructive. Moreover, they are the very best critics of each other's work, and once trained well, of their own. The boy or girl who always says 'I don't like mine' is the most dangerous, for he is usually courting flattery from his teacher and his fellows: but the child who will stand before his own picture now and then and say 'I think mine is the best' has proved his confidence in himself not only as an artist, but as an unbiased critic.

In being critical, however, the teacher must not avoid Scylla only to fall a victim to Charybdis. However good the children are, they will not produce adult work. Their work will be essentially child-like, and to assess this work anyone is up against a very real difficulty. For though he was a child himself once, though he may have made a serious study of child psychology and development, though he may have spent years at work among children, the fact is inescapable that he is an adult now. His memories of childhood are remembered with an adult memory, his knowledge of children is an adult's knowledge, and his conception of what is child-like is adult, too. The absolutely impossible thing for most people is too see anything as a child sees it, unclouded by maturity, and not through the mirror of assimilated experience. So in being critical he must beware of judging by what *he thinks* a child should do, or what a child should like; the criterion is what the child does do, and what he likes.

B *Educational Conservatism*

Black Paper Basics

(From Cox, C. and Boyson, R. (Eds) 1975, *Black Paper 75*. Dent, p. 1.)

Educational conservatism found its most vocal expression in the polemical set of Black Papers issued from 1969 onwards. Initially, these were dismissed very easily by those in schools and higher education, but later they had to be taken very seriously indeed as their criticisms struck raw nerves in both politicians and parents. Educational conservatism represented a reaction to the so-called 'libertarianism', believed by Black Paper writers to have characterized education in the sixties. Black Paper slogans included 'Back to the basics', 'The preservation of standards', and 'The importance of structure'. As this first extract shows, liberal romantic (as well as social democratic) notions of 'freedom', 'equality of opportunity' and 'non-competitive ethos' were violently attacked and, reinterpreted, were used as weapons against the purveyors of 'left-wing radicalism' in the schools. Primary education was singled out as a major cause of student unrest and other unwelcome tendencies and phenomena both within education and the wider society. Though some of the ten points do not apply directly to primary education, 'Black Paper Basics' is reproduced in full here; it represents educational conservatism at its most assertive and strident. The ten points advanced are regarded by their authors as self-evident; there is no invitation to discussion, only pressure to concur. The emotional appeal of such confident assertions to anxious politicians, parents and teachers cannot be disputed; their intellectual validity is much more open to question.

Black Paper Basics

Ten Points

1   Children are not naturally good. They need firm, tactful discipline from parents and teachers with clear standards. Too much freedom for children breeds selfishness, vandalism and personal unhappiness.

2   If the non-competitive ethos of progressive education is allowed to dominate our schools, we shall produce a generation unable to

maintain our standards of living when opposed by fierce rivalry from overseas competitors.

3   It is the quality of teachers which matters, rather than their numbers or their equipment. We have sacrificed quality for numbers, and the result has been a lowering of standards. We need high-quality, higher-paid teachers in the classroom, not as counsellors or administrators.

4   Schools are for schooling, not social engineering.

5   The best way to help children in deprived areas is to teach them to be literate and numerate, and to develop all their potential abilities.

6   Every normal child should be able to read by the age of seven. This can be achieved by the hard work of teachers who use a structured approach.

7   Without selection the clever working-class child in a deprived area stands little chance of a real academic education.

8   External examinations are essential for schools, colleges, polytechnics and universities. Without such checks, standards decline. Working-class children suffer when applying for jobs if they cannot bring forward proof of their worth achieved in authoritative examinations.

9   Freedom of speech must be preserved in universities. Institutions which cannot maintain proper standards of open debate should be closed.

10 You can have equality or equality of opportunity; you cannot have both. Equality will mean the holding back (or the new deprivation) of the brighter children.

Putting Primary Education Back on the Right Track

(From Froome, S., 1974. 'Back on the right track', *Education 3–13*, 2, 1, pp. 13–16.)

Educational conservatism has spoken with voices other than the shrill tones of the more extreme Black Paper writers. It has found intellectual justification in some of the work of Bantock, part of whose critique of progressivism is reproduced later in the reader (pp. 134–138). Here, it finds relatively moderate expression in the views of Stuart Froome, former primary head and member of the Bullock Committee. In this extract he offers a reasoned critique of post-war developments in primary education and makes his own suggestions for getting education back on the *right* track. By seeking to portray children and schools 'as they really are', he attacks some of the assumptions outlined by Brearley earlier in this book. His concern for 'more systematic and structured methods of schooling', the importance he attaches to the acquisition of knowledge by primary children, and his unwillingness to allow children too much freedom in what or how they learn, are representative of the views of a substantial proportion of primary teachers, many more than the advocates or detractors of liberal romanticism or educational conservatism may care to admit.

When Edmund Burke, the eighteenth century political thinker remarked that one sure symptom of an ill-conducted state was the propensity of the people to resort to theories, he was not thinking about education, but this cogent observation might well be applied to the situation in which we find ourselves today. Since the last war there has been a greater expansion of education in terms of money and manpower than had ever before been contemplated, and at the moment the cost of education exceeds what is spent on national defence. It would, however, be foolishly complacent to claim that the vast expenditure on schooling of all kinds has significantly improved standards of achievement in what used to be called the basic subjects of the curriculum. Indeed, during the past five years there have been significant murmurs of discontent from a number of quarters about the many school-leavers who cannot spell, write accurately or cipher satisfactorily, while the public at large is beginning to think that a return to more systematic and structured methods of schooling is long overdue.

After the passing of the Butler Act in 1944, which laid it down that every child must be educated in accordance with his age, aptitude and ability, the public was generally agreeable to vast sums of money being spent to achieve this highly desirable end. As Professor Parkinson would have warned however, increased expenditure on a project does not necessarily result in increased efficiency or productivity, and it is certain that the appointment of too many cooks is quite likely to water-down the nutritional strength of the educational broth.

With the dissatisfaction expressed with reading standards in a number of surveys made, after the war and the general willingness to spend money to improve education came a spate of untried theories, nostrums, stunts and gimmicks which were only notable for their transience and impracticability. It was claimed that many of these innovatory ideas were based on the child-centred philosophy of John Dewey, who it was said had advocated the abandonment of the traditional scholastic approach to education and the replacement of it by a method of teaching in which the child was the sole agent of his own learning. Dewey had certainly criticised the formal, didactic, 'chalk and talk' mode of teaching because of its 'passivity of attitude, its mechanical massing of children, its uniformity of curriculum and method.' While it must be admitted that there were some valid grounds for such criticism, it was extremely doubtful if the ordinary run-of-the-mill teacher would ever be capable of organising his approach to pupils on any but the most formal, traditional lines. Certainly with the huge classes and cramped accommodation of the post-war era, it was quite unrealistic to attempt to put Dewey's child-centred notions into practice.

However, the limitations of the average school establishment did not in any way deter the theoretical educationists from promulgating the Dewey dogmas and urging on the schools educational methods which were remarkable more for their plausible attractiveness than for their soundness and practicability. For myself, I was in no way convinced by the champions of informal child-centred schooling, because I did not think such methods were appropriate for schools and children as they really are, not as they exist in the minds of dilettante advisers who seldom have to carry out in practice the theories which they so strenuously advocate.

I have moreover, always felt that there was a wide gulf between the theoretical advice offered to teacher-students by college of education lecturers and educational advisers and the practicalities of classroom procedure. Having begun my teaching career as a student-teacher at the age of seventeen, I had largely learnt how to cope with the problems of class control and the complications of organising a programme of work with overlarge classes before I entered upon my college training. I had thus served a useful practical apprenticeship, and with this behind me I could absorb educational theory and psychology with a certain critical appraisal. I confess however, that I never felt that what was regarded in colleges of education as ideal teaching methodology, could ever be equated with the humdrum pedestrian practices which of necessity were the mainspring of the teacher's daily round. It was fascinating to read Rousseau, William

James and Dewey and to feel that what they said might have some relevance in an ideal classroom situation and with small groups of amenable children, but I knew that real-life schools had classes of fifty or sixty and that the children were in the main unwilling participators in the educational struggle. After college training, to return to the schools was to begin a further period of disillusionment with current educational thinking, and since that time it has appeared to me that the purpose of most advice proferred by both county and Her Majesty's Inspectors has been not to improve the amount of quality of learning to be assimilated by the child, but both to water . . . down the content of knowledge and at the same time to prolong the period over which children are to be taught. This process of dilution appears to me to have been deliberate, but it was done so gradually and insidiously that those who suffered under it were hardly conscious of the changes taking place.

First of all there came an attack on what was called rote-learning. It was alleged that to commit to memory the facts of such subjects as history or geography was rather an unworthy accomplishment, and in any case what was the point of remembering and repeating facts like a parrot when they could be so easily discovered in a reference book? Having made the retention of information sound rather disreputable it was an obvious sequitur to suggest that the learning of multiplication and other tables was equally obnoxious because a table-book or ready-reckoner could provide all that was necessary to be reasonably successful at elementary arithmetic.

At the same time as this general condemnation of rote-learning was being thrust upon the schools as official policy, came the universal move towards 'look-and-say' as the most efficient method of teaching children to read. Because practised readers do not need to spell-out the sounds of letters but are able to recognise whole words at a glance, it was naively claimed that little children starting to read would be capable of the same skill, and would in fact learn to read altogether by this means. This putting the result at the beginning, which Professor Jacques Barzun has described as a 'preposterism', is in my view wholly responsible for the parlous state of reading in the schools of this country. I recently visited a large ILEA comprehensive school where the Head of the Remedial Department which employs no less than five teachers, informed me that of the school's yearly intake of 240 children aged eleven, no less than one-third had reading ages of eight or below, while the average reading age of the entire intake was 9.3 years as against their actual average age of 11.6. This number of retarded readers moreover was increasing year by year and was attributable in the Head of Department's opinion partly to 'look-and-say' and partly to the lack of teacher pressure in the contributing infant and junior schools.

What an indictment of current reading methods is revealed in these gloomy statistics! Indeed, 'look-and-say' which seeks to replace the tedium of repetitive drill in letter-sounds by something akin to pure guess-work is in the view of many teachers, largely responsible for the decline which has been revealed in the two latest surveys of children's reading ability. Reading is certainly the basis of writing and so it was inevitable that with the slowing-down of this skill should come a decline in the art of children's written expression. This was contributed to, by persistent advice from inspectors to teachers not to worry children unduly with writing-form, spelling, punctuation and grammatical sentence-construction. These so-called 'pedestrian and mechanical aspects of writing' were regarded as impediments to the fluent flow of ideas which children were bursting to communicate. It is of course not surprising that while older and more experienced practitioners were sceptical of this free-writing notion, the new laissez-faire approach to written expression was welcomed by younger teachers because there was now a legitimate excuse to avoid the tedious labour of marking and correcting the unimpeded upsurge of creativity which flowed unrestrainedly from so many juvenile pens. It is moreover also not surprising that after a decade or two of uncorrected creative writing, it is now common to find newly-qualified teachers who cannot spell, punctuate or write their sentences according to the rules of syntax. It would seem that their ability to communicate accurately has been stultified by the exuberance of their own creativity, and those who have shamefully advised them against excessive care in composition might well ponder the opinion of Dr Johnson on this subject. That which is written without much effort, is likely to be read without much pleasure.

Effort however, is a word to be avoided in modern educational parlance. Even though a distinct decline in the basic subjects has been apparent to many older teachers and even to the public at large, no steps have been taken to halt the downward slide, or to tighten-up the slackness which inevitably accompanies excessive freedom in educational practice. On the contrary. The Plowden Report endorses unreservedly what is called freedom and flexibility of curriculum whereby teaching on a subject base is replaced by topic-teaching and the integrated day.

Now the idea of topic-learning through which a child or group adopts some theme or subject of current interest such as air-travel or water-pollution and by consulting reference-books and making general enquiries is able to use reading, written-expression art and modelling as aids to investigation, seems at first sight an altogether admirable alternative to the dull routine of following subjects on a conventional time-table. However, like all such attractive innovatory practices, topic-learning can, and does in many instances, degenerate into mindless copying of information from books on to pages in 'project-folders' and interspersing these plagiarised extracts with cuttings from newspapers and magazines. In a recent HMI's report on reading for information in a number of schools in connection with project and topic work, it was stated that it was much less successfully practised than might have been expected, and extensive and selective consultation of reference books and sources appeared rare. More usually, the child just sought an encyclopedia or single-reference book and copied down what he found there, while often, questioning showed that this was done without any any real understanding of its meaning.

It would be manifestly unfair to condemn all modern innovatory practices in school because of the misapplication of them in some cases. However, it is the fact that most such innovations are foisted on to a long-suffering body of teachers without any real evidence of their usefulness, that has prompted my suspicion of such unproven methods, for I do at least know from personal experience that working from a subject timetable with stipulated schemes of work, and using straightforward didactic approach did ensure that attainable stages of schooling were reached at certain stated intervals. Could such a claim be seriously made by the advocates of topic-learning, the integrated curriculum and the open classroom?

Now while I freely admit that scholastic method is in need of periodic critical assessment, reform and redirection if it is not to become ossified and out of touch with contemporary thought and social change, I believe that the hostile reaction against the somewhat rigid and narrow conception of schooling as typified in some of the old elementaries, has been emotional rather than intellectual, and those who urged teachers to follow Dewey's child-centred theories, conveniently forgot that in emphasising the need for children's freedom of activity and experience, he also stressed the necessity for systematic training, accuracy and plain hard work. 'Play should not be fooling,' he said, 'the only way to prevent this consequence is to make regard for results enter into even the freest play activity.'

I have spent longer than I had intended on attempting to trace how the pattern and methods of British education have altered substantially during the past three or four decades, and how in consequence standards in the basic subjects of the curriculum have deteriorated. Such a critical review however, would have little point unless some suggestions were offered on how past errors can be rectified, and the mischievously misdirected educational train be put firmly, 'back on the right track.'

First, we must clearly define what it is we want our children to learn during that vital 3 to 13 period of their schooling. It would I think be generally agreed that reading should come at the top of the list of priorities, and it should be mastered with the aid of early phonics as soon as possible (three is not too early for some) without any regard for that chimerical notion 'reading readiness', which in my view was specifically invented to excuse an unnecessary prolongation of the reading process. After reading, whose function it is to enable the child to garner information and to be instructed as well as entertained, come speech and writing for articulacy, and number for computation. With the mastery of these basic skills children can express, research and solve, for with this competence comes a self-reliance which is necessary for true discovery.

Secondly, there is a need for a structured programme, where teacher, the expert, will build step-by-step understanding. The acquisition of knowledge is much too important to be left to the spontaneous whims and fancies of little children. It must be laid down in a systematic sequential pattern easily understood by teacher and taught, so that both participants can observe and measure the progress which is being made, while school inspectors should regard it as part of their task to ensure that viable schemes of work do exist.

Thirdly, because of the brevity of school life, every minute must be utilised fully, and that means the use of teacher demonstration followed by much general practice of skills to improve both group and individual standards. To avoid monotony, children can do individual assignments on choice, or specified tasks, but they must be able to follow instructions, work to plan and must always complete their chosen projects.

Fourthly, it must be recognised that learning is a difficult process involving much conscious effort and memorisation. Without this there can be no progress. It is not a jolly, pleasant game and so Dewey's activity and experience are not enough to bring it to a successful conclusion. Consequently, there must be stated aims, a timetable, an observable overall framework and a corpus of knowledge in every discipline to be transmitted from the teacher to the class. Informality of procedure is time-wasting and inefficient, and although some group-work is necessary to let children learn the value of co-operation, thus becoming aware of their fellows' strengths, the teacher must at all times be in charge. He cannot abdicate. Periodic testing of accomplishment, although today unfashionable, is also necessary not only for the teacher's benefit but so that pupils and parents can see the progress being made. Moreover, there should be recurrent national surveys of children's attainment which could best be carried out under the guidance of the Schools Council.

Fifthly and finally, I think it is time to dispel the romantic illusion that schooling must always be a joyful, agreeable and largely entertaining experience in which the child is always self-motivated. We may not desire a return to the rigid imposed discipline of the past when the schoolmaster was, in Goldsmith's words, 'a man severe, and stern to view'. On the other hand, the teacher's recent public image has become badly tarnished by association with methods which are more noteworthy for their sloppy informality than for their effectiveness. If we wish to refurbish this image it is necessary to disassociate the teaching profession from that popular anti-intellectualism which derides verbal learning, deplores structure, system and sequential scholastic attainment, seeks to abolish standards and examinations and above all desires to make the teacher a bosom pal of the pupil.

Goldsmith's schoolmaster may have been a somewhat forbidding character, but he was at least loved and respected for his wide knowledge and integrity. He is certainly preferable to the current Joyce Grenfellian caricature of the genial child-minder who, with toothy inane smile and sentimental posturing, waits hopefully in the background for her little charges to read, write and computate in their own good time. We should remember that firmness and sympathy are not incompatible qualities in a teacher, a fact which Goldsmith noted in his poem: *Yet he was kind, or if severe in aught, the love he bore to learning was in fault.*

C *Liberal Pragmatism*

The Importance of Planning, Organization and Assessment

(From DES, 1979, *Mathematics 5–11*, London, HMSO, pp. 7–11).

Judging from the surveys reported by Ashton (1975, *The Aims of Primary Education*, Macmillan), Bennett (1976, *Teaching Styles and Pupil Progress*, Open Books) and Taylor (1974, *Purpose, Power and Constraint in the Primary School Curriculum*, Macmillan), liberal pragmatism may well be the most widely held of the four ideologies outlined in this section of the reader, but paradoxically it is the most difficult to characterize and to exemplify clearly and concisely through extracts. At the primary stage advocates of liberal pragmatism advocate a broad curricular grounding for all children, in part preparatory for secondary education, but a grounding which takes account of the fact that children learn through both first- and second-hand experience, which uses children's knowledge and interests as starting points and contributions to ongoing work, but which shapes and refines children's experience along teacher-directed lines. Liberal pragmatism is characterized by a concern for planning and policy-making, for 'systematic progression and continuity', and for evaluation and assessment of children's learning. The ideology finds intellectual justification in the work of writers such as Dearden (pp. 139–145) and Richards (Volume 2), and underlies many of the recent HMI statements on primary education, such as (1980) *A View of the Curriculum* (London, HMSO, Volume 2) and (1978) *Primary Education in England* (London, HMSO). Neither of the latter contains a short passage which neatly exemplifies the ideology. Here, an extract from the HMI book, *Mathematics 5–11*, is reproduced. The concerns it voices about primary mathematics are very much the concerns that liberal pragmatism has for each area of the curriculum.

The primary teacher today is faced with a considerable task, brought about by the changes which have taken place in the teaching of mathematics. These have involved new content, new terms, new concepts and what many regard as a new approach to the teaching of the subject (although this approach has a very long history).

Today, the child is encouraged to make enquiries, investigate, discover and record; learning is not looked upon only as something imposed from without. It is recognised that it is through his own activity that the child is able to form the new concepts which will in turn be the basis of further mathematical ideas and thinking. These early experiences provide the foundation on which future learning is built.

The school which concentrates single-mindedly upon arithmetical skill alone is neglecting the whole range of important logical, geometrical, graphical and statistical ideas which children can meet before the age of 12. The school which stresses 'modern' topics and practical work for its own sake at the expense of consolidating number skills, systematic thought and learning, is equally guilty of neglecting its charges. The challenge is to encourage children to develop their mathemetical education along a broad front of experience while ensuring systematic progression and continuity.

The primary teacher, confronted with the task of providing a wide experience for her children, can be bewildered by the wealth of apparatus, material and equipment which are now available. *She must be capable of informed choice, bearing in mind the needs of her individual class within the school.* Planning is vital; and it cannot be achieved by teachers in isolation. Infant and junior teachers need to plan together within the school and between schools.

Although most schools have a scheme of work for mathematics, in many schools this needs to be revised, what is perhaps a greater problem is that large numbers of teachers experience difficulty in translating the scheme into an effective mathematics programme.

Within some primary schools today, teachers are endeavouring to work for some of the time in such a way that subject barriers are not emphasised. Many 'integrated' studies, resulting from this way of working, lend themselves admirably to the introduction of mathematics. This mode of working requires understanding of the mathematical potential of a wide variety of situations, and this in turn demands more mathematical knowledge than many teachers possess. As a result, the opportunities for developing mathematics from an integrated topic are too often under-developed. The thematic approach is unlikely to motivate all the mathematics which most children need to cover within the age range 5–11 years; it is necessary to provide adequate time for mathematics, to cover a scheme of work systematically, and to include sufficient regular revision of those skills which have been identified as necessary for further progress.

Organisation

The school or classroom organisation can be critical in determining the effectiveness of mathematical learning. Any decision on organisation needs to take into account the aims and objectives decided by the school or by teachers themselves.

It is essential for the teacher to intervene appropriately and give support and help, not only in the later stages of mathematical learning but also in structured 'play'; otherwise these activities are not fully utilized and can easily become meaningless and result in time wasting and a lack of progression. An activity which does not have the teacher's attention can seem to be less important to the children. In addition, the only work which draws the teacher's attention is that written in a book, it is quite natural that children should desire to work in this way however inappropriate it may be, in order to attract the teacher's approval. There are occasions, particularly with the younger children when the teacher needs to recognise that participating with the children in the activities she arranges might sometimes be the best use of mathematical time.

When the activities of a class are well organised children are able to work with much less direct supervision and teacher support. This allows the teacher to work with smaller groups and individuals within groups Class organisation which allows children the opportunity to exercise an informed choice needs not override the wish of the teacher to withdraw a group of children in order to teach them. Indeed, professional time can easily be wasted if on one day a teacher finds that she needs to introduce or teach the same skill eight times with eight individuals separately. In general, it is the extremes in classroom organisation which militate most acutely against the effective learning of the subject.

Forms of organisation which require children and their teacher to change their activity after a set period of time inhibit sustained work in mathematics. This is particularly true if the child has been working constructively with material or apparatus and needs an extension of time to complete his task before the equipment is packed away or used again for something else. A child will often work with deep concentration and effort on a task which has interested him, and to ask him to move off quickly on to some other area of experience can be unwise. If it is decided to impose timetabling restrictions these should be interpreted flexibly, bearing in mind the needs of the individual child. Over-fragmentation of the child's day should be avoided.

A further cause for concern is the quality of mathematical education which is available to those children who are able in the subject. Too often, schools present an insufficient challenge to the more able or highly gifted. In primary schools the problem is as important as at the secondary stage.

The efficacy of an organisation for mathematics can be judged by the following criteria.

Does the organisation provide opportunities for:

  i.   direct teaching of individuals, groups of various sizes and the whole class,
 ii.   practical work with appropriate material in a range of situations,
iii.   children to use mathematics across the curriculum and to see the relevance of mathematics in the different areas of study which mathematics pervades,
 iv.   discussion and consolidation of mathematical ideas with individuals, groups and the class,
  v.   project work or studies,
 vi.   effective remedial work for a variety of ability levels,
vii.   extended experiences for the more able pupils.
viii.   children to reflect on their experience and the kind of thinking they are engaged in, so that they are aware that the activities in which they are involved are mathematical,
 ix.   children to learn relevant work skills;
        recording and clear presentation, including an understanding of why this is important,
        the use of reference books,
        the use of measuring instruments.

Assessment

If teaching is to be successful, it is essential that the teacher should assess what is happening. *Assessment, evaluation, diagnosis* and *prescription* are all important and should feature in the planning of work in school, in a particular class or for groups or individuals. These forms of assessment are essential if children are to learn mathematics effectively and to make progress that is in accord with their ages and abilities.....

As a first step, the school should decide the purpose of its assessment procedures. The aim may be to grade children in order to assist transition to the next stage of education, and in this case there is little choice. A uniform scheme devised by the LEA would seem almost essential. Where the school has discretion, assessment may be part of a philosophy which embodies a belief in the stimulus of competition, or its purpose may primarily be diagnostic (seeking to reveal the learning problems of individual children), or it may be part of a more general strategy seeking to modify the future teaching planned for a group of children in the light of the collective progress made. All of these objectives imply different types of tests and appropriate record-keeping procedures.

It is necessary to evaluate what both individuals and groups are learning; the results may or may not reflect what the teacher believes she has taught. These procedures demand great courage and professionalism. A teacher should not feel a failure if, on occasion, what has been taught has not been learnt, providing that assessment is continually being carried out. Following the evaluation of the work done by pupils, it may be necessary for the teacher to diagnose the difficulties of a group of children or of a single child within a group. When a difficulty has been identified a prescription which gives specific help should follow, if success is to be achieved.

It is all too easy to restrict assessment to those aspects of mathematics teaching which are most easily tested. Efforts should be made to broaden assessment procedures to include as many as possible of the initially planned objectives of the course.

It is essential to know the ability of the child to apply skill and knowledge to problems associated with the world in which he lives. The teacher needs to know the child's attitudes towards mathematics, his perseverance, creativity (elaboration, fluency, flexibility and originality), his understanding, visualisation and psychomotor skills. At the present time, skills which are described as mathematical are applied across the curriculum. It is necessary to assess this — to assess the ability to generalise, to classify and to identify and select the essentials which determine the solution of a practical problem.

Formal examinations, based on syllabus content, frequently limit the teaching of mathematics to that which is to be tested. Objective tests. although they give a wide coverage and facilitate rapid marking, seldom reflect good methods of teaching or satisfactory levels of learning. In addition, the existing tests in no way assess mathematical creativity.

Oral questioning is an important method of checking particularly for some areas of the curriculum and for some pupils. Certain aspects of the work can be reliably tested particularly well in this way (for example, rapid recall of number facts). For other work, judgement based on this type of testing, unless very carefully prepared, can be unreliable. Oral questioning is usually very time consuming.

There are certain long established standardised tests. The use of a well validated test will not of itself be helpful unless the teacher takes the trouble to learn the purpose of the test, studies the appropriate method of administration, and appreciates the limitations. Some teachers prefer to plan their own assessment tests, believing that such tests can be more closely related to the teaching objectives. Where this is the practice, an attempt should be made to learn something of the expertise laboriously acquired by professional testers over many years, and to apply it appropriately.

It is also necessary for schools and for teachers to evaluate the teaching methods and materials they use. This involves the careful scrutiny of materials, schemes of work, text-books, work-cards, equipment and apparatus, to see if they are providing what is required.

Assessment might be regarded as a procedure which challenges the teacher to define aims and objectives more clearly, and subsequently leads to more effective teaching and learning. It allows the teacher to check if the aims have been achieved and the objectives reached. Most learning experiences need to be planned, and it is at the planning stage that the fullest assessment (evaluation, diagnosis and prescription) is important if the experiences are going to meet the real needs of the children. For this there are no standardised tests, and the teachers involved must rely on their professional judgement. This judgement can often be sharpened by collaborative work within the school or at a teachers' centre.

Finally, no methods of assessment are sacrosanct. From time to time, the methods themselves require reappraisal in order to decide whether or not the purposes they are intended to serve are being achieved.

D *Social Democracy*

The Community School and Community Education

(From Midwinter, E., 1972, *Priority Education*, Harmondsworth, Penguin, pp. 19–20, 22–5).

Unlike the writing of the educational conservatives, where the political underpinning is implicit though easy to detect, social democratic views of primary education have an explicit political stance. They are concerned with the promotion of social justice and with the role of the school as an essential (though by no means the only essential) agency in the creation of a fairer society. In the words of the last sentence in this extract, social democracy as an educational ideology seeks 'to make the state's educational system more truthfully the people's system and to deploy it more beneficially as a support and as a keystone for grassroots democracy and community involvement.' Social democracy was powerfully represented by certain members of the Plowden Committee and was reflected in the report's recommendations on educational priority areas and on the importance of home-school-community links (see pp. 179–183, 184–186). With some influential individuals in primary education such as Schiller (pp. 68–70) social democracy seems to have co-existed along with liberal romanticism. As an ideology, social democracy was particularly influential in schools associated with the Educational Priority Area action research projects (see pp. 187–192) set up after the publication of Polwden and in inner-city areas such as Coventry. One of its leading spokesmen has been Eric Midwinter. In this extract he develops his ideas of social education, community education, and community development, all aimed at 'self-renewal and community revitalisation' in the disadvantaged areas of inner cities. [He begins by suggesting that there is an alternative to the kind of education usually offered children in disadvantaged areas:]

The alternative might be to offer the majority of children a social education; one that might give them the social competences to examine the depressing reality of their world, in the hope that they might learn to repair or change it in ways agreeable and pleasing to them. Through a close investigation of their social environment, the children might be that much readier to understand their own needs with more clarity. From that standpoint, they might come to invent ways and means of satisfying those needs. This is the opposite of persuading children to resign themselves stoically to their lot.

This is an attempt to make them think and act boldly and inventively about their lot. What it does not do is pretend the lot is necessarily a happy one. One hopes to replace resignation and negative rebelliousness with a positive reformist attitude.

Such an open-ended investigation of the social environment (not just, let it be noted, the *local* environment: for example: television and advertising are non-local forces in the children's environment) might be the foundation of the EPA Community School. There would be an attempt to tap the potential and the experience of the city child in his own right, with rather less of that escapism with which teachers have superficially attempted to polish the urban child. It has been as though they wanted to paint a quick-dry cultural gloss on to the pupil. The social environmentally-based curriculum is psychologically more accurate. It begins with the child's experience and works purposefully *outwards*. So much teaching of the urban child has, in the past, postulated new experiences without lifelines from the old.

Such a radical re-think of the EPA syllabus would, of course, require many changes in the structure of the school and of teaching and it would imply a much more exciting and intimate relation of the school to its catchment area. It means long looks at the school's situation vis-a-vis many social institutions, the most prominent of these being, naturally enough, the home. But the other social and economic amenities around the school must also be introduced into and related to the exercise, so that the school might become the hub of a thriving, socially-based educational process, rather than the exclusive and sometimes withdrawn agency of education.

[This kind of social education requires a particular kind of school, a community school, if it is to flourish and help equip future citizens with the means to respond creatively to the challenge of disadvantage.]

The Community School, then, emphasizes the differences rather than the similarities of schools precisely because it attempts to relate fluently and productively with the ethos, character and values of the community it serves. This is what makes it a relevant school. By establishing school-community interconnections, it constructs a stable basis upon which a three-cornered partnership of parent, teacher and child might harmoniously operate. The Community School ventures out into the community. The Community School welcomes in the community. Ideally, the barriers would collapse completely and the borders become indistinguishably blurred. Physically, one might foresee a time when, architecturally, the school, along with all other social agencies, might be subsumed into the community. The shopping precinct prampark might run into the nursery unit; the school clinic and the civic group surgery might be one; and the children might eat their school dinner in what is also the local café and snack-bar.

Gone would be the seclusion of the traditional English school, with children drawn in and instructed behind closed doors and high walls. The Community School requires a highly socialized format because it has a social rather than an academic aim. Its long-term purpose is to equip the critical parent, worker, consumer and citizen of the next generation, in the hope that that generation might respond creatively to the challenge of deprivation. It is an attempt to break the poverty cycle, in which deprived parents have bred deprived children in deprived situations to become, in turn, the deprived parents of deprived children. It is an attempt to replace the ad hoc sporadic governmental palliatives with a fullrun policy of self-renewal and community revitalization.

As such, it turns the traditional school approach on its head. The school has always been a relatively uninfluential agency for social change. It is an affirming mechanism. It is not going to Eton or to St Pancras RC Primary in Braddersfield that transforms you into an overemployed cabinet minister or an unemployed cabinet maker; it is being born into that particular avenue of life in which Eton or St Pancras stands and which you experience as you pass down the avenue. This is the lesson of the home and school researchers. It is home and neighbourhood that is important; the school merely accepts and confirms.

Willy nilly, schools have tended to defend the status quo, and there are countless social and professional pressures upon teachers to continue this hundreds-year-old convention. But, in our deprived urban districts, it is the status quo that is wrong. The Community needs to be changed and thus the Community School has to be involved in changing and not in standing still. Teachers will have to become social prosecutors rather than social defenders, if the school is, in effect, to shift itself massively and become a positive influence on social change.

It is immediately obvious that the school cannot operate alone, and here one meets one of the first golden rules of the Community School; namely, one cannot have community education without community development and one cannot have community development without community education. It would be, on the one hand, frustrating to turn out a sane, critical, well-balanced product, eager for the participatory democracy fray, only to find that participatory democracy — in the workplace, on the streets, over local issues, in the shops and so on — was absent. It would, on the other hand, be wasteful to create a grassroots community organism, if the people had not been given the opportunity to develop the essential social skills for its most fruitful usage. The planner, paying his lipservice to consultation, knocks on the door and asks the client what sort of home or environment he would like. The answer should properly be: 'I was never educated to hear that question; I was never educated to articulate an answer; if you'd like me to tell you about Who Flung, the little Chinese boy, a day in the life of Egbert, the little Anglo-Saxon boy or the story of Tobias, the little boy who knew St Paul, come round in the morning and we'll give it a whirl'.

Community education should provide an important servicing agency for community development ensuring that, if all the elements — law and order, housing, welfare, transport, social and utility services — are drawn into a unified communal enterprise, its patrons would be well-versed in how to cope with the operation. Children in school should be, in A.H. Halsey's compelling phrase, 'eager apprentices for community life'. Community education for the socially disadvantaged should be part of the gamut of community development for the socially disadvantaged. Perhaps, indeed, it should be first among equals. It is increasingly apparent that, of itself, education cannot compensate for the malpractices and injustices of society. It can contribute, but it can only contribute profitably in a propitious community clime.

The community module is no stranger to political science. Aristotle anticipated us for one. It has respectable medieval and nineteenth century antecedents. Now it is the task of the community developer to modify the ideal of autarchy to twentieth century conditions and, assuredly, education has a significant role to play. The community educationist is at once more long-sighted and more pessimistic than the compensatory educationist. He looks far beyond the short-term blandishments of an improved reading age to the sunny vision of a highly skilled citizenry recreating high quality civic life in our cities. In so doing he notes, at base, that education cannot go it alone — he is not, then, optimistic about the school as a kind of Lone Ranger solving all educational and thereby social problems, with the silver bullets of language programmes and numeracy drives. To hack at a fearful metaphor, this particular Lone Ranger would need a number of Tontoes to be guarding the flanks of all the other social factors in civic life.

Of course, it is a spiral process. It is not a question of solving problems independently. Community education does not have to be perfected, it need only be well under way, to provoke articulate and valid pressures for reform through an improved utilization of existing possibilities; as reforms in other spheres are accomplished, the confidence in and investment in commuity education could grow, and so on. For example, a more socially aware community could use the existing channels of social welfare benefits or the existing avenues of political protest with increased skill. This, in turn, might bring about alterations in welfare administration or an acquaintance with political techniques (such as school management) and both could visibly affect the everyday life of the Community School.

There is a circular argument surrounding the promulgation of democracy. Can the individual be trusted to exercise democratic power fully or must he be content with his quintennial excursion to the polling station; if he be given sovereign power, will the efficiency and productivity of our society be undermined because of his lack of know-how and his insufficiency or responsibility? We tend to keep democracy at arm's length or, rather, at ballot-box length. It seems we cannot afford the risk of popular as opposed to constitutional democracy; naturally, the only way to discover the truth of the argument is to give it a try, but we flinch from this. In terms of the schools, there are many ready to argue that we should leave well alone and tamper but gently with a reasonably effective system which produces a modicum of scientists, doctors, engineers and clergymen. Parents, it is still argued, would be in the way and would not be expert enough to join in a total discussion about their own children's future.

Here is the crux. It is the age-old state versus individual dilemma. But the state is an aggregate of individuals. As for the state education system, it is a remarkable illustration of the point, for — as community developers have been quick to observe — it is the highest common multiple of community development. Everyone has been to school; many have children at school; education should and could be a lifelong process; everyone lives near to and recognizes the school as an ongoing social agency; rate-payers and taxpayers both fork out mightily for it. It is the goal of community education to make the state's educational system more truthfully the people's system and to deploy it more beneficially as a support and as a keystone for grassroots democracy and community involvement.

Education for Life

(From Kitwood, T. and Macey, M., 1977, *Mind that Child!*; Writers and Readers Publishing Cooperative, pp. 41–8).

The booklet from which the extract is taken attempts to explain the issues underlying the debate over standards in primary education which took place as a result of the Black Papers (pp. 40–44), the William Tyndale Affair (pp. 45–50, 209–219), and the publication of Bennett's research, *Teaching Styles and Pupil Progress* (Volume 2). The authors argue that the issues go well beyond the question of how children should be taught in primary classrooms, and involve the kind of society we want to create. They characterize our present society as unjust and believe that schooling is a major means through which this unjust society reproduces itself. They argue that the focus of education needs to shift away from individual competition and narrowly conceived 'standards' towards an emphasis on cooperation, social responsibility, caring, creativity and joyfulness. Their social democratic stance is evident in the final paragraph: 'The message we have inherited is outmoded and unjust. "To the many — education for drudgery; to the few — education for power". This must now be replaced by a different message, the one to which so many of the positive changes in our schools have been pointing. "To all of society — education for life".'

The claims of this booklet thus far can be summed up in seven simple points. First, while primary schools must maintain high standards of literacy and numeracy, these are not the only things that matter. Second, it is unrealistic and unhelpful to force a division between 'traditional' and 'progressive', as rival styles of education. Third, the debate about standards is part of a much larger issue, from which it cannot be separated. Fourth, our judgement must take into account the long-term educational history of Britain, looking both back into the past and forward into the future. Fifth, the research which has been cited by those who cry out for a return to the old ways is unsound, even by its own standards. Sixth, the debate, including the research, has generally been carried out on a false basis, because it has forgotten the most important element — people. Seventh, education must be seen not as a factory for producing exam passes, but as a means for enabling people to live more fully human lives.

Now the argument must be pressed further. We must face the vital question of the broader purpose of education in relation to society, both now and in the future. For it is not just an individual matter; education and society affect one another constantly, and sometimes in powerful ways. Here, perhaps, the controversy over standards has reached its highest level of confusion. Probably we all realise, if dimly, that Britain is still a society with great inequalities, inherited from the past. This is true on an indiviual level, but also for whole social groups. If we compare, say, the life-prospects of solicitors with those of unskilled labourers in the chemical industry, the point is immediately clear. There are vast differences between the various sectors of society, extending over virtually every aspects of life — and death. The statistics, which are well documented, tell their own story. A person's chances of surviving at birth, of receiving adequate and timely medical care, of moving easily through the educational system, of remaining employed, of avoiding insanity (or being well cared for when insane), of having a pension, of living to a ripe old age, are all related to social class. This is not simply a matter of income, status, power, or wealth, though these are included. Fundamentally, the quality of life is at stake.

It is, of course, the job a person does which mainly determines lifestyle. It is the education which mainly determines the job. And it is the social background (in other words, the lifestyle of the parents) which mainly determines the education. Of course there are exceptions, the success-stories which seem to reassure us that our society provides the means of advancement to everyone. These, however, are conspicuously rare. The main fact is that we have a social system which inexorably seems to reproduce itself. Education is one of the main means by which it does so.

People sometimes talk as if Britain were gradually becoming a classless society. This is largely a fiction, as the statistics make very plain. It is easy to draw false conclusions here, on the basis of casual impressions. Indeed, it is very difficult for anyone to gain a balanced picture of the whole of society, because we all tend to gather among people of our own kind; our friends are generally like ourselves. Unless we make a very deliberate effort to find out the truth, other parts of the social system remain hidden from us. Of course some of the centres of power and wealth in that system have shifted to some extent. There is, however, little indication that we have gone very far towards creating a society with genuinely human prospects for all.

Teachers, probably more than most, are aware of the divisions and inequalities which surround us. They know that education provides the main tickets to success, and therefore what power and responsibility are in their hands. They may well feel that the main way they can help their pupils on to a 'better' life is by getting them through exams: from some this is the main expression of their caring. If they can convince themselves that they have gone some way towards providing equality of opportunity to school children, they can feel slightly more comfortable when faced with the disheartening reality of a social system which is a society only in name.

There is a fatal flaw, though, in this way of thinking, if everyone were to adopt it. The number of privileged jobs in any country is strictly limited; schools have no direct effect on the structure of opportunity. Suppose, then, we could wave a magic wand and turn all today's academic failures into tomorrow's successes, what would be the result? Society would not change so as to create privileged positions for all who had then achieved the necessary qualifications. Universities, colleges and employers would simply raise or alter their bases of selection, so that there would again be the right number of people to fill the posts. The rest would still be the failures, at a higher educational level.

The realistic conclusion, then, is this. As long as we live in a country where access to advantage is via educational qualifications, education as a means to that end can only benefit the few, never the many. Under this arrangement schools are bound to confer the label of failure on the majority of children, in the process of enabling a few to succeed. It seems likely that the loss of zest for living and learning which occurs in many during their 11 or so years at school is partly the result of this fact. Children from all social backgrounds show great promise at 5 or 6 years old. Somewhere, en route to adulthood, their potential becomes lost or deeply hidden. Many of those who are on the way to acquiring the 'failure' label are psychologically 'camping' at school, accepting it sullenly or with defiance, truanting when they can or dare, and waiting day by day for the farce to end.

This might appear a depressing and inevitable picture, but it need not necessarily be so. We ought always to remember that social structures are man-made, not God-given: they *are* amenable to change. To bring this about on a large scale will require understanding, persistence and moral courage.

One radical change of attitude is required. We should look on the future, not from the narrow vantage-point of personal gain, but considering society as a whole. This is difficult for parents, because naturally they want the best possible foundation for life for their children. It is often hard for teachers, too, who are eager that their own pupils should get as much as they can from the opportunities education provides. But this, by itself, is shallow thinking. On the present system, if one child is an educational success, four others will be failures; if the children in one class do well, the price will be that others have done badly. The same system that makes some, breaks others.

In the long run, however, the sucesses and the failures will have to live side by side. Judging by the last hundred years, and the state of the country at present, this is not a satisfying or harmonious form of social existence. If we perpetuate it for our children, strife will certainly continue, and democracy itself may well collapse.

So it is essential that we change our view of education, and see it as serving a larger and more human purpose. It must be something for every person, a means towards the unfolding of the abilities which they undoubtedly have. Education is not just about 'standards', as narrowly conceived. It is about the natural world, about human relationships, about social responsibility, about culture, about responding to the wonder of being alive. Of couse, amongst this, both literacy and numeracy are important. But it would be sadly mistaken to see them as merely part of the technique for gaining personal advantage, or as tools of the trade in a complex technological society. Institutions exist for people, and not the other way round.

So our schools must not be allowed to be no more than heartless academic factories, turning out people dominated by self-interest, as has so often happened in the past. This is why we have stressed the need to see the current debate in a broad context — and this includes an historical one. For the controversy about falling standards seems to be taking us in the direction of a system which contains remarkable similarities to the very early days of 'universal' education. When the notion of education for one's station on life was replaced by some notion of equality of opportunity, the way to achieve this was seen as being via a national core curriculum (the 3 R's) and by nationally implemented testing procedures. Under this system, school classes were 'inspected' to ensure that the children had 'attained' to a certain level — and if they hadn't their teachers were deemed to be failures.

Now, at first glance, this does not seem to be a totally unreasonable situation. But a moment's thought tells us, as it told eminent educationalists of the day, that the consequences of such a system are purely mechanical learning on the part of the children, and purely mechanical (rote or drill techniques) on the part of the teachers. Little 'real' learning takes place in this kind of situation, although it was, and is, relatively easy to train children to pass tests in a 'parrot-type' fashion. Yet this is the kind of farcical situation to which the Black Paper writers would have us return; this is the kind of situation to which certain politicians would have us return. But now they do this by reference to 'scientific' research, and in the name of equality and objectivity.

And the real tragedy is that the present educational system contains many promising signs. Some of our schools are becoming centres of community, serving not only children, but people of all ages. Library facilities are being used more. There is an increased demand among young and old for education which is not geared to exams and qualifications. There is greater parental and community involvement with schools than there ever has been in the past. There are some indications of increased social and political concern, and of a greater sense of caring among young people. It is quite false to claim that these work against high academic standards. There is now, throughout the country, a higher level of education than there has been at any other period.

Putting it another way, it is the dominant conception of human worth — at present accepted by many of the 'failures' as well as the 'successes' — which must be altered. In our traditions we lay stress on individual competition and put people into rank orders. We implicitly teach that possessing much and consuming more are the outstanding human achievements. Now is the time for the focus of our education to be placed elsewhere: on co-operating with others, being creative, caring, joyful, making the most of the conditions of life. Of course we need people to carry forward our industrial and commercial effort, but industry and commerce need humanity too.

And the point that must be stressed again is that none of this implies a lowering of standards in any sense at all; if anything it implies a much higher — though broader — conception of standards. But the widespread belief in our society that we can, and should, rank people according to their performance on so-called 'objective' tests tends to mitigate against this broader conception of standards, talent and general human worth. Here we would make two points. The first is that our ability to measure intelligence, 'talent' and even attainment, is far more limited than some people would have us believe. The second is quite simply that even if we had perfected the techniques required to measure such aspects of persons, would we really wish for a society dominated by the 'able' as measured only by such tests? Would we really want all our decisions to be made by people who scored highly on so-called intelligence tests, with no reference to qualities of personality, humanity and so on?

The relevance of this to our education system in general, and to the heated debate about standards lies in the fact that testing and measurement seem to be accepted as being the 'right' and 'proper' way of going about things. Our secondary education sector, in general, is dominated by exams which make reference to the concept of intelligence. Now it seems that our primary sector is to be 'brought back into line' — it was apparently straying too far away from routine testing as a means of assessing children's ability and attainment. The threat of a reactionary, retrograde movement is a very real one. The recommendations of the Black Paper writers for national testing at prescribed stages have been accepted. One of the editors of these publications has received 'formal ' recognition at Central Political Party level; and the education system is characterized by increasing bureaucracy at all levels and in all forms. The wheel appears to have turned full-circle. The only 'basic' difference between the modern call for maintaining standards by regular testing, and that same call nearly 100 years ago, is that we now have bigger and better tests. But what *kind*? Tests to process people more accurately and efficiently?

The world is changing, whether we like that fact or not. It is time for us to take responsibility for change, and turn it to the social good. There can be little doubt that during the next decade hours of work will become shorter and retirement will generally be younger. There will be less work for society to share around. If we hold onto the conception of education which is built into our history it means that large parts of life are going to be very empty for many people. The message we have inherited is outmoded and unjust. 'To the many — education for drudgery; to the few — education for power.' This must now be replaced by a different message, the one to which so many of the positive changes in our schools have been pointing. 'To all of society — education for life.'

E *An Alternative Perspective*

The 'Progressive', 'Elementary' and 'Technological' Traditions

(From Golby, M., 1982, 'Microcomputers and the primary curriculum', in Garland, R. (Ed.), *Microcomputers and Children in the Primary School*, Lewes, Falmer Press, pp. 206–7, 208).

This short extract provides a rather different ideological perspective from that presented in the rest of this section. Golby distinguishes three traditions in primary education:

1 an elementary tradition concerned with the inculcation of essential knowledge into passive pupils;
2 a progressive tradition celebrating self-expression, individual autonomy and personal growth, but lacking an adequate theory of knowledge to help it define the primary curriculum; and
3 a technological tradition stressing utilitarian values associated with the pursuit of science and technology.

His brief characterization of the progressive tradition is particularly interesting.

It may be of value to distinguish three broadly separate 'traditions' ... which are still discernible in the primary field. They are discernible ... both in the practice and in the discourse about primary education. Two of the traditions represent the familiar antithesis of elementary and progressive ideologies while the third, which I shall call the technological tradition, is a relatively new arrival.…

  We could perhaps deal with the first two traditions summarily. The elementary tradition takes as its guiding metaphor the inculcation of essential knowledge into passive pupils. Most of us learned to reject or at least become highly sceptical of this utilitarian tradition in our early training but many of us returned to it in various modified forms later in our careers. I suggest that this tradition is by no means dead and the modern primary curriculum is still heavily underlain by a 'drills and frills' approach. The nineteenth century elementary curriculum lives in many schools' division of the curriculum into the 'basics', consisting of the three 'R's and the 'extras', consisting in an uncertain melange of literary, aesthetic, humanistic and now scientific ingredients.… The elementary tradition expressed a political will to 'gentle the masses' through the controlling power of a curriculum which would be limited in scope. This curriculum is an education (though today's philosophy might deny it the title of education at all, and substitute socialization or training as the appropriate concepts) for subservience. The elementary curriculum survives, despite the abolition of the 'eleven plus', in the deeper structure of many schools by emphasizing certain conforming performances rather than the expansive qualities of questioning and imagination.

The progressive tradition has very largely gained its identity not through the coherent expression of new rationales but through its romantic opposition to the elementary tradition. Thus, instead of stressing control, subservience and conformity, it celebrates self-expression, individual autonomy and personal growth. None of these formulae have, in my opinion, been adequately defended in philosophical terms. The tone of progressive teaching has always been enthusiastic and evangelical. The contents of the curriculum have always been poorly defined and this for the simple reason that content is not to the fore in this line of thinking. Indeed, it is the weakness of the progressive tradition that it has no adequate theory of knowledge to help it define the curriculum above the rhetorical level. Accusations of incoherence in *practice*, however, seem to me to be less well substantiated that those against the theory of progressive education. In practice, progressive educators know very well how to bring to bear all manner of subject matter in the interests of individual children as they individually grow and develop. There is, I believe, a practical logic composed of a blend of fundamental opposition to the values of elementary education with a perception of children not as empty vessels but, rather, as centres of consciousness and potentialities beyond what we can preconceive. It is also possible, I believe, to assert that progressive ideas have a romantic and rural texture much in contrast with the practical and urban fabric of the elementary tradition.

These contrasts are vastly over-simplified. This should go without saying but needs repetition here as I am about to offer a third, also over-simplified, opinion. There exists, I believe, a more recent tradition which may be broadly labelled technological. This tradition has emerged most noticeably in the years since 1976 when education has come under a closer political scrutiny. What I have in mind here is the recent emphasis since the Great Debate on the utilitarian values associated particularly with the pursuit of science.... The technological tradition I perceive has its most tangible emphasis in the continuing and developing concern of HMIs, for example in their Primary and Secondary working papers and surveys. In both of these endeavours the place of science and in the secondary field of Craft. Design and Technology is taken for granted as an aspect of the 'core curriculum'. The debate about the core curriculum has not as yet penetrate beyond the level of such atavistic assumptions as the above concerning science and we have to look into still relatively unknown theoretical literature for a clear defence of the position of Science, Craft, Design and Technology in the 'protected core' of the curriculum. Perhaps most obviously this new technological tradition comes into view in the Primary survey where the conclusion is drawn that improvements in science teaching in primary schools are greatly to be desired. Yet no rationale for the inclusion of science, a subject of very low visibility historically in the primary curriculum, is to be found in the survey itself. While we should not expect of the kind of research which the survey was an accompanying philosophical statement on the rationale for the 'whole curriculum', we could hope to see the issues raised somewhere. And the literature, both from official quarters and from the research community seems to me deficient in this major respect. I assert then, that I perceive a new tradition, building on old assumptions, making inroads into the primary curriculum. 'Hard science' — and, perhaps, especially, 'science that works' or technology — is making a claim; a claim I do not reject or concede here but merely hold up for inspection. It is no part of my task here to take up a side in this as yet unformed debate but rather to point out that the primary curriculum, though it has seen the rather successful innovation of *Science 5–13*, has traditionally not found space for the sort of utilitarian emphasis on technical skills that may be implied in the crudest form of this new technological imperialism over out curricular thinking.

3   *Primary Education: Philosophical Perspectives*

Introduction

The philosophy of education has developed into a distinctive branch of study in Britain during the last twenty years. It has established itself as a foundation discipline in the study of education with its own distinctive group of theorists, a developing tradition of enquiry, and a considerable number of publications, including the *Journal of Philosophy of Education*. For a review of its development, readers are referred to an article by Dearden (1982), and, for an overview of the current state of play in the discipline, to a collection of papers edited by Barrow (1982).

According to Hirst (1982), 'three distinctive features' have characterized the kind of philosophy of education which first developed in England in the 1960s. Philosophy of education has used the techniques of conceptual analysis to examine major terms used in educational discussion (for example, 'education', 'teaching', 'growth', and 'creativity') so as to explore the complexities in their meanings. This has led to greater clarity in the meanings of educational beliefs and principles employing such terms. Secondly, philosophy has examined the justifications offered for educational principles (such as those associated with 'liberal romanticism' or 'educational conservatism'). This work 'has sharpened up an awareness of the value-judgements often implicit in educational doctrines and of the philosophical beliefs about the nature of knowledge, mind and moral values that were being presupposed' by adherents of such doctrines or ideologies. Thirdly, philosophy of education has helped in the development of more adequate educational theory by contributing more justifiable philosophical beliefs, based on contemporary work in the general field of philosophy.

These 'three distinctive features' are useful in characterizing the philosophical material related to primary education, which is featured in this section of the source book. The first two extracts illustrate the work done on the analysis of important concepts. Much of this work has focused on concepts applicable to education generally, but some attention has been given to concepts of particular significance in primary education. Dearden, for example, has analyzed concepts such as 'needs' (pp. 109–112), 'growth' and 'play', while Wilson has examined the concept of 'interest' and its connection with 'education' (pp. 113–116). The next four extracts illustrate the contribution made by philosophers to the critical examination of educational ideologies or doctrines. In particular, philosophers have examined the justifications offered for 'child-centred' education; it is regrettable that the same degree of attention has not been accorded the ideologies of 'liberal pragmatism' or 'social democracy'. The remaining two extracts reveal how philosophers can contribute to the development of more adequate theories of primary education.

The extracts in this section exemplify some of the points made by Dearden (1982) in his discussion of the potential contribution of philosophy to study and debate in education:

> It should make any necessary distinctions to clarify meaning, explore conceptual possibilities and try to identify what is necessary and what is contingent. It should expose question-begging, misleading claims and inconsistency. It should draw implications, show the full extent of someone's commitments, reveal absurd consequences, highlight by parallel arguments, draw attention to unnoticed alternatives and test assumptions. It should probe the validity of justifications, draw attention to areas of undeserved neglect, redress serious imbalances and assemble pertinent reminders.
>
> Further, philosophy of education should expose narrow conceptions, probe presuppositions and reveal hidden connections, or expose spurious unity. It should clarify ideas and articulate imaginative new conceptions. It should re-describe to bring into focus, show how certain notions will or will not do the work expected of them, show how one thing prevents the recognition of another, identify misplaced emphases or misdirected attention and set things in a wider illuminating context.

References

BARROW, R. (Ed.) (1982) 'Philosophy and education', *Educational Analysis*, 4, 1.

DEARDEN, R. (1982) 'Philosophy of education, 1952–82', *British Journal of Educational Studies*, 30, 1, pp. 57–71.

HIRST, P. (1982) 'Philosophy of education: The significance of the sixties', *Educational Analysis*, 4, 1, pp. 5–10.

Children's Needs

(From Dearden, R., 1968, *The Philosophy of Primary Education: An Introduction*, London, Routledge and Kegan Paul, pp. 14–18.)

Of all contemporary English philosophers of education, Dearden has contributed most to clarifying thinking in the area of primary education. In his book, (1968) *The Philosophy of Primary Education* (Routledge and Kegan Paul), he analyzed a number of very important concepts (including 'interests', 'play' and 'experience'), and he put forward a carefully argued theory to underpin the primary school curriculum. (This is summarized in the seventh extract in this section of the source book.) Here he analyzes the concept of 'need', as exemplified in the phrases 'The needs of children are ...' or 'In the primary school children need ...'. He argues that needs-statements do not simply describe what children lack but go beyond that to imply that what children lack is in some ways desirable or valuable. He maintains that 'one has to look behind statements of need to the values that are guiding them, for it is here that the issue substantially lies.' This explains why proponents of any educational ideology can argue their case by reference to children's 'needs' and why the nature of these 'needs' differs crucially from ideology to ideology.

Statements of 'need' abound in educational writing. One of the most recent examples relevant to primary education is to be found in *Primary Education in Scotland* (HMSO, 1965), the first chapter of which is not, as one might reasonably have expected it to be, devoted to setting out aims, but rather gives a statement of the 'needs of the child', which are apparently five in number. Furthermore, this statement of needs concludes a chapter the character of which is almost purely psychological, so that one is led to suppose that if one wants to know what children need, then it is to psychology that one ought appropriately to turn. Empirical research will show the way, or so it is implied.

There are, however, two serious defects in any attempt to by-pass a discussion of aims by furnishing statements of need instead. The first of these defects relates to the logical impossibility of passing from statements of psychological fact to value-based judgements about what one ought to do. The second defect concerns some hidden assumptions behind thinking, as indeed is often thought, that an education which starts from the 'needs of the child' will solve the problem of motivation. Each of these defects merits some further elaboration, though for a more fully developed discussion, with due qualifications added, one would have to look elsewhere (see Komisar, 1961, or Dearden, 1966).

The first defect, then, concerns the attractiveness of the apparently empirical, or observationally based, character of statements of need. And indeed, on the face of it at least, needs-statements are simply empirical. If someone says that teachers need a salary increase of three hundred pounds per year, or that students need at least two advanced levels to enter university, or that owners of dogs need a licence, is it not simply a matter of fact that this is so? If one had occasion actually to make a categorical assertion of the form '*x* needs *y*', would it not simply be a matter of fact that *x* had not already got *y*, and furthermore that getting *y* would indeed achieve whatever results were regarded as desirable of achievement. Surely these would be matters of fact, and some appropriate method of fact-finding, whether ordinary observation or sophisticated research, would be not just relevant but absolutely indispensable. The catch, however, lies in the implication of there being a condition desirable of achievement; for this brings to light the *valuational* basis of needs-statements, and the necessary subservience of the empirical data to such values.

Teachers *need* an increase of three hundred pounds only if it is a good thing to have one's salary so advanced. Students *need* two advanced levels only if going to university is regarded as something desirable, or worthwhile. Owners of dogs *need* a licence only because the law backs with an obligation the desirability of having one. Simply that someone does not actually have something, or that he would have to have it *if* he wanted to do something else, does not establish a need. Teachers do not have classes of seventy children, but no-one will therefore detect a *need* here. Yet if we thought mass instruction a good thing, as it was thought to be in one phase of the elementary school tradition, then we might well say that classes of seventy were needed. Confronted with statements of need, then, it is appropriate to inquire into the valuational basis of such statements. What values are being assumed here? What is being assumed to be desirable? And to see this is to see through the merely apparent empirical character of needs-statements. It is also to see that psychology, or indeed any other empirical science, logically must fail at some point as a sufficient warrant for asserting something to be needed.

Of course, often there is wide and proper agreement as to what is valuable, or desirable, or obligatory, and against a background of such consensus it is the researcher who has the important points to make. Thus when Bowlby claimed to have found, and let us assume for the sake of discussion that it really was there to be found, that maternal deprivation in early childhood caused an 'affectionless' character to be formed, then he was warranted in asserting the need of maternal care in childhood, for we all agree that being an 'affectionless' character is *undesirable*.

But we do not always agree over what is desirable. The child-centred reformers did not agree with the architects of the elementary tradition over what was desirable. In such circumstances, it is simply begging the question to talk about needs, or to pretend that there is nothing at issue that cannot be settled by empirical research. One has to look behind statements of need to the values that are guiding them, for it is here that the issue substantially lies. Defenders of the elementary school tradition could, with perfect propriety, talk of the 'needs of the child'. On their view, the needs of the child would be to pay attention and to listen, to do as he was told and then wait for further instructions, to show obedience and respect towards adults in authority, and so on. What was *desirable* was that the proclivities of a bad nature should be curbed and re-directed, that future responsibilities should be prepared for, and that certain social attitudes should be inculcated.

A further illustration of this same important point about the valuational basis of needs-statements is provided by a consideration of educational books which are imported from other cultures or societies significantly different from our own. For here one may find needs-statements the warrant for which is culture-relative, and which are therefore invalid when exported, in spite of all their research support. P.T. Young mentions 'the need to maintain one's status within one's group, the need to win pre-eminence, the need to save one's face, the need to avenge an affront . . .' (Young, 1943, 150), which nicely illustrate this point. In connection with cultural relativity, however, mention might be made of Maslow's useful distinction between 'basic' or 'deficit' needs and 'growth' needs (Maslow, 1955). 'Deficit' needs are those without which we become 'mentally ill', such as safety, love and respect, and which are therefore needed by anyone. Much more relative, however, both to cultures and to individuals within cultures, are 'growth' needs. By these Maslow means, for example, the need to be a good artist, carpenter or scientist. . . .

The second of the defects earlier mentioned related to the assumption that an education which starts from the 'needs of the child' will solve the problem of motivation. But the trouble here lies with the equation of what a person *needs* with what he *wants*, for the motivational problem is only in some degree solved when the relevant item comes to be wanted. From the judgement that '*x* needs *y*' it by no means follows that '*x* wants *y*'. John may need Latin to enter university though he loathes the subject. The patient may need to convalesce for a month though what he wants is to return to work immediately. And certainly such an optimistic conclusion was unwarranted in the elementary school, where it was not even expected that children would want what they were judged to need.

Child-centred theorists, however, are sometimes apt to take wanting as a *criterion* of needing. If a child in an infant classroom wants to play with sand, *ergo* he needs to. Sometimes perhaps indeed he does: if, for example, he would in that way work out some phantasy or emotional problem which it is desirable that he should work out. But even here, to say that he needs to play with the sand is to say more than simply that he wants to. It is to sanction his desire as being an urgent or important one that *ought* to be satisfied, and plainly not all wants come into that category. Taken as an unrestricted generalization, the statement that what children need is what they actually want would be as near as makes no difference to saying that we should start from children's *interests*. Such a shift in the argument is at least to be desired for giving up talk about a curriculum based on children's needs, for as Komisar has pointed out, every curriculum is a needs-curriculum (Komisar, 1961). No-one dreams of including in the curriculum anything that is not needed, and hence no criterion of choice is or could be furnished by resort to bare statements of 'need'. As has already been argued, the heart of the matter lies in the prior notions of what is valuable or desirable. It is here that a criterion of choice must be found.

References

DEARDEN, R. (1966) '"Needs" in education', *British Journal of Educational Studies*, 14, 3, pp. 5–17.

KOMISAR, P. (19761) '"Need" and the needs-curriculum', in SMITH, B. and ENNIS, R. (Eds), *Language and Concepts in Education*, Rand McNally.

MASLOW, A. (1955) 'Deficiency motivation and growth motivation', in JONES, M. (Ed.), *Nebraska Symposium on Motivation*, University of Nebraska Press.

SCOTTISH EDUCATION DEPARTMENT (1965) *Primary Education in Scotland*, HMSO.

YOUNG, P. (1943) *Emotions in Man and Animal*, Wiley.

Interests and Education

(From Wilson, P., 1971, *Interest and Discipline in Education*, London, Routledge and Kegan Paul, pp. 66–8, 68–9.)

The book from which this extract has been taken was described by Peters in 1971 as 'one of the first attempts at a precise and well-argued defence of a point of view associated with "progressive" education'. This description remains true more than a decade later. In the interim, little has been done in England to put liberal romanticism on a sound philosophical footing (though see pp. 146–153). In the book, Wilson explored the meanings of 'interest' and 'discipline' in a variety of contexts and attempted to tease out the connection between such concepts and that of 'education'. He was careful not to imply that 'education' and 'schooling' were co-extensive: 'Although most of what takes place in schools could be called "schooling", only some of it (and not necessarily any of it) is "educative". 'In this extract he argues for a very tight connection between 'education' and 'whatever is of intrinsic value', such that a person's education 'can only proceed through the pursuit of his interests, since it is these and only these which for him are of intrinsic value'. On this view, an individual's education, 'whether in or out of "school", consists in whatever helps him to develop [his] capacity for valuing and [his] inclination to pursue what is valued'. In the light of his analyses of 'education' and 'interest', Wilson indicates in general terms what he believes the educative function of the teacher to be.

Interests and Education.   What I am advocating here has often been called 'child-centred education', but a teacher who stands back and just *allows* children to pursue whatever interests come into their heads is practising, as I have argued elsewhere (Wilson, 1969), a travesty of 'child-centredness'. The feature of the concept of education which 'child-centred' educators were concerned to stress was its connection with the development of whatever is of intrinsic value, and thus, in the case of children just as much as in the case of adults, its connection with the notion of 'interest'. The point of calling education 'child-centred' lies in emphasizing that even when the person who is being educated is a child, and even, therefore, when his interests often seem 'childish' or silly or undesirable from the point of view of his adult teachers, nevertheless his *education* can only proceed through the pursuit of his interests, since it is these and only these which for him are of intrinsic value. However ridiculous a child's interests may seem, there is nothing else in terms of which he can become *more* 'educated'. He can be 'schooled' to adopt adult values, but only at the expense of leaving his own in their present childish and uneducated state.

A person's interests, dispositional and occurrent, represent his capacity (such as it is) to find intrinsic value in the circumstance of living, and his inclination to pursue or seek such value in terms of feeling and understanding and of activity which seems appropriate to its practical point. Such a person's 'education', I believe, whether in or out of 'school', consists in whatever helps him to develop this capacity for valuing and this inclination to pursue what is valued. Thus, whatever enables him to appreciate and understand his interest more fully, and to pursue it more actively and effectively, is 'educative'. But this does not mean that teachers, even when they are thinking about 'educating' children rather than just about 'schooling' them, should give assistance in the pursuit of anything and everything which catches the interest of a particular child. Still less does it mean that they should stand aside, or merely 'follow' the child down 'divergent paths'. There is a difference between helping a child to follow an interest for himself, and abandoning him to get on with it *by* himself. A merely tolerated child is apt to wonder in the end what his teacher is doing at school at all, if all that he ever hears from that teacher is 'Yes, Billy. On you get with it, then.' Ultimately Billy will be bound to start asking what *teacher* is 'getting on with'. Meanwhile, the interest which he had been casting around for ways of pursuing 'appropriately', founders for lack of help.

There is a constant risk involved in pursuing an interest, since no one can ever say in advance exactly how it is going to turn out. In it, one is not trying to approximate to a *norm* of action, or in other words to do what the majority of people might agree that one 'needs' to do. It is not a matter of trying to conform to *proven* or *consensual* standards or norms of value. It is more like trying to find out more about what it is which gives value to norms, or like *seeking* a measure of value against which to *evaluate* norms. In principle, this is a risky business. There might turn out to be precious little value in the direction in which we have taken it to lie. Or, in gaining what is of value in an interest, we might lose other values which previously we had achieved in other directions, or jeopardize the future achievement of further values in store. Just as each new understanding which we gain restructures our entire conceptual grasp of the world in which we live, so each new value which we find or seek, in pursuing an interest, brings about a shift — and sometimes a radical shift — in our entire current *scale* of values. Such changes, although pursued for their interest, are by no means always in *our* interest, let alone in the interest of anyone else. The inherent uncertainty of life's outcomes is what makes possible its interest. It also makes unavoidable its risk. Children, therefore, and perhaps especially children educationally speaking, need constantly the kind of confidence to proceed which comes from receiving effective help. This effective help is the educative function of teachers, and it *includes* the weighing of each risk against its possible gains.

By contrast, then, with the kind of manipulative changing of behaviour which I described [earlier in the book], 'teaching' of an *educative* kind consists in helping children to structure their experience and activity in ways which enable them to see more of its intrinsic point and value ...

... What I am trying to suggest..., is that children benefit 'educationally' by *learning* how to pursue their interests both more effectively and in an increasingly selective and discriminating way, and that 'educative teaching', therefore, is whatever intentionally serves to bring about this end. '"Ought",,' as philosophers would say, 'implies "can"' (e.g. Henderson, 1966; 1969), but not everything which *can* be done *ought* to be done. It would be unintelligible to say that a person 'ought' to be interested in *anything*, unless from time to time he were inclined already to see intrinsic value in *something*. But this means only that a sense of the intrinsic value of *some* thing or things in life cannot be induced in people solely by manipulating the external conditions in which they live. It does *not* mean that anything and everything which a particular person values is *bound* to prove valuable or to be most worth pursuing here and now.

A child's interests are already selective. Through them he begins to discriminate intelligible and possibly valuable features of the world. Trying to pursue an interest means always, then, trying to see those features more and more clearly, and in doing so, *trying out* (as it were) their possible value. The child's *educational* need is to be sustained and helped through these trials, so that his interests neither become fixed in some stereotyped form through his inability to see how to develop them further, nor remain at the fleeting level which, by themselves, his own unaided efforts might achieve. But neither on educational nor on any other grounds does the child 'need' to pursue *all* his interests. Indeed, it is only on educational grounds that he 'needs' to pursue *any* of them. There is room, then, for other grounds such as prudence, practicality and morality to be considered, when the selection is being made as to which of his interests should be pursued in school.

If *only* these 'other grounds', however, are being considered both by children and by teachers, then school becomes a place where no education can possibly be going on at all. If one were *always* to be prudent, it would be unwise *ever* to pursue an interest for its own sake, because of the *unavoidable* risks involved. A school staffed by teachers who are never more than prudent becomes, therefore, a sort of value-dump of supposedly good things whose *intrinsic* value is the one feature of them which no one can ever afford to consider. The prudent children, meanwhile, become artists in stagies for *concealing* their interests from adults whom they know, from bitter experience, will merely make use of those interests for well-intentioned but unintelligible purposes of their own. The child's own culture or sense of values, such as it is, is the price which he is required to pay, in such schools, for the acquisition of adult norms. There is no other reason for his going to school, in that case, than that he must.

References

HENDERSON, G. (1966) '"Ought" implies "can"', *Philosophy*, 41.
HENDERSON, G. (1969) 'Moral pragmatism', *Philosophy*, 44.
WILSON, P. (1969) 'Child-centred education', *Proceedings of the Philosophy of Education Society of Great Britain*, 3.

A Critique of Plowden's 'Recognisable Philosophy of Education'

(From Peters, R. (Ed.), 1969, *Perspectives on Plowden*, London, Routledge and Kegan Paul, pp. 3–4, 4, 5, 6, 6–7, 7–8, 10, 11–12, 12, 13, 13, 14, 14, 15, 15–16, 16, 20.)

In their report, the Plowden Committee stated that teachers 'should bring to bear on their day-to-day problems astringent intellectual scrutiny.' Two years after their comments were published, their own report was subject to such 'astringent intellectual scrutiny' by a group of educationists from the London Institute of Education, led by Professor Peters. Peters provided a hard-hitting critique of the 'half-truths' underlying Plowden's 'recognisable philosophy of education' summarized in paragraph 505 (reproduced on p. 71 of this source book). Here, he examines some of the principles enshrined in the report, including the importance attached to development and self-direction, the approval given to the non-compartmentalization of knowledge, and the image of the teacher. He finds many of the report's notions 'suspect', in particular its neglect of the 'inescapably social character of thought and language, of processes of transmission, and of motivation.'

[Plowden's] 'recognizable educational philosophy' proliferates in important half-truths that are paraded as educational panaceas. It is necessary, therefore, to separate out its various components and to attempt to place them in a more adequate perspective. They are as follows:

(a) That the child has a 'nature' which will 'develop' if the appropriate environment is provided. What will he develop into? Presumably a 'mature adult' who can 'be himself' and be critical of his society.

(b) Self-direction is very important in this development. 'The child is the agent of his own learning' (Para. 529). 'Sensitivity and observation are called for rather than intervention from the teacher' (Para. 527). Children have an intense interest in the world around them together with powers of concentration which will ensure learning if they are provided with materials for which they are 'ready' (Paras. 533, 534).

(c) Knowledge cannot be divided into separate compartments. Self-chosen activity within an 'integrated curriculum' is desirable.

(d) The teacher must be a guide, an arranger of the environment, rather than an instructor....

A Constructive Critique

Development. What is to be made of the notion that children have a 'nature' or that the individual has a 'self' which will emerge if the right environment is provided? This raises, of course, a host of old questions about what is innate and acquired; but it also raises equally crucial questions about the concept of 'development'. . . .

How is such development to be conceived? In most books on child-development 'development' is divided into physical, intellectual, social, moral and emotional aspects, as if social and moral development were devoid of 'intellect', as if morality and the use of the intellect were free from passion, and as if emotional development was separable from thought and social awareness. This indefensible type of classification should surely be scrapped and replaced by a more logical division into forms of thought and awareness, each of which has its affective aspect. This would include scientific, mathematical, moral, historical, inter-personal, aesthetic, and religious forms of awareness; proper attention should also be paid to the developmental aspects of various forms of skills — 'basic' and linguistic ones included.

What is urgently needed is a new approach to child-development in which the logical aspects of these form of awareness and the values inherent in them are more closely related to facts about the learning process of young children. . . .

But even if one tidied up these various aspects of 'development' how would this help to determine the emphasis of education? Is a man more 'developed' if he is highly trained scientifically but aesthetically insensitive or if he is aesthetically sophisticated but a scientific ignoramus? Is a man more developed who is 'well-rounded' but with a thorough knowledge of nothing, than one who is a brilliant mathematician and musician but ignorant of most other things? Was Lenin more 'developed' than Gandhi? . . .

There was a time, of course, when forms of awareness were comparatively undifferentiated and when the religious one, in the form of various brands of Christianity, provided some kind of unifying ideal of man against which a man's development could be roughly measured. But those times have passed. We now live in a pluralistic type of society without any such unifying ideal, and as educators we must come to terms with this. Those who stress the importance of individual self-realization as an educational aim are, perhaps unwittingly, lending their support to a pluralist conception of the good life. . . .

But what tends to be forgotten by those who identify themselves with this type of ideology is what Dewey called the 'shared experience' which such individual development presupposes. On the one hand there are high-level moral principles such as toleration, respect for persons, fairness, and consideration of people's interests which underpin democratic institutions and which provide the interpersonal framework within which individuals can be encouraged to pursue a variety of interests that are thought to be worth-while. Without some such consensus, into which children must be initiated, the pluralist pursuit of value would be impossible. On the other hand all the different options open to individuals are inescapably social in character. No individual can embark on science, singing or tool-making without being introduced to a vast body of knowledge and skill that has gradually been accumulated, and in most of them he will share a form of life with others who are also engaged on them. Furthermore when we encourage children to be themselves we surely take for granted a vast array of activities and forms of awareness that we think *worthwhile* within which we encourage children to find the ones to which they are particularly suited. As teachers we must make value judgments when we think of any sort of curriculum; for we do not offer blowing up live frogs with bicycle pumps or bingo as possible options. Talk of 'development', like talk of children's 'needs', is too often a way of dressing up our value-judgments in semi-scientific clothes. . . .

Self-Direction. Obviously enough the stress on self-direction and self-chosen activities is closely connected with the ideal of individual self-development. But it incorporates additional doctrines, one proclaiming a value judgment, the other relating to theories of learning. I will briefly consider each of them in turn.

(i) *Autonomy as a moral principle.* On the one hand a powerful plea is being made for the value of individual autonomy, for the importance attached in a democratic society to individual choice, independence of mind, and to more recondite virtues such as creativeness and originality. I need not expatiate on the importance of this in a pluralist society. But three types of comment are in place. Firstly this, like any other value, must surely be asserted not absolutely but with an 'other things being equal' clause. . . .

Secondly too little is known about how such autonomy independence, and 'creativeness', is developed. It may well be that a very *bad* way of developing this is to give children too many opportunities for uninformed 'choices' too young. One thing, however, is obvious enough — that the notion of 'autonomy' makes very little *sense* unless a child first has a grasp from the inside of what following rules means and has taken rules into himself between which he has to choose. Similarly general talk of 'creativeness' is cant; for there is no such general faculty. One can be creative in science without being a creative cook. And to be 'creative' in any sphere presupposes some mastery of the skills and body of knowledge appropriate to it. As Whitehead wisely put it, the stage of 'generalization' or autonomy comes after the stage of precision. The implication of all these points is that it is essential for children to be initiated into skills and bodies of knowledge which are part of our public heritage, before they can sensibly strike out on their own.

Thirdly, if we accept that there are many ways in which an individual can strike out on his own in a pluralist type of society, and if we think that children should be encouraged to stand on their own feet and find their own way, then we must think seriously about equipping them to do this effectively. This means not only taking them a certain distance in the various options so that they may have experience on the basis of which they may choose; it also means paying special attention to activities such as literature, history, and social studies which are an aid to them in this sort of choice. . . .

(ii) *'Discovery' methods*. The doctrine of self-direction relates, on the other hand, to a theory of learning. It suggests that children learn things better if their activities are self-chosen and approximate to 'discovery'. This claim is based almost entirely on teacher's hunches not on objective evidence . . . *too much* emphasis on self-chosen activities may lead to a certain type of promiscuity amongst children against which Liam Hudson recently warned us in his stimulating book called *Contrary Imaginations* (Hudson, 1966, p. 49). What has happened in this case is a further example of what has happened too often in psychology — a method for learning some things has become puffed up into *the* method for learning almost anything. . . .

Non-Compartmentalization of Knowledge. The committee, predictably enough, made its obeisance to the fashionable view that knowledge cannot be split up into distinct slabs and that the curriculum should therefore be undifferentiated though, interestingly enough, little attention is paid to this conviction when in Chapter 17 'Aspects of the Curriculum' were set out in a traditional way with few suggestions for 'integration. Again there are important truths in this view, but the various issues need to be disentangled. Firstly though it is perfectly true that many problems require a combination of forms of knowledge for their solution it does not follow from this that distinctions between forms of knowledge are arbitrary. It took acute thinkers such as Hume and Kant a considerable time to establish that mathematics is different from empirical science in important respects. . . . Surely one of the great achievements of our civilization is to have gradually separated out and got cleared about the types of concepts and truth-criteria involved in different forms of thought. . . .'

Secondly, in these discussions about the curriculum, forms of knowledge are often confused with school subjects which may or may not

correspond to pure forms of knowledge. Mathematics and science obviously do; classics and geography obviously do not, and educational theory is, of
course, one of the biggest bastards of them all. Whether forms of thought
should be taught separately or linked together in some kind of 'topic' or
'project' approach is a matter which cannot be settled without empirical
investigation into how successful the various alternatives are in relation to
agreed criteria....

Too often, so it seems to me, reformers pass from the undeniable truth
that the present 'subject-centred' curriculum is often boring to the conclusion that it should be abandoned and a topic centred one substituted
for it. They do not consider sufficiently seriously the less radical suggestion
that the more traditional type of curriculum could be both more imaginatively and more realistically interpreted. As with the emphasis on 'discovery' methods one can detect in all this a yearning for some overall recipe
for teaching. My contention is that no such overall recipe is possible. What
is needed is a down-to-earth, clear-headed, experimental approach which
takes due account not only of general criteria but of the differences in what
is taught and the children to whom it is taught.

The Role of the Teacher. The image of the teacher presented in the
Plowden Report is of a child-grower who stands back and manipulates the
environment so that children will proceed from discovery to discovery
when they are 'ready'. There is so much wrong with this image that one
scarcely knows where to begin in criticizing it. Most of what is wrong with
it can be summed up by saying that it systematically ignores the inescapably
social character of thought and language, of processes of transmission, and
of motivation. The notion that children can peel concepts off the world
without sensitization to selected aspects of it incorporated in a public
language, that most of their interests are self-originated rather than caught
from others, that children become 'ready' by some kind of internal ripening
without imitation, identification, and instruction — all such notions are
highly suspect....

The derogatory impression created by the statement 'The school is not
a teaching shop' is again characteristic of this one-sided approach to
teaching. For what is teaching? There is masses about learning in the
Plowden Report, but almost nothing about teaching. Yet teaching can take
the form of instruction, and explanation, of asking leading questions, of
demonstrating by example, of correcting attempts at mastery, and so on. It
can be done with a whole class, with small groups, and with individuals....

The moral of all this is not, of course, that we should throw overboard
all that has been learnt from 'progressive' methods and revert to archaic
systems of undiluted mass instruction. It is rather that we should do all in
our power to help teachers to develop a critical, empirical, adaptable

attitude to methods of teaching and encourage them to learn to think on their feet and experiment with different ways of teaching different types of subjects to different types of children. If only this critical, experimental attitude to teaching could be more encouraged we might soon cease to turn out teachers who thought that if they can only keep talking — or stop talking — then children are necessarily learning something, or teachers who practice something approximating to a free day without keeping a careful check on what in fact each child has learnt. Better still, we might turn out no teachers for whom 'teaching' has become a dirty word.

Reference

HUDSON, L. (1966) *Contrary Imaginations*, Methuen.

Plowden's 'Facts' about Children: A 'Child-Centred' Critique

(From Wilson, P., 1974, 'Plowden aims', *Education 3–13*, 2, 1, pp. 52, 54–5.)

The principles underlying the Plowden Report were attacked by some critics for being too 'child-centred' and for neglecting the importance of teaching as a way of initiating the young into public forms of knowledge (pp. 117–122). Here, one of the report's sympathizers criticizes it for not being consistently 'child-centred'. Wilson accepts the overall aim of the report — to place the child in the centre of the educational process — but criticizes the document for failing to work out the implications of this central aim, owing to its reliance on so-called experts (psychologists and sociologists) who provide misleading 'facts' about children's nurture, nature and education. He attacks passages in the report which, he argues, assume that education is a manipulative process conducted on passive children. He argues that the child's nature cannot be regarded simply as the product of the interaction between nature and nurture but that it depends crucially on the view the child himself takes about his life and the way it might develop. In line with the thinking in his book (pp. 113–116) Wilson maintains that education should aim to help the child develop his capacity to pursue 'possibilities of value' leading to personal development and transformation.

In spite of pooh-poohing the value of overall educational aims, the Report's own overall educational aim is stated right at the beginning and, in various more specific reformulations, again and again all the way through. There's nothing trite, perfunctory or apologetic about it. Teachers have not dismissed it but have responded to it, perhaps recognising in it the central concern of the deliberative aspects of their own best practice, or the core in other words of the known and valued ends which as educators they are already continually trying to reach.

This statement of overall aims is as follows: 'Underlying all educational questions is the nature of the child himself . . .' (p. 1). 'At the heart of the educational process lies the child. No (educational) advances . . . have their desired effect unless they are in harmony with the nature of the child, unless they are fundamentally acceptable to him . . .' (p. 7).

What is unfortunate, and what has led (I believe) to the bulk of the criticism by philosophers and others of the Report is that instead of trying to work out the implications of this central aim, by reflecting and deliberating further on the best *educational* practices which they could find, the reporters for some extraordinary reason turned aside at this point and consulted 'experts' — not *educational* experts (i.e., not those whom they considered most expert in the practice of placing the child at the heart of the educational process), but experts at everything under the sun *but* education, and principally of course experts in psychology and (to a lesser extent) in sociology....

Fundamentally, I believe, the error of the Report lies in its reliance upon non-educational experts. It has ... presented us with a picture of 'the facts' about children on an analogy with facts about the nature of merely physical processes such as skeletal growth in babies or the nutrition and 'training' of plants or the neurological development of brain cells, which in turn are thought of on a further analogy with the invariably law-following motions of inanimate objects such as stones rolling downhill or waves rippling inevitably towards some shore.

We thus emerge from our reading of the Report with a picture of children as passive object. We see them as no more than 'products' of the interreaction of their 'nature' and their environment or 'nurture'. Children become no more than links in a causal chain. What they themselves happen to think, feel and do about their nature, their environment and their education can make as little intelligible difference to their behaviour, on this view, as a stone's 'thoughts' about itself or about the law of gravity could make to its rolling downhill. Of themselves, children such as these cannot be imagined as capable of doing anything educationally significant, any more than by 'taking thought' they could add inches to their physical stature. Their education, on this view, must depend entirely (like the movement of a stone) on the manipulation of their environment by external agencies for ever beyond their control or influence (and principally, of course, by external agencies such as teachers, parents and others with whom they come into the most immediate environmental contact).

Just as we may dislodge a stone to get it moving, or shine light into the pupil of the eye to make it contract, or put compost around a row of vegetables to get the best development of their best natures (or the highest possible development which is 'in harmony with' their natures), so education is therefore conceived of in the Report as a manipulative process which 'motivates', 'stimulates' and 'nourishes' objects which may be moved about, grown and developed in desirable directions, but whose *own* views and values can never be taken seriously into account any more than could those of stones, cabbages, or the pupil of someone's eye: 'There is a strong association between the circumstances which affect the nutritional conditions underlying progress in physical development and those other conditions which nourish, as it were, intellectual and emotional growth,' (p. 15).

Exactly! and whether the children are left to forage about for sustenance or to suck up their educational chemicals and nutrients for themselves ('learning by discovery'), or on the other hand are supported by teachers of good character (as plants by string and strong stakes), or given compensatory doses of 'enrichment' like ailing chrysanthemums, or instructed individually in ways designed to meet special deficits or 'needs', the educational position of the child remains the same: he is an object or organism to be manipulated, or as the Report puts it: 'The child's physique, personality, and capacity to learn develop as a result of continuous interaction between his environmental [*sic*] and genetical inheritance. Unlike the genetic factors, the environmental factors are, or ought to be, largely within our control ... (p. 26) but never to any extent within his! At no time, then, can the child's own thoughts and feelings about his education be seriously considered. How *could* they be? One might as well ask a chrysanthemum if it wants to win the prize for which you are growing it, or a young police-dog what it thinks of the laws which you are training it to help enforce.

If children were like chrysanthemums and so on, this theory of education might be useful — although, even then, we'd still have to decide what goals we were cultivating the children for (other than for the question-begging end of a 'good' or 'adaptable' adult life). But children, in fact, are more like persons than like plants, insects, animals, machines, or inanimate objects, and 'the facts' about persons and their development cannot be verified or given attested universal description in the way that 'the facts' about plants and so on can.

Not only their educational development but, really, anything at all about persons (their health, for example, or whether they have to have certain physical characteristics such as two arms and legs in order to qualify as persons') exists as a 'fact' only in a conjectural and provisional sort of way, since it always depends in part upon the views of those persons themselves. In particular, however, the 'facts' of a person's educational development are especially and distinctively provisional, since our theories about people's educable 'natures' are interdependent with our theories about the sorts of valuable life which people *might* live and the sorts of valuable person whom possibly they *might* become. With chrysanthemums, the interreaction of their nature and their environment governs the 'facts' of their development entirely. With children and other persons or person-like beings, however, their own view *of* their nature and nurture is itself a factor in what they may become. In other words, their view of how they *might* develop or what they *might* become or prove to be, is itself an uncontrollable constituent *in* their development and its outcomes.

It is this interpenetration of fact and value in the 'nature' of persons and of their education, by contrast with the nature and motions of plants, stones and so on, which makes the Report's error a basic one. When I want 'the facts' about a person or about what I should do for his education. I must consult his opinion as well as my own or anyone else's, since 'the facts' both of his life and of his education will depend, at least in part, upon the view which that person himself is forming *of* his life and of his education. A person's 'nature' is thus provisional, open to agreement and disagreement, open to thought and feeling — open to education. Education is not something which we should regard as being determined, then, by a person's nature, nor by his environment, nor by the 'interaction' of the two. Indeed, we should not, I believe, regard it as determined, fixed, settled, by anything at all. Whatever a person might valuably become, may be an educational aim for him. Our own educational aim for him, in turn, should be to keep those possibilities of value as open as we can, not to close them off prematurely by making particular children conform to merely statistical 'facts' about children in general. By following non-educational experts in leading us to believe that 'the facts' about children's nature and nurture are as fixed and therefore as theoretically discoverable (through research, etc.) as the facts about the repair and maintenance of machines, the trajectories of falling stones, the maturation and sensitisation of bones and brain cells, or the domestication and control of animals and plants, the Report makes inconceivable the personal developments and transformations in which the value of education lies.

What is so unfortunate about this is that it was with persons, not with statistical regularities, that the Report began and with which (in its child-centred spirit at least) I believe that it was concerned. 'At the heart of primary education lies the child', not universal child-nature. The child is always a person. It is because he *is* a person, from the start, that we can hope to educate him, rather than just to push him around like a machine with a row of buttons, fill him up like a digestive tract, train him up against a wall like a plant, or domesticate him like an animal to our house-rules, however 'universal' we conceived those rules to be.

'Child-Centred' Education: A Critique

(From Dearden, R., 1976, *Problems in Primary Education*, London, Routledge and Kegan Paul, pp. 53–9.)

In the first half of the chapter from which this passage has been extracted, Dearden outlined what he saw as the 'broad principles of the child-centred tradition'. Such principles included the importance of respect for the child as a person in his own right, the acknowledgement of each child's unique individuality, the necessity for an imaginative and sympathetic insight into the world of each child, and the need for the teacher to structure the educational environment to provide the child with much freedom of choice, chance to pursue interests and many opportunities for discovery and self-expression. In this passage, he provides a constructive, not unsympathetic, critique of such principles, indicating to what degree he believes them to be justified and to what degree deficient. He believes that fundamentally, the deficiency of 'child-centredness' lies 'in what it neglects rather than in what it celebrates', especially 'its failure, or perhaps refusal, to come to terms with the need for adult authority' — a view shared by Peters in his critique reproduced earlier in this section (pp. 117–122).

'Strong on methods, but weak on aims', is a judgment that has often been expressed on child-centred educational theory. But it may be questioned whether it is possible at all to be strong on methods if one is weak on aims. How could a sequence of activities be regarded as the expression of a method at all if there were no aims, no end-in-view? Is blowing a whistle a good method? Well of course, it all depends on the circumstances and what you are aiming at in those circumstances. Is it to get a train started, or a game stopped, attention in a playground, the boiling of the water advertised, the rescue team directed, or extra help in making the arrest? Blowing a whistle may be a good method of doing all of those things, but we cannot judge that until we know the aim. So if child-centred educational theory is strong on methods it can hardly be weak on aims. Perhaps all that was meant by this epigram was that child-centred teachers can easily get children going on activities, without any motivational problems. But simply to achieve that, without any closer specification of which activities, could be an achievement of little educational value. By all accounts, bedlam is a state of considerable activity.

Then what are the characteristic child-centred aims? Aims there must be, even if they are left implicit and unstated, because choices and decisions constantly have to be made. Materials and equipment have to be selected and ordered, an environment has to be chosen and constructed, and decisions have to be made about the questions one asks and the possible lines of development one sees. In all of these lie value-judgments implying a set of aims. And the characteristic child-centred aims, ... are relational rather than prescriptive of content to be learned. They specify the various desirable ways in which the child should be related to what he does and learns, rather than the content of the learning. What he learns is thought to be of less importance than that he should develop good attitudes in learning it. These relational aims can be conveniently grouped under three main headings: (i) intrinsic interest (eagerness, curiosity, learning to learn, absorption, etc.); (ii) self-expression (expressing one's own individuality, being oneself, etc.); (iii) autonomy (making independent judgments, choosing with confidence, self-direction, learning by discovery, etc.). But such relational, or attitudinal, aims leave undeclared the directions in which they will be pursued. As Edmond Holmes resoundingly declared 'let the end of the process of growth be what it may; our business is to grow'. But Hitler grew.

In practice, many child-centred teachers are no doubt more sensible than the pure doctrine might lead one to expect, but to a degree many teachers are also misled by the doctrine (as we can see from several of the firsthand reports in the series of booklets *British Primary Schools To-day*, prepared under the aegis of the Schools Council). Often the necessary value-judgments are there in practice, though disguised in the horticultural language of nourishing or feeding and of not stunting or forcing. But again, plants can be trained to go in different directions, some better than others. Yet one does not really want to depreciate child-centred values as such. To quote from the Plowden Report in a way which reverses the direction of its own concession: 'these are genuine virtues and an education which does not further them is faulty' (para. 506). The relational aims mentioned above are very important. The deficiency of child-centredness, however, is surely to be found in what it neglects rather than in what it celebrates.

Two things especially it neglects, both of them to do with the selection of the content of what is to be learned. First of all, it neglects the importance of achieving a certain balance of spread of activities over a period of time, not necessarily daily, or perhaps even weekly, but within a manageable period over which the teacher can keep steadily in view where the educational process is going. Of course, ideas of all-roundness are often found in child-centred literature. But it is, as we should expect, the all-round child rather than the all-round curriculum which is in mind. The five- or six-sided child is to benefit from an all-round development: emotionally, physically, socially, morally, spiritually and (always last nowadays) intellectually. But what of the kind of all-roundness traditionally celebrated in the concept of a liberal education? That implies an initiation, to whatever degree time and individual ability allow, into a selection of the main forms of knowledge or understanding which have historically developed.

It is none the less true for sounding platitudinous to say that a child has a culture to inherit as well as a self to express. And a selection from that culture made according to the best judgment available ought surely to complement child-centred 'relational' aims. We might even say that the latter can be realized only through the former. In practice, if one scratches a child-centred teacher one usually uncovers the traditional subject curriculum. The Plowden Report in fact proceeded from its child-centred principles to a chapter on the curriculum which was mainly divided into ten very traditional sections. But this does not necessarily mean that virtue triumphs in the end, since the traditional subject curriculum is not necessarily the best conception of a modern liberal education.

The second neglected perspective on content is that of future usefulness, whether for the later stages of education itself or by way of 'preparation for life'. Plowden may say that 'children should live first and foremost as children and not as future adults', but children unavoidably are future adults. It is undoubtedly a great educational and human gain when children are respected as persons in their own right, and childhood is seen as part of life and not just as a preparation for life. But the suggestion here is not that schools should be just a preparation for later life; it is only that that is one important aspect of it. Children still need basic skills if they are to take full advantage of their subsequent education, and it is no service to them, let alone to the wider society in which they will live, if they are unemployable or incapable of social co-operation.

Historically, child-centred theories have usually been wedded to a belief in the natural goodness of children. This is an obscure doctrine, but to the extent that clear sense can be given to it, then it is false. In the first place, it is a fallacy though a popular one to infer from the fact that some characteristic is natural that it is therefore good. What is natural might also be good, but it cannot follow simply from its being natural that therefore it is good. In reality, much that seems to be natural (spontaneous and untaught) would normally be judged to be bad, such as spite, selfishness, aggressiveness, boastfulness and jealousy. These tendencies take their turn along with sympathy, generosity, kindness and other more amiable characteristics. It may have been necessary historically for crude ideas of original sin to be corrected by the contradictory doctrine of natural goodness, but the truth seems to lie somewhere between the two.

Again, the epistemological status of the doctrine is unclear. Is it an empirical generalization? When pressed with apparent counter-examples, a determined advocate of the doctrine, such as A.S. Neill, will retreat until even the foetal environment is blamed for bad tendencies. The fault, he clearly thinks, must be found in some environment or other, and not in the intrinsic nature of the child. The problem of the status of the doctrine is further complicated by the fact that nature is often only too obviously read into the child from whatever unconscious assumptions prevail at the time. Thus Rousseau found it entirely natural for Sophy, destined to be Emile's wife, to have an authoritarian upbringing, to be dependent on the good opinion of others, and to be taught a dogmatic religion. 'Nature', here, is made to bear a face which no women's liberationist would recognize as her own. In contemporary versions, 'nature' is perhaps more apt to look like someone's highly-reflective and articulate niece at play in some middle-class back garden. But whatever the truth of the matter may be, it is evident enough that by school age, even nursery school age, nature has taken on many socially determined characters, some of which are remarkably recalcitrant to any change initiated by the teacher. Language and interests, or their absence, are prominent examples. True or false, 'natural goodness' seems to be an eminently dispensable doctrine.

The relativity of conceptions of 'nature' is sometimes matched by the relativity of the child-centred observer's special insights into the inner world of childhood. The problem of how we can know other minds is a long-standing one in philosophy, though most would agree that we do have such knowledge, however difficult it may be to give an adequate account of its possibility. And it would also be widely agreed that different people have very different degrees of insight into others' minds and experience. There is a world of difference between the one extreme of the person so full of prejudices and self-preoccupations that others appear before him as little more than physical presences, and the other extreme of the person who can immediately read intentions and respond to feelings on the slightest cues and indications. And, since in general ability follows interest, a teacher of child-centred sympathies might be expected to have developed greater perceptiveness and sympathy in this respect. There is no evident reason to doubt that this is often so. But, equally, there is no reason to doubt that many a traditional teacher has, through experience, gained considerable insight into children. But here a caution needs to be sounded. Error is also possible, and is likely to be more frequent if we have a preconceived doctrine as to the nature of the child. For this may lead us to read into children's activities a significance which either is not there at all or else which ought to be set against other features which the doctrine leads one altogether to fail to notice. A reasonably objective and often very rewarding exercise is closely to watch a given child's activities over a period, then to ask the teacher what he thinks the child has been doing. In that teacher's situation, we should probably all be to some degree surprised by the discrepancy, but to the extent that it is doctrinally induced it is not inevitable. Respect for children as persons is not incompatible with respect for truth. It may well be dependent on it.

A further respect in which child-centred views on the nature of children may be questionable concerns the idea of development. Frequently presupposed is an idea of development as an unfolding according to an inner principle. And in physical respects there may be much in this. There may also be much in it to the extent that the development of mind has physiological and especially neurological necessary conditions. It may even be, though doubts have been cast on it, that something very like Piaget's development through distinctive stages is unalterable in its order and not to be hastened in its evolution. But it does not follow from any of this, even if it is all true, that education must be an unfolding. Even Piagetian stages require experience for their emergence. And if we consider the acquisition of objective knowledge, as in mathematics, the sciences and history, then if the truth is to be known belief has to agree with reality and the external discipline of fact is unavoidable. Nor is it just that matters of fact are independent of what we think. The critical standards which have been historically developed in these disciplines also present themselves initially as external, as do moral standards, which would have no point if we did by nature all that morality requires. Getting everything from the child and always starting from an existing interest may therefore be frequently useful practical principles, but cannot be universally appropriate. But in relation to every aspect of children's natures and their development detailed observation, unprejudiced by general doctrinal prescriptions, is really what is most appropriate. That is not to say that we can ever observe without making assumptions, but we can at least be ready to observe on the assumption that we may be wrong in our particular expectations.

In many ways the principal deficiency of child-centred educational theory, where it is deficient, is its failure, or perhaps refusal, to come to terms with the need for adult authority. One is given the overwhelming impression that though teachers may be formally in authority, they should not really exercise that authority in any overt or noticeable way. All can be accomplished in the way of discipline by utilizing the child's own strong interests and purposes, or by appealing to the rules imminent in the playing of a game or the accomplishment of a purpose. And if the reality should stubbornly turn out to be otherwise, then the child concerned is plainly not ready for whatever it is. Doubtless there are instances, education being a highly complex and varied enterprise, where this is indeed so. Nevertheless, justice is still not done to the need for authority, the more so the younger the children.

The fact is that what children do, or do not do, affects their later lives. So too do the experiences which they now have, or miss, involve consequences for their futures. Dewey amongst the traditional child-centred theorists was perhaps the most aware of this. He even tried to extract a value criterion from it. But a child's life now and later is all part of a single life. It is all his life, even though he may now be conscious of nothing beyond to-day or even the present moment. Since he often does not know of his own future, and of the consequences for it of what he does now, he cannot form a judgment of his best interests on any adequate basis. Even his interest in becoming autonomous is subject to this deficiency.

On the frankly paternalistic ground of being in his best interests, it therefore falls to adults who have a special knowledge of him, and a natural or professional care for him, to try to discover those interests and secure their satisfaction on his behalf.. Parents and teachers therefore rightly exercise a certain directive influence over him for his good, though to the extent that autonomy is one of his interests then that authority should set itself as one of its tasks its own demise in the face of growing powers of self-direction. This authority is, of course, dependent for its justification on the relevant adult being able and willing to discover the child's best interests, or at least to do so better than can the child himself. Mistakes will no doubt be made, and in the transition period the child will in fact sometimes know better, all of which makes a responsible task that much more difficult. But so far as schooling is concerned, it seems clear that throughout the primary stage general judgments of interest will still have to be made by the teacher and the headteacher. The curriculum cannot simply follow felt interests, but should be liberal in its balance and scope, and it must to some extent prepare for life. Again, true knowledge of fact and the acquisition of the critical standards involved in the discovery of fact are external disciplines which will not always be in perfect harmony with mood and interest. The best accommodation between these sometimes conflicting interests must be judged by the teacher.

Teaching well is a difficult art if only because it requires balancing conflicting claims in order to find the best course in a great variety of circumstances. The individual has claims but he is also part of a group containing others who have equally valid claims on the teacher's limited time. Present interests are sometimes at variance with future needs, of which needs the child himself may even be unaware. Then the tension between the claims of different parts of his own life becomes the tension between the child's freedom and the adult's authority. Eagerness and confidence are sometimes misplaced or misdirected in the light of critical standards and objective fact, so that self-esteem and respect for truth may be in conflict. It is a one-sided simplification in such conflicts to resolve them all by the expedient of always 'starting from the child', just as much as it is an illusion that teaching can ever be an entirely conflict-free, happy and harmonious affair. As well as having a sensitive and sympathetic insight into the world of childhood experience, a teacher also needs determination and a will directed towards the future. It is not too harsh to say that fascinated spectatorial absorption in children and their world sometimes usurps the role of teacher. An essential and valuable source of insight then becomes the object of a form of self-indulgence.

Principles Governing the Content of Education: A Critique of Progressivism

(From Bantock, G., 1980, *Dilemmas of the Curriculum*, Martin Robertson, pp. 42–6.)

The author of the passage below is a leading intellectual proponent of 'educational conservatism' which views the 'business' of education as the transmission of culture, and the curriculum as the repository of worthwhile activities and values into which the young have to be initiated (p. 62). Bantock uses his extensive knowledge of the history of educational ideas to contrast the underlying principles of 'traditional, "liberalizing" education' and those of progressivism (or liberal romanticism). He argues that whereas the former was informed by conceptions of excellence, the latter is guided by the immediately useful or the temporarily relevant. He asserts that in 'the modern British primary school in its more progressive guise', temporary interest and immediate need are guiding principles and too easily foster 'a magpie curriculum of bits and pieces, unrelated and ephemeral. In the interests of a temporary relevance a more permanent and deeper comprehension is often sacrificed.' He concludes that principles which favour the exploitation of the immediate and the everyday in order to provide stimulation and interest may be more appropriate with younger children but that 'even at this stage, such principles governing the content of education should be treated with some caution as at best limited guides.' The importance Bantock attaches to confronting the young with the achievements of others in the past and to getting them inside the concepts and developments of various subject fields finds echoes in the arguments of Peters and Dearden reproduced elsewhere in this section (pp. 117–122 and 139–145).

There is one general point of great importance, concerning the whole orientation of the traditional education vis-à-vis the progressive [education].

As I have made clear earlier, the enterprise of traditional 'liberalizing' education was informed by conceptions of excellence, by the search for perfection, for the Idea in its highest form. Whether the aim is to produce the Philosopher-King (Plato), the Orator (Quintilian), the humanist Courtier (Castiglione) or the Autonomous Mind (initiated by Locke) — all, incidentally, intended to take an *active* part in affairs — in each case it is a notion of the Ideal type which exercises the controlling influence over the content of their education. It would be absurd to deny that a philosopher is a lover of truth and reality; or that his nature, as we have described it, is allied to perfection' (Plato). 'The Orator whom we are educating is the perfect orator, who can only be a good man' (Quintilian). 'I would like our game this evening to be this: that one of us should be chosen and given the task of depicting in words a perfect courtier' (Castiglione); and the tradition was carried on into the nineteenth century by Herbart, Arnold, Cardinal Newman and others. It is this 'vision of greatness' — in Whitehead's phrase — which has informed the determination of curriculum in the past; and, as the social role aimed at has been conceived of in its perfection, so the contributory activities, whether mental or physical, have been conceived of in their own specific perfections. Hence the frequent emphasis on 'imitation' — of the best models; and any 'usefulness' was to be informed by an antecedent liberalization. The autonomy of mind was, in fact, an autonomy from daily exigencies. In these ways, the accidental events of everyday life would be encountered by a mind already prepared to assess such accidents by reference to 'philosophic' principle and contextual significance, by a mind initiated into the circle of knowledge.

But the principle behind the progressive view of the curriculum is essentially that of the accidental; Rousseau wishes for an education that will be immediately useful — 'Life is the trade I would teach him' (1943, p. 9) — and the motivating force is provided by the incidents of daily existence: the activities of the gardener, a conjurer at a fair, a note from Emile's parents, an attempt to gather the cherries from the tree in the garden. Clearly Rousseau is still sustained by the Christian-humanist ethic — 'life' for him would not have included the activities of a Fagin — but his approach involved little ordered attempt to convey the structures of knowledge in a coherent fashion that fastened attention on the primary importance of mastering disciplines and their essential natures. And the same is true of the modern British primary school in its more progressive guise — as it is becoming of many middle and comprehensive schools. Temporary *interest* and immediate *need* are the guiding principles implicit in the attempt to 'psychologize' learning; hence the emphasis on motivation and endogenous development too easily fosters a magpie curriculum of bits and pieces, unrelated and ephemeral. In the interests of a temporary *relevance* a more permanent and deeper comprehension is often sacrificed.

Let us, with this indictment in mind, consider the current fashion for the interdisciplinary. Subject divisions are often dismissed as 'artificial', largely on the grounds that everyday living constantly involves the crossing and recrossing of subject boundaries and 'life as real as the home or the playground' is the object of our endeavour. But, of course, our 'living' is only interdisciplinary, as it were, in our moments of inattention and of imperfect consciousness. As soon as we focus our attention, seek to transcend the often mindless play of our daily existence, we enter an essentially specialized world. That building is a certain shape — what is the meaning of that shape, of the way the space has been deployed? Only a knowledge of architecture in its central concern with mass, space and line can provide the answer. A study of 'Our Town' (a popular subject) involves historical, economic, geographical features (among others) that, to take on significance beyond the most superficial, imply some degree of inwardness with the concepts and developments of the various subject fields involved; otherwise all that occurs is a meaningless copying from books and authorities (a not infrequent manifestation, it can be said), in undifferentiated enthusiasm.

The error implicit in an exclusive diet of this sort of thing lies in its haphazardness — and its subjectivity. It is to see the world as an appendage of self, without a meaning to be sought or guessed at apart from the meaning temporarily assigned in relation to one's immediate interests; it marks a failure to appreciate the integrity of the other, of what lies outside the self. All action, of course, is personal action and depends in the last resort on the responsibility of the self. But that self, to be wisely formed, must display some humility before the achievements of other selves, which is what is implied by a culture, and which it is the business of education to transmit. The danger of an education based totally on imitation is, of course, atrophy; the danger of an education based on novelty, the 'dominance of the foreground' as Santayana puts it, and immediacy is instability and parochialism, with the eccentricities, and worse, that accompany these conditions.

As a child, I was brought up in a way that would currently seem barbaric — with an almost exclusive emphasis on rote learning. Between the ages of five and ten, I learnt chunks of the Bible, gobbets of Shakespeare, fifty spelling words a week, the names of the kings and queens of England and the chief battles, the names of county towns, chief manufactures, capes, bays, isthmuses, rivers — sometimes in blank incomprehension. (Never tell a child what he cannot understand, advised Rousseau; cf. 1943, p. 76). I have forgotten much of this — but I have not forgotten the lesson it implied: that the world, physical and cultural, existed as an entity apart from myself and that if I wished to learn about it I must come to terms with its existence. The famous remark in the Primary School Report of 1931 perpetuates a false dichotomy: 'the curriculum is to be thought of in terms of activity and experience rather than of knowledge to be acquired and facts to be stored.' Knowledge, as I have tried to indicate above, is an essential part of experience: mind is selective and left to itself only focuses meaningfully on what it already knows about.

I am far from saying that occasional projects of an interdisciplinary nature should not be undertaken; but it should be realized that even their value as stimuli is limited to an essentially restricted attraction unless the ephemeral configurations of daily existence are informed by a deeper understanding of the parts that are brought into temporary contiguity in the project — and that have been studied as 'subjects'. For 'subjects' are precisely ways 'in which the incoherence of everyday experience is made meaningful, broken down into its constituent elements and illumined by study in depth. Such study is not to be dismissed as artificial but is an essential element in that very comprehension of the foreground the progressives wish to promote.

Furthermore, it is a psychological error to think that even young children are attracted only by the immediate — the assumption being that their world is bound in by the scope of their sense experiences and their present, and often temporary, 'interests'. In contradistinction to Rousseau's analysis of La Fontaine's fable of the 'Fox and the Crow', with its emphasis on the scientific inaccuracy of the elements of the fable, Coleridge urged the need for the remote and the imaginative:

For from my early reading of fairy tales and genii, etc. etc. my mind

had been habituated to *the Vast*, and I never regarded *my senses* in any way as the criteria of my belief. I regulated all my creeds by my conceptions, not by my *sight*, even at that age... I have known some who have been *rationally* educated, as it is styled. They were marked by a microscopic acuteness, but when they looked at great things, all became a blank and they saw nothing, and denied (very illogically) that anything could be seen ... [1933, p. 532]

Even very young children appreciate some amplification of their surroundings. The theory behind a recent set of readers for young children, Leila Berg's *Nippers*, is that children appreciate the familiar and are at home among the actualities of language and sights assumed to belong to their everyday life. But many find it embarrassing to read out loud: 'Cor, don't it pong', which represents a degeneration into a patronizing uncouthness, and are bored with the mundaneness. They much prefer the 'unreality' of Sheila McCullogh's charming imagination or Dr Seuss's *A Cat in the Hat*.

The argument in favour of the exploitation of the immediate and the everyday in the name of stimulation and interest would seem to be most compelling at the younger ages, when children are, arguably, in the terminology of Piaget, at the level of 'concrete operations' and need the stimulus of the actual. What I have tried to show is that, even at this age, such principles governing the content of education should be treated with some caution as, at best, limited guides — limited both in the way in which sense experience itself is a limited principle to guide curricular choice and also in the way in which this is meaningless unless it is enforced by comprehension of significance — and significance is not a characteristic of surface.

References

COLERIDGE, S.T., (1933) quoted in POTTER, S. (Ed.), *Select Poetry and Prose*, Nonesuch Press.
ROUSSEAU, J. (1943) *Emile*, trans. by B. FOXLEY, Everyman.

The Aims of Primary Education: Towards a More Adequate Educational Theory

(From Dearden, R., 1969, 'The Aims of Primary Education', in Peters, R. (Ed.) *Perspectives on Plowden*, Routledge and Kegan Paul, pp. 29–31, 32–3, 33–4, 35–6, 36–7, 38–41.)

Philosophy of education is sometimes criticized for being concerned merely with words and usages and for not providing guidance for the conduct of educational activities. Here, Dearden draws on the conceptual analyses of Peters on 'education' and Hirst on 'forms of knowledge' to arrive at a philosophically defensible theory to underpin his conception of the primary school curriculum. Dearden's argument is based on the ideal of personal autonomy, which is exercised through the expression of choice, which in turn presupposes that the person so choosing has a well-grounded understanding of his situation in the world. Such an understanding involves 'an insight into certain basic ways in which human experience has, as a matter of historical fact, been developed and elaborated.' It is these forms of understanding — mathematics, science, history, the arts and ethics — which Dearden argues should form the basis of the primary curriculum. For further elaboration of his arguments readers are referred to his book, (1968) *The Philosophy of Primary Education* (London, Routledge and Kegan Paul).

Education implies processes of learning in which we come to understand and appreciate what is valuable in human life. But about what *is* valuable there is endless dispute, including now, and on an extensive scale, dispute about religion as a possible answer to the question of values. As between these differing values and ideals of life the state schools, which in practice the majority of children are legally compelled to attend, ought not to be partisan. There are other educational agencies, such as the family, church and Sunday School, or even the extra-curricular parts of the school's own provision, which can present partisan views to those who can be persuaded to listen to them. But having said that much, one's problem then is to see what is left from which to construct a common curriculum. There are, I shall argue, at least two valid, and partly overlapping, approaches to this problem.

First Approach. The first approach is to recall that, in spite of the fact that our society is pluralist in regard to values, there does remain a quite substantial and acceptable consensus on what is basically valuable for personal and social competence in our form of life. These are the things hinted at in Plowden when the Committee mentions the society into which our children will eventually grow up. What is involved here is perhaps all rather obvious, but I will briefly spell it out.

To begin with, there is the importance of being economically viable, which points at the very least to a constantly revised component in the curriculum of traditional linguistic and arithmetical skills. Next, there is living with others in a justly ordered form of social life, which points, perhaps to social science, and certainly to some form of basic moral education. Again, there is the worthwhile use of leisure, which would point to a rich range of optional extra-curricular activities, such as field games, and clubs and societies, both religious and secular. Furthermore, there is the enjoyment of physical and mental health, which points to physical education and also to an informed sensitivity in teacher-pupil relationships and in general classroom arrangements. Finally, there are valued forms of personal relationship, such as those of love, family life and friendship, which point to several things, including perhaps sex education, 'domestic science' and moral education once again.

This first approach, then, of inquiring into the basic necessities of personal and social competence, can be made to yield a limited set of aims and corresponding curricular recommendations. But the result is clearly minimal, and certainly would not normally occupy the whole of primary schooling, still less the full ten years of compulsory schooling. Some further basis for enriching the school's programme is therefore clearly necessary.

Second Approach. The second approach that I mentioned is, perhaps, rather less obvious, but nevertheless very fruitful. It stems from the view I put forward that state schools ought not be partisan as between the various differing but morally acceptable ways and ideals of life, differing choices of how to live, to be found in our pluralist society. Compatibly with maintaining a basic level of morality, we may choose a life of scholarship, or pursuit of the arts, or active membership of some church, or being close to nature, or family life and intimate friendships, or risk and adventure — or a life of some combination of these and many other valued activities. The logic of this situation must force upon the school the view that children should choose for themselves what suits them best and where their loyalties are to lie.

To present the matter in this way is to say that we will indeed choose, and not just plump for, or be told what to believe and do. And this is already to take for granted the value of personal autonomy which I detected earlier behind a number of Plowden's proposals. There are two aspects to such an autonomy, one negative and one positive. The negative aspect is that of independence of authorities who dictate what we are to believe, or direct us in what we are to do. The complementary positive aspect is, first, that of testing the truth of things for ourselves, whether by experience or by a critical estimate of the testimony of others, and secondly, that of deliberating, forming intentions, and choosing what we shall do, according to a scale of values which we can ourselves....

If personal autonomy is indeed of such fundamental importance among values, then it is most highly deserving of respect, in others by us and in us by others. Furthermore, such a value will be rich in the guidance which it gives over the procedures to be adopted in teaching. For if understanding for ourselves and responsible agency are constitutive of autonomy, then methods of teaching should be devised which bring about such an understanding and which cultivate such a sense of personal agency. Vague notions such as 'the needs of the child' now begin to get some specification and backing. 'Starting from interests' recommends itself as one possible approach that does not call for authoritarian imposition and overruling. And development in the direction of greater autonomy would seem to me to be the valuable heart in such child-centred doctrines as that children should 'grow', that they should 'learn by discovery', and that they should be allowed to choose and to do as much as possible for themselves....

But if personal autonomy is indeed of fundamental importance among values, this is already to admit there to *be* other values. Granted that it is I who am to understand and choose, then what is worth understanding, and what deserves to be chosen? The curriculum problem now shows itself to have been far from solved by the acceptance of the procedural principle of respect for autonomy, for how is account of these other values to be taken? If it is in teaching subjects, then which subjects? If in developing interests, then which interests are to be encouraged or stimulated, and what is it for them to 'develop'? And if the teacher does not take it upon himself to direct the whole of the proceedings, mistakes and unwise choices will sometimes be made, and effort will sometimes be misdirected. Such mistakes may be acceptable, on a long-term view, as the inevitable accompaniments of gaining independence, but up to what point are they acceptable? A teacher is as much responsible for what happens if he withdraws as if he intervenes....

To summarize this second approach as so far presented, then, I have argued from a recognition of the fact that choices have to be made between ideals and ways of life, and from an acceptance of the principle that the public school ought not to be partisan as between these choices. The first implication to be drawn from this is the important tautology that if I am to *choose*, then *I* am to choose. That is to say, the logic of the situation forces personal autonomy into prominence as a value. But the choices actually made will themselves scarcely be of any value unless they are made with as great a degree as possible of understanding of what the situation is and of the possibilities it contains.

Choice and Understanding. To begin to develop this fast point, I want to introduce here the notion of a 'form of understanding', which immediately shows itself to be a notion connected with knowledge and experience. (I have particularly in mind here, and am greatly indebted to, the views developed by Professor P.H. Hirst (1965).).... There are two aspects of forms of understanding which are important here, First, they are systems of interconnected concepts and organizing principles. Secondly, they have distinctive validation procedures for determining the truth, rightness, or adequacy of various statements or judgments that may be made....

Forms of understanding, then, are distinguished by their concepts and their validation procedures, or, if you like, by the ways in which they answer the questions 'What do you mean?', and 'how do you know?' In grasping these concepts and procedures our experience is gradually transformed, and new realities are disclosed which extend and enrich our understanding of our situation in the world. They show us what 'the world' *is*. Each of these forms has its own style of critical thinking, its own ways of being creative and of exercising imagination, and its own ways of refining feeling and guiding activity. These forms are, I suggest, and with the primary school in mind, mathematics, science, history, the arts and ethics....

To draw all this together then: the exercise of choice which is the expression of one's autonomy presupposes a well-grounded understanding of one's situation in the world. Such an understanding in turn is neither just having a load of information loosely carried behind, not is it just having good attitudes, together with an information-getting skill of mythical potency. It is rather an insight into certain basic ways in which human experience has, as a matter of historical fact, been developed and elaborated.

The claim is not that *all* knowledge is of one or other of these forms. Primitive abilities such as knowing how to raise one's arm, or how to locate sensations, are not included, nor are the more everyday sorts of perception and memory, such as the perception that this is a flower, a farm or a frying pan, or the recollection that I had eggs for breakfast last Monday. Nor is it claimed that every one of these forms of understanding enters into every choice that anyone ever makes.

The claim is rather this. First, these forms of understanding are structural of what have historically turned out to be very wide-ranging modes of experience, and hence are basic ingredients in one's understanding of one's situation in the world. Secondly, as such they are relevant to very many, and probably to all of the more important, choices that we have to make, both in our work and in our leisure. And thirdly, their consequent essential connection with the exercise of personal autonomy, together with the requirement of a systematic schooling for their development, make them obviously central candidates for education in the curriculum of our primary schools. . . .

The aims and curriculum for the primary school at which one arrives, then — and in suggesting these I am not attempting a straight deduction, so much as exercizing a certain practical judgment in the light of the two approaches I have described — is as follows. First of all, there would be made at least a beginning in developing an understanding of mathematics, science, history and the arts. Mathematics and the arts would be introduced from the start, in the infant school, while science and history, as distinct from the rovings of a promiscuous and uninstructed natural curiosity, would probably best be left until the second year or so of the junior school. I cannot myself see any justification for dividing further either the sciences or the arts at the primary stage. At some point in the primary school, what *we* know to be physics, chemistry, biology, meteorology, geology, astronomy and physical geography would all be touched upon, as would elementary anthropology, economic geography and some aspects of the psychology of perception. But there seems to be absolutely no point in making explicit these ponderous distinctions.

Where the arts are concerned there seem to be great advantages, in addition to having the truth, in an explicit recognition that they belong together as aspects of aesthetic education. I have in mind here poetry, 'creative writing', drama, singing, instrumental music, dancing, painting, drawing and clay modelling as examples of the relevant aspects of aesthetic education. The advantage of recognizing their common contribution to aesthetic understanding is that by tying them together in this way it makes it much less easy for perpetuators of the elementary school tradition to ignore them, in the pursuit of 'English and arithmetic', or something of that sort. It also helps to direct attention to these activities themselves, so that poetry is not treated just as a spring board for a geography lesson, drawing is not treated as a chance to do some more geometry, and painting and drama are not regarded just as occasions for some lay psychoanalysis.

In drawing up an actual syllabus, of course, further sub-criteria would be needed. These might include: (i) logical priority; (ii) the particular interests shown by children; (iii) special knowledge and abilities of staff; (iv) utility in relation to some other part of the curriculum; (v) economic value; (vi) exemplification in our own particular form of social life or local area. Doubtless there would also be other such sub-criteria.

The second major component in the primary school curriculum would be the 'basic skills'. These would include the mechanics of reading and writing, perhaps learning to speak a foreign language, learning to speak English in the case of immigrants, some of the Welsh, and some English children, a constantly reviewed amount of social arithmetic, and finally, I think also map-reading ought now to be included as a basic skill of high utility.

The third component would be physical education in its various aspects. This would include activities of a gymnastic kind, team-games, swimming, some athletics and also some incidental health and sex education, both of which at this pre-adolescent stage might well be treated as sub-criteria in the choice of topics for science.

Fourthly, there could well be a wide range of extra-curricular activities which a primary school might arrange. These might include chess, stamp, and art and craft clubs as well as outdoor games, though this would all be an optional matter for children and staff alike, of course.

So far I have said nothing concrete about the fifth of the forms of understanding that I mentioned earlier, namely ethics. It would seem best for this to enter into primary education mainly through other activities rather than as a formally structured piece of learning on its own, and hence would be shown in the procedural principles adopted. Fundamental amongst these, I argued, should be respect for personal autonomy. But autonomy is enhanced in value as we increase in our understanding and appreciation of other sorts of value, which ought not to be depreciated in a one-sided adulation of 'the child'. Doing justice all round here poses nice problems of judgment for the teacher, problems which could be thought to be solved in advance of all circumstances only by the doctrinaire.

In addition to respect for autonomy, I take also to be included under ethics such general moral principles as fairness and consideration of interests, and such more particular specifications of these as have to be made explicit as rules. Many more particular moral rules, however, can remain implicit at this stage, as part of a general climate of expectation regarding acceptable standards of behaviour. (I have attempted a much more extended discussion of moral education at the primary stage in Dearden, 1968).

Beyond such a basic morality as this, the ethical includes also a multitude of more or less divergent ideals and ways of life, and hence of possible self-concepts in terms of which to identify oneself and to achieve integrity. Here, on the views which I have presented, the teacher's task is not that of firm instistence but of the disclosure of possibilities. Such a disclosure of ways and modes of life should not be accompanied by subtle, or often very unsubtle, pressures towards compliance and initiation, but should take place through history, including the history of religion, literature, including religious literature, and also those aspects of science concerning men and how they live.

Finally, it seems to me that there is really no such thing as *primary* education, if by that is meant anything more than an administratively and developmentally convenient *stage* in an education which is one. The education which is given in the primary school must therefore always be incomplete and cannot be autonomous. The success of the primary school is to have made a good start.

References

DEARDEN. R., (1968) *The Philosophy of Primary Education; An Introduction*, London, Routledge and Kegan Paul.

HIRST, P., (1965) 'Liberal education and the nature of knowledge', in ARCHANBAULT, R. (Ed.), *Philosophical Analysis and Education*, London, Routledge and Kegan Paul.

The Beginnings of a Reformulation of 'Progressive' Education

(From Armstrong, M., 1977, 'The informed vision: A programme for educational reconstruction', *Forum*, 9.3, pp. 76–80.)

As the extracts in this section illustrate, 'progressive' education (or liberal romanticism) has been the subject of considerable philosophical criticism since the publication of the Plowden Report in 1967. Apart from the work of Wilson (pp. 113–116), little has been done in England to provide a closely argued philosophical basis for this educational ideology. Significantly perhaps, the beginnings of more adequate 'progressive' educational theorizing have been provided by an American philosopher of science, David Hawkins, who was himself greatly influenced by his contacts with English primary schools arising out of his development work on elementary school science in the 1960s. Some of the most important points in his (1974) book of essays, *The Informed Vision* (Agathon), are synthesized here by Armstrong and represent ideas for the reformulation of 'progressive' education along more justifiable philosophical and psychological lines.

Most of the themes that dominate *The Informed Vision* emerge in the title essay [the first essay in Hawkins' book]. For David Hawkins an informed human vision is the ultimate goal of education. Education is not, not first and foremost, a utility, a means of growth, of 'producing a population increasingly ready to embrace and further the new industrial technology which development requires'; nor is it primarily a means to economic or political power, either for individuals or for classes. It is, in its essence, a way of informing and enhancing the human vision, of sustaining a sense of involvement and of commitment within our world, of 'being at home in the world', a quality which also implies 'that we very well understand the opposite condition of non-involvement, the many moods of alienation'. The most important kind of estrangement in our own world, 'derives from the fact that the extraordinary technological and material evolution of the last century or two expresses a way of life and thought that has been genuinely available only to a minority among us. To the rest it is, in essence, and alien affair'. The consequence is twofold: the majority are deprived both of a proper sense of involvement and commitment in our world, and of access to the means of power which depend upon a knowledge they do not share, while the select and privileged minority who do possess the knowledge, divided as they are from the rest of society, are inevitably 'subject to all the corruptions of caste and status'. 'A world so deeply committed to science', and to other forms of symbolic knowledge, 'cannot survive with a vast majority of its population intellectually and aesthetically alienated from' these forms.

It is the purpose of the essays [in Hawkins' book] to describe and to defend 'a style of education that would permit correction, in our culture, of this basic defect'. Hawkins seeks an analogy for the style he has in mind in Colin Turnbull's account of education and among the Pygmies in his book *The Forest People*. 'It is an education which begins in play suffused with enjoyment and evolves into an apprenticeship premised on commitment'. He acknowledges the vast difference between our needs and those of the Pygmies. 'What we must learn is in part more remote from the immediate environment, more abstructed and dependent on symbolic skills. And that is the challenge to our education; to recover for our world', a world of abstraction and symbol, 'the ways of learning that are concretely involving and aesthetically rewarding, that move from play toward apprenticeship in work'.

It is characteristic of any achievement of learning of this order that it possesses a quality of spontaneity which Hawkins, quoting John Dewey, defines as 'complete absorption in subject matter that is fresh, the freshness of which holds and sustains emotion'. Spontaneity of human expression 'is no mere display or outburst: it is a synthesized achievement compatible, as Dewey goes on to say, "with any amount of labour provided the results of that labour emerge in complete fusion with an emotion that is fresh" '. Among the conditions that foster and nourish such an achievement two are pre-eminent. One is the child's 'freedom for active involvement', for exploration and for choice; the other is the teacher's provisioning of an environment rich in exploratory potential. To reinforce 'the natural probings and explorings of children' is, as Dewey saw, 'the basis of all true education'. But that is only one side of the story. Content is no less important than method and 'absorption in subject matter requires a major effort of provisioning for that subject matter'. In its preoccupation with the child's freedom for active involvement 'progressive education' has sometimes neglected to show an equal, matching concern for provisioning 'the world of children's exploration with subject matter they could explore well, could penetrate deeply.'

Exploration with Explanation

Education, then, requires the freedom to explore 'the order and organisation of the world' through 'complete absorption in subject matter that is fresh' and in the company of teachers who have made ample provision for that subject matter. But the emphasis on exploration does not preclude the value or necessity of explanation. 'There comes a time for harvesting, gathering, organising, even programming, and here individual learners must be drawn together under a common discipline. In our schools, this time comes much too early. Or, better, it is too little preceded and followed by periods — long periods — of individualised and diversified work of a more exploratory and self-directed kind.... We must learn better to instruct children, when, after absorption in subject matter, they communicate by their behaviour those directions which they are prepared to find meaningful because they themselves have begun to define and seek them. And then there is the opposite transition, when formal instruction has brought children to new levels of understanding and interpretation; to open again the door to less directed probing and testing at these new levels — and thus to consolidate what has been learned, to use it for further learning.'

Of all the themes presented in [the] opening essay the foremost is that of autonomy. In essay after essay Hawkins insists that it is 'a fundamental aim of education to organise schools, classrooms and our own performance as teachers in order to help children acquire the capacity for significant choice' and that 'learning is really a process of choice'. 'If children are deprived of significant choice in their daily activities in school then the most important thing that education is concerned with is simply being by-passed.' Traditionally, autonomy has been viewed as one of the ends of education but not as part of its means, or at any rate not an essential part. It is from this mistake that much of the failure of traditional education derives. Thus 'it is often conceded that a superordinate aim of education should be the cultivation of competence in children to fashion well their own lives. But it is NOT supposed steadily that such competence is gained through exercise of it. It is supposed, rather, that self-organisation will appear magically AFTER years of schooling subordinated to a quite different principle, according to which children are DEPRIVED of autonomy. They are deprived in the interest of what is conceived to be an efficient imparting of information and guidance. During all this time, and in the interest of such efficiency, children are essentially deprived of any significant exercise of autonomy in choice, discrimination and judgment. They are coerced, however politely, into a frame of organisation intended to promote their acceptance of information and exercise in specific curricular topics, these being justified on the ground that they are necessary to competent adult functioning. This induced organisation is thought of as a kind of scaffolding to be torn down after the process is finished and the product certified as complete. But it is in fact a powerful moulding of character, and of a kind of character antagonistic to the superordinate aim which education professes to serve. The scaffolding gets built into the structures and cannot be removed'.

Already Advantaged

Hawkins suggests that the children who succeed under such a programme do so because they already possess a capacity for individual choice, acquired OUTSIDE of school. 'But children are very unequally endowed by previous condition and experience with this capacity for independent choice, which the schools do little to help them cultivate. No one can catalogue all the conditions of such relative success but it is a conspicuous statistical fact that the successful come commonly, though not universally, from a background which could be called the folk-culture of the already well-educated. The deeper conditions of academic success, which schools often unconsciously work against, are in fact supplied from another cultural source. But for vast numbers of children the mismatch between their own developing capacities and the experience available in school is so great that they are unable to avoid the induced pattern, with its constant accompaniment for them of failure and boredom, withdrawal, manipulation or rebellion'.

Alternative Learning Theory

To remedy this deep defect in 'standard educational practice' and theory we require a radically new theory of education, reflecting an alternative conception of learning and of knowing, 'the theory of a design which seeks to optimise the eolithic component in education, to optimise children's capacity to conduct their own learning and to become their own teachers.... The key proposition in this theory is that learning, in its most significant educational dimensions, is not something of a different kind from self-government, self-organisation, choice, but is a species of that very genus. Learning in an educationally important sense is an active process of self-organisation and reorganisation which takes place through the mediation of choice among significant alternatives available to the learner'. Hawkins opposes such a theory to classical Learning Theory, and, in an essay entitled 'Mind and Mechanism in Education' and again in the long philosophical essay which closes his collection, he discusses the relationship between the alternative conception of learning and knowing which he proposes and the philosophical and psychological theories of Kant and of Piaget. Tentative and schematic though it is, this discussion is of great importance in the development of an adequate theory of 'progressive' education. However I do not have space to discuss it further here. I would like, rather, to draw attention to some of the implications which Hawkins extracts from his conception of the primacy of autonomy in education, implications which are often ignored in traditional discussions of 'progressive' education.

'Progressive' thought has seemed on occasion to make a mystery of autonomy as if it were a quality of mind that was self-generating, self-sustaining and self-sufficient, an innate and inexplicable flowering of intellect and character. Nothing could be further from Hawkins' intention. The proper exercise of autonomy in learning is inseparable, he insists, from communication with others — adults, teachers, other children — and communion with things — the subject matter of their common concerns. 'No child, I wish to say, can gain competence and knowledge, or know himself as competent and as a knower save through communication with others involved with him in his enterprises. Without a Thou there is no I evolving. Without an It there is no content for the context, no figure and no heat, but only an affair of mirrors confronting each other'. This triangular relationship, between teacher, pupil and task, he explores in one of the few essays in this collection that is already relatively well known in England, an essay entitled 'I, Thou and It'.

He begins his discussion by considering 'a kind of electronic analogy for what goes on in a child's mind. Think of circuits that have to be completed. Signals go out along one bundle of channels, something happens, and signals come back along another bundle of channels; and there's some kind of feedback involved. Children are not always able to sort out all of this feedback for themselves. The adult's function, in the child's learning is to provide a kind of external loop, to provide a selective feedback from the child's own choice and action. The child's involvement gets some response from an adult and this in turn is made available to the child. The child is learning about himself through his joint effects on the non-human AND the human world around him. The function of the teacher is to respond diagnostically and helpfully to a child's behaviour, to make what he considers to be an appropriate response, a response which the child needs to complete the process he 's engaged in at a given moment.'

Intervention Strategy

'Progressive' teachers sometimes give the impression of forgetting 'the unique importance of the human role'. 'We tend to say "Oh well, if children just have a good, rich, manipulable and responsive environment, then everything will take care of itself...." But, of course, that's a dangerous illusion. It's true only in those periods — in good schools frequent periods — when children don't need the external loop. When they do need it and there's no-one around to contribute the adult resonance, then they're not always able to carry on the process of investigation, of inquiry and exploration, of learning, because they need help over a hump that they can't surmount through their own resources. If help isn't available the inquiry will taper off, and that particular episode, at least, will have failed to accomplish what it otherwise might have.'

Of all the many kinds of intervention a good teacher is required to make, the most important is the kind of intervention that encourages, or helps to sustain, a child's absorption in subject matter, in the various objects of children's and teachers' inquiries. It is here that we can see most clearly 'how the "It" enters into the pattern of mutual interest and exchange between the teacher and the child', and why it is that Hawkins attaches supreme importance to the interrelationship of teacher, pupil and task.

'The investment in the child's life that is made in this way, by the adult, the teacher in this case, is something that adds to and in a way transforms the interest the child develops spontaneously. If, as sometimes happens, a child gets particularly interested in a variation on a soap bubble theme that you've already given him, you can just happen to put nearby some other things that might not at first seem related to soap bubbles — some geometrical wire cubes, tetrahedra, helices, and wire with a soldering iron. The resulting soap films are almost bound to catch the fancy of many human beings, including children. What have they got? Well they've got a certain formal geometrical elegance, they've got colour; when you look at the films in the right kind of light you see all those marvellous interference colours. Such a trap is bristling with invitations and questions. Some children will sample it and walk on; but some will be hooked by it, will get very involved with it. Now, this kind of involvement is terribly important, I think. It's aesthetic, or it's mathematical or it's scientific. It's all of these potentially, and none of them exclusively. The teacher has made possible this relation between the child and "It" even if this is just by having "It" in the room; and for the child even this brings the teacher as a person, a Thou, into the picture. For the child this is not merely something which is fun to play with, which is exciting and colourful and has associations with many other sorts of things in his experience: it's also a basis for communication with the teacher on a new level and with a new dignity.

'Until the child is going on his own the teacher can't treat him as a person who is going on his own, cannot let him be mirrored there, where he may see himself as investigator or craftsman. Until he is an autonomous human being, who is thinking his own thoughts and making his own unique, individual kinds of self-expression out of them, there isn't anything for the teacher to respect, except a potentiality. So the first act in teaching, the first goal, necessary to all others, is to encourage this kind of engrossment. Then the child comes alive for the teacher as well as the teacher for the child. They have a common theme for discussion, they are involved together in the world'.

They have proved, as Hawkins puts it at the end of his essay, 'that we're all in "It" together'.

Authority of Teachers

The I-Thou-It relationship is the indispensable complement to Hawkins' insistence on the primacy of autonomy in learning, and it is this feature of his work, above any other, that helps him to escape from many of the stereotypes that bedevil discussion of 'progressive' education. Thus his emphasis on adult intervention belies the common accusation that 'progressive' is synonymous with 'permissive'. Indeed Hawkins is at pains to point out that 'authority is one of the primary sources of learning. To be an authority in this sense (the sense of being one whose activities or contribution to your existence you value because it has proved itself to BE valuable), to be a teacher whom children honestly respect because you give them something which helps them on the way and which they know they couldn't get for themselves, is to be a teacher. If you are not that kind of authority, you are not a good teacher, you're not functioning properly as a teacher'.

Worth of Content

Similarly, his deep concern for subject matter, 'the order and organisation of the world' which children and teachers investigate together, makes nonsense of the presumption that 'progressive' education is inevitably weak on content or curriculum, on 'the public forms of experience' as Hirst and Peters have it. 'Adults involved in the world of man and nature bring that world with them to children, bounded and made safe to be sure, but not thereby losing its richness and promise of novelty.... Adults and children, like adults with each other, can associate well only in worthy interest and pursuits, only through a community of subject matter and engagement which extends BEYOND the circle of their intimacy. The attitude of deprecating subject matter, and of deprecating curriculum as a guide to the providing of worthy subject matter, reflects therefore the half-truth badly used.'

Even his insistence on the necessarily informal, unpredictable and incommensurable nature of education, of learning and teaching, is balanced by a recognition of the appropriate moment for formality, didacticism, rote-learning. 'One has to fight against the belief that because the central priority is self-directed learning there is never any value in instruction or didactic teaching. There are times when a group of children is very ready to be instructed about something, or to engage in a set task which might even be rote learning under certain circumstances. Their readiness to do this means that it has become for them a significant choice and it is therefore by no means violating the principle of choice to say there is room, and sometimes a significant amount of room, for quite formal instruction.'

There is, then, a salutary note of caution in many of the details of Hawkins' account of education, which helps to guard his argument against the misconceptions to which 'progressive' education is particularly prone. Yet, when all is said and done, this cannot, as indeed it should not, blunt or blur the radical and demanding nature of his vision.

4   Primary Education: Sociological Perspectives

Introduction

The sociology of education is now a major branch of educational study. During the last thirty years, its theories, methodologies and areas of enquiry have been the subject of development and controversy (Banks, 1982). At no time during this period have primary schools been the main focus of its attention. Nevertheless, the foundations of a sociology of primary education have been laid through a variety of studies, extracts from some of which are reproduced in this section.

During the 1950s and 1960s, sociologists were interested in the ways in which the educational system was related to structural features of society such as social stratification, industrialization, and the division of labour. At that time education was viewed by policy-makers as a means of providing a literate and adaptable labour force and as a way of promoting social mobility for individuals from 'lower' socio-economic groups. There was particular sociological interest in documenting how far children from different social classes had access to selective education and in explaining how these class-related inequalities came about. The extracts from Floud, Halsey and Martin (pp. 166–169) and Davie, Butler and Goldstein (pp. 170–178) illustrate some of the class-related differences in educational attainment in primary schools and the 11+ examination, revealed by a large number of investigations. Attempts were made to search for the factors responsible for these differences and for the resulting inequalities of opportunity. The factors investigated included family size, briefly referred to in the extract from Floud, Halsey and Martin (p. 168–9), socio-linguistic codes investigated by Bernstein and others (pp. 193–199), and parental aspirations, values and attitudes, which were the subject of many inquiries, including a major one sponsored by the Plowden Committee (pp. 179–183). Some sociologists such as A.H. Halsey were involved not just in documenting and explaining class-related inequalities, but in devising strategies to help alleviate them (pp. 187–192). As part of the general interest in the social and economic functions of education, some sociologists studied the patterns of social structure, methods of social control, and processes of social change in particular institutions, as illustrated by the first extract from Alan Blyth on the five social functions of primary schools (pp. 158–160).

Around the end of the 1960s, the structural-functional approach to the sociology of education was challenged by the interactionist perspective which stressed, not the constraints of social structures and functions, but the ways in which man was able to create and define his own social reality. In Banks' words, 'the central task of the sociology of education, therefore, was seen as an examination of the participants in the educational process through an exploration of their perceptions and assumptions as well as their interaction with each other. There was a change in method, most significantly, in the exchange of observation for the social survey, and a change in what were seen as problem areas.' The brief extract from Nash (pp. 229–231) illustrates the concern for the way in which participants build up identities and bodies of knowledge about educational reality through day-to-day interactions. Two new foci of attention emerged: the study of classroom interaction, as illustrated here by the work of King on infant education (pp. 232–236), and the study of curricula as socially organized knowledge 'processed' by schools — an area of enquiry aided by the theoretical work of Bernstein (pp. 200–205).

In addition to the other two sociologies of education, a third emerged in the 1970s. This neo-Marxist perspective viewed the educational system as an agency for the social and cultural reproduction of capitalist society, with teachers cast very largely as unwitting collaborators and with working-class pupils largely as unknowing victims. On this view, schools socialize the young by getting them to accept the way things are and by preventing them from considering alternative possibilities to the existing social order. Most of this neo-Marxist theorizing has been conducted at a highly abstract level, not often accompanied by detailed empirical work to test the arguments advocated. In the context of primary education, an exception is the study by Sharp and Green (pp. 225–228). Another strand to the neo-Marxist perspective has been a critique of recent educational policies — a concern illustrated here by Dale's paper on control, accountability and the William Tyndale affair (pp. 209–219).

The extracts in this section of the source book do not constitute a complete course in the sociology of primary education. They need to be supplemented by more extensive general reading, but they do illustrate the value of a sociological perspective, or more accurately a variety of perspectives, on primary education. For more detailed overviews on developments in the sociology of education, readers are referred to Banks, O. (1982). 'The sociology of education 1952–1982', *British Journal of Educational Studies*, 30, 1; and Robinson, P. (1981) *Perspectives on the Sociology of Education: An Introduction*, Chapters 1 and 2, London, Routledge and Kegan Paul.

The Five Basic Roles of the Primary School

(From Blyth, W., 1965, *English Primary Education*, Vol. 1, London, Routledge and Kegan Paul, pp. 17, 17–8, 19, 20, 20–1).

This extract has been taken from an analysis of primary schools as social institutions — an analysis written in the first half of the 1960s and informed by a structural-functional approach to the sociology of education. Through discussion of the primary school in terms of social structure, social function and control, and social change, Blyth placed it in relation to the education system and to the wider social structure. Here, he suggests that the primary school discharges four basic roles — instruction, socialization, classification and welfare — to which he adds a fifth, and less clear dimension, that is, the creation of a distinctive, semi-autonomous identity. In discussing the five roles, he draws on his analysis of traditions within primary education, which is featured elsewhere in the source book (pp. 3–7). Though the theoretical perspective adopted here is no longer fashionable, the sociological description offered provides a useful and still recognizable view of the primary school as an institution.

There are five basic roles which primary schools may be said to discharge in contemporary English society: to instruct; to socialise; to classify; to promote social welfare; and to develop autonomy for themselves....

First: *instruction*. Whether one judges from the volume of controversy or from the nature of the formal structure of primary schools, there is no doubt about the importance attached to instruction, especially in the basic skills. Despite the impact of the developmental tradition, there is still general support for the view that primary schools instruct, and that the expansion of children's cognitive horizons is among their principal objectives. However, instruction is often broadly and generously defined, so that this role may at its best involve an exciting intellectual adventure and concurrently an extension of social learning.

The second role is that of *socialisation*. This is more directly associated with the developmental tradition, and implies that primary schools are places where children learn to live together in such a way that they will continue to live, in later years, in a manner appropriate to a civilised community. This may also involve some instruction; but socialisation is more than instruction, and it is doubtful whether social values can be acquired in any other way than through participation in collective living, even though the excellence of the social values may depend heavily on the quality of the social living and the influences with which it is surrounded, and the wisdom with which this environment is adjusted to the developing capacities and vision of the children. The actual patterns of socialisation in primary schools vary according to the fundamental beliefs of the teachers and others who influence policy, but there can be little room for dispute about the importance of the socialising role itself.

Next in the series comes *classification*. In England today, one aspect of classification — that of selection for secondary education — is so prominent that the very existence of others is masked. But in fact, classification is a continuous and ubiquitous process in primary schools. Children come to be classified informally according to the aspects of the curriculum in which they do well or badly, and also according to their physical and social abilities and attainments. From all of these they may derive a general reputation which adheres to them as a stereotype, as tends to happen also in their peer-life outside school. For some of these classificatory processes official records are kept — of physique, for example, and of general and specific abilities and attainments, and of personality ratings — but others are informally but decisively committed to the children's own minds and those of their associates....

The fourth role is that of *welfare*.... In England, ... the welfare role of primary schools has a statutory basis ... and indeed several observers (Mellor, 1950, p. 88; Gray, 1955) have pointed out that schools have become focal points of the Welfare State, just because almost the whole child population passes through them. This welfare function is derived in part from traditional religious and philanthropic concepts of social service, and in part from widely-accepted views about the functions and responsibilities of the modern State. In addition primary schools have a specific welfare role for, as Mays (1962) points out, they are nowadays the only true neighbourhood institutions....

Last in order of consideration comes the *autonomous* role, and it is the most difficult to define. It is closely associated with the developmental tradition; ultimately, it is the role which obliges each school to be itself. For this purpose it must draw on the collective experience and talents of its staff, and on the support of various elements in the community, but for the rest it grows spontaneously....

A school must do more than reflect the culture of part or even all of its pupils. It cannot even be content to reflect that culture in its idealised form. The only way in which it can realise its autonomous role is by cutting purposefully adrift from the culture-patterns associated with the various parts of its clientele and creating something new and worth-while in itself. Once this is achieved, it can lead to the establishment of a social climate in which the operation of the usual conventions and counter-conventions of society and of its subdivisions are minimised, so that individuality and initiative can develop within an accepted framework of stable and considerate behaviour. Feeling that theirs is a good and satisfying school, the children are then more favourably disposed towards it, more ready to go along with it in the implementation of its other roles, and incidentally thereby more tolerant towards others whose cultural background differs from their own. The effective implementation of the autonomous role involves the consummation of the other roles also.

References

GRAY, K. (1955) 'Social welfare and the teacher', *Social Welfare*, 9, 5, pp. 104–10.
MAYS, J. (1962) *Education and the Urban Child*, University of Liverpool Press.
MELLOR, E. (1950) *Education through Experience in the Infant School*, Blackwell.

Socialization into School

(From Newsom, J.; Newsom, E.; and Barnes, P., 1977, *Perspectives on School at Seven Years Old*, Allen and Unwin, pp. 41, 41–2, 42–3, 44, 44–5, 47–8).

Socialization is one of the main roles or functions of the primary school according to Blyth's analysis summarized in the first extract of this section (pp. 158–162). The material reproduced below is written within the same structural-functional framework and examines how children's socialization into the school's structure, norms and values is achieved. According to the Newsoms, 'school is the contact which crystallises the child's transformation into a social creature, which formalises his experience of the peer group and of outside authority, and which presents a new set of demands which may be totally alien to the expectations of home but which are too powerful for the child to reject altogether.' The passage describes how infant children adjust to the dynamic social structure of the primary school (helped by the infant teacher as a key mediator of their experience), how they develop very considerable knowledge of how teachers, fellow pupils and schools operate, and how they acquire an evolving social status. The material for this analysis is derived from the Newsom's large-scale longitudinal study of child-rearing in Nottingham and complements the authors' parallel study of the home environment of 7-year-olds (Newsom, J. and E., 1976, *Seven Year Old in the Home Environment*, Allen and Unwin). For a contrasting interpretation of socialization into school, at least as far as lower working-class children are concerned, see the first extract by Bernstein later in this section (pp. 193–196), and that by Sharp and Green (pp. 225–228).

The teacher, . . . as well as being the key figure in the child's introduction to formal learning, also mediates his experience of the school world in which that process of learning takes place; and the school itself serves (for most children) as the earliest model of the complicated patterns of behaviour and social interaction which evolve in the institutional or organisational settings that will continue to be important to a greater or lesser extent as the child grows up. . . . It is part of the teacher's role not only to identify herself with the school, but to cause the child to do so too, usually via the transitional stage of himself identifying with her. If the child's relationship is only with the teacher and not with the school beyond her, she has failed to wean him from the purely personal bond of which the mother was the first model. Eventually the child must familiarise himself with the corporate entity of the school, come to feel that he belongs to it and it to him, and learn in his turn to initiate younger children into its customs and values. In becoming socialised in the school as social institution, children are carried onward by repeatedly experiencing the rhythms and rituals of the school day and the school week, as well as by innumerable encounters with other people who themselves have a known place in the pattern: children from their own class and their own year, children from the 'babies' class' or the 'top class', in-between children who are not 'the big ones' but yet are bigger than themselves, teachers who are soft and motherly from looking after the little ones, teachers who are bright and brisk from keeping nine-year-olds in order, the head and the deputy head, the school secretary, the dinner-ladies and the caretaker. Through such encounters, in which he may be either participant or observing bystander, the child begins to appraise his own position within the hierarchical age-graded structure of the school as a whole.

Probably no one person has full knowledge of all the customs, beliefs and practices which make up the social organisation of a single primary school. In our daughters' school, for instance, it was only the lower junior girls who knew about the Green Lady behind the cupboard in the hall, and how she needed to be propitiated; and no doubt any group one could identify, among children and staff alike, would be found to have its own beliefs which contribute to the total social edifice. But even understandings which have the status of 'common knowledge' must be acquired gradually over time by any given child, by piecing together a thousand scraps of experience. . . .

From all these diverse sources of information, then, children gradually absorb a rather different set of standards from those which have come to govern their behaviour in the intimate family environment. Because the seven-year-old is an extremely social animal, the child approaching this age will be very responsive to a philosophy of 'This is the way we all do it, so this is how it has to be'. Schools are thus enabled to guide and mould the behaviour of their children in hundreds of different and subtle ways, often without resort to any coercion other than the social pressure which is implicit in the example of the majority being willing to conform to group expectations. The compelling difference between home socialisation and socialisation to the school lies in *the degree of tolerance accorded to egocentricity*. At school, egocentricity must fairly quickly accept subordination to group needs. Obviously the pre-school child *is* developmentally more egocentric than the primary school child; but it is not just a question of age. Obviously, too, parents subscribe in general terms to the idea that one child cannot be allowed to dominate the whole group; it is their own conscious endeavour that one member of the family should not ride roughshod over the others. None the less, children of any age, including adolescents, do dominate their families egocentrically for brief or longer periods according to their special problems or needs or preoccupations of the moment; and it is perhaps the family's special function to put up with such episodes of domination because they are necessary to the child's development at the time and because no other institution in society will tolerate them.

In fact, although children of seven still respond to their teachers in a highly personal way, it is a mistake to suppose that the relationship between teacher and pupil is at all similar to that between parent and child. The teacher's role, however democratic or benign he or she may be, is deliberately formalised; and in the school environment all sorts of social forces are in operation to constrain the behaviour of both adults and children. Teachers themselves naturally assume — and are indeed accorded — a respect proper to their status within the institution, which is quite different from that which parents would nowadays expect from their own offspring at home. Related to this is another consideration: that teachers behave, and are expected by parents to behave, according to a code of professional conduct. . . .

The development of group norms of acceptable school behaviour is a factor of considerable practical importance, since it is only this development which enables such a small number of adults to cope effectively and benignly with such large numbers of children. Many parents express deep admiration for the way teachers surmount what appears to be the almost impossible task of controlling such an enormous 'family', and it is clear that their admiration stems from this false comparision with their own parental role. Surely teachers must be almost superhuman if they can deal with thirty children single-handed! Imagine what it would be like if their own families were to be increased by a factor of ten! It is this mixture of awe and sympathy which can lead parents to ignore their children's complaints, feeling that they themselves could not do such a job and therefore have no right to criticise if something goes wrong. This is interesting, since not being able to do a job ourselves does not normally prevent our criticism of, say, an inefficient television repair or an inept comedian; and it does appear to be the sense of comparability, *coupled* with parental feelings of inadequacy, which produces this reaction. . . .

What needs to be understood, however, is that the attempt to teach such a large group of children would indeed present an impossible task were it not that they are already, by the time they reach junior school age, in bond to a substantial network of group conventions. The average benign primary school is a complex social institution with a tightly knit and well-ordered social structure. The hierarchy is dominated at one level by older children whose own status is served by assisting in the socialisation of the younger ones; and at another level by experienced adults who are deliberately accorded considerable power over the children in their charge. As in most social organisations, the participating members, whether higher or lower in the hierarchy, are constrained within a system of values and customs which govern when, where and how the participants are expected to behave towards each other. Some few of these customs will be made explicit as school rules or school information, to which the attention of children and parents will be deliberately drawn; but many more will be absorbed through the pores, as it were, as 'natural' and established usage — the accepted ways in which pupils and teachers do behave in school. The child imperceptibly comes to adopt and make his own a quite complicated notion of a dynamic social structure and his own evolving status within it, by a long accretion of incidental learning.

When we say that children adjust or 'settle down' to school, then, we may be in danger of missing the crucial point: that they are being subjected to a compelling socialisation process, much of which offers persuasive rewards, but as a result of which they learn to accept their place as very junior members of an elaborate social hierarchy. This is by no means to say that the child simply learns passive conformity to rules and conventions: on the contrary, the power of the system lies in the fact that the child internalises its values in a very active sense. . . .

Schools today, as parents often pointed out, offer much more freedom of choice than many of these parents themselves remember from their own early schooldays. The style of control has changed; the atmosphere is more child-centred and permissive. Harshness of punishment or threat of punishment is only rarely encountered. This does not, however, mean (as some parents supposed) that children can do whatever they like, or that teachers have given up any control over their pupils: only that teachers, like parents, have moved towards a democratic image, and have learned to use group forces, at least in the primary school, to maintain an illusion of democratic choice within a relatively unyielding framework. Within this framework, parents and teachers are at some pains to keep the child contented, and with goodwill and easy communication can often smooth the difficulties which the child encounters. However, problems of communication can arise, both between parents and teachers, and between parents and their own children: home and school *are* different worlds, and the two worlds foster myths about each other which may not be helpful to the child moving between them. Certain facts, beyond the myths, have to be lived with. Teachers have always been aware that some parents provide a frankly damaging environment for their children, and that these children will continue to be at risk however compensatory the education that may be devised for them. It is also true that some teachers are incompetent and that some are unsuitable for their profession and damaging to the children they teach: when this happens, both parents and children are likely to find that there is very little to be done to change the situation, other than to sweat it out as best they can. It is here that both communication for parents and democratic choice for children break down.

In this introduction to the parents' perspective on school, we have attempted first of all to present the school situation from a more objective perspective than parents are usually themselves able to take: they are, after all, usually too immediately concerned with the individual personalities involved and the actual activities being undertaken from day to day. We have tried to show how the child extends his horizons from home and family, to school, peers and less intimate authorities, and how his adaptation to the more formal social system takes place. In his first months in the infant school, the child's teacher will make considerable allowance for his individual quirks and foibles: less responsive than his mother to his egocentricity, she is still a tolerant, nurturant figure, to whom he can ascribe a mothering image and who can offer him a protective transition from home to school expectations. Loving his teacher uncritically, yet also compelled to share her with a greater number of peers than he has been used to, he learns two massive adaptations: he identifies with his teacher, and thence with the school world which she represents; and he is introduced to a discovery for which he is now intellectually ready — the discovery that group co-operation brings its own rewards in greater achievement and more complex and satisfying play. These crucial social lessons of the infant school, mediated chiefly by the teacher herself, allow him to become fully integrated with the peer group and with the school as social institution, and bring him under the powerful influence of both: and in this way he is enabled to wean himself from the protective nurturance of his teacher, and become an independent 'junior'. At this stage, while retaining a close and friendly relationship with his class teacher, he is also more able to look beyond her to other teachers with whom he enjoys more casual contact; and, detached from his personal dependency, he begins to show the emergence of 'us and them' loyalties in relation to peer group *vis-à-vis* teachers, turning more frequently towards other children as a source of comfort and support in meeting difficulties at school. Socialisation takes on a new emphasis.

Social Class and Educational Opportunity

(From Floud, J.; Halsey A.; and Martin F., 1956, *Social Class and Educational Opportunity*, Heinemann, pp. 142–7.)

The major preoccupation of the few sociologists studying the English educational system in the 1950s was the relationship between social class and educational opportunity. Sociologists documented the access to selective secondary education (through the 11+ examination) by children from different social classes and attempted to provide explanations of what brought about these differences of access. The passage below comes from the conclusions of a major sociological study of the social distribution of access to grammar schools by boys in South-West Hertfordshire and in Middlesbrough. In their investigation the authors documented the marked differences in the chances which boys of different social classes had of obtaining grammar school places in both the areas studied. They concluded that although there was a close relationship between 'ability' (defined as 'measured intelligence' on IQ tests) and 'opportunity' (defined as access to grammar schools), 'the problem of inequality of educational opportunity' was 'not thereby disposed of ', since material and cultural differences in the environment of children from different social classes affected their performance on tests and hence their access to selective secondary education through the 11+ examination. The social determinants of 'educability' in which the authors were interested became a major focus of sociological investigation at the end of the 1950s and the early 1960s, as illustrated by the work of Bernstein (pp. 193–196) and the 1964 National Survey conducted for the Plowden Committee (pp. 179–183). At that time there was general agreement with the concluding sentences of the study from which the passage below has been extracted:

> The problem of equality of educational opportunity is now more complicated than when it took the simple form of the need to secure free access to grammar schools on equal intellectual terms. With the expansion of educational opportunity and the reduction of gross economic handicaps to children's school performance the need arises to understand the optimum conditions for the integration of school and home environment at all social levels in such a way as to minimise the educational disadvantages of both and to turn their educational advantages to full account.

It is obvious that the number of working-class boys entering the grammar schools each year has been increasing fast, and that there are more in the schools today than ever before. Nevertheless, the probability that a working-class boy will get to a grammar school is not strikingly different from what it was before 1945, and there are still marked differences in the chances which boys of different social origins have of obtaining a place. Of those working-class boys who reached the age of 11 in the years 1931–41 rather less than 10 per cent entered selective secondary schools. In 1953 the proportion of working-class boys admitted to grammar schools was 12 per cent in Middlesbrough and 14 per cent in South West Hertfordshire. Thus, approximately one working-class boy in eight was admitted in Middlesbrough, as compared, for instance, with nearly one in three of the sons of clerks; and approximately one working-class boy in seven in South West Herfordshire, as compared with nearly one in two of the sons of clerks.

Our findings as to the social distribution of measured intelligence are closely consistent with those of earlier enquiries, and provide an adequate explanation of these differences. Virtually the full quota of boys with the requisite minimum IQ from every class was admitted to grammar schools and the distribution of opportunity stands today in closer relationship to that of ability (as measured by intelligence tests) than ever before. Yet the problem of inequality of educational opportunity is not thereby disposed of.

We have considered some of the material and cultural differences in the environment of the children who succeed, as distinct from those who do not succeed, in the selection examination for secondary education, and we have shown how the success of children varies with the distribution of these features of the environment even at the same social level. Since measured intelligence is so closely related to the results of the selection procedure our findings are relevant to the problem of the influence of environment on intelligence test scores. But this was not our direct concern, and the features of the environment we have selected for study cannot, of course, be regarded as social determinants of intelligence. Nevertheless, though they touch on less fundamental problems, certain conclusions do emerge concerning the part played by differences of environment in the social distribution of educational opportunity.

In the past, the problem of social waste in education could be seen in comparatively simple terms, for gross material factors overshadowed all others. Poverty caused ill-health and poor attendance; facilities for study could not be provided in slum homes, nor proper instruction given in over-crowded schools; grammar school places were refused by parents who could not afford to forgo adolescent earnings. But the influence on the distribution of educational opportunity of the material environment in which children live at home and are taught at school before the age of selection, is tending to diminish in importance in face of the general prosperity and the measures of social reform which are characteristic of post-war Britain. Social factors influencing educational selection reveal themselves in more subtle forms today.

The present situation at its most favourable is illustrated by the position in South West Hertfordshire where a generally high minimum degree of material comfort is enjoyed at all social levels. In that area, in 1952, material conditions in their homes did not, at a given social level, distinguish the successful from the unsuccessful candidate in the selection examination. At a given social level, the children who secured grammar school places were not those whose parents earned the highest income, nor those who enjoyed superior standards of housing. On the other hand, differences in the size of the family, and in the education, attitudes and ambitions of parents were reflected in the examination performance of children in all classes. In Middlesbrough the situation was less favourable. In 1953 in that area, purely material conditions at home still differentiated the successful from the unsuccessful children even at the same social level. If poor parents were favourably disposed towards their children's education this attitude was less likely than in South West Hertfordshire to be reflected in the performance of their children in the selection examination. Moreover, the traditional association between poor homes and poor schools persists in Middlesbrough, and places an additional handicap on the child of poor but educationally well-disposed parents. There is still scope for attack on gross economic disabilities. In South West Hertfordshire, however, virtually everyone enjoys an adequate basic income and good housing which, together with the security of the social services, provide something like the basic ingredients of a middle-class or at least lower middle-class existence. The influence of the home on children's educational prospects is more subtle, and the problem of developing and utilizing their ability to the full is educational rather than social.

Once the grosser material handicaps are eliminated, the size of the family emerges as the most important single index of the favourable or unfavourable influence of home environment on educational prospects. Very little is known as to what determines the size of families at different social levels, but there is no doubt about the existence of a relationship between family size and educational opportunity. This relationship obviously has its economic aspect, even in the Welfare State. It is a well-established fact, however, that children from small families, at all social levels, tend on the average to do better in intelligence tests and therefore also in the selection examination for secondary education. Dr Nisbet has suggested that the child of a large family learns verbal skills less effectively from his peers than does the child of a small family from adults, and that he carries the handicap at least until the age of eleven. But the evidence from Middlesbrough suggests that the educational disadvantages of a large family are far less marked for the children of Catholic parents, and if generally true this would cast doubt on the notion that there is some distinctive quality of educational value in the environment of a small family. It may be suggested that family limitation amongst Catholic parents does not correspond so closely to intelligence as it tends to do amongst non-Catholic parents, so that the average level of ability of children from large Catholic families is likely to be higher than of those from large non-Catholic families. In fact, the mean IQ of the children of Catholic unskilled workers, who constituted the largest single social group amongst the Catholic children, was found in 1953 to be slightly higher than that of others at this social level. This finding cannot be interpreted without more information, particularly as to the geographical origins of Catholic parents, and their length of residence in Middlesbrough. Recent immigrants to the area might be temporarily employed in occupations below their capacities, so that their offspring might show greater ability than the average for the unskilled group. However that may be, this problem, and others in the same field of the relations between social class, family environment and educational opportunity, can only be effectively examined through intensive enquiry into children's home environment on case-study lines.

Social Class Differences in Attainment and Ability at Seven

(From Davie, R.; Butler, N.; and Goldstein, H., 1972, *From Birth to Seven*, Longman, pp. 98–105).

The previous passage provided data and comment on social class differences in access to selective secondary education. This one gives information on pupils' attainments in infant schools and departments and relates these to social class (defined here in terms of the occupational group of the children's fathers). The figures come from the National Child Development Study which examined the overall development of about 16,000 children born between 3 March and 9 March 1958. This particular study of the children at the age of 7 was followed up when they were 11 (Wedge and Prosser, 1973) and again at 16 (Fogelman, 1976). Each of the studies revealed a similar picture, suggesting that 'whatever the factors are which social class indirectly measures, they are fairly sharply differentiated as between middle-class and working-class homes, at least as far as their effect on attainment or ability is concerned.' The particular figures reproduced here indicated the extent of class-related differences in attainment after only two years of compulsory education. A similar longitudinal study of a 1946 cohort of children (Douglas, 1964; Douglas, Ross and Simpson, 1968) indicated that the gap between social classes continued to widen during the period of formal schooling, at least as far as scores on reading and arithmetic tests were concerned.

This particular extract has been chosen as an example of the kinds of data which were provided by psychologists, medical personnel and others, and which required sociological study. In the event, the social determinants of educability proved elusive to pin down.

In interpreting the data in the extract, readers need to know the classifications of occupations adopted by the National Child Development Study as an indicator of social class:

Social Class I	Higher professional
II	Other professional and technical
III (non-manual)	Other non-manual occupations
III (manual)	Skilled manual
IV	Semi-skilled manual
V	Unskilled manual

References

DOUGLAS, J. (1964) *The Home and the School*, MacGibbon and Kee.
DOUGLAS, J.; ROSS, J.; and SIMPSON, H. (1968) *All Our Future*, Peter Davies.
FOGELMAN, K. (Ed.) (1976) *Britain's Sixteen-Year-Olds*, National Children's Bureau.
WEDGE, P. and PROSSER, K. (1973) *Born to Fail?*, Arrow Books (in association with National Children's Bureau).

Social Class Differences in Attainment and Ability

There has been a great deal of discussion in recent years about the relationship between social class and school attainments. This has tended to centre upon the issue of social inequality which, it has been alleged, is reinforced by our educational system.

For example, Douglas's (1964) results indicate that during the years of primary schooling the gap in attainment between children from different occupational groups widens. Although this finding has been subjected to criticism on statistical grounds (e.g. Carter, 1964), there seems little doubt

Figure 26.　*Percentage of children with below average oral ability (teachers' ratings)*

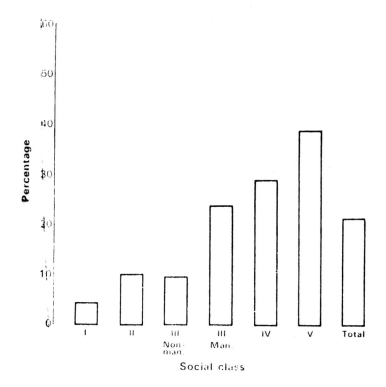

that the phenomenon is a real one. Douglas's later work (Douglas, Ross and Simpson, 1968) suggests that this process is continued in the secondary school.

However, in the discussions and controversies which have followed these and other findings, relatively little thought has been given to the role of the primary school. Attention has tended to centre upon the eleven-plus examination and the selective secondary education which follows. In particular, the laudable attempts to provide equal educational opportunity for all children have perhaps overlooked the very marked inequalities which exist even before children transfer to junior school. This is partly because very few studies have been concerned with attainments in infant schools or departments, and even fewer have related these attainments to social class. . . .

. . . It is not difficult to see why there should be some relationship between a father's occupation and his children's progress at school. . . .

First, heredity is likely to play a part. The relative contributions of heredity and environment to children's abilities and attainments is a difficult question and psychologists, sociologists, geneticists and others will no doubt continue to debate it until we know a great deal more about brain

Figure 27. *Percentage of children with below average 'awareness of the world around' (teachers' ratings)*

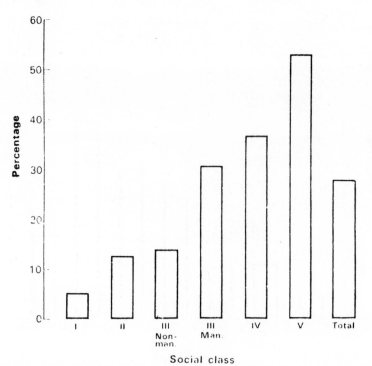

function. However, that heredity plays some part in perhaps setting limits to the rate of intellectual development or to its ultimate peak can hardly be doubted. Since, in general, parents in a competitive society who have risen to occupations demanding a high level of skill will show a higher level of general intelligence than those in less skilled occupations, it would follow that there will be corresponding differences in their children.

Over and above this, environmental influences will shape a child's abilities and influence his capacity or readiness to learn. A great deal — if not the major part — of learning takes place outside of school and much of this is accomplished even before the child enters school. The vocabulary and concepts used by those around him are vital in providing a framework within which his own intellectual growth can take place. If this framework is bare or impoverished, his own development is likely to be slow; a rich framework of words and ideas will provide the food for more rapid growth. More advanced or abstract thought processes are usually clothed in more elaborate and highly structured language (Bernstein, 1961). A home conducive to learning is one where there is a feeling for the spoken and written word as a tool for conveying precise meaning; and where children are stimulated to question the world around them and receive explanations appropriate to their age.

Figure 28.   Percentage of children with 'little' or 'no' 'creativity' (teachers' ratings)

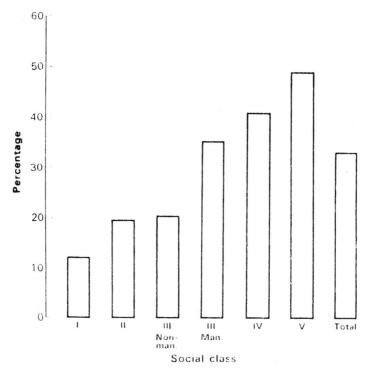

There are two senses in which a child from such a home comes to school ready to learn. He is intellectually ready in that his language and concepts are already well structured, so that the school is building upon established foundations. But he is also psychologically ready to acquire new skills. For example, he has learned that reading provides pleasure and he wants to be a part of the literate community as soon as possible. His whole attitude to school is conditioned by his parents' high regard for education.

This kind of home is certainly not a monopoly of professional or other non-manual workers. However, it is more frequently found amongst occupational groups which possess a high level of education and skill. Thus, in examining social class differences, we are examining the effects both of environment and of heredity upon children's abilities and attainments.

The results in Figs 26 to 31 show the relationship between poor ability and attainment and social class. The groups of children included are by no means at the extremes. For reading and arithmetic, where test results were available, the children whose results appear in the histograms are those whose score placed them in the bottom 30 per cent of the sample.

Figure 29.   Percentage of children with 'poor' copying designs score (0–5)

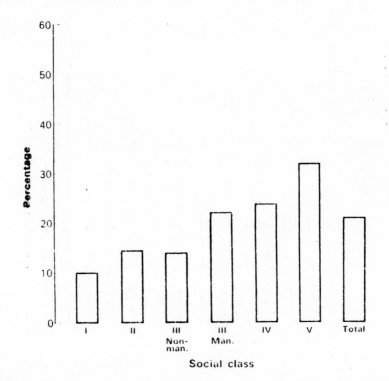

Two important points emerge in these two analyses. First, there is clearly a strong association between social class and reading and arithmetic attainment at seven years of age. The chances of an unskilled manual worker's child (Social Class V) being a poor reader are six times greater than those of a professional worker's child (Social Class I). If the criterion of poor reading is made more stringent, the disparity is much larger. Thus, the chances of a Social Class V child being a *non*-reader are fifteen times greater than those of a Social Class I child.

A second point which emerges is that the gradient from Social Class I through to Social Class V is not regular. There are little or no differences between the results for Social Class II and Social Class III (non-manual) children but very considerable differences between the results of these groups and those for Social Class III (manual) children.

The results for the abilities assessed by teachers' rating and for the copying designs test show the same general pattern with increasing proportions of children with poor ability accompanying lower social class. Again, the gradient of proportions through the social classes is not regular.

It is difficult to draw firm conclusions about the relative differences in the proportions in the social class groups since these are dependent upon

Figure 30. *Percentage of children with 'poor' problem arithmetic test score (0–3)*

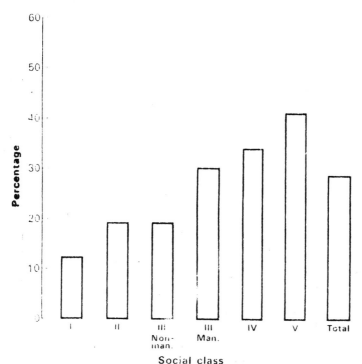

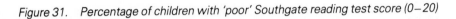

Figure 31.   *Percentage of children with 'poor' Southgate reading test score (0–20)*

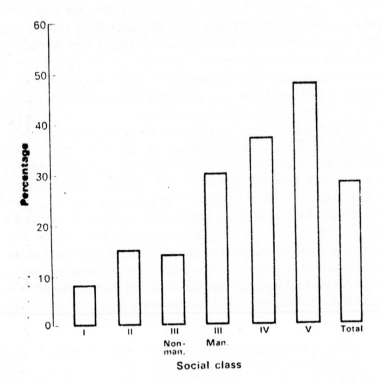

the abilities being assessed, the measures used and the stringency of the criteria adopted. However, there appears to be a substantial division between the children from non-manual, or middle-class, homes on the one hand, and those from manual, or working-class, homes on the other. This suggests that whatever the factors are which social class indirectly measures, they are fairly sharply differentiated as between middle-class and working-class homes, at least as far as their effect on attainment or ability is concerned. The results also suggest that there is a meaningful division within the middle-class group between Social Class I children and the others. In the working-class group, the Social Class V children appear to be at a particular disadvantage in respect of poor ability or attainment in school.

Of course, these speculations do not throw light directly on the reasons for the differences. Some of the results in [a previous chapter] might suggest that environmental factors are relevant. For example, the proportions of parents who discussed their children with the schools followed the same social class pattern as for the children's abilities and attainments. However, hereditary factors cannot be entirely ignored.

Social Class and the Need for Special Educational Treatment

The teachers were asked whether the children were receiving any help within the school because of educational or mental backwardness, 'apart from anything which the teacher may be able to do in the normal way'; and, if No, they were asked whether the children would benefit from such help. Five per cent of the children were receiving help and a further 8 per cent were not but would have benefited. The size of this last figure, as was pointed out in the first report...indicates an urgent need to re-examine the provision of special educational treatment in infant schools.

A further question asked of the teachers was whether the children 'would benefit *now* from attendance at a special school'. Some 2 per cent of children fell into this category. The teachers were not asked to choose between special schooling and special educational treatment within the normal school, so that virtually all of the children who would have benefited from special schooling were also said to be in need of help in the normal school.

The results presented in Fig. 32 show the proportions in the social classes. The proportion of children in Social Class V who, it was reported,

Figure 32. *Percentage of children needing special educational treatment by social class*

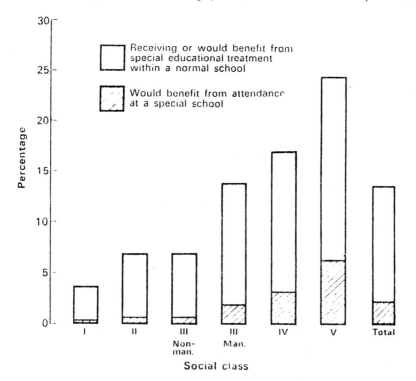

would have benefited from attendance at a special school was forty-five times larger than the corresponding proportion in Social Class I.

References

BERNSTEIN, B. (1961) 'Social structure, language and learning', *Educational Research* 3, pp. 163–76.

CARTER, C. (1964) review of *The Home and the School, Eugenics Review*, 56, 2, pp. 93–6.

DOUGLAS, J. (1964) *The Home and the School*, MacGibbon and Kee.

DOUGLAS, J.; ROSS, J.; and SIMPSON, H. (1968) *All Our Future*, Peter Davies.

Factors Affecting Children's Performance in Primary Schools

(From Central Advisory Council for Education (England), 1967, *Children and Their Primary Schools*, Vol. 1, London, HMSO, pp. 31, 32, 33–4, 35, 36.)

Concern over the 'wastage' of ability, particularly working-class ability, created an alliance between sociologists and policy-makers, as illustrated by this passage from the Plowden Report. The Committee accepted the sociological findings concerning the relationship between social class and educational disadvantage and believed that the publication of their report presented 'an opportunity for reform'. The part of the report dealing with the relationship between home and school was imbued with a 'social democratic' stance towards the reduction and, preferably, elimination of inequality (see p. 62).

As part of the background to its deliberations, the Plowden Committee instigated a national survey to investigate the relationship between home and school and the attainment of children. Data were collected on about 3000 children in 173 schools through interviews with the pupils' mothers, information on their schools from headteachers and HMIs, information on the children from their class teachers and assessments of children's attainments on reading comprehension tests and, for top juniors, on a picture intelligence test.

The passage reproduced below stresses as 'the most striking feature' of the comparisons made in the survey the large part played by parental attitudes in accounting for the variation in children's performance within and between schools. The Committee optimistically claims that since parental attitudes are not monopolized by any one class, the attitudes of large numbers of parents can be altered in the direction of supporting their children's efforts to learn. Some sociologists, however, later criticized the Committee's loose definition of 'parental attitude' and argued that parental attitudes might be more resistant to change than the report suggested, since attitudes could be regarded as dimensions of deep-rooted social class differences (Bernstein, B. and Davies, B., 1969, 'Some sociological comments on Plowden', in Peters, R. (Ed.), *Perspectives on Plowden*, London, Routledge and Kegan Paul, pp. 55–83).

... we are far from realising the potential abilities of our children. To reveal the influence of parental occupation is a criticism of society; but it is also an opportunity for reform. There must always be a great diversity of parental occupations; but they need not continue to have their present severe discriminatory effect on children's educational prospects. The grosser deprivations arising from poverty can be removed. More parents can be brought to understand what education can do for their children, and how they can work with the schools. The educational disadvantage of being born the child of an unskilled worker is both financial and psychological. Neither handicap is as severe as it was. Both are more severe than they need be. Educational equality cannot be achieved by the schools alone: but the schools can make a major contribution towards ensuring (as Sir Edward Boyle wrote in his foreword to the Newsom Report) 'that all children should have an equal opportunity of acquiring intelligence'.

86. The last three reports of the Council drew attention to the numerous exceptions to the rule that they established. They pointed to the homes and the schools which produce good or even brilliant results in spite of adverse circumstances. Our own enquiries have been directed to throwing light on the reasons for these exceptions. If we can pinpoint the factors which make good work possible in apparently unlikely circumstances, we may see what most needs to be done to enlarge the numbers of those who succeed. What is it about the home that matters so much? That was the main question we wished to have explored....

89. The main purpose of the survey was to relate what we could learn about home and school to the attainment of the children. For the summarised table in this chapter [Table 1] the variables used are grouped into three categories.... The first category is broadly called 'Parental Attitudes'. These attitudes were assessed by parents' answers to such questions as the age at which they wanted children to leave school and the secondary school they preferred. The initiative shown by parents in visiting the school, in talking to heads and class teachers and asking for work for children to do at home was also taken into account. Parents were asked about the time they spent with children in the evening and whether they helped children with school work. There was also an assessment of the literacy of the home as judged by what parents and children read, whether they belonged to a library and the number of books in the home. The second category is 'Home Circumstances', including the physical amenities of the home, or lack of them, the occupation and income of the father, the size of family, the length of parents' education and the qualifications they had obtained. The third category is the 'State of the School'. It covers facts about school organisations such as size of school, size of class and the ways children were put into classes. It also includes facts provided by the head about the experience of the staff and their attendance at short courses, and

judgments by H.M.I.s on the quality of the school and the competence of teachers. . . .

91.   The figures given in Table 1 show, for different ages, the percentage of the variation in performance which can be accounted for by the three main categories of variable. For each age group the comparisons made in the table are of two kinds, between pupils *within* schools and *between* schools. The object of this division was to bring out the extent to which a school's situation depends on the neighbourhood it serves. For comparisons between schools the unit of analysis was the school, and the variables were based on the average for each school of the original variables. For comparisons within schools the variables were the deviations of each pupil from the school average. If neighbourhood were unimportant, and the parents, pupils and teachers in each school were merely random samples of the general population, the two kinds of analysis would give the same result. In fact, they do not; the comparisons between schools account for more variation than those within schools. This is because pupils, parents and teachers in the same school and neighbourhood resemble one another more than they resemble pupils, parents and teachers in general, just as

Table 1   *Percentage Contribution of Parental Attitudes, Home Circumstances and State of School to Variation in Educational Performance*

| | Infants | Between Schools | | All Pupils |
		Lower Juniors	Top Juniors	
Parental Attitudes	24	20	39	28
Home Circumstances	16	25	17	20
State of School	20	22	12	17
*Unexplained	40	33	32	35
	100	100	100	100
	Infants	Within Schools		All Pupils
		Lower Juniors	Top Juniors	
Parental Attitudes	16	15	29	20
Home Circumstances	9	9	7	9
State of School	14	15	22	17
*Unexplained	61	61	42	54
	100	100	100	100

* The unexplained variation is due to differences between children which have not been covered by our variables, and also to errors in measurement. That so much variation has been explained — the amount in the between-schools analysis is remarkable for an enquiry of this kind — is due in part to the comparatively simple nature of the criterion variable, a reading comprehension test.

apples growing on the same tree resemble one another more than they resemble apples in general. The apples on a tree in a good situation will do better than those on a tree in a poor situation, unless the latter receives special attention —....

92. The most striking feature of both these sets of comparisons is the large part played by parental attitudes, and the fact that it tends to be greater among the older than the younger children. Not surprisingly, there are changes of emphasis within the attitudes of parents as children grow older. Parents' interest is likely to be greater in the children's early years at school when, as the interviewers found, they were more confident about helping children in their work, because they understood it better. It yields some ground to parental aspiration as the children reach the top of the junior school. By that time the children's very success or failure in school work may increase or weaken parental aspiration.

93. The influence of the home has always been known to be important, and the importance of parental attitudes began to emerge in earlier studies such as those of Fraser (1954), Floud, Halsey and Martin (1956), but now its importance can be better understood. Broadly the same results stand out from other surveys made for us by Professor Wiseman in Manchester on a small group of children (1967), and by those responsible for the National Child Development Study (1967), which deals with a national sample, considerably larger than ours, of children born in one week in 1958....

98. Some explanation may be needed about the relatively low weight which attaches to two of the three variables in Table 1. Some readers may be surprised at what they suppose to be the comparatively small influence of the school. To feel thus is to misunderstand the table. What emerged as important about the schools was the experience and competence of teachers. Most teachers have had a similar education and training, and differ less from one another than parents. The parents have usually had their children in their care for their whole lives, whereas most of the class teachers about whom information was collected had been with the children only for the best part of one school year. It must, therefore, be expected that differences between parents will explain more of the variation in children than differences between schools. It is obvious, too, that parental attitudes may themselves be affected by children's performance at school and by the contacts parents have with schools....

100. [A] point that will occur to readers is whether the differences in circumstances account for the differences in attitudes. Our evidence ... suggests that parents' occupation, material circumstances and education explain only about a quarter of the variation in attitudes, leaving

three-quarters or more not accounted for. This implies that attitudes could be affected in other ways, and altered by persuasion.

101.   Our findings can give hope to the school, to interested parents, and to those responsible for educational policy. Parental attitudes appear as a separate influence because they are not monopolised by any one class. Many manual workers and their wives already encourage and support their children's efforts to learn. If there are many now, there can be even more later. Schools can exercise their influence not only directly upon children but also indirectly through their relationships with parents.

References

FLOUD, J.; HALSEY, A.; and MARTIN, F. (1956) *Social Class and Educational Opportunity*, Heinemann.

FRASER, E. (1954) *Home Environment and the School*, University of London Press.

NATIONAL CHILD DEVELOPMENT STUDY, (1967) 'First Report', in Central Advisory Council for Education (England), *Children and Their Primary Schools*, Vol. 2, Appendix 10, London, HMSO.

WISEMAN, S. (1967) 'The Manchester Survey', in Central Advisory Council for Education (England), *Children and Their Primary Schools*, Vol. 2, Appendix 9, London, HMSO.

Policy Informed by Research: Proposals for the Establishment of Educational Priority Areas

(From Central Advisory Council for Education (England), 1967, *Children and their Primary Schools*, Vol. 1, London, HMSO, pp. 50, 51, 52–3, 57, 65.)

Within education, the relationship between sociological research and proposals for educational policy was never more clearly demonstrated than in the Plowden Committee's recommendations for the establishment of educational priority areas. Drawing on sociological research and the findings of their own national survey (pp. 179–183), the Committee acknowledged the 'central' role played by schools in disadvantaged areas, either in helping maintain a 'vicious circle' of 'cumulative deprivation', or in helping create a 'virtuous circle' of increased parental interest in education and higher standards of performance from children. In the passage below the Committee makes very strong claims for the importance of the primary school in combatting disadvantage: 'What these deprived areas need most are perfectly normal, good primary schools alive with experience from which children of all kinds can benefit.' Arguments are then advanced for 'positive discrimination' for schools in areas of educational priority and for both an increase in, and a redistribution of, resources devoted to education to help achieve this priority.

132.   In a neighbourhood where the jobs people do and the status they hold owe little to their education it is natural for children as they grow older to regard school as a brief prelude to work rather than an avenue to future opportunities. Some of these neighbourhoods have for generations been starved of new schools, new houses and new investment of every kind. Everyone knows this; but for year after year priority has been given to the new towns and new suburbs, because if new schools do not keep pace with the new houses some children will be unable to go to school at all. The continually rising proportion of children staying on at school beyond the minimum age has led some authorities to build secondary schools and postpone the rebuilding of older primary schools. Not surprisingly, many teachers are unwilling to work in a neighbourhood where the schools are old, where housing of the sort they want is unobtainable, and where education does not attain the standards they expect for their own children. From some neighbourhoods, urban and rural, there has been a continuing outflow of the more successful young people. The loss of their enterprise

and skill makes things worse for those left behind. Thus the vicious circle may turn from generation to generation and the schools play a central part in the process, both causing and suffering cumulative deprivation....

What these deprived areas need most are perfectly normal, good primary schools alive with experience from which children of all kinds can benefit. What we say elsewhere about primary school work generally applies equally to these difficult areas. The best schools already there show that it is absurd to say, as one used to hear, 'it may be all very well in a nice suburb, but it won't work here'. But, of course, there are special and additional demands on teachers who work in deprived areas with deprived children. They meet special challenges. Teachers must be constantly aware that ideas, values and relationships within the school may conflict with those of the home, and that the world assumed by teachers and school books may be unreal to the children. There will have to be constant communication between parents and the schools if the aims of the schools are to be fully understood. The child from a really impoverished background may well have had a normal, satisfactory emotional life. What he often lacks is the opportunity to develop intellectual interests. This shows in his poor command of language. It is not, however, with vocabulary that teaching can begin. The primary school must first supply experiences and establish relationships which enable children to discriminate, to reason and to express themselves. Placing such children in the right stance for further learning is a very skilled operation....

138. In our cities there are whole districts which have been scarely touched by the advances made in more fortunate places. Yet such conditions have been overcome and striking progress has been achieved where sufficiently determined and comprehensive attack has been made on the problem. In the most deprived areas, one of H.M. Inspectors reported, 'Some heads approach magnificence, but they cannot do everything... The demands on them as welfare agents are never ending'. Many children with parents in the least skilled jobs do outstandingly well in school. The educational aspirations of parents and the support and encouragement given to children in some of the poorest neighbourhoods are impressive. Over half of the unskilled workers in our National Survey want their children to stay at school beyond the minimum leaving age. One third of them hoped their children would go to a grammar school or one with similar opportunities. (The educational aspirations of unskilled workers for their children have risen year by year. It has been stressed to us that the range of ability in all social classes is so wide that there is a great reservoir of unrealised potential in families dependent on the least skilled and lowest paid work. A larger part of the housing programme than ever before is to be devoted to rebuilding and renewing obsolete and decaying neighbour-

hoods. The opportunity must be seized to rebuild the schools as well as the houses, and to see that both schools and houses serve families from every social class. It will be possible to make some progress in reducing the size of classes in primary schools in these areas as well as elsewhere. Colleges of education which have taken a special interest in deprived areas report that their students respond in an encouraging fashion to the challenge of working in these neighbourhoods. Most important of all, there is a growing awareness in the nation at large, greatly stimulated, we believe, by our predecessors' Reports, of the complex social handicaps afflicting such areas and the need for a more radical assault on their problems. These are the strengths on which we can build. How can they be brought to bear?

139.   We propose a nation-wide scheme for helping those schools and neighbourhoods in which children are most severely handicapped. . . .

The principle, already accepted, that special need calls for special help, should be given a new cutting edge. We ask for 'positive discrimination' in favour of such schools and the children in them, going well beyond an attempt to equalise resources. Schools in deprived areas should be given priority in many respects. The first step must be to raise the schools with low standards to the national average; the second, quite deliberately to make them better. The justification is that the homes and neighbourhoods from which many of their children come provide little support and stimulus for learning. The schools must supply a compensating environment. The attempts so far made within the educational system to do this have not been sufficiently generous or sustained, because the handicaps imposed by the environment have not been explicitly and sufficiently allowed for. They should be. . . .

173.   Positive discrimination accords with experience and thinking in many other countries, and in other spheres of social policy. It calls both for some redistribution of the resources devoted to education and, just as much, for an increase in their total volume. It must not be interpreted simply as a gloss upon the recommendations which follow. . . . This would not only be a misunderstanding of the scheme; it would destroy all hope of its success. For it would be unreasonable and self-defeating — economically, professionally and politically — to try to do justice by the most deprived children by using only resources that can be diverted from more fortunate areas. We have argued that the gap between the educational opportunities of the most and least fortunate children should be closed, for economic and social reasons alike. It cannot be done, unless extra effort, extra skill and extra resources are devoted to the task.

Policies and Practices in Pursuit of Equality

(From Halsey, A. (Ed), 1972, *Educational Priority, Vol. 1: E.P.A. Problems and Policies*, London, HMSO, pp. 3, 6, 7–8, 8, 9, 11–12, 12, 180, 198.)

Some sociologists have not only been concerned to investigate the relationship between social class and the educational system, but have gone further and participated in the formulation of and, less often, the enactment of policies directed towards reducing inequalities. For example, in the late 1960s A.H. Halsey who had made a major contribution to demonstrating the relationship between social class and educational opportunity (see pp. 166–169) became national director of an action-research programme set up in response to the Plowden Committee's call for 'research to discover which of the developments in the educational priority areas have the most constructive effects, so as to assist in planning the longer term programme to follow.' Action-research projects were carried out in five urban areas between 1968 and 1971, and their findings published in a series of books. The material reproduced below is taken from the introductory volume to the series, which analyzes 'the E.P.A. problem' and reflects on the work undertaken in relation to pre-schooling, the community school curriculum, and links between the community school, the family and the community. The first passage is a hard-hitting review of past policies and principles used 'to find a strategy for educational roads to equality'. It asserts firmly that 'egalitarian policies have failed' and it outlines how the debate about education and equality has shifted ground over the years. It clearly demonstrates the complex interconnections between political ends and educational means. The second passage outlines the major conclusions of the action-research programme and is curiously optimistic compared with the pessimistic policy analysis presented earlier. In the event, its optimism proved largely misplaced and its initial analysis largely justified. The 'framework of organisation for pre-schooling and community schooling' which it advocated did not materialize on a national scale.

Political Ends and Educational Means

To find a strategy for educational roads to equality! That has been a central theme of educational discussion from the beginning of the twentieth century. It has produced a prolific sociology of education over the last generation in which the centrality of educational systems to the structure and the functioning of industrial societies has become a commonplace. In the nineteen fifties education in these societies was seen as having a crucial role for economic growth and change. More recently the emphasis has shifted to the part played by formal educational organisations in defining what is and what is not knowledge, and as selective agencies allocating individuals to social positions, moulding their social personalities and their definitions of the world around them. But the underlying question is whether, and if so under what circumstances, education can change society ... the essential fact of twentieth century educational history is that egalitarian policies have failed. This must be the starting point for understanding the significance of our studies and to reach it we must review past principles and policies. There appears to us to have been a developing theoretical and practical debate in three stages about the way education can be used as a means towards the political and social end of equality.

In the first phase, from the beginning of the century to the end of the nineteen fifties, the definition of policy was liberal — equality of opportunity. It meant equality of access to the more advanced stages of education for all children irrespective of their sex or social origin in classes, religious and ethnic groups or regions. It therefore expressed itself in such measures as building the scholarship ladder, abolishing grammar school fees, doing away with a system of separate secondary education for the minority and elementary education for the majority and substituting a system of common schooling with secondary schools "end-on" to primary schools. In the later years of this phase it also meant expansion of higher education....

The essential judgement must be that the 'liberal' policies failed even in their own terms. For example, when, in a large number of the richer countries during the nineteen fifties, a considerable expansion of educational facilities was envisaged, it was more or less assumed that, by making more facilities available, there would be a marked change in the social composition of student bodies and in the flow of people from the less favoured classes into the secondary schools and higher educational institutions. This has certainly not happened to the degree expected. While expansion of education was accompanied by some increase in both the absolute numbers and the proportions from poor families who reached the higher levels and the more prestigious types of education, nevertheless progress towards greater equality of educational opportunity as traditionally defined has been disappointing. It is now plain that the problem is more difficult than had been supposed and needs, in fact, to be posed in new terms (Frankel and Halsey, 1971).

Too much has been claimed for the power of educational systems as instruments for the wholesale reform of societies which are characteristically hierarchical in their distribution of chances in life as between races, classes, the sexes and as between metropolitan/suburban and provincial/

rural populations. The typical history of educational expansion in the nineteen fifties and nineteen sixties can be represented by a graph of inequality of attainment between the above-mentioned social categories which has shifted markedly upwards without changing its slope. In other words relative chances did not alter materially despite expansion.... There has been a tendency to treat education as the waste paper basket of social policy — a repository for dealing with social problems where solutions are uncertain or where there is disinclination to wrestle with them seriously. Such problems are prone to be dubbed 'educational' and turned over to the schools to solve. But it was now increasingly plain that the schools cannot accomplish important social reforms such as the democratisation of opportunity unless social reforms accompany the educational effort. And it also became more evident that the schools are hampered in achieving even their more traditional and strictly 'educational' purposes when, in societies changing rapidly in their technologies and in the aspirations of their populations, a comparable effort to make the required change in social structures and political organisation is lacking.

In summary, it may be said that liberal policies failed basically on an inadequate theory of learning. They failed to notice that the major determinants of educational attainment were not schoolmasters but social situations, not curriculum but motivation, not formal access to the school but support in the family and the community.

So the second phase began with its new emphasis on a theory of non-educational determination of education. In consequence of the experience of the first phase in trying to bring about greater equality of educational opportunity, there had to be a change in the meaning assigned to the phase. Its earlier meaning was equality of access to education: in the second phase its meaning gradually became equality of achievement. In this new interpretation a society affords equality of educational opportunity if the proportion of people from different social, economic or ethnic categories at all levels and in all types of education are more or less the same as the proportion of these people in the population at large. In other words the goal should not be the liberal one of equality of access but equality of outcome for the median member of each identifiable non-educationally defined group, i.e. the *average* woman or negro or proletarian or rural dweller should have the same level of educational attainment as the average male, white, white-collar, suburbanite. If not there has been injustice....

The Plowden Report belongs to this phase in the development of our understanding of the egalitarian issues in education and relates them to the social setting of the school.... In reading the Plowden Report, one could hardly escape the view that equality of opportunity was without equality of conditions, a sham. Home circumstances were obviously critical and these in turn were adversely affected by class and neighbourhood patterns. The school, where, after all, the children spent only five hours of the day, seemed comparatively powerless to alter matters radically of its own volition. Assuredly, a decision to consider the E.P.A. school in its communal setting was a wise one, and the Plowden Committee had been well advised to recommend that community schools should be developed in all areas but especially in E.P.A.s.

Our own definition of the problem in 1968 was consonant with the debate up to this point and was in accord with the Plowden approach accepting that positive discrimination held out the hope of further steps towards the new definition of equality of opportunity.

But in the early months of our work we began to realise that there were unsolved issues behind the equality debate even in its advanced formulation and especially when applied to the children of the educational priority areas. The debate could be taken beyond equality of educational opportunity to a third phase which involves reappraisal of the functions of education in contemporary society. Education for what? The debate over equality as we have summarised it — a movement from preoccupation with equality of access towards concern with equality of outcomes as between social groups — is essentially a discussion about education for whom and to do what. In planning our intervention in schools we were forced sooner or later to consider both questions and in doing so to question whether an E.P.A. programme is anything more than a new formula for fair competition in the educational selection race.

What assumptions could or should be made about the world into which our E.P.A. children would enter after school? Were we concerned simply to introduce a greater measure of justice into an educational system which traditionally selected the minority for higher education and upward social mobility out of the E.P.A. district, leaving the majority to be taught, mainly by a huge hidden curriculum, a sense of their own relative incompetence and impotence — a modern, humane and even relatively enjoyed form of gentling the masses? Or could we assume a wide programme of social reform which would democratise local power structures and diversify local occupational opportunities so that society would look to its schools for a supply of young people educated for political and social responsibility and linked to their communities not by failure in the competition but by rich opportunities for work and life? Even short of the assumption of extra-educational reform how far should we concentrate on making recognition easier for the able minority and how far on the majority who are destined to live their lives in the E.P.A.? And if the latter did this not mean posing an alternative curriculum realistically related to the E.P.A. environment and designed to equip the rising generation with the knowledge and skills to cope with, give power over and in the end to transform the conditions of their local community?

It was, and is, commonly felt that a discriminatory boost was needed in the backward areas to bring education up to scratch.... The Plowden Report argued this respectable and widely held thesis with admirable spirit. It detailed a programme of 'positive discrimination' and 'a new distribution of educational resources', through priority building and minor works, improved staffing and auxiliary help, supplemented salaries and so on. This was designed to cater for 'a great reservoir of unrealised potential', for 'what these deprived areas need most are perfectly normal good primary schools'. Twice over Plowden decreed that the E.P.A. schools should be as good as the best in the land.

Because the national system of education was seen not to operate efficiently in its uniform application across the country, it was accepted that a differential application would help close, to quote Plowden again, 'the gap between the educational opportunities of the most and least fortunate children ... for economic and social reasons alike.' But, logically, an alternative existed. It was worth considering that what was wrong was a uniform system, and that differing areas required different educational formats.

This viewpoint, Eric Midwinter insisted in our early conferences, does no disservice to the pioneers who campaigned for parity of opportunity. They doubtless imagined that equality of opportunity would beget conditions in which forthcoming generations would automatically start at par. This has not, unhappily, transpired. Those working in a deprived area are typically sympathetic to the egalitarian tradition and find the alarums and the postures of the anti-egalitarian commentators laughable. They shout before they are hurt. One might recall the words of R.H. Tawney (1921): of the nation's children, he wrote '... if, instead of rejuvenating the world, they grind corn for the Philistines and doff bobbins for the mill-owners, the responsibility is ours into whose hands the prodigality of nature pours life itself'. Eventually an E.P.A. community must stand on its own feet like any other and rejuvenate its world, and that is a dogma which might hold good on both political wings...

Conclusions

Our major conclusions from the four English E.P.A. action-research projects are that:

(1) The educational priority area, despite its difficulties of definition, is a socially and administratively viable unit through which to apply the principle of positive discrimination.

(2) Pre-schooling is the outstandingly economical and effective de-

vice in the general approach to raising educational standards in E.P.A.s.

(3) The idea of the community school, as put forward in skeletal outline by Plowden, has now been shown to have greater substance and powerful implications for community regeneration.

(4) There are practical ways of improving the partnership between families and schools in E.P.A.s.

(5) There are practical ways of improving the quality of teaching in E.P.A. schools.

(6) Action-research is an effective method of policy formation and practical innovation.

(7) The E.P.A. can be no more than a part, though an important one, of a comprehensive social movement towards community development and community redevelopment in a modern urban industrial society. . . .

We must finally return to the fundamental question raised [at the beginning of this extract] — the limits of an educational approach to poverty. These limits cannot be removed by any kind of E.P.A. policy. But within them we think we can see a viable road to a higher standard of educational living for hundreds of thousands of children in the more disadvantaged districts.

We have outlined a wide range of policies around the development of pre-schooling and the community school, and we have called for a co-ordinated advance of statutory and voluntary effort. The action-research project method, adroitly constituted to work with 'the system' but with a small but essential element of independence from the normal administrative procedures, has proved itself to be an effective agent of educational change and a magnet for voluntary effort from a wide range of public and private organisations. Such projects, perhaps linked in some cases to the current Community Development Projects, could carry forward the development of E.P.A. policy as we have done in three years from its inception in the Plowden Report. At the same time we would hope that there is sufficient confidence in our results from the first projects for the Government and the local education authorities to create the framework of organisation for pre-schooling and community schooling that we have advocated. If so there will be a new landmark in British educational progress.

References

FRANKEL, C. and HALSEY, A. (1971) 'Introduction', *Educational Policies for the 1970s*, Paris, OECD.
TAWNEY, R. (1921) *The Acquisitive Society*, Bell.

Language and Educability

(From Bernstein, B., 1971, *Class, Codes and Control, Vol. I: Theoretical Studies towards a Sociology of Language*, London, Routledge and Kegan Paul, pp. 194–5, 196–7, 199–200.)

The theoretical work of Bernstein 'is not only complicated and subtle but extremely general and comprehensive' (Banks, O., 1976, *The Sociology of Education*, 3rd ed., Batsford, p. 110). In his work on a sociology of language, he has been concerned with the interrelationships among culture, social organization, orientation towards certain uses of language, and social class differences in school achievement. He has argued that there is a relationship between social class, forms of family control and communication, and the linguistic codes used by parents and children. Elaborated codes, characteristic of many middle-class homes, involve speakers in elaborating their meanings and making them both explicit and specific; such codes give children access to universalistic orders of meaning conveyed by teachers in schools. Restricted codes, found particularly but not only in lower working-class homes, are characterized by implicit meaning, simplification and rigidity; such codes give children access to particularistic orders of meaning, which are discontinuous with the universalistic meanings transmitted and developed by teachers in schools. Such linguistic discontinuity forms a crucially important part of the total cultural discontinuity between the culture of the school and that of the working-class child. Though difficult to follow and requiring background reading to fill out and explain many of its points, the extract below summarizes Bernstein's sophisticated explanation of how social class differences in language use are related to social class differences in school achievement. (For a critique see pp. 197–199.)

We can distinguish between uses of language which can be called 'context bound' and uses of language which are less context bound. Consider, for example, the two following stories which Peter Hawkins,... constructed as a result of his analysis of the speech of middle-class and working-class five-year-old children. The children were given a series of four pictures which told a story and they were invited to tell the story. The first picture showed some boys playing football; in the second the ball goes through the window of a house; the third shows a woman looking out of the window and a man making an ominous gesture, and in the fourth the children are moving away.

Here are the two stories:

(1) Three boys are playing football and one boy kicks the ball and it goes through the window the ball breaks the window and the boys are looking at it and a man comes out and shouts at them because they've broken the window so they run away and then that lady looks out of her window and she tells the boys off.

(2) They're playing football and he kicks it and it goes through there it breaks the window and they're looking at it and he comes out and shouts at them because they've broken it so they run away and then she looks out and she tells them off.

With the first story the reader does not have to have the four pictures which were used as the basis for the story, whereas in the case of the second story the reader would require the initial pictures in order to make sense of the story. The first story is free of the context which generated it, whereas the second story is much more closely tied to its context. As a result the meanings of the second story are implicit, whereas the meanings of the first story are explicit. It is not that the working-class children do not have in their passive vocabulary the vocabulary used by the middle-class children. Nor is it the case that the children differ in their tacit understanding of the linguistic rule system. Rather, what we have here are differences in the use of language arising out of a specific context. One child makes explicit the meanings which he is realizing through language for the person he is telling the story to, whereas the second could does not to the same extent. The first child takes very little for granted, whereas the second child takes a great deal for granted. Thus for the first child the task was seen as a context in which his meanings were required to be made explicit, whereas the task for the second child was not seen as a task which required such explication of meaning. It would not be difficult to imagine a context where the first child would produce speech rather like the second. What we are dealing with here are differences between the children in the way they realize in language-use apparently the same context. We could say that the speech of the first child generated universalistic meanings in the sense that the meanings are freed from the context and so understandable by all, whereas the speech of the second child generated particularistic meanings, in the sense that the meanings are closely tied to the context and would be fully understood by others only if they had access to the context which originally generated the speech. Thus universalistic meanings are less bound to a given context, whereas particularistic meanings are severely context bound. . . .

We can . . . say that certain groups of children, through the forms of their socialization, are oriented towards receiving and offering universalistic meanings in *certain contexts*, whereas other groups of children are oriented towards particularistic meanings. The linguistic realization of universalistic orders of meaning are very different from the linguistic realization of particularistic orders of meaning, and so are the forms of the social relation (e.g. between mother and child) which generate these. We can say then that what is made available for learning, how it is made available and the patterns of social relation are also very different.

Now when we consider the children in school we can see that there is likely to be difficulty. For the school is necessarily concerned with the transmission and development of universalistic orders of meaning. The school is concerned with the making explicit and elaborating through language, principles and operations, as these apply to objects (science subjects) and persons (arts subjects). One child, through his socialization, is already sensitive to the symbolic orders of the school, whereas the second child is much less sensitive to the universalistic orders of the school. The second child is oriented towards particularistic orders of meaning which are context bound, in which principles and operations are implicit, and towards a form of language-use through which such meanings are realized. The school is necessarily trying to develop in the child orders of relevance and relation as these apply to persons and objects, which are not initially the ones he spontaneously moves towards. The problem of educability at one level, whether it is in Europe, the USA or newly developing societies, can be understood in terms of a confrontation between the universalistic orders of meaning and the social relationships which generate them, of the school, and the particularistic orders of meanings and the social relationships which generate them, which the child brings with him to the school. . . .

I have stressed that the school is attempting to transmit uncommon-sense knowledge, that is, public knowledge realized through various meta-languages. Such knowledge I have called universalistic. However, it is also the case that the school is both implicitly and explicitly transmitting values and their attendant morality which affect educational contents and contexts of education. They do this by establishing criteria for acceptable pupil and staff conduct. Further, these values and morals affect the *content* of educational knowledge through the selection of books, texts, films *and* through examples and analogies used to assist access to public knowledge (universalistic meanings). Thus the working-class child may be placed at a considerable disadvantage in relation to the *total* culture of the school. It is not made for him; he may not answer to it.

Now I have suggested that the forms of an elaborated code give access to universalistic orders of meaning in the sense that the principles and operations controlling object and person relationships are made explicit through the use of language, whereas restricted codes give access to particularistic orders of meaning in which the principles and operations controlling object and person relationships are rendered implicit through the use of language.... Because the sub-culture or culture through its forms of social integration generates a restricted code, it does not mean that the resultant speech and meaning system is linguistically or culturally deprived, that the children have nothing to offer the school, that their imaginings are not significant. Nor does it mean that we have to teach the children formal grammar. Nor does it mean that we have to interfere with their dialect. There is nothing, but nothing, in the dialect as such, which prevents a child from internalizing and learning to use universalistic meanings. But if the contexts of learning, the examples, the reading books, are not contexts which are triggers for the children's imaginings, are not triggers on the children's curiosity and explorations in his family and community, then the child is not at home in the educational world. If the teacher has to say continuously, 'Say it again darling, I didn't understand you', then in the end the child may say nothing. *If the culture of the teacher is to become part of the consciousness of the child, then the culture of the child must first be in the consciousness of the teacher.* This may mean that the teacher must be able to understand the child's dialect, rather than deliberately attempt to change it. Much of the contexts of our schools are unwittingly drawn from aspects of the symbolic world of the middle class, and so when the child steps into school he is stepping into a symbolic system which does not provide for him a linkage with his life outside.

It is an accepted educational principle that we should work with what the child can offer: why don't we practise it? The introduction of the child to the universalistic meanings of public forms of thought is not compensatory education — *it is education*. It is in itself not making children middle class. The implicit values underlying the form and contents of the educational environment might. We need to distinguish between the principles and operations, that is our task as teachers to transmit and develop in the children, *and* the contexts we create in order to do this. We should start knowing that the social experience the child already possesses is valid and significant, and that this social experience should be reflected back to him as being valid and significant. It can be reflected back to him only if it is a part of the texture of the learning experience we create. If we spent as much time thinking through the implications of this as we do thinking about the implications of the Piagetian developmental sequences, then possibly schools might become exciting and challenging environments for parents, children and teachers.

Continuity or Discontinuity between Home and School Experience of Language: A Critique of Bernstein's Views

(From Edwards, A., 1976, *Language in Culture and Class*, Heinemann, pp. 145–7.)

The previous extract and its editorial introduction could not do justice to the subtlety and complexity of Bernstein's contribution to a sociology of language. Likewise, this passage is simply illustrative of the critiques of Bernstein's work undertaken by linguists, socio-linguists and sociologists of education. Much of the criticism has centred on the ambiguous concept of 'code' and on the interpretation of 'restricted code' as referring to an inferior form of speech. For examples of criticisms the reader is referred to Coulthard (1969), Jackson (1974), Grimshaw (1973) and Rosen (1972). The passage below, taken from an extended scrutiny of Bernstein's work, has been chosen to complement the previous extract where Bernstein suggested a cultural and linguistic discontinuity experienced by lower working-class children in schools. Edwards argues that 'the school end of this discontinuity of experience is described with infuriating vagueness.' He maintains that in the absence of extensive research into the forms and functions of classroom language, it could equally well be argued that in some schools (described as 'highly ritualized' and 'hierarchical'), there might be 'too much continuity between home and school experience of language'. At the very least, Edwards throws doubt on the adequacy of Bernstein's account of how social class differences in language use are related to social class differences in school achievement.

References

COULTHARD, M. (1969) 'A discussion of restricted and elaborated codes', *Educational Review*, 22, 1, pp. 38–50.

GRIMSHAW, A. (1973) 'On language in society, Part I', *Contemporary Sociology*, 2.

JACKSON, L. (1974) 'The myth of elaborated and restricted codes', *Higher Educational Review*, 6, pp. 65–81.

ROSEN, H. (1972) *Language and Class: A Critical Look at the Theories of Basil Bernstein*, Falling Wall Press.

Bernstein's argument is *not* reducible to a matter of stylistic elaboration because of its emphasis on the functions of language, and the kinds of meaning being transmitted. The 'discontinuity' which he identifies is not 'linguistic', but what he calls 'cultural' and might have called 'sociolinguistic'. The lower working-class pupil is described as having had less experience of elaborated speech variants in two areas of experience obviously relevant to school, those of control and instruction. He has learned to look to adults as the source of directives, but not for the reasons for their orders, or the principles by which he should control his own behaviour. He faces problems in school because he is not used to feeling a personal responsibility for his actions, or to lengthy probing of his motives, or to subtly-phrased and indirect commands. He has special difficulties in learning because his curiosity has been less often rewarded, his questions have less often been answered in ways directly relevant to them, his awkward questions have been more often evaded, and his attention has been drawn less often to the general principles underlying concrete examples. Above all, he has had less experience of being offered alternatives to explore, and problems to solve for which the solutions are diverse or uncertain. He will be ill at ease with the universalistic orders of meaning which are emphasized in schools.

There are two main directions from which this summary can be questioned. Are the lower working-class children like this? And are schools like this? The school end of this discontinuity of experience is described with infuriating vagueness. Justifiably enough, the main efforts of the SRU [the Sociologial Research Unit] went into the intensive investigation of family roles and relationships. The orientation of the lower working-class child was towards 'closed' roles and particularistic meanings. Schools, however, 'are predicated upon an elaborated code and its system of social relationships' (1973. p. 212; also 1970, p. 117). Does this mean *all* schools, at all age levels, in all degrees of selectivity, in all varieties of expressive or instrumental orientation? There is an interesting contrast between the 'global' assumptions about schools in Bernstein's writing on language, and the carefully differentiated analysis to be found in his writing on organization and curriculum (Bernstein 1967; 1971). If disbelief is suspended, the idealization takes the following shape. In formal education, principles and operations are made verbally explicit. They are freed from their immediate context, and from the implicit background knowledge made available by a shared cultural identity. Such universalistic meanings can be self-consciously examined, the grounds for them scrutinized. Though at some risk of insecurity and even alienation, alternative realities can be contemplated. Meanings are therefore provisional, open to change. They can arise only from relationships that are themselves open to change — which are personal and achieved, not positional and ascribed. Entering such an environment, the lower working-class child steps into a symbolic system which provides few links with his life outside (Bernstein 1970, p. 120). Yet all this would not be true of the highly ritualized, hierarchical school; or the 'closed' school: or the school where what counted as knowledge was strongly 'classified' and 'framed'. Selecting some 'traditional' characteristics of schools (such as are described in Bernstein's own writing), it could be argued that meanings are too often 'given' as part of a natural order which cannot be questioned; that children are too rarely encouraged actively to enquire, experiment, and 'create their own world on their own terms in their own way'; that the boundary between teacher and learner is too clear, the latter having too little discretion; and that the individual child is so submerged in the pupil role that meanings relate not to him but to the category in which he is fitted. The counter-argument is as tendentious and over-generalized as the original target. But when Bernstein describes, in relation to the critical contexts of socialization, the underlying system of communication which is regulated through a restricted code, it is tempting to see some schools as fitting that picture without undue distortion. In so far as they do, their lower working-class pupils should, in Bernstein's own terms, feel perfectly at home. An underlying restricted code is found where communication is 'realised through forms of speech where meanings are implicit, principles infrequently elaborated, qualified or explored, infrequently related to the specific experience of the child or the specific requirements of the local context, where alternative possibilities are infrequently offered, where questioning is less encouraged' (in Gahagan and Gahagan 1970, p. 116). If *some* schools resemble this description, then extending their working-class pupils' range of control over language (crudely, 'teaching them' an elaborated code) will require new roles, functions and communicative tasks more demanding than the traditional classroom routines. Otherwise there will be too *much* continuity between home and school experience of language. That suggestion must be tentative because we know so little about the forms and functions of classroom language, and about how the sociolinguistic rules relevant to them are learned and applied.

References

BERNSTEIN, B. (1967) 'Open schools, open society', *New Society*, 14 pp. 351–3.

BERNSTEIN, B. (1970) 'A critique of compensatory education', in RUBINSTEIN, D. and STONEMAN, C. (Eds), *Education for Democracy*, Harmondsworth, Penguin.

BERNSTEIN, B. (1971) 'On the classification and framing of educational knowledge', in YOUNG, M. (Ed.), *Knowledge and Control: New Directions in the Sociology of Education*, Collier-Macmillan.

BERNSTEIN, B. (1973) *Class, Codes and Control; Vol. 1: Theoretical Studies towards A Sociology of Language*, Paladin Books.

GAHAGAN, D. and GAHAGAN, G. (1970) *Talk Reform: Explorations in Language for Infant School Children*, London, Routledge and Kegan Paul.

The Sociological Study of Educational Knowledge

(From Bernstein, B., 1975, *Class, Codes and Control. Vol. 3: Towards a Theory of Educational Transmissions*, 2nd ed., London, Routledge and Kegan Paul, pp. 85, 86–7, 87–9, 90–1, 91, 93–4.)

As indicated in the general introduction to this section of the source book, one of the 'new directions' taken by the sociology of education during the last decade or so has been the study of educational knowledge, including teachers' professional knowledge (see pp. 220–224) and knowledge enshrined in curricula. Bernstein has made a major contribution to this study, as he has done to the sociology of language. In his (1981) *Perspectives on the Sociology of Education* (Routledge and Kegan Paul), Robinson argues that Bernstein's 'work on the organisation of knowledge is an extension of [his] earlier work and has been running parallel to the language theories since 1964. The essential problem that he addresses is common to both aspects of his work, namely the reproduction of the conditions through which social control is managed, how consciousness is structured by the pattern of class relationships in which the individual is located.' The passage below is taken from an influential paper in which Bernstein makes a number of important conceptual distinctions to aid in the study of curricula as socially organized knowledge. In the paper he distinguishes between curriculum, pedagogy and evaluation, and then (in this extract) goes on to use his concepts of 'classification' and 'framing' to generate a typology of educational knowledge codes which can be used to conceptualize the curricula of primary or secondary schools. In a later part of the paper (not reproduced here) he speculates on the consequences of the use of these knowledge codes for the exercise of social control and the shaping of children's consciousness in schools.

Introduction

How a society selects, classifies, distributes, transmits and evaluates the educational knowledge it considers to be public, reflects both the distribution of power and the principles of social control. From this point of view, differences within, and change in, the organization, transmission and evaluation of educational knowledge should be a major area of sociological interest (Bernstein, B., 1966, 1967; Davies, D.I., 1970a, 1970b; Musgrove, 1968; Hoyle, 1969; Young, M., 1971). Indeed, such a study is a part of the larger question of the structure and changes in the structure of cultural transmission. For various reasons, British sociologists have fought shy of this question. As a result, the sociology of education has been reduced to a series of input-output problems; the school has been transformed into a complex organization or people-processing institution; the study of socialization has been trivialized. . . .

Two Types of Curricula

Initially, I am going to talk about the curriculum in a very general way. In all educational institutions there is a formal punctuation of time into periods. These may vary from ten minutes to three hours or more. I am going to call each such formal period of time a 'unit'. I shall use the word 'content' to describe how the period of time is used. I shall define a curriculum initially in terms of the principle by which units of time and their contents are brought into a special relationship with each other. I now want to look more closely at the phrase 'special relationship'.

First, we can examine relationships between contents in terms of the amount of time accorded to a given content. Immediately, we can see that more time is devoted to some contents rather than others. Second, some of the contents may, from the point of view of the pupils, be compulsory or optional. We now take a very crude measure of the relative status of a content in terms of the number of units given over to it, and whether it is compulsory or optional. This raises immediately the question of the relative status of a given content and its significance in a given educational career.

We can, however, consider the relationship between contents from another, perhaps more important, perspective. We can ask about any given content whether the boundary between it and another content is clear-cut or blurred. To what extent are the various contents well insulated from each other. If the various contents are well insulated from each other, I shall say that the contents stand in a *closed* relation to each other. If there is reduced insulation between contents, I shall say that the contents stand in an *open* relationship to each other. So far, then, I am suggesting that we can go into any educational institution and examine the organization of time in terms of the relative status of contents, and whether the contents stand in an open/closed relationship to each other. . . . I shall now distinguish between two broad types of curricula. If contents stand in a closed relation to each other, that is if the contents are clearly bounded and insulated from each other, I shall call such a curriculum a *collection* type. Here, the learner has to collect a group of favoured contents in order to satisfy some criteria of evaluation. There may of course be some underlying concept to a collection: the gentleman, the educated man, the skilled man, the non-vocational man.

Now I want to juxtapose against the collection type, a curriculum where the various contents do not go their own separate ways, but where the contents stand in an open relation to each other. I shall call such a curriculum an integrated type. Now we can have various types of collection, and various degrees and types of integration.

Classification and Frame

I shall now introduce the concepts, classification and frame, which will be used to analyse the underlying structure of the three message systems, curriculum, pedagogy and evaluation, which are realizations of the educational knowledge code. The basic idea is embodied in the principle used to distinguish the two types of curricula: collection and integrated. Strong insulation between contents pointed to a collection type, whereas reduced insulation pointed to an integrated type. The principle here is the strength of the *boundary* between contents. This notion of boundary strength underlies the concepts of classification and frame.

Classification, here, does not refer to *what* is classified, but to the *relationships* between contents. Classification refers to the nature of the differentiation between contents. Where classification is strong, contents are well insulated from each other by strong boundaries. Where classification is weak, there is reduced insulation between contents, for the boundaries between contents are weak or blurred. *Classification thus refers to the degree of boundary maintenance between contents*. Classification focuses our attention upon boundary strength as the critical distinguishing feature of the division of labour of educational knowledge. It gives us, as I hope to show, the basic structure of the message system, curriculum.

The concept, frame, is used to determine the structure of the message system, pedagogy. Frame refers to the form of the *context* in which knowledge is transmitted and received. Frame refers to the specific pedagogical relationship of teacher and taught. In the same way as classification does not refer to contents, so frame does not refer to the contents of the pedagogy. Frame refers to the strength of the boundary between what may be transmitted and what may not be transmitted, in the pedagogical relationship. Where framing is strong, there is a sharp boundary, where framing is weak, a blurred boundary, between what may and may not be transmitted. Frame refers us to the range of options available to teacher and taught in the *control* of what is transmitted and received in the context of the pedagogical relationship. Strong framing entails reduced options; weak framing entails a range of options. *Thus frame refers to the degree of control teacher and pupil possess over the selection, organization, pacing and timing of the knowledge transmitted and received in the pedagogical relationship.*

There is another aspect of the boundary relationship between what may be taught and what may not be taught and, consequently, another aspect to framing. We can consider the relationship between the non-school everyday community knowledge of the teacher or taught, *and* the educational knowledge transmitted in the pedagogical relationship. We can raise the question of the strength of the boundary, the degree of insulation, between the everyday community knowledge of teacher and taught and educational knowledge. Thus, we can consider variations in the strength of frames as these refer to the strength of the boundary between educational knowledge and everyday community knowledge of teacher and taught. . . .

A Typology of Educational Knowledge Codes

In the light of the conceptual framework we have developed, I shall use the distinction between collection and integrated curricula in order to realize a typology of types and sub-types of educational codes. The *formal* basis of the typology is the strength of classification and frames. However, the sub-types will be distinguished, initially, in terms of substantive differences.

Any organization of educational knowledge which involves strong classification gives rise to what is here called a collection code. Any organization of educational knowledge which involves a marked attempt to reduce the strength of classification is here called an integrated code. Collection codes may give rise to a series of sub-types, each varying in the relative strength of their classification and frames. Integrated codes can also vary in terms of the strength of frames, as these refer to the *teacher/pupil/ student* control over the knowledge that is transmitted.

Figure 5.1 sets out general features of the typology.

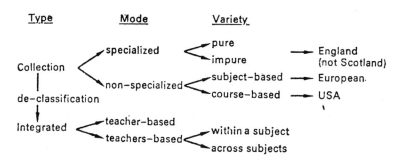

Figure 5.1

Collection Codes

The first major distinction *within* collection codes is between specialized and non-specialized types. The extent of specialization can be measured in terms of the number of closed contents publicly examined at the end of the secondary educational stage. Thus in England, *although there is no formal limit*, the student usually sits for three 'A' level subjects, compared with the much greater range of subjects which make up the Abitur in Germany, the Baccalauréat in France, or the Studente Exam in Sweden.

Within the English specialized type, we can distinguish two varieties: a pure and an impure variety. The pure variety exists where 'A' level subjects are drawn from a common universe of knowledge, e.g. Chemistry, Physics, Mathematics. The impure variety exists where 'A' level subjects are drawn from different universes of knowledge, e.g. Religion, Physics, Economics. . . .

Within the non-specialized collection code, we can distinguish two varieties, according to whether a subject or course is the basic knowledge unit. Thus the standard European form of the collection code is non-specialized, *subject*-based. The USA form of the collection is non-specialized, course-based. . . .

Integrated Codes

Integration, as it is used here, refers minimally to the *subordination* of previously insulated subjects *or* courses to some *relational* idea, which blurs the boundaries between the subjects. We can distinguish two types. The first type is *teacher*-based. Here the teacher, as in the infant school, has an extended block of time with often the same group of children. The teacher may operate with a collection code and keep the various subjects distinct and insulated, or he can blur the boundaries between the different subjects. This type of integrated code is easier to introduce than the second type, which is *teachers*-based. Here, integration involves relationships with other teachers. In this way, we can have degrees of integration in terms of the number of teachers involved.

We can further distinguish two varieties according to whether the integration refers to a group of teachers *within* a common subject, or the extent to which integration involves teachers of different subjects. Whilst integrated codes, by definition, have the weakest classification, they may vary as to framing. During the initiating period, the frames the teachers enter will be weak, but other factors will effect the final frame strength. It is also possible that the frames the *pupils* enter can vary in strength.

Thus integrated codes may be confined to one subject or they can cross subjects. We can talk of code strength in terms of the range of different subjects co-ordinated by the code, or if this criterion cannot be applied, code strength can be measured in terms of the *number* of teachers co-ordinated through the code. Integrated codes can also vary as to frame strength as this applies to teachers or pupils or both.

References

BERNSTEIN, B. (1967) 'Open schools, open society?', *New Society*, 14 September.

BERNSTEIN, B.; ELVIN, L.; and PETERS, R. (1966) 'Ritual in education', *Philosophical Transactions of the Royal Society of London*, Series B, 251, No. 772.

DAVIES, D.I. (1970a) 'The management of knowledge: A critique of the use of typologies in educational sociology', *Sociology*, 4, 1.

DAVIES, D.I. (1970b) 'Knowledge, education and power', paper presented to the British Sociological Association Annual Conference, Durham.

HOYLE, E. (1969) 'How does the curriculum change? (1) A proposal for enquiries (2) Systems and strategies', *Journal of Curriculum Studies*, 1, 2; 1, 3.

MUSGROVE, F. (1968) 'The contribution of sociology to the study of the curriculum', in KERR, J. (Ed.), *Changing the Curriculum*, University of London Press.

YOUNG, M. (1971) 'Curricula as socially organised knowledge', in YOUNG, M. (Ed.), *Knowledge and Control*, Collier-Macmillan.

Visible and Invisible Pedagogies: An Introductory Overview

(From Robinson, P., 1981, *Perspectives on the Sociology of Education: An Introduction*, London, Routledge and Kegan Paul, pp. 120–1.)

Bernstein's interest in the sociology of educational knowledge has involved not just the curriculum (the focus of the previous extract) but also pedagogy — the way the curriculum is transmitted. In this summary by Robinson, Bernstein's distinctions between 'visible' and 'invisible' pedagogies are discussed and related to his previous work on classification, framing, and educational knowledge codes (pp. 200–205). An 'invisible' pedagogy, believed by Bernstein to be institutionalized at the level of the infant school, is seen to be a pervasive influence for the exercise of social control and thus important in the process of social reproduction in capitalist society. For further elaboration, readers are referred to Bernstein's original paper, 'Class and pedagogies: Visible and invisible', in Bernstein, B. (1975) *Class, Codes and Control, Vol. 3: Towards a Theory of Educational Transmissions*, 2nd ed., London, Routledge and Kegan Paul, pp. 116–56.

[In his discussion of pedagogy, Bernstein] suggests three factors which regulate the teacher-pupil relationship. These are the factors of hierarchy, sequencing rules, and criteria, each having an explicit and implicit dimension. Hierarchy refers to the power within the relationship, either unambiguously explicit as in 'I am in control because I am the teacher', or implicitly where there are no *overt* rules. The stress on 'overt' is crucial — the paradox of implicit hierarchies is that although on the surface there may appear to be no rules nevertheless rules exist. In the infant classroom the teacher may invite the children to 'do your own thing', to take responsibility for their own learning. The children quickly come to appreciate, however, that 'doing your own thing' does not include setting fire to the Wendy House or throwing sand across the classroom! Under the apparent freedom there is control and the child must learn the markers to that control.

The second aspect to the teacher-pupil relationship is the sequencing rules which regulate the order in which transmission takes place. If the rules are explicit, there is a clear recognition of what is appropriate to the child at any particular stage. Every teacher has experienced, for example, going into a noisy classroom and saying, 'What class is this?' and, on being told a fourth-year class, responding, 'I thought it was the first year, the amount of noise you were making.' There is appropriate behaviour at appropriate stages; if the rules are implicit, 'the sex and chronological age of the child do not become strong marking features of the sequencing rules'. In this case only the teacher will be aware of what is appropriate, picking up cues from the child's behaviour as to his reading readiness or developmental stage.

Finally the transmission realizes criteria of accomplishment which also may be explicit or implicit. If explicit the teacher on asking, for example, the child to draw a house will criticize the production if it does not have windows, or if the windows are in the 'wrong' place. If the criteria of accomplishment are implicit, the child is invited to 'Tell me all about your painting'. The criteria are apparently the child's. However the paradox reappears when at the end of the lesson not every picture is put on the wall for all to see; or if we had given the example of a piece of written work, not every piece is typed-up and placed in the class story book. Under the openness of the relationship there are criteria, there is control though its nature changes. Where the hierarchy, sequencing rules and criteria are *explicit* Bernstein labels the form of transmission one of *visible pedagogy*; where they are *implicit* he labels the form of transmission one of *invisible pedagogy*.

. . . Bernstein argues that under an integrated code, more of the pupil and teacher enter the pedagogical relationship. This can now be expanded by linking to his discussion of visible and invisible pedagogies. As the strength of classification weakens, so what counts as knowledge becomes more open to negotiation, the child may bring more of his world into the classroom. But in doing so he introduces more of himself as a unique person. Within a visible pedagogy (that is strong framing and strong classification) the teacher need not know her pupils as people; symbolically she enters the classroom through one door and the pupils through another and the two need never meet. This type of relationship is epitomized by the mass lecture in higher education — the personal biography of both lecturer and student is not relevant to the occasion. Within an invisible pedagogy, (weak framing and weak classification), the teacher knows more about the child as a person and must also reveal more of herself, if only to admit ignorance in answer to a pupil's question. But as more of the pupil is available so less of his unique self is protected from the school's influences, hence the paradox that although the invisible pedagogy appears to be the open, liberal pedagogy, it is also more pervasive in its control, the child begins to internalize the requirements of the classroom.

Bernstein is talking about the curriculum [and pedagogy] at a high level of theoretical abstraction, necessarily so if we are to begin to understand the place of education in the process of social reproduction.

The curriculum is not a neutral package of knowledge which responds to the natural demands of the wider society. [Together with pedagogy] it is a vehicle both for increasing the child's knowledge of the world but also for moulding her stance towards that world, as Wylie puts it, 'From the attitude of teachers, from the way in which school work is presented, from the textbooks, the children learn to make basic assumptions concerning the nature of reality and their relationship to it' (1973, p. 73).

Bernstein has begun an exploration of how children might come to make basic assumptions about the nature of reality; the strength of his model lies in bringing together content and form, curriculum and transmission, and linking both to the process of social reproduction within society. Its weakness is that some of the links in the argument are ambiguous and await further development.

Reference

WYLIE, L. (1973) *Village in the Vaucluse*, Harvard University Press.

Control, Accountability and William Tyndale

(From Dale, R., 1981, 'Control, accountability and William Tyndale', in Dale R. *et al.* (Eds), *Education and the State, Vol. 2: Politics, Patriarchy and Practice,* Falmer Press/The Open University Press, pp. 308–14, 314–16.)

The increasing prominence of neo-Marxist scholarship in the sociology of education has helped redirect attention to the relationship between the educational, political and economic systems at national level. Because of Marxist preoccupation with problems of historical change and process, it has also led to a renewed emphasis on historical perspectives to this relationship. Dale's paper, from which this extract has been taken, analyzes aspects of the recent history of education and relates these to political forces. It is an example of what Ahier and Flude (1983) term 'a more policy-oriented and politically aware sociology of education'. In it, Dale examines changes in the control of schooling and the accountability of teachers, and the role played in these changes by the William Tyndale affair (pp. 45–50). He argues that the affair facilitated, but did not cause, changes in the structure of the educational system towards greater central control. In particular, it dealt a final blow to the basis of the management of the English educational system enshrined in the 1944 Education Act (pp. 34–36); it helped justify the replacement of teachers' professional judgement by bureaucratic accountability; and it contributed to the erosion of the teaching profession's influence on educational policy.

Reference

AHIER, J. and FLUDE, M. (Eds) (1983) *Contemporary Education Policy*, London, Croom Helm.

The Management of Education

The Tyndale affair has been widely regarded as a management problem. It is seen as posing questions both about how conflict between individuals and groups can be settled, and about what institutional machinery is most likely to bring about this desirable end. Yet, as in so many other areas, what happened at William Tyndale served to bring concentrated attention to bear on a problem which was far from novel, through a dramatic demonstration of some of the more extreme difficulties the problem might entail.

It was already clear before 1975 that the basis of the management of the English education system, enshrined in the 1944 Education Act, was in a rapidly advancing state of decay. The social, economic and educational context of 1944 had been transformed by the late 1960's, placing an increasingly unabsorbable strain on the assumptions on which the system was based. The two most crucial assumptions were those of a balance of power, and a supra-political consensus. The 1944 Act sought to create a balance between central and local government and the teaching profession such that:

> power over the distribution of resources, over the organization and context of education was to be diffused among the different elements and no one of them was to be given a controlling voice...
> the DES was not given strong formal powers to secure the implementation of its policies because it was assumed that both central government and local education authorities were managed by men of good will whose main concern was to improve the service and whose reflective judgements remained untainted by the intrusion of party ideology (Bogdanor, 1979).

The second part of that quotation is shot through with an ideology of supra party consensus on education; this was to be achieved through consultation with all interested parties. Thus, as Bogdanor (1979) further states:

> Were any element in the system to seek to use its formal powers to the full, the system could not work. Mutual constraint, as in the Hobbesian universe, is the precondition of success, and the war of all against all would make progress in education impossible. There must, therefore, be limits on the degree of politicization of the education service if it is to operate successfully.

There are at least five shortcomings to be noted with respect to this system of education management. First of all, it quite clearly does not reflect the situation in the system it was set up to control at all accurately. The comprehensive schools issue alone, culminating in the Tameside judgement, knocks the props out completely from under a system premissed on the exclusion of party politics from educational matters and some sort of permanently available central-local consensus. Second, as Bogdanor too points out, the system is ineffective in directing the education system into new pathways. Since 1944, the potential contribution of education to both individual and national economic prosperity has been widely acknowledged, but a system which rests on no one party taking an undue initiative in its direction has responded only slowly to the challenges contained in the role of education in the development of human capital. (This is not to suggest that the system of education management alone is responsible for this failure, very far from it.) Third, again as noted by Bogdanor, such a system is able to operate much better in periods of expansion than in periods of retrenchment, when squabbles between the parties to the consensus over the distribution of even scarcer resources may become inevitable. Fourth, there has been in recent years evidence of a change in the style of education management, at both national and local level, towards a 'managerialism' emphasising efficiency rather than broadening access (see David, 1978), with the DES coming under the influence of a manpower planning ideology (see Tapper and Salter, 1978). At a local level this has been accompanied by a growth in the size of local authorities following the 1974 reorganization of local government, and by the introduction in many of them of a system of 'corporate management' drawn from industrial and business use and intended primarily to increase efficiency (see Cockburn, 1977). Finally, the assumptions have been challenged by an increasing desire for participation in the control of the education system by many of the groups affected by it but excluded from influence over it. As Bogdanor (1979) puts it,

> in particular the move towards greater participation in education has done much to undermine traditional arrangements. For the system of consultation worked best, when only a small number of interests were involved whose rank and file were content to defer to elites, and could, therefore, be relied upon to act 'sensibly'.

(And what did William Tyndale do to that?!) As David has shown, pressure towards greater participation in the control of education was already building up in the late 1960s. At that time such pressure was associated with radical efforts at securing greater community control over schools; it is interesting that such moves were nowhere near as successful as the articulation of 'parent power' to a much more conservative political stance in the past three or four years, and it is difficult to avoid seeing an effect of William Tyndale here. What the Tyndale case was used to demonstrate was the importance of parents having some say in what was going on at their children's school, rather than an example, albeit rather flawed, of an attempt to set up a school more responsive to its local community than to perceived national priorities.

It is fairly clear that the Tyndale affair did have some effects in the area of the management of education. It served to deliver the final blow to the 1944 system by demonstrating that its several shortcomings could jointly lead to disaster. It had, perhaps, two particular effects in this area. First, it appeared to show that the pursuit of national economic goals could be not merely ignored but actually frustrated in a system where clear central leadership was absent; in this way it made the path to greater DES intervention in the education system much smoother. And second, it greatly enhanced the likelihood that the progress of parent participation in schooling would be articulated in a conservative rather than any kind of progressive or radical philosophy of schooling.

Teachers' Classroom Autonomy

The assumption that the education system was governed by a more or less implicit consensus about aims and objectives, strategies and tactics had considerable effects at the level of the management of individual schools, too. For, as Pateman (1978) argues, where the goals of schooling were expressed in terms of implicit understandings rather than explicit targets, this:

> increased the power of both teachers and inspectors. In the case of teachers it made it difficult for them to be held to account by either parents or managers with whom it was possible, if desired, to play a 'catch us if you can' game. In the case of inspectors, it required of them a hermeneutic understanding of the schools, the efficiency of which they were assessing ... Education, like medicine and the law, had its mysteries to which teachers and inspectors were privy, and parents and politicians were not.

This approach is developed further in Dale and Trevitt-Smith (1976). In a consensual situation teachers' classroom autonomy has plenty of space to develop — in such a situation:

> the extent to which a school board can hold teachers or a school to account for its performance is strictly limited, since by definition its members are not expert and can at best only claim to be able to identify cases of gross incompetence, gross inefficiency and plain corruption — and even here they may well feel constrained to rely on the advice of the head teacher or an inspector.

Two common explanations of the Tyndale case, one from 'sympathetic liberals', and the other from more cynical radicals, become pertinent here. A common argument from people not unsympathetic to the Tyndale teachers is that what they were attempting was fine in theory (and some versions go on to indicate that similar things are being done with impunity in other schools) but they just were not very good at carrying through these admittedly very difficult practices and policies. Chaos inevitably ensued, to a degree that was interfering with any kind of effective education of the children. The more cynical view suggests that what happened to the

Tyndale teachers merely confirms what we knew all along, namely that all the talk about professional autonomy was just a hoax — when it is put to the test, when someone actually treats it seriously, then its bogus nature is immediately revealed.

Both these arguments seem to be too simple and to ignore some of the complexities of the situation. The first argument assumes the persistence of a consensus about education; according to Pateman (1978), a logical precondition for teacher autonomy '. . . when the ends of education cease to be consensual . . . the claim to professional freedom logically collapses. For in such a situation there is no longer a neutral professional dealing in expertly-assessable means', albeit one that has changed over the years and is now represented, in primary schools at any rate, by what might be called 'Plowdenism'. John White (1977) puts this very clearly: 'It is one of the ironies of this case that they were, after all, only putting into practice in a radical form the theories that had been pumped into them in their own training and which have, between Hadow and Plowden, become the official gospel of the primary world'. Two points need to be made about this. First, the teachers at William Tyndale saw themselves as going well beyond Plowdenism — in April 1975 Brian Haddow had attacked 'the late 1960's style of informal progressive repression', advocated the abolition of 'point-less structure' and called for more egalitarian systems for staff and children. (The teachers' views on progressive education are set out in Ellis *et al.*, 1976). Thus, 'incompetent Plowdenism' seems an ineffective charge to lay at their door. Second, I have argued elsewhere (1979a, 1979b) that the period of dominance of the Plowden consensus was already very much on the wane, and was yet another educational phenomenon whose end was hastened rather than directly brought about by its being dragged into the Tyndale affair. Effectively, then, teacher autonomy was being treated under a form assuming a consensus regime some time after a consensus could in fact be established. Hence the conditions for the kind of teacher autonomy premissed on consensus were absent; it was only a matter of time before their absence was discovered.

The other pat response to the Tyndale affair — its exposure of the hoax of teacher autonomy — also rests on a number of rather fragile and vague assumptions about the nature of teacher autonomy. Essentially, they make the exercise of teacher autonomy far too voluntaristic, indeed far too easy. What they miss is the situated nature of teachers' classroom autonomy, and even, indeed, its political nature. Only its suppression is seen as a political act; its practice by teachers in situations like that at William Tyndale is seen rather as the expression of inalienable professional rights. Yet Pateman's argument shows that it is only in the relatively narrow — and in a sense self-defeating — context of working within a consensus framework that the assertion of teacher classroom autonomy — if that means doing something different from what is officially expected of them, which it usually implicitly does — is anything other than a political challenge which must be interpreted and acted on as such.

Oddly similar in some ways to this cynical interpretation of the Tyndale affair is the more popular and more right wing view which sees the teachers as abusing their power and deserving everything they got. This account, too, turns on a particular interpretation of teacher autonomy. There are very many, very widely recognised, constraints on teacher autonomy, some of which it is impossible for individual teachers to overcome — such as the teacher pupil ratio, the inability of schools to choose whom they will teach and so on — others of which it is possible, if very difficult, to overcome — such as the expectation that children will be taught the 3 R's or that they will not be tortured. Teachers have an implicit mandate to combat ignorance and indiscipline and they have to carry it out in particular circumstances (such as the teacher — pupil ratio, external examination demands) which themselves entail certain constraints (Dale, 1976, 1977). Within these constraints, teachers are relatively free to carry out their duties as they will. They are only relatively free since, first, they remain at the bottom of a hierarchy of authority and subject to the immediate control of their head teacher and, second, the ways in which they exercise the freedom available to them are subject both to the constraints of the classroom situation, its 'hidden curriculum', and to the assumptions about what it is to be a teacher which they distil from their own pupil experience, their teacher training and their teacher experience (Daie, 1977). One result of this, for instance is to make a cognitive style of individualism very prominent among teachers (Dale, 1978). It is for this reason, rather than any lack of imagination or initiative on the part of teachers, that what autonomy teachers have has both tended to be minimized in much writing about teaching, and to have had so confirmatory, rather than disruptive an effect on the education system. Consequent to this modifying of possible autonomy, it was possible for teachers to be granted a 'licensed autonomy' within the education system without danger of this leading to a revolutionary, or even radical, transformation of the system.

What the Tyndale teachers appear to have done, however, and what led to the charges of abuse of autonomy, was to step outside the implicit and internalized guidelines as to how what autonomy they had should be used, as much as to extend the area of autonomy itself. In exercising their autonomy, the Tyndale teachers both ignored their mandate (by reversing the priorities it contained) and ignored the prescriptions for practice contained within the sedimented common sense of the teaching profession. This dual negation in the exercise of their professional autonomy is the basis of the accusations of its abuse.

The effects on educational policy of this perceived abuse of their autonomy by the Tyndale teachers have derived from the two sides of that negation. Steps have been taken to ensure both that the mandate (to teach certain subjects like maths and reading) is actually made mandatory (through the specification of the remit of the APU) and to reinforce the already potent effect of experience and professional common sense (through more frequent and more detailed monitoring of teachers and school activities). It has led to an increasing emphasis on how educational knowledge is *consumed* at the expense of how it is *produced* — symbolized in the waxing of the Assessment of Performance Unit while the Schools Council wanes. It has led to a recognition of the political nature of teachers' classroom autonomy in a period when there is no clear consensus on educational goals, and a consequent attempt both to specify the aims and objectives of the education system more clearly and more explicitly, and to routinize teachers' accountability for the performance of their (newly specified) roles. What is involved is the replacement of teachers' professional judgement by bureaucratic accountability. No longer will teachers be able to use their professional expertise to play 'catch me if you can'; they will now have to play 'jumping through the hoops'.

The Influence of the Teaching Profession

The effect which the Tyndale case had on teacher autonomy was not, however, limited to the moves to limit teachers' classroom autonomy just outlined. The affair also had a notable effect on the whole standing of the teaching profession and on its power and influence in the corridors and conference rooms where education policy is made. This is particularly important, for it is possible to distinguish two rather different conceptions of teacher autonomy which frequently are combined with consequent confusion and lack of clarity. The first conception of teacher autonomy, which we might call the weak conception, would limit it to the free exercise of acknowledged expertise in executing in the school and classroom educational programmes designed elsewhere, over which teachers should have no greater say than anyone else. It is this conception which underlay the discussion in the previous section. The second, 'strong', conception would include the creation as well as the execution of educational programmes within the scope of teacher autonomy, on the basis that the teachers are the experts about education and that they alone, or they best, can decide what should be taught as well as how to teach it. Now these issues are the subject of a continuing philosophical and political debate which is not strictly relevant here. What is relevant is that the Tyndale affair had an important effect not only on the weak conception of teacher autonomy, an effect which as we saw in the previous section led to it being curtailed, but also on the strong conception. This is not because the Tyndale teachers were in any way closely associated with those levels of the teaching profession which exercise its influence over educational policy, or because they were in any way attempting directly to bring pressure to bear on national educational policy themselves. Far from it. They were, in fact, repudiated by their union, the National Union of Teachers, which represented not them, but the Deputy Head, Mrs. Chowles, at the Auld Inquiry and, though they received some initial support from their local association of the NUT in the form, for instance, of asking other local primary schools not to enrol children removed from William Tyndale, this appears not to have continued in the same way.

The two conceptions of teacher autonomy broadly divide the two major teachers unions, with the NUT holding very much more to the strong conception than the NAS/UWT.... It had been and continues to be, however, increasingly difficult to sustain [the strong conception], for a number of reasons, several of which appeared to be strengthened by what happened at William Tyndale. One basic cause was the generally declining economic state of the country. This inevitably led to ever more severe cuts in budgets for education, affecting both resources and manpower. The zenith of the NUT's influence had been reached, inevitably, in the decade of rapid educational expansion from the late 50's on, and such contraction not only closed off possible avenues of further expansion, but made it very difficult even to maintain the *status quo*. Again the Tyndale affair had no direct effect on this, but the atmosphere it created made it very much easier for such cuts to be implemented. That atmosphere had a similar effect on the teaching profession retaining its central role in educational decision making. As has been hinted above, the DES was very keen to give a more decisive lead to the education service, to bring it more into line with perceived national priorities, and 'clipping the teachers' wings' seems to have been regarded as an important part of this. Before Tyndale, though, this would have been politically very difficult to achieve, given the very entrenched and apparently well legitimated position the teaching profession held. Tyndale, together with other evidence (such as the alleged decline in literacy) of the failure of the schools to do what the nation required of them made this 'wing clipping' much more feasible. It did this through creating a situation where the scapegoating of the education system for the nation's parlous economic condition could be converted into the scapegoating of the teachers, and thus absolve all other levels of the system from responsibility. Thus, the educational policy makers and implementers emerged from the attacks on the system they directed scot free, while the reputation of the teaching profession received a very damaging blow.

As well as being squeezed from the one side by the more aggressive stance being taken by central government, the NUT's influence was also being pressured from the other side by the development of 'parent power', and once more this development was far from being hindered by the Tyndale affair.

So, notwithstanding the NUT's explicit repudiation of the Tyndale teachers, what they are popularly interpreted as having done has made a significant contribution to the erosion of the teaching profession's influence on education policy. Its wings *have* been clipped by the DES — note, for instance, the Schools Council's new (1978) constitution which effectively removed it from teacher control. It has been forced onto the defensive both by cuts in educational budgets and by falling rolls, with the pressure they put on the maintenance of teachers' jobs. And the public reputation of the teaching profession has not been lower for a long time, something which has further weakened its ability to defend its influence and its interests; this is symbolically reflected in a public mention, however tentative — in the Green Paper — of the possibility of setting up machinery to sack incompetent teachers, a further erosion of teacher power which the effect of Tyndale made it much more difficult to resist.

Conclusion

It should by now be clear that the role attributed to the William Tyndale affair in respect of changes in the control of schools and the accountability of teachers is essentially a facilitative one. What happened at the school did not initiate or cause these shifts, whose consequences are not yet clear, but whose broad aim quite clearly is to restructure and redirect the education system. Both the successful completion and an intended outcome of this process involve cutting back the influence of the teachers at both classroom and policy levels. However, stating that the Tyndale affair enabled rather than caused these changes is not an entirely satisfactory way to conclude this analysis and I would like in this final section to examine, extremely briefly, what might be some of those causes.

...many of the trends and tendencies which Tyndale brought to fruition were present long before the school achieved its notoriety, and I want now to look at some of these trends and tendencies. Why, for instance, did the DES want to increase central control over education? Why did the dominant consensus break down? Why did parents want more say in their children's education? In sum, how had all these problems arisen and why was it necessary to solve them in these particular ways?

Very briefly (the arguments in this paragraph are spelled out much more fully in Dale, forthcoming), over the period since 1944, the economic, political, and ideological climates in which education operates had changed, and so had the contributions which it was assumed education could make at each of these levels. However, the changes at these levels are far from being mutually complementary but are in fact contradictory; it is from these contradictions that the education system gains its dynamic. Similarly, changes at one level do not always, or often, keep pace with changes at other levels, which results in considerable strain during the catching-up period. Concretely, over this period both the pressure to national economic success, and the contribution which it seemed education could make to it, increased. The manpowering function of education became dominant. Yet, because it was governed by a system set up with a different set of priorities in mind, and dominated ideologically by approaches which were often hostile to the manpowering function, the implementation of what the priority of that function entailed was substantially obstructed. Furthermore, the removal of these obstructions was no easy matter; what were seen as obstructions from the viewpoint of an increasingly frustrated central government were widely legitimated features of a well established education system. As I have suggested some of these features were beginning to lose their legitimacy well before the Tyndale affair blew up. There is, though, no doubt that it hastened the pace of educational change, even if the broad direction of that change was already clear.

References

BOGDANOR, V. (1979) 'Power and participation', *Oxford Review of Education*, 5, 2, pp. 157–68.

COCKBURN, C. (1977) *The Local State*, Pluto Press.

DALE, R. (1976) *The Structural Context of Teaching*, E202, Unit 5, Open University Press.

DALE, R. (1977) 'Implications of the rediscovery of the hidden curriculum for the sociology of teaching', in GLEESON, D. (Ed.), *Identity and Structure: Issues in the Sociology of Education*, Driffield, Nafferton Books.

DALE, R. (1979a) 'From endorsement to disintegration: Progressive education from the Golden Age to the Green Paper,' *British Journal of Educational Studies*, 28, 3, pp. 191–208.

DALE, R. (1979b) 'The politicization of school deviance: Reactions to William Tyndale', in BARTON, L. and MEIGHAN, R. (Eds), *Schools, Pupils and Deviance*, Driffield, Nafferton Books, pp. 95–112.

DALE, R. (forthcoming), *The State and Education Policy*, London, Routledge and Kegan Paul.

DALE, R. and TREVITT-SMITH, J. (1976) 'From mystique to technique: Completing the bourgeois revolution in education', unpublished paper.

DAVID, M. (1978) 'Parents and educational politics in 1977', in BROWN, M. and BALDWIN, S. (Eds), *The Year Book of Social Policy in Britain 1977*, London, Routledge and Kegan Paul, pp. 87–106.

ELLIS, T. *et al.* (1976) *William Tyndale: The Teachers' Story*, Writers and Readers Publishing Cooperative.

PATEMAN, T. (1978) 'Accountability, values and schooling', in BECHER, A. and MACLURE S, (Eds), *Accountability in Education*, NFER.

TAPPER, E. and SALTER, B. (1978) *Education and the Political Order*, Macmillan.

WHITE, J. (1977) 'Tyndale and the Left', *Forum*, 19, 2, pp. 59–61.

Teachers and Their Pupils' Home Background

(From Goodacre, E., 1968, *Teachers and Their Pupils' Home Background*, NFER, pp. 15–18, 18–19.)

This material comes from an investigation of infant teachers' attitudes towards their pupils' home backgrounds and their expectations and assessments of individual pupils. In the passage, a summary analysis is provided of replies from infant teachers in middle-class, upper working-class and lower working-class areas. The extract has been chosen to illustrate two areas of interest in the sociology of education, one long-established, and the other more recent. The latter involves the examination of the origins, content and consequences of teachers' 'professional knowledge', including the labels and categories teachers employ which help define reality for them and, in part, for their pupils. The way the infant teachers categorized pupils into those from 'good' and 'poor' home is discussed, and the argument is advanced that teachers' stereotypes of the type of pupil and home they could expect 'were related to their ideas concerning the relationship of occupational level, social conditions and intellectual ability'. The second area of interest illustrated by the extract is the concern of sociologists to provide explanations for working-class failure in schools. Goodacre's evidence suggests that, in the case of some of the teachers, their knowledge of children's social class background influenced their conceptions of pupils' ability and might have lowered their expectations of what pupils could achieve. Some sociologists certainly argue that a partial explanation of why working-class children underachieve in schools is the result of lowered expectations on the part of their teachers.

1.   *What importance do infant teachers attach to pupils' home background in the teaching of reading?*

Generally the teachers considered that the pupils' home background was an important factor in learning to read; they described those aspects of the home which they believed could actively assist that process, and the abilities pupils used in learning to read which they most readily associated with differences in home conditions. They most valued the provision of suitable reading material in pupils' homes on which pupils could practise their newly acquired skill, and the type of atmosphere in which it was taken for granted by parents and child that reading was a desirable skill to be acquired. Differences in home background were most readily connected with a child's desire to learn to read and his rate of learning.

2.   *How do teachers categorize their pupils in relation to home background?*

The teachers in this study appeared to be familiar with the terms 'good' and 'poor' homes as a means of categorizing pupils. When asked to describe them in their own words, they used more motivational and cultural characteristics in describing the 'good' home. The 'good' home tended to be described as one which facilitated the teacher's task of instruction by preparing the child for participation in the formal learning situation and also for acceptance of the teacher's role in it. If a child showed no eagerness to learn to read, teachers believed that the difficulty of imparting the techniques of the skill was increased, because not only did they have to provide the appropriate systematic instruction (difficult enough if teacher and pupil used different types of language systems, dialect etc.) but they had also to demonstrate to pupils that reading was a desirable and necessary skill.

When teachers rated the different characteristics of a 'good' home, the school's social area assumed importance. For instance, there was little difference between the ratings of teachers in middle and upper working-class areas, but particular motivational and cultural items assumed importance as distinguishing characteristics between the two working-class groups. These items were the ability of the parents to answer their children's questions, to provide stimulating experiences in the home and to help with school work; parents' own levels of education and intelligence, and the presence of 'good' conversation and manners in the home. Comparing the extreme social area groups, the items regarded as most important were a religious faith, parental help with school work, stable emotional home life, and a mother who did not go out to work.

Each teacher's ratings for the various items were added up to give a total score for this question, and if high scores can be interpreted as indicative of an interest in the contribution of the 'good' home, it seems likely that such an interest is related to the individual teacher's age and general personality type. The findings suggest that it is more likely to be the older or more authoritarian type of teacher, with unfavourable attitudes to pupils and their homes, who is most likely to categorize pupils in terms of 'good' or 'poor' homes.

3.   *What is the extent of teachers' personal contacts with pupils and their homes, and what clues do they use as a basis for their impressions of pupils' home conditions?*

It was found that amongst these urban infant teachers, contacts with parents seldom extended beyond meetings on school premises. Few school heads had established parent-teacher organizations, and few teachers ever visited pupils' homes. Two out of three parents[1] were said to visit the school, usually for reasons connected with the child's physical well-being, and since these questions were asked of teachers of young children, parental interest at this stage was largely an expression of maternal concern.

Pupils' records of attendance and lateness were not indicative of social class differences in attitudes towards the value of education, but pupils' reasons for being away or their excuses for lateness provided teachers, to some extent, with information about the pupils' home circumstances. There was, however, some evidence to suggest that certain types of schools might find particular reasons more 'acceptable' than others.

Teachers seemed to have little difficulty in finding evidence of a child's economic circumstances. Conversations, class 'News', or actual observations of personal belongings, etc. brought to school were considered to be indications of a family's pattern of conspicuous consumption. The type and quality of a child's clothing, even in today's welfare state, still seems to be a major 'clue' for most teachers. Obvious signs such as the bare feet of the nineteen-thirties have disappeared, but indications such as the suitability of clothing from the point of view of climate and weather conditions, and the care and quality of underclothing provide a basis for comparison to the practised eye of the observer.

The teachers suggested a variety of ways in which the actions of parents could be construed as constituting parental interest in the child's reading progress. However, analysis of their answers indicated areas of difference which could well be the basis of misunderstandings between teachers and parents. There were, for instance, the different responses to the practical suggestion that parents should provide pupils with a copy of the reader in the school reading scheme, so that the child could practise at home. Firstly, provision of the reader and parents 'hearing' their children read at home was more often suggested as a sign of parental interest by the heads than by the class teachers. Secondly, the head's views as to whether the parent was expected to borrow or to buy the book appeared to be related to his own social class origin. A head of working-class origin would be likely to consider a request from a parent to borrow a school reader as a

---

[1] Since one in three parents are not seen by the teachers at school (even from the beginning of the child's schooling), one wonders to what extent lack of face-to-face relationships influences the teachers' assessments of parental interest — it may well be that the unknown, unmet parent soon comes to be regarded as the parent who 'takes little interest'. Douglas (1964) assessed parental encouragement by using the class teachers' comments at the end of the first and fourth years in the primary school and their records of the number of times parents visited the school to discuss their children's progress. It was found that on the basis of this assessment of parental interest, when parents took little interest, their children lost ground in tests and gained rather fewer places in the selection examinations than would have been expected from their measured ability.

sign of interest, but the same request to a head of middle-class origin might be considered as a 'trivial' reason for a visit to the school.[1]

There was evidence to suggest that the type of school organization has a bearing on the role expected of parents. For instance, more heads of the smaller, combined department school expected parents to take an active interest in the work of the school to the extent of visiting the school to ask about the methods in use, whereas more class teachers in the infant only schools emphasized the parents' supportive role, expecting them to encourage and sustain their children in their efforts but not, at this early stage in their children's education, to want to help with school work.

5.   *What inferences do teachers make about pupils whose parents follow different types of occupation?*

The teachers' lack of knowledge regarding the gradients of status in the manual classes was reflected in the tendency for teachers in lower working-class areas to see their classes as homogeneous groups, and pupils as predominantly children of fathers with manual occupations. Their tendency to stress the power and responsibility of occupations which, in the past, were related to educational mobility and hence intellectual capacity, also led them to think of pupils from the lower working-class areas not only as *socially* homogeneous groups, but also as being *intellectually* homogeneous; more teachers in the lower working-class areas tended to accept that they had no pupils of above average intellectual ability. Further, it appeared from the teachers' comments that their own language system and academically biased education might make it extremely difficult for many of them to recognize unfamiliar forms of intellectual functioning.

6.   *To what extent do such inferences affect teachers' ratings of individual pupils?*

In reply to the request to complete estimates, records and predictions of individual pupils' abilities, attributes, reading attainment and progress, it was found that the teachers in the extreme social areas were less reluctant to supply information about pupils' home conditions than the teachers in the

---

[1] DEPARTMENT OF EDUCATION AND SCIENCE (1967). 'National Survey of Parental Attitudes and Circumstances Related to School and Pupil Characteristics', Appendix 3, *Children and Their Primary Schools* (Plowden Report) reported that just over a third of the parents had *bought* copies, to have at home, of some of the textbooks their children were using at school. Considerably higher proportions of parents from the non-manual than manual worker families had bought textbooks.

upper working-class areas. This suggested that the teachers in the extreme social areas tended to have well-structured stereotypes of the type of pupil and home they could expect. It seemed likely that these expectations were related to their ideas concerning the relationship of occupational level, social conditions and intellectual ability. . . .

References

CENTRAL ADVISORY COUNCIL FOR EDUCATION (England), (1967) *Children and Their Primary Schools* Vol. 2, Appendix 3, London, HMSO.
DOUGLAS, J. (1964) *The Home and the School*, MacGiddon and Kee.

Primary Education and Social Control

(From Sharp, R. and Green, A., 1975, *Education and Social Control*, London, Routledge and Kegan Paul, pp. vii-viii, 216–7, 217, 217–18, 218, 221–2, 224, 224–5, 227.)

English infant education has been the subject of two important sociological case-studies, which are featured in this extract and the next. Sharp and Green's study was conducted with the headteacher and infant teachers in one junior and infants school and, though small-scale and exploratory, raised a number of important issues, both for theoretical work in the sociology of education and for primary school policy and practice. The authors provided an abstruse but thought-provoking critique of 'progressive education'. Their main argument (summarized in the first paragraph of the extract) is that such an approach may not be as liberal or emancipatory as it appears; they suggest it 'is an aspect of romantic radical conservatism', since it involves a subtle process of sponsorship and stratification among pupils (equally as effective as the process of differentiation in traditional approaches to education) and it provides enhanced opportunities for the exercise of social control 'in both the narrow sense of achieving discipline in the classroom and the wider sense of contributing to the promotion of a static social order generally' (see also pp. 206–208). Their interpretations (both sociological and educational) have not gone unchallenged.

The child centred teacher sees him, or herself as engaging in a radical critique of the authoritarian-élitist assumptions of the more formal, traditional approaches to education. He does not wish to subordinate the child's individuality to some predefined social requirements or impose 'high culture' upon the child in an arbitrary fashion because these would frustrate the realization of the child's inner potential. We attempt to show some of the ways in which the well-intentioned 'radical practices' of the progressive educator produce effects very similar to the hierarchical differentiation of pupils characteristic of formal methods. Whilst laying emphasis upon the freedom of the child, the teacher who has adopted the ideology of child centredness may well find himself unwittingly constrained to act in ways which pose serious problems concerning the efficacy of accommodating to and encouraging the 'spontaneous development of the child from within himself'. In our explanation of these and other phenomena which we have researched, what is being suggested is that the child centred educator, with his individualistic, voluntarist, and psychologistic solution to the problem of freedom fails to appreciate the ways in which, even in his own practice, the effects of a complex, stratified industrial society penetrate the school. It is suggested that the radicalism of the 'progressive educator' may well be a modern form of conservatism, and an effective form of social control in both the narrow sense of achieving discipline in the classroom and the wider sense of contributing to the promotion of a static social order generally.... In our analysis of the theory and practice of the teachers in their classroom activity, we observed them subject to conflicting expectations and ambivalencies stemming from several sources. The practical implications of the child centred methodology were not clearly articulated amongst the staff community. In operation they tended to mean the 'free day' or the 'integrated curriculum', both these and other notions being loosely formulated. These became, in practice, organizational precepts whereby children tended to be given wide discretion to choose between many activities, and in so far as they appeared to choose to do things, i.e. satisfied the conditions for 'busyness', the child centred approach was assumed to be in operation. The teachers seemed to be left unclear as to their precise role in interacting with their pupils to further their development in various approved areas of knowledge. The vocabulary appealed to such concepts as 'needs', 'interests' and children's 'readiness' without specifying their operational indicators. The teachers' rationales fall back upon the idea that 'what children do they need to do', 'it is important for children to be happy at school' or 'play is work'. These are operationalized or informed in practice by the teachers' common sense concerning how normal children behave, derived from their immediate colleagues, from the wider context of their professional relationships and from their continuing biography as lower middle class members of society.... [In the primary school studied] the teachers are able to organize the environment of their classrooms to allow a wide range of choice but have to generate their own theory of instruction for the children.

The headmaster publicly endorses the view that the school is committed to the teaching of both traditional and new types of knowledge. As a progressive school the children should be allowed to integrate their own knowledge, develop at their own pace, according to their own present needs and interests. But the school has also to account for itself in the established way by teaching literacy and numeracy. The teaching of reading, writing, mathematical concepts and computing skills are thus recognized as important in the teacher's work. The teachers are, however, in a difficult position because it is not immediately clear how these can be 'developed from within' the child rather than through the routine intervention and structuring by the teachers of their pupils' activities. They are confronted with the complex problem of cognizing, monitoring and further facilitating the children's development without adopting a too directive or formal approach. This is compounded by the age range of the children and their clearly differentiated levels of achievement.

The solution adopted by the different teachers we have observed consists of operationalizing in varying ways the 'integrated day' with a tendency to adopt the therapeutic ethos or image of the school as presented by the headmaster. Publicly, the school operates as a progressive educational establishment while in the practice of these teachers and in the private views of the headmaster, it is also a socializing institution, civilizing a deprived portion of the population. . . .

Perhaps the central paradox of the substantive level of our study relates to the operationalization of the child centred methodology and the relationship between intentions and outcomes. In the abstract, child centred ideology, the teacher operates by 'knowing the child'. . . . The individual child in this situation, unlike in more formal and traditional approaches to education, really matters. At the level of the teachers' classroom practice and in the ethos of the school, the aim is towards a fluid harmony of co-operative actors allowing full and free expression on the part of the children. . . . We have tried to show how the constraints beyond and within the classroom situation prevent the teacher from achieving the high degree of consociality which the abstract ideology requires . . . whilst the teachers display a moral concern that every child matters, in practice there is a subtle process of sponsorship developing where opportunity is being offered to some and closed off to others. Social stratification is emerging.

We have tried to show how these practices are a function of the constraints both ideological and material which influence the practice of the individual teacher. . . .

. . . The processes we have observed in the classroom and referred to as the social structuring of pupils' identities can be seen as the initial stages of the institutionalization of social selection for the stratification system. As studies of differential achievement have shown, early success and failure in the classroom is of crucial importance for entry into the occupational structure, and hence the class structure at different levels. Moreover we have suggested not merely that there is a developing hierarchy of pupils but also the content of education is being selectively organized and socially transmitted. The social stratification of knowledge and ignorance which characterizes the wider society thus impinges on the child in his earliest encounters with formal institutional mechanisms. In addition within the school, social control is being maintained through the initiation of pupils, teachers and parents into appropriate attitudes and modes of action and, when these break down, through the operation of constraint against those who challenge established interests. . . . Whilst educators and parents may view the educational system as the locale where talent is developed and individual needs responded to, its 'real' function may be very different and related more to the social demands of established interests in the macro structure than to the requirements of individual pupils. As we have observed in the classroom, the social advancement of the few depends upon a denial of the same for the many, as pupils' careers are socially structured through the activities of educators who are themselves enclosed within a wider structure of constraints over which they have little control.

It is here that the real irony and paradox of child centred progressivism as an educational ideology is revealed. Developing as a reaction to what was held to be the rigidity of traditional educational structures which denied opportunity to the many, the progressive child centred movement was impelled by a moral rhetoric which sought to re-establish the rights of the individual for freedom, self-development and individual expression over and above the demands of the society....

We suggest that the rise of progressivism and the institutional supports it receives are a function of its greater effectiveness for social control and structuring aspirations compared with more traditional educational ideologies whose legitimacy was already being questioned. Within child centred progressivism, far wider ranges of the child's attributes become legitimate objects of evaluative scrutiny and explanatory variable in the construction of success and failure. Not merely intellectual but social, emotional, aesthetic and even physical criteria are often employed in the processing of pupils in educational institutions, the social control possibilities thus being enhanced.... We are suggesting that modern child centred education is an aspect of romantic radical conservatism.

Classroom Interactions and Pupils' Perceptions

(From Nash, R., 1973, *Classrooms Observed*, London, Routledge and Kegan Paul, pp. 16–17, 90–2, 101–2.)

This material has been taken from the report of a three-year observational study in primary and secondary schools, which explored how children through day-to-day interactions with teachers and fellow pupils formed concepts of themselves (their ability, status, identity) and developed consistent patterns of behaviour appropriate to their self-concepts. As Nash argues elsewhere in his book,' the essential cultural messages of the school are conveyed through an incalculable number of interactions between teachers and pupils. These messages are only marginally concerned with school learning in the normal sense of the term but they have everything to do with the child's status, with his self-image, and with his aspirations for the future.' The two small-scale studies reported here (the first in a primary school and the other in a secondary school) support the author's interactionist stance and demonstrate how close were children's and teachers' perceptions of the class positions of individual pupils. Nash's work suggests a partial explanation of why working-class children are in general less successful in school than their middle-class counterparts. It may be that teachers' lower expectations for working-class children, documented in a number of studies, are conveyed directly or indirectly through day-to-day interactions to the pupils who use them to build up their identities which in turn influence their future behaviour and progress in school (see also pp. 220–224).

I set out to establish precisely how accurate children's perceptions of their class positions were. First of all I obtained from three teachers rank orders of ability on three measures; number, writing, and reading, for the children in their classes. Each child was then seen individually and asked to point to the names, written on cards arranged randomly on the desk before him, of the 'people a wee bit better than you at number'. The same procedure was followed for testing whom the child thought better than himself at reading and writing. From these data it was possible to estimate each child's self-perceived class position. For example, if a child pointed to ten children as a 'wee bit better' than himself, he was assumed to regard his position in the class as eleventh. It is necessary to be quite clear about what was happening here. The teachers' rankings were made at my request and were not communicated to their pupils. In theory the children should have had no idea of their class positions and had I directly asked children what their positions were I suspect I should have got some strange answers. But tested in this indirect way children aged as young as eight gave themselves positions which correlated highly with those assigned them by their teacher. The complete figures are given in Table I....

Table 1 *Correlations between teachers' ranks on school subjects and pupils' own estimates of their positions*

Age	Reading	Writing	Number	Totals	N
8	0.69	0.44	0.64	0.85	28
10	0.31	0.20	0.45	0.46	30
11	not applicable	0.47	0.80	0.82	33

[A similar investigation was carried out in a secondary class.] ... Each pupil was seen individually and presented with a set of thirty-five cards on each of which was written the name of one of the children in his class. The pupil was asked to sort the cards into three groups: (i) a group 'a bit more clever than you', (ii) a group 'about the same as you', and (iii) a group 'not so clever as you'. The names of the pupils placed in each group were noted. To establish the child's estimate of his position he was given those he had named 'about the same' as himself and asked to 'put them in the right order'. His own name is included in this group. If, for example, a child placed ten pupils in group (i), and twelve in group (iii), his estimate of his position must lie between eleventh and twenty-third. If the pupil then places himself fourth in group (ii) his position must be fourteenth. This procedure avoided giving children the rather tedious task of ranking thirty-five cards. The resulting positions were rank-ordered. Ties were permitted.

A second measure was obtained by counting the number of times each pupil was named by his classmates as 'more clever than me', subtracted from the number of times he was mentioned as 'slower than me'. For example, a child named as 'more clever than me' by twenty of his classmates and as 'slower than me' by twelve would receive a score of +8. These scores which ranged from −31 to +34 were ranked. Ties were permitted. This rank was assumed to correspond to the position each child was collectively seen to hold.

There are now two ranks: (i) derived from pupils' estimates of their own positions, and (ii) derived from pupils' estimates of each other's positions. These were found to be significantly correlated, r. 0.72. Analysis of the data shows that for thirteen of the thirty-three pupils tested (two were absent) the two ranks were within plus or minus 3 points. Another eleven pupils saw themselves as within plus or minus 6.5 points of their position as seen by others. Five children badly underestimated their position as seen by others and were not thought to be as poor as they thought themselves. Four overestimated their positions and thought themselves better than their classmates believed.

The interactionist theory discussed [previously] predicts that children perceived unfavourably by their teachers will develop unfavourable self-concepts and that these will be reflected in the low class positions these children will believe themselves to have. Conversely it predicts that children favourably perceived will believe themselves to be highly placed in the class. This hypothesis may be tested by correlating the teachers' perceptions of their pupils (construct rank) with the rank derived from the pupils' own estimates of their positions. The correlation was r. 0.54, which is significant at the 0.05 level. From this it follows that the correlation between the teachers' perceptions and the pupils' estimates of each other's class positions will be high. It is, in fact, r. 0.69, a result which may be taken to reflect the high degree of agreement between the pupils' and the teachers' perceptions of the relative abilities in the classroom. . . .

. . . I have argued that from an interactionist standpoint the child can be understood to be actively engaged in working out through his day-to-day interactions in the classroom a pattern and style of behaviour from which he and others build up expectations for his future behaviour. That others in the classroom are engaged in a continual process of evaluation has been demonstrated by the high correlation between the perception a child has of his class position and the perception his classmates have of it. It is becoming clear that within the classroom there is a commonly agreed body of knowledge about the relative abilities of all its members. These results may be taken to support the interactionist theory that children are continually engaged in forming a concept of themselves and developing a consistent pattern of behaviour appropriate to this self-concept. There is evidence that the firmer these patterns of behaviour become the more unshakeable the models of them constructed by others will be and the more power their expectations will have in confirming the others' behaviour. And the models and expectations children have of each other may be as important in determining academic behaviour as those of the teacher.

The Nature of Infant Education: A Sociological Perspective

(From King, R., 1978, *All Things Bright and Beautiful?: A Sociological Study of Infants' Classrooms*, Wiley, pp. 143–6, 146, 147, 148–9.)

In his book from which this extract is taken, King provides a detailed sociological account of English infant education based on close observation and discussion of practices in three infant schools, including one (Burnley Road) designated as a social priority school because of its high proportion of disadvantaged children. In describing and explaining the activities occurring in the classrooms, he relates teachers' actions to the 'child-centred' educational ideology they hold with its elements of (i) developmentalism (belief in the existence and importance of physical, intellectual and emotional development); (ii) individualism; (iii) play as learning; and (iv) childhood innocence. (This constitutes a variant of 'liberal romantic' ideology discussed on pp. 63–77.) He shows how this ideology gives teachers a sense of what infant children and infant education are and how they should be. He argues that where (as at Burnley Road) there is a discrepancy between how children actually behave and how teachers assume they should behave, the latter resort to a 'family-home background theory' which, in crude summary, suggests that children's poor behaviour and progress are due to the conditions and the way they are brought up by their families (see Goodacre's 'good' and 'poor' homes, pp. 220–224). Through this means teachers preserve their belief in the innocence of childhood and their own identity as effective practitioners. The passage below indicates some of King's summary reflections on the nature of infant education in the light of his empirical work.

I pointed out that the child-centred ideologies which represent what is 'real' about children and their learning to infants' teachers, are social constructs; there was a time when they did not exist and they are not accepted by everyone. Children have learnt and still learn, in some parts of the world, basic skills by methods far removed from those I have described. Within this perspective, classroom practices and ideologies may be discussed and evaluated independentally of any claims for their being the best or the truth.

Play

Among the many purposes they attributed to play. the teachers emphasized 'play as learning'. Children have learnt and do learn the three R's in other times and places without any play elements, so that this cannot be essential. Since all children did 'learning by playing' I have no adequate way of estimating its effectiveness in the three schools. The only easy judgement possible is whether it is desirable. Whether they learnt what their teachers thought they did or not, most children seemed happy when they played, and on this account alone it could be considered worthwhile, particularly at Burnley Road, especially if the teachers' ideas about the limited nature of their activities outside school were correct.

But does play get in the way of learning? Would the children at Burnley Road have mastered the basics better if they did them all day and never played? This idea was part of the pre-school intervention programme described by Bereiter and Engelmann (1966) in the U.S.A. English infants' teachers would find the old-fashioned didactic methods they used an affront to their child-centred ideologies, but of all the programmes tried, it seems one of the most effective in terms of improved test scores.

Classroom Control

[Previously] I suggested that a major element in the oblique forms of social control used by teachers was the idea that young children were innocent in their intentions, even if their behaviour was defined as naughty. There are two important considerations that follow from this practice, one theoretical and the other practical.

This particular view of innocence touches upon the relationship between man and society and the issue of free will. It is recognized that men make society but are also constrained by it. The phenomenologists stress the first part of the relationship, the marxists and functionalists the latter. Weber tried to contain both in his sociology, in that, given the inseparable nature of man and society, it was still possible to pose that an individual may freely choose a course of action against societal constraints. At what point may children be regarded as being in this position? When may it be judged that a child has freely chosen to break the rules established by the powerful in the society of the classroom? I have suggested that the teachers' actions were such that the children tended to conform with the definitions that informed those actions, which were based upon child-centred ideologies. At Burnley Road the definition of innocence was difficult for the teachers to sustain. Would their dilemmas about the children's behaviour have been eased or solved if they had interpreted naughty behaviour as an outcome of the children's free choice, that they intended or chose to be naughty? Would the occasional pinching, punching, and pushing have stopped if they had not ignored it?

The forms of child behaviour approved by the teachers included being quiet, busy, tidy, helpful, kind, and conventionally polite, and much of their control was directed towards promoting them. Are these desirable qualities in a child, or should they be changed?

Children's Interests

Many classroom activities were based upon teachers' imputations of children's interests, but [elsewhere] I described how interests could be induced and others ignored by the teacher. Should the children's 'true' interests have been completely acknowledged and incorporated into the educational process as part of the idea of child-centredness? At Burnley Road this would have meant a curriculum for the boys which legitimated their manifest interest in fighting, wars, and violence in general, an interest which posed a problem for the teachers because it contradicted the definition of the children as innocent.

Given that many interests were induced by the teachers, the range and nature of these could be questioned. This might involve enquiry into the education of infants' teachers, and how, in my observations, its products claimed no special body of knowledge other than that of children and their learning, but were sometimes ignorant of that knowledge which they defined everyone should have. This implies that the child-centred education of teachers requires supplementing with more general education.

The Three R's

[In a previous chapter] I reported the primacy that teachers gave to the three R's. It may be thought an absurd question to pose whether children should learn to read, write, and do sums. Most people would regard these as being basic competences for adult life in contemporary British society, although Neil Postman (1973) has questioned the necessity of being able to read, a skill required in order to understand the argument he has written.

The child-centred ideology does not justify the learning of the three R's, but the methods of teaching and learning them were based upon the presumed nature of the child, and his presumed interests. Given the varying definitions of reading readiness by teachers and their invariably real consequences, the concept of readiness would appear to be very questionable, indeed at Burnley Road some teachers had laid it aside. This suggests that some children not manifesting 'readiness' could be started reading earlier in their school careers. This does not automatically mean that they would become better readers.

The content of the reading provided for children is based upon their imputed interests and upon assumptions about the need to protect their innocence. Does the nature of the story worlds so presented contribute to the sex and social class differences in reading attainment? (The latter was suggested by the Plowden Committee.) The worlds of Peter and Jane, and of Ken, Pat, and Pipkin are clearly more middle class than working class. Would their reading levels rise if the children of Burnley Road read stories reflecting their own family lives, including absent fathers and successions of 'uncles'?

The Family-Home Background Theory

Teachers created and managed classroom situations in which children exhibited behaviour and progress which the teachers sometimes found incompatible with their definition of what children should be, and they explained the discrepancies by means of the family — home background theory, which preserved the innocence of the children and their own identities as good teachers and left unquestioned their child-centred ideologies and practices. The posing of the family — home background theory was made easier, if not actually made possible, by their child-centred practices, which presented them with the 'evidence' of the children's homes and families through their writing, drawing, and talking. Taking an interest in the whole child legitimated knowing about his or her life outside the classroom. Thus the child-centredness permitted the family-home background theory and was protected by it.

It is not easy to imagine a case where a teacher would know nothing of a child's background without changing many established practices. If teachers were to abandon the family-home background theory they would have to conclude that any 'problems' were either due to the children's deficiencies or to their own. The acceptance of either would seriously question their ideologies.

Infant Education — A Middle-Class Institution?

The nature of infant education has been explored mainly in terms of the children's behaviour and progress that were defined as problems by the teachers. From this it might be concluded that it is basically a middle-class institution. There are a number of initial reservations that should be made about this view. Firstly, although there were social class differences in mean reading ages and in teachers' assessments of behaviour and attitude to work, it was not the case that all or even most middle-class children did better than all or most working-class children in the same school. Many working-class were assessed as well behaved and hard working, and had high reading quotients. Statistical differences between social groups draw attention away from their similarities. Secondly, the sex differences in these assessments were arguably bigger than the class ones. Do these make infant education a female education or even a middle-class female one, since it is this group who are assessed most highly?

The analysis of the existing system of infant education cannot ignore its relation to the social and economic structure, but this relationship is not a sufficient criterion for its evaluation, which depends principally upon the acceptability of the value-judgements upon which it is based. In the teachers' terms these were that children should be able to read, write, and do sums; they should experience painting, drawing, craft work, singing, dancing, and physical exercise; they should be happy, helpful, quiet, tidy, clean, and kind. They should learn through play and through their presumed interests, and treated in such a way as to protect and respect their imputed innocence. These are posed as intrinsically valuable for all young children irrespective of their sex, social origins, or social destinies. From this point of view infant education may be regarded as the most egalitarian sector of English education.

References

BEREITER, C. and ENGELMANN, S. (1966) *Teaching Disadvantaged Children in the Pre-School*, Prentice-Hall.

POSTMAN, N. (1973) 'The politics of reading', in KEDDIE, N. (Ed.), *Tinker, Taylor: The Myth of Cultural Deprivation*, Harmondsworth, Penguin.

Sex and Social Class: A Case-Study

(From Hartley, D., 1978, 'Sex and social class: A case-study of an infants' school', *British Educational Research Journal*, 4, 2, pp. 75–81.)

The concern of sociologists with class-related inequalities has been complemented in recent years by developing interest in the study of sex-related inequalities in education, particularly the ways schools play a part in reproducing the traditional gender relationship, which works to the disadvantage of women. Studies have been conducted of the differential treatment accorded the sexes in schools, but almost all of these have been concerned with secondary-aged pupils. This case-study, dealing with class- and sex-related differentiation, is an exception. The author examines the definitions held by infant teachers of boys and girls as pupils and explores in a preliminary way the consequences of these definitions for the ways in which the teachers treated the children in class. The small-scale, exploratory nature of the research and the tentative nature of its findings need to be stressed.

. . . The research setting was a large (n = 393) urban infant school in the Southwest of England. The sex and social class composition of the school was as follows: working class boys, 24.8 per cent; working class girls, 25.1 per cent; middle class girls, 22.2 per cent; and middle class boys, 27.9 per cent. Social class was determined by the father's occupation and was classified using the Registrar General's (1971) classification of occupations. A simple manual/nonmanual dichotomy was used. It should be noted, however, that these working class pupils might tend to resemble the children of what Toomey (1969) has called 'home-centred' working class parents who are owner-occupiers of well-decorated homes and who tend to vote Conservative. Such parents tend to have high aspirations for their sons. Some 72.5 per cent of the parents in the present study were owner-occupiers; 4.5 per cent were council house tenants. Over the last decade, voters in the area have returned Conservative candidates. The pupil-teacher ratio was 25.5:1, there being fifteen full-time classroom teachers, of whom two were men. The pupils were taught in a manner more traditional than 'progressive'. There were no open-space teaching areas.

The study had two main aims. The first was to obtain the definitions held by teachers of the pupils in each of the aforementioned sex/social class categories. The second was to find out if these definitions had consequences for the ways in which teachers treated these pupils in the classroom.

Related to the first aim were two subsidiary ones: how did the pupils themselves nominate the classroom behaviour of their classmates? How did the teachers report the classroom behaviour of their pupils in their year-end reports? Thus these subsidiary aims can be regarded as different indicators focusing on the same issue — the classroom behaviour of pupils who belong in these different sex/social class categories.

Methodology

The Teachers' Definitions

Rather than impose the researcher's constructs on the teacher for the latter to respond to, it was decided to generate second-order constructs from the teachers' commonsense definitions of boys and girls as pupils. Each teacher was interviewed and asked to define any differences she saw in boys and girls as pupils in the school. A content analysis of the interview transcripts revealed a set of the most frequently mentioned constructs and their semantic equivalents. This is not to suggest that all of the teachers would completely agree on the meaning of each construct but, having shared a common professional setting, it may be suggested that these meanings may approximate each other (Becker *et al.*, 1961). From these first order constructs, a set of five pairs of semantic opposites was compiled so as to form the scales of a seven-point semantic differential type of rating scale. The scales thus generated were: able/unable to concentrate; immature/ mature; tidy/untidy; gentle/rough; and noisy/quiet. Each pupil was then rated by his classroom teacher against each of these five scales. The scores were then grouped on the basis of sex and social class.

The Consequences of the Teachers' Definitions

'If men define situations as real, they are real in their consequences.' So said W.I. Thomas (1928). To apply his theorem here, it would be necessary to ask: What are the classroom consequences of these teachers' definitions of their pupils? To partly answer this, a three-hour nonparticipant observation period of each teacher was undertaken. In a period of observation such as this the observer enters a 'naturalistic' setting. Although the setting here was not prestructured by the researcher, the observational procedure was. There were two reasons for this. Firstly, since the purpose of the observation was to see if there existed a 'link' between the two research instruments; the rating scales and the observation. This was itself provided by the employment of the ten behavioural dimensions used in the five ratings scales, which themselves were derived from the interviews: noisy; quiet; rough; gentle; tidy — and so on. During the observation, whenever a teacher nominated a pupil as revealing one of these types of behaviour, this, and the situation in which the nomination was made, was noted. In all cases an attempt was made to interpret the meaning of the teacher's utterance or gesture. Secondly, the observational procedure was kept constant so as to permit inter-classroom comparison. That said, in theory each pupil would have ten scores, one for each behaviour dimension, at the end of the observation period. In practice, however, most teachers were more concerned with pupil concentration, noisiness and tidiness. Their thoughts on the maturity of the pupil were rarely uttered except to inform a pupil that he was 'acting silly' or 'acting like a baby'.

The Pupils' Nominations of the Classroom Behaviour of their Classmates

Research with young children is difficult. They are suggestible to clues and lack the rudiments of reading and writing. In order to find out how the pupils defined their classmates' behaviour, a sociometric device, the *Guess Who?* Test, was orally administered to each pupil. The procedure is as follows: A pupil is asked a question such as, 'Can you think of anyone in your class who is often noisy?' The pupil then names those pupils whom he feels fit that description. Here, each pupil was asked that question and nine others which contained the remaining nine behavioural categories mentioned in the rating scales. Thus: 'Can you think of anyone in your class who is often noisy/tidy/rough/quiet?' — and so on. One point should be noted. An attempt was made to use their teacher's own semantic equivalent of each of these ten dimensions so that they would be recognisable to the pupil. Instead of being asked, say, which pupils were often 'noisy', this could be replaced by, 'someone who is always chattering', or whatever utterance the teacher usually made to convey the meaning of 'noisy'.

The Teachers' Year-end Reports

These reports are succinct verbal records of how the teacher defines a pupil's work and behaviour. The comments probably would tend not to go into detail about each of the ten behavioural categories so far referred to; indeed there would be no guarantee that the teacher would mention any of these. Thus, if the comment itself is general, so the analytical method of them should mirror this. A simple three-choice evaluation of each report was made ('positive', 'negative', and 'undecided'). Of course this evaluation is that of the researcher, not the teacher. To help interpret the intended meaning of the teacher a semantic differential, using scales generated from the interviews, was constructed and each teacher rated the concept: 'The Successful First School Pupil'. The results of this, and the researcher's own recall of the teacher actually teaching, were of help in evaluating each report. A second, female researcher also rated the reports and a 90.3 per cent agreement was reached (the names of the pupils were deleted from the record cards to minimise sex-bias).

Results

The Teachers' Rating Definitions

Table I shows that on three scales working class pupils were rated less 'favourably' (more unable to concentrate; untidier; and noisier). Significant sex differences obtained within both social groups, the more so within the middle class, nonmanual sample. Within the latter, boys were rated as significantly rougher, noisier, untidier and more unable to concentrate when compared to girls. Within the working class group, girls were significantly more gentle and quiet. If, as a crude indicator, the mean scores of Table I are inspected, nonmanual girls are the most favourably rated on four scales whilst manual boys are the least favourably rated on all scales.

The Consequences of the Teachers' Definitions

The results in Table II indicate social class differences in the teachers' treatment of the pupils but these are not significant except that nonmanual pupils were more frequently nominated for not concentrating. But manual, as opposed to nonmanual, pupils were in receipt of more teacher utterances, as were boys, as opposed to girls. This might suggest that teachers prefer manual pupils and boys, but this is to be doubted since, within both social classes, boys received significantly more nominations for being noisy.

The Pupils' Nominations of the Behaviour of their Classmates

Table III reveals an absence of any significant social class differences, but, within each social class group, the sex differences are highly significant. Boys received significantly more 'unfavourable' nominations for being rough, noisy, untidy, immature and not concentrating. If the percentages are inspected it can be seen that of the four categories of pupil, manual boys were the most frequently nominated for being noisy, Rough, untidy and for not concentrating, whilst nonmanual girls were the least nominated on these dimenstions. With regard to the 'favourable' nominations, nonmanual girls received significantly more for being gentle, concentrating, quiet and tidy. Within the manual sample, the only significant sex difference was that girls were the more nominated for being gentle.

The Teachers' Year-end Reports

Table IV indicates both social class and within-social class sex differences. The reports of manual pupils were rated significantly less positively than those of their nonmanual counterparts. Within both social class groups, girls were given significantly more favourable reports. Again, if the percentages are inspected, nonmanual girls were reported upon the most favourably and manual boys the least favourably.

Discussions

Whilst interpreting the results, a number of considerations should be kept in mind. Firstly, the findings are based on aggregated data. Within classrooms, the data was subdivided into four sets: nonmanual/manual boys; nonmanual/manual girls. However, the sample sizes within these subdivisions were too small for statistical analysis. As such, an aggregative fallacy may have been perpetrated since events within individual classrooms may not reflect the findings given here. Secondly, the study makes no claims about sex and class differences on cognitive matters save to say that there may be some correlation between cognitive and behavioural dimensions in the ways in which teachers define their pupils (Williams, 1976). Thirdly, the results show some correspondence between the teachers' rating definitions and classroom practice. Table I revealed trends, though not significant, for manual pupils and boys within both social class groups to be more frequently nominated for revealing inappropriate behaviour. It might have been the case that had the classroom observation been longer, then more discernible and perhaps significant trends might have emerged. Fourthly, the present study is an exploratory case study and extrapolations to other settings should be made cautiously.

That the teachers' ratings should have revealed such significant social class differences is surprising since, as mentioned, the working class pupils here would seem to come from 'educogenic', 'home-centred' families. Noteworthy too is the absence of social class differences in the pupils' nominations of their classmates' behaviour, and this may indicate a lack of

Table I. Teachers' ratings of the pupils in their classrooms

	All manual x̄	All non-manual x̄	t	df	NM boys x̄	NM girls x̄	t	df	M boys x̄	M girls x̄	t	df
Able/unable to concentrate	3.898	3.218	3.055**	396	3.734	2.693	4.221***	199	3.989	3.823	0.728	195
Immature/mature	4.294	3.905	1.926	396	4.133	4.307	0.676	199	3.926	4.039	0.252	195
Tidy/untidy	3.796	3.239	2.632**	396	3.672	2.682	3.143**	199	3.958	3.509	1.911	195
Gentle/rough	3.472	3.512	0.234	396	3.708	3.261	2.180	199	3.970	3.009	3.302**	195
Noisy/quiet	3.695	4.448	2.776**	396	3.946	5.091	5.066***	199	3.832	4.676	3.221**	195

*p<0.05   **p<0.01   ***p<0.001

Table II. Teachers' classroom nominations of pupil behaviour

	All manual (n = 176) % nominated[1]	All nonmanual (n = 183) % nominated	X²	NM boys (n = 104) % nominanted	NM girls (n = 79) % nominated	X²	M boys (n = 104) % nominated	M girls (n = 86) % nominated	X² (n = 90)
Concentrating	31.25	24.04	NS	21.15	27.85	NS	32.56	30.00	NS
Not concentrating	46.02	28.96	11.09***	34.62	21.52	NS	53.49	44.30	NS
Noisy	25.57	19.67	NS	26.92	10.13	6.829**	33.72	17.78	5.06*
Tidy	7.95	6.56	NS	7.69	5.06	NS	5.81	10.00	NS
Untidy	7.38	7.10	NS	10.58	2.53	NS	10.47	4.44	NS

*p<0.05   **p<0.01   ***p<0.001 (1 df)   NS not significant

[1]Pupils are regarded as having been 'nominated' or 'not nominated'; the number of nominations is disregarded.

Table III. Pupils' 'Guess Who' nominations of the behaviour of their classmates

Behaviour	All manual (n = 184) % nominated[1]	All nonmanual (n = 189) % nominated	X²	NM boys (n = 105) % nominated	NM girls (n = 84) % nominated	X²	M boys (n = 87) % nominated	M girls (n = 97) % nominated	X²
Gentle	69.57	67.72	NS	57.14	80.95	11.037***	51.72	85.57	15.563***
Rough	50.00	40.74	NS	60.95	15.48	38.86***	87.76	20.62	68.96***
Concentrating	70.65	71.43	NS	60.95	84.52	11.576***	75.86	65.97	NS
Lacks concentration	61.41	52.91	NS	67.62	34.52	19.261***	70.11	53.61	4.599*
Noisy	69.02	65.08	NS	77.14	50.00	13.95***	89.66	50.52	31.32***
Quiet	70.65	75.66	NS	66.67	86.90	9.254**	65.50	75.25	NS
Immature	57.07	52.91	NS	70.48	30.95	27.418***	75.86	40.20	22.34***
Mature	62.50	60.34	NS	55.24	66.67	NS	55.17	69.07	NS
Tidy	70.11	71.43	NS	57.14	89.29	22.076***	73.56	67.00	NS
Untidy	63.04	55.56	NS	74.29	32.14	31.87***	77.01	50.52	13.786***

*p<0.05   **p<0.01   ***p<0.001 (1 df)   NS not significant
[1]Pupils are regarded as having been 'nominated' or 'not nominated'; the number of nominations is disregarded.

Table IV. Analysis of year-end reports of pupils

All manual (n = 159) % rated as:			All nonmanual (n = 170)				M boys (n = 83)			M girls - 76)				NM boys (n = 97)			NM girls (n = 73)			
+ive	−ive	?	+ive	−ive	?	X²	+ive	−ive	?	+ive	−ive	?	X²	+ive	−ive	?	+ive	−ive	?	X²
50.31	27.67	22.90	65.88	11.18	43.53	13.98***	39.8	38.6	21.7	61.8	15.8	22.4	10.053**	54.6	16.5	28.9	80.8	4.10	15.1	11.486**

**p<0.01   ***p<0.001 with 2 df

social class awareness on the part of very young children. But the importance of the study is that within-social class sex differences are highlighted by three indicators; teachers' ratings, pupils' nominations, and the year-end reports. These sex differences appear to obtain more within the middle class sample. The findings suggest that the pre-school sex-roles of children within the same social class background do not equally prepare them for the pupil role. Indeed there is good evidence that pre-school sex-role socialisation does differ within both social class groups (Newson & Newson. 1968). In short, the notion that working class pupils of both sexes may be ill-prepared for classroom life may be as unfounded as the notion that middle class pupils of both sexes are well-prepared.

References

BECKER, H.S. (1961) *Boys in White: Student Culture in Medical School*, University of Chicago Press.

BRANDIS, W. and BERNSTEIN, B. (1974) *Selection and Control*, London, Routledge and Kegan Paul.

HUTCHISON, D. and MCPHERSON, A. (1976) 'Competing inequalities: The sex and social class structure of the first year Scottish university student, 1962–1972' *Sociology*, 10, pp. 111–16.

KING, R.A. (1971) 'Unequal access in education — sex and social class', *Social and Economic Administration*, 5, pp. 167–75.

NEWSON, J. and NEWSON, E. (1968) *Four Years Old in an Urban Community*, London. Allen and Unwin.

REGISTRAR GENERAL (1971) *Classification of Occupations* London, HMSO.

THOMAS, W.I. (1928) *The Child in America*, New York, Knopf.

TOOMEY, D.M. (1969) 'Home-centred working class parents' attitudes towards their sons' education and careers', *Sociology*, pp. 299–320.

WILLIAMS, T. (1976) 'Teacher prophecies and the inheritance of inequality' *Sociology of Education*, 49, pp. 223–35.

5 Primary Education: Perspectives on Children's Learning

Introduction

Psychology, the study of behaviour, encompasses a broad field, and attempts to explain how and why living creatures come to act as they do. From psychological research as a whole, together with specific studies directed towards educational issues, there has emerged a psychology of education and child development, which has particular relevance for teachers and education. Among other things it is concerned with questions of how people acquire and use language, of how they come to think and solve problems in a variety of situations, of how social and emotional development takes place, and of how all these are represented to themselves and for others.

Each of these aspects involves complex interactions of biological and social factors. As a result of these interactions, people learn to make moral judgements and decisions, know about sex-appropriate behaviour and increasingly come to understand the viewpoint of others and so modify their own behaviour. How it all takes place is far from clear and over its history, psychology has offered models to explain processes in behavioural developments. Those most influential on education have been the Piagetian school of thought (see pp. 247–261) and the radically different view of the behaviourists, notably B.F. Skinner. Piaget's detailed studies, first of his own children, and later of others in Geneva, have given us a picture of the child's thinking and construction of reality proceeding in qualitatively different stages. From the first reflex actions of the newborn infant to the highly developed, flexible, internalized actions which constitute the thoughts of the adolescent and adult in Western cultures, the human being is seen as acting upon his physical and social environment in the development of logical intelligence. Although in his later years, Piaget took more account of the effect of specific experiences in developing thought structures, his theory in general has tended to underplay the role of the child's environment in development and particularly problems of representing action in language forms. By contrast, radical behaviourist psychologists have regarded the child at birth as being a ' "tabula rasa", a blank slate, on which experience writes'. This child is seen as passively reacting to stimuli, and all behaviours including language are viewed as learned by means of the reinforcements which the environment provides. Much of the research on which behaviourist theories rest has been carried out with rats, pigeons and monkeys and applied to human beings. In the field of language which only humans possess, the theory would limit human beings to production of what has been learned through imitation, and cannot account for the novel, creative aspects of language, as can generative theories of language. In turn, the latter have been criticized for their assumption of innate competences which are believed to be triggered off simply by exposure to language.

Neither view is complete. Whereas Piaget's work has led to a greater understanding of developmentally-based changes in the child's thinking, and conversely behaviourists have stressed the importance of the environment in learning, psychologists now think in terms of a complex interplay between biologically given tendencies to act in particular ways and the quality of the environment to facilitate or impede their realization. A reconciliation of the two extremes is emerging in psychology, and has been given impetus through a social learning modification of behaviourist research (see pp. 295–301). In this, the social environment has importance as a source of models for learning, and the child is seen as active in extracting key features from experience. The child is thought of as approaching each social and natural-physical experience with intention, using hypothesizing and testing to build a model of representation or cognitive map. This is a set of understandings about the world, and undergoes considerable refinement and extension by means of developing abilities to perceive similarities and differences, identity, equivalence, contrasts and relationships. The existing set of understandings is brought to bear on a given new experience and what makes sense to the child at the time is the means by which new understandings or confusions follow. The process is an active one of distillation of experience mediated through the social environment of family, peer group, teachers, other adults and media. It is this process which interacts with the child's unique characteristics.

The extracts selected for this section exemplify the transactional nature of the relationship between the uniqueness of the individual child and features of his environment. Through this, the child understands past and present, and brings meanings to bear on future experience.

The Implications of Piaget's Work

(From Isaacs, N., 1961, *The Growth of Understanding in the Young Child*, Ward Lock, pp. 9–14, 32–5.)

Isaacs was one of a number of psychologists who have interpreted the writings of Piaget and have discussed their implications for education. Here he draws the readers' attention to the importance of not misunderstanding Piaget's work so to constrain expectations of what a child can or cannot do by virtue of chronological age. Development proceeds in stages which are only very approximately age-related. Piaget merely cited the ages at which children in Geneva solved particular problems. These ages are not to be generalized to all children irrespective of culture and individual differences. Of special importance are the implications that the present level of thought structure sets limits to what can be meaningfully learned at a given time, and, from that, that the teacher needs to match work sufficiently closely to extend from existing understanding. This point recurs in other extracts. Isaacs rightly stresses that environment is not ignored by Piaget, but is very much a feature of his theory. According to the latter, development is essentially a question of the child's actions upon the environment, and higher levels of thought represent internalized action in which language comes to substitute for overt action. The weakness here, which is not drawn out by Isaacs, is that Piaget did not differentiate qualitative nor quantitative features of the milieu in which the child grows.

The Piagetian Picture of the Child's Development

1. Keys to the Child's Mental Growth

The main keys to the child's mental growth, as Piaget brings them out, are (i) the paramount part played from the start by his own *action* (ii) the way this turns into a process of *inward building-up*, that is, of forming within his mind a continually extending *structure* corresponding to the world outside.

(i) The Child As Agent (a) Piaget shows how from the beginning, the infant himself takes a controlling hand in procuring and organizing all his experience of the outside world. He follows with his eyes, explores with them, turns his head; explores with his hands, grips, lets go, pulls, pushes; explores with his mouth; moves his body and limbs; explores jointly and alternately with eye and hand, etc. All this brings experiences which come to him as the products of his activities and are formed into psychic schemes

or patterns *keyed* by them. That keying becomes even more clearly marked when, happening upon an interesting experience, he is stimulated to repeat the activity that led to it, and then *goes on* with it or, after an interval, returns to it. This process of absorbing and organizing experiences round the activities that produce them Piaget calls '*assimilation*'. He regards it as our most fundamental process of learning and growth, which indeed goes on for the rest of our lives. However, assimilation is always being modified by an accompanying process of *accommodation*. Many situations or objects resist the activity patterns the child tries on them, and in so doing impose some changes on these patterns themselves. Still others yield *new* results which go to enrich the range or scope of the patterns.

Thus the assimilative processes constantly extend their domain whilst at the same time accommodation steers them into ever more successful *adaptation* to the world. This dual process, and the endeavour to maintain an equal balance between the two sides, are for Piaget the chief controlling factors of intellectual growth.

(b) To begin with, the activities that organize patterns of resulting experiences round them can only be physical, directed to outward objects and situations. Their scope indeed widens all the time, as the child's powers grow and above all as he masters locomotion and his range of exploration and action is thus immensely multiplied. But in the course of the second year, these external activities also develop a great new inward dimension. Language comes in and with it a more and more settled power of evocation and representation of absent things. This power is the main foundation for the unfolding activity of thought. The latter begins essentially as a form of *action in terms of internal images*, and presently of their verbal symbols, extending the range of the child's *physical action on outward objects*. Thought is in fact for Piaget just action carried on inwardly and thus started on a new career of internal organization and growth.

(c) That story goes on developing through all the child's activities, outward and inward, during the next few years; but his most decisive advance usually comes only towards 7–8, when, by various related moves forward, he establishes himself on the level of *structured thinking*. This Piaget calls the stage of *concrete* operations of thought, because it still remains tied to tangible starting-points and goals, taken over from the real world. In the years that follow, the child exploits and consolidates these new-found powers of controlled thinking; but at the same time he prepares the ground for his next and final advance. Between 11 and 14 he attains the power of *abstract* thought — that is, thought emancipated from the given facts of the real world and able to operate freely with its own imagined possibilities and hypotheses. It can work out the logical consequences of these, or vary them or even reverse them, and draw a fresh set of consequences. How much use the child makes of this ability will depend on his bent, interests and native capacity; but in suitable subjects it can lead all the way to the most abstruse forms of logical, mathematical or scientific thought. Yet the link with action remains unbroken. All thought, as Piaget sees it, is operation, and operation is internalized action; it is this that determines the whole of our human experience, all our throught-life and learning, and all human mental growth.

(ii) The Child as Inward Builder   Piaget thus directs our attention to what in fact lies behind our characteristic behaviour as human beings. Right from the start we build up in our minds a kind of working model of the world around us; in other words, a model of a world of persisting and moving objects and recurring happenings set in a framework of space and time and showing a regular order. Piaget shows how far this model-building is carried, in a functional yet unmistakable way, even in our first eighteen months, that is, prior to the help of language or explicit thought. Once the basic model is in our minds, the rest is merely a matter of building on, filling in and organizing; the structure remains the same, even though it is immeasurably expanded and enriched. In fact we carry it with us for the rest of our lives and although we normally take it for granted, it continually *regulates* all our planning and action. We are drawing on it — and relying upon it — whenever we start to *think out* any course of action: its space aspect when we want to get somewhere; its scheme of material objects when we want to make or construct something; its order of events, when we want to bring about or to prevent some happening.

From the appropriate part of the model in our minds we then work out the actual sequence of movements or actions which we shall have to follow. In a great number of cases this process is virtually automatic; our purposes bring into our thoughts the programmes needed to give effect to them, and we get on with these without worrying how we have come by them. If, however, we stumble on a difficulty and need to stop for some real thinking, this may well make us explicitly aware, first, of the scheme in our minds which has carried us so far, secondly of the nature of the present gap in it, and thirdly of what help we might be able to get from bringing further parts of our thought-resources to bear.

If then we consider the whole range of planned courses of action on which we constantly launch ourselves, we can get some measure of the connected and organized scheme of things in our minds on which they must rest. Our plans of course always contemplate the real world itself, in which they are to be realized; but the point is that when we are making them, we are *foreseeing*, *forethinking* and *foreplanning*, and can therefore only be doing so from the model of that real world in our *minds*. We are naturally thinking of the real world, but at that stage we are only *thinking* of it. However our model so truly corresponds to it, at any rate in its main structure, that we can pass straight over from the model to the real world without any further thought. It is only in matters of comparative detail that it is liable to prove wrong or insufficient.

Piaget's work can greatly help us to grasp this situation, since it shows more clearly than anything before just how we build up that structured model of the world in our minds. We are not born with it, but have to construct it piecemeal, right from its foundations. Piaget demonstrates in detail how the child does this, from the first few weeks of his life onward. Here is the briefest outline of the process as he exhibits it.

2.   The Main Building Stages

(i)   First 18 Months; Sensori-Motor Phase   Through a series of revealing tests on his own three infants, Piaget brings out the stages by which the first building up proceeds. The earliest behaviour shows not the least sense of persisting objects or of the most rudimentary space or time relations. But presently it is seen to change, and month by month it takes more account of these features of the world, until the child clearly has in his mind a scheme that corresponds to them. We see him *recognizing* different objects as such and expecting them to persist, to move in space and to display spatial characters and relations. Similarly he *recognizes* different happenings and expects them to take a certain course, expects some of them to lead on to others, and so on. The infant's conduct is now visibly *pre*-adjusted to all this; i.e. it is controlled by something in his mind which regularly anticipates just those features. How he is led to form that controlling schema has already been referred to; he learns by doing and trying, by assimilating all the different experiences that thus come to him, and by constantly varying and extending his experimental activities. And by eighteen months the range and variety of his purposive behaviour already bears witness to the controlling presence in his mind of the sort of basic world-model I have described.

(ii)   18 Months to 4–5 Years: Stage of Intuitive Thought   So much having already been achieved, the child has only to go on to exploit all the further instruments and powers that come to him. He now incessantly expands and enriches, works over, organizes and re-organizes, his inward model of the world. He does so mainly through imaginative play on the one hand and through more exploring and experimenting, combined with questioning, listening and talking, on the other hand. The different kinds of objects and happenings which he can recognize, pre-adjust to, remember and imagine continually increase, whilst at the same time his sense of space-relations and time-relations becomes more varied and better articulated. Yet most of the detailed images and ideas in his mind tend to remain vague and unstable,

and his thinking cannot move away from present situations without losing itself.

(iii) 4–5 Years to 7–8 Years: Advance to Stage of Concrete Operations

Piaget now concentrates above all on the state of the child's main *framework* notions and what happens to them. Thus he examines how children progress in their notions of different aspects of space, of time, of movement and speed, of number and measure, and of elementary logical relations such as those of whole and part, classes and sub-classes, or serial order, etc. By numerous experiments he shows that most 4–5 year olds of average intelligence have as yet no settled notions in any of these fields. Everything is still in a state of flux, nothing is clear or stays put. Size, shape, arrangement, etc. are mixed up with number; distance and length with movement; rate of movement with overtaking or catching up; time with speed, and so on.

The same experiments, however, carried out with children only about a year older show the *beginnings* of a notable change. At least in the simpler cases they can, by trial and error, sort their ideas out, and thus get some first inklings of the true meaning of distance, length, number and the rest. Thereafter there is usually further piecemeal progress and then, perhaps another year on, the scene is transformed. By 7–8 years children deal with most of the concrete experimental situations much as an ordinary adult would. Each of the basic structural concepts is now clear and stable. In Piaget's language, the level of 'conservation' has been reached. That is, distance, length, number, speed, mass, class-inclusion, etc., now each stand for something *constant*, whichever way round it is taken, however it is sub-divided, and, in the case of number however it is arranged in space, concentrated or spread. Moreover we have here concepts that can be linked together in larger structures which in turn have the same character of conservation. In fact various sets of these concepts taken together come to form distinctive schemes of operational thought. That means, schemes of connected relational *reasoning*, either mathematical or logical, such as eventually make up geometry, arithmetic, mathematics at large, mechanics, and the formal logical aspects of all other sciences. That may seem to be looking a long way ahead, and is not properly realized till the stage of full abstract reasoning is reached at 11–14 years. What Piaget establishes, however, is that the first prototypes of these operational ideas, that is, concepts that possess the minimum characters needed, are present in most children's minds from the age of 7–8 years. Thus the basic structure of their world is now properly laid down in their thought, not of course in words, but in functioning ideas. Therefore they can think out, flexibly and successfully, the simple everyday space relations (distances, sizes, etc.), time-relations (intervals, successions, overlaps, etc), or mechanical, numerical and logical relations which we all continually need. How far they have had to travel in order to get to this level is shown in the most illuminating way be Piaget's work on the earlier stages, from about 4–5 years onward. . . .

Educational Bearings of Piaget's Work

1. We should note first of all that whilst Piaget's studies of the earliest years cover the whole basic pattern of learning, later he deals almost solely with *structural* growth, the framework concepts of space, time, number, and so on. We must thus distinguish between the more general bearings of his psychology as a whole, and what his *structural* enquiries imply for the specific education of children in arithmetic, geometry and related fields. There is of course no inconsistency between the two; the latter are a special case of the former. Both merit our most careful attention; the first for educational theory and practice at large, the second for some of its most troublesome applications. [As a preliminary, it is essential to] clear out of the way a double misunderstanding of Piaget's findings, which often hinders their true assessment.

On the one hand his results have been taken to refer to the processes of native growth, or inward *maturation*, of the child's mind. On the other hand, they have been held to establish — or to claim to establish — the actual *age* to which each stage of this maturation is tied. Thus, on such an interpretation, children of 4–5 would be incapable of the idea of number, or of most spatial ideas, or of certain elementary logical ones, etc. Those of about 6 would only just be able to grope their way forward in very easy cases. One would, in fact, have to wait till about 7–8 before one could expect any real grasp of even apparently simple numerical, spatial, temporal or logical relations. This then, if valid, seems to call for drastic re-thinking of much of the work of all our ordinary Infant Schools; but it seems to set a barrier also to what the most 'active' and progressive methods can do for children under 7–8.

However, as already said, all this is but of misunderstanding, even if it has been fostered at times by some a Piaget's own ways of presenting his results. Careful consideration of his work as a whole shows how mistaken is such a reading. First, as regards the relation of age and stage Piaget claims nothing more than that the ranges he cites represent his actual findings on the Genevan school-children who were tested. We find in fact that the ranges given are very wide, besides being mere averages. Furthermore, his detailed figures plainly show a large *overlap* between the stages. Thus some 4–5 year olds produce replies characteristic of the 7–8 average, and some

7–8's respond like average 4–5's. Piaget has himself insisted that his age-ranges are no more than a useful framework of reference for the way in which the stages *succeed* one another; it is the order of succession that matters, and not any particular chronological age.

On the other point, the apparent heavy stress on maturation, the answer is simply that what Piaget is setting out to study is not the differences which different environments might make, but the *common* stages and laws of *all* children's mental growth. There is enough scope in such a study to keep any investigator fully engaged without his going outside that task. This does not, however, mean *denying* the influence of outward factors, or treating mental growth as resulting only from inward maturation. On the contrary, Piaget's whole psychology rests on the principle of continuous *interaction* between the child and the world around him; it is this that furnishes all the material, as well as the motive force, for his intellectual advance. Thus there can be no question for Piaget of any purely internal process of development irrespective of the quality of the environment.

He would hold, of course, like most of us, that the way our human minds grow is at bottom prescribed by our human endowment and capacities, so that if growth goes on at all, it must assume certain characteristic forms. It is these in which he is most interested and on which he concentrates. But on his own premises one would expect that favourable or unfavourable outward conditions would bear strongly on the success and extent of development. The former might go far to promote it; the latter to arrest or warp it. Piaget would certainly have the utmost sympathy with any enquiry that aimed at establishing the *optimum* setting for mental growth. He might indeed well consider that his own findings pointed to what that setting should be, even though it was not for him as a psychologist, but rather for teachers, to work out the practical implications.

These implications do not in fact diminish the teacher's powers and responsibilities in any way, nor do they in the least support any attitude of just waiting whilst the child inwardly matures. The *order* of stages in mental growth is what Piaget is concerned to make clear; but whether they will be passed through with greater or less speed or zest or all-round gain, or whether the later stages will be reached at all, is a wide-open question. From that angle, it may be vitally important whether the educator has or has not provided the right conditions and help for the child.

2. This brings us directly to the light thrown on these conditions by Piaget's own new psychological picture of intellectual growth. Here we can first of all say broadly that what his psychology does is to supply a solid new foundation and a fresh weight and authority for just those pregnant insights which we already owe to the great educational reformers of the past. That

of course becomes very clear, once the false 'maturational' interpretation is corrected, but the actual elements of this new accession of strength to 'active' education merit a special glance.

(i) First and foremost, Piaget brings out all the *psychological* gulf between the true learning that is growth and the so-called learning which is mere verbal training, habit formation, or the mechanical mastery of skills and knacks. The former is our great human achievement, which starts practically from birth and in some degree goes on all our lives. Its main motor throughout is the child's own active doing, and learning from doing. Above all else, it is *cumulative*. That is, it forms a structure in the child's mind which he himself keeps building up. Each new level is only made possible by what has been built before, but then leads on to a further advance, and a greater and richer whole. The second kind of learning, on the other hand, has real value only as far as it provides *working means and tools* for the first type. If treated as an end in itself (whatever show it may make) it becomes worthless. Verbal 'learning' can be 'taught' by drilling and cramming at any time, but tends to be shed almost as soon as the cramming stops. Moreover, if it remains merely verbal, it is only a meaningless 'act', even while it lasts. To *some* extent, of course, it can join up under favourable conditions with the 'real' learning that goes on all the time, and to that extent it achieves true value; but how little that amounts to among average school children is only too lamentably plain.

(ii) True learning is learning not only by doing but also by understanding. That however again means *genuine* understanding, which is intimately linked with doing and largely dependent upon this. As already emphasized, the child constructs in his mind in his first 18 months a basic working model of the world which he can then use for the assimilation of all his new experiences. That assimilation to what he already firmly holds is what brings the sense of understanding to him.

In the course of these further assimilations the original model is itself constantly extended and further filled in. At the same time its content is being sorted and grouped and *ordered* in diverse ways, by various kinds of likenesses and relationships. Furthermore, as 'accommodation' operates, and shortcomings and errors come to light, the model gets revised and, where necessary, re-organized. Thus if the conditions are right, it should steadily grow more comprehensive and better adapted to the real world, and this in turn should make it capable of ever more effective assimilation of new experience. Such assimilation can then more and more truly be called *integration*; that is, integration into an already existing organic scheme.

In this way growth should of its own momentum lead to further growth. It will be seen how essential here is *continuity* of doing and experience. *All the way through, further integration can only be built on effective past integration.* To the extent to which the wrong kind of learning (that is, learning without doing and experiencing without understanding and integration) intrudes into the process, continuity is broken. Thus the very power of future integration, and so of future true learning, is in some degree impaired.

Comprehending the Task: A Re-Examination of Piaget

(From Donaldson, M., 1978, *Children's Minds*, Fontana, pp. 18–24.)

This extract is taken from an influential book which seeks to modify and reinterpret the Piagetian view of children's development outlined earlier (pp. 247–255). This reinterpretation is based partly on a number of studies with children carried out by Donaldson and her associates. One such investigation is described here and relates to children's ability to take account of someone else's spatial perspective. Not only is Piaget's claim disputed, but an important point is made about factors affecting children's performance on tasks. When a child understands what is wanted, performance is better than when the task is not clearly comprehended. This truism is tested in experimental form by Donaldson and her associates, and except for its significance for education, might have been thought to be too obvious to merit research. The extract outlines two important implications for teaching. First, if a task is outside our comprehension, if it does not make sense, then we have only our own point of view to fall back on — an egocentric view. Donaldson argues that this is the case with tests of egocentricity in understanding spatial relations in Piaget's Three Mountains Task. A second implication is that understanding is at first specific to the context in which it occurs and in order to abstract general principles or to form what Piaget called '*structures d'ensemble*' a child needs a variety of related experiences. Experiences of counting with acorns, buttons, peanuts and the like, as examples from the classroom, are necessary to the formation of concepts about ordinal and cardinal number. Each separate experience, rooted in everyday life, provides the '*aliment*' from which concepts develop in a fusion of nature and nurture.

It has been claimed that children under the age of six or seven are very bad at communicating, precisely for the reason that they are bad at decentring — or that they are highly 'egocentric'.

This claim has been made most forcibly by Jean Piaget, and it has been backed by much supporting evidence. He has made it central to his theorizing about the capacities of children in the pre-school and early school years. He has constructed such a far-reaching and closely woven net of argument, binding together so many different features of the development of behaviour, that it is hard to believe he could be wrong.

Yet there is now powerful evidence that in this respect he *is* wrong.

In recent years Piaget has collected most of his data by devising tasks for children to do and then observing their behaviour when they deal with the task, questioning them about it, noting what they say. One of the best known of these tasks is concerned with the ability to take account of someone else's point of view in the literal sense — that is, to recognize what someone else will see who is looking at the same thing as oneself but from the other side.

For this task, a three-dimensional object or set of objects is needed. Piaget uses a model of three mountains. (See *The Child's Conception of Space* by Piaget and Inhelder.) The mountains are distinguished from one another by colour and by such features as snow on one, a house on top of another, a red cross at the summit of the third.

The child sits at one side on the table on which this model is placed. The experimenter then produces a little doll and puts the doll at some other position round the table. The problem for the child is: what does the doll see?

It would clearly be hard for the child to give a verbal description ('He sees a house on top of the mountain on his right ...' etc.) for that description would have to be of considerable complexity. So in one version of the task the child is given a set of ten pictures of the model taken from different angles, and he is asked to choose the one which shows what the doll sees. In another version he is given three cardboard 'mountains' and he is asked to arrange them so that they represent what would be seen in a snapshot taken from the doll's position. Children up to the age of around eight, or even nine, cannot as a rule do this successfully; and there is a powerful tendency among children below the age of six or seven to choose the picture — or build the model — which represents their own point of view — exactly what they themselves see.

Piaget takes this to indicate that they are unable to 'decentre' in imagination. He points out that in one sense they know perfectly well that the appearance of a thing changes when you walk round it. And yet he maintains that they are bound by what he calls 'the egocentric illusion' as soon as they are called upon to form a mental representation of some view which they have not actually seen. They 'really imagine that the doll's perspective is the same as their own'. They all think the doll sees the mountains only as they look from the child's position. What the child lacks is held to be the ability to see his own momentary viewpoint as one of a set of possible viewpoints, and to co-ordinate these possibilities into a single coherent system, so that he understands the ways in which the different perspectives relate to one another.

We are urged by Piaget to believe that the child's behaviour in this situation gives us a deep insight into the nature of his world. This world is held to be one that is composed largely of 'false absolutes'. That is to say, the child does not appreciate that what he sees is relative to his own position; he takes it to represent absolute truth or reality — *the world as it really is*. Notice that this implies a world marked by extreme discontinuity. Any change in position means abrupt change in the world and a sharp break with the past. And indeed Piaget believes that this is how it is for the young child: that he lives in the state of the moment, not bothering himself with how things were just previously, with the relation of one state to those which come before or after it. His world is like a film run slowly, as Piaget says elsewhere.

This is by no means to say that Piaget thinks the child has no memory of the earlier 'stills'. The issue for Piaget is how the momentary states are linked, or fail to be linked, in the child's mind. The issue is how well the child can deal conceptually with the transitions between them.

All this has far-reaching implications for the child's ability to think and reason...let us consider how children perform on a task which is in some ways very like the 'mountains' task and in other extremely important ways very different.

This task was devised by Martin Hughes. In its simplest form, it makes use of two 'walls' intersecting to form a cross, and two small dolls, representing respectively a policeman and a little boy. Seen from above, the lay-out (before the boy doll is put in position) is like this:

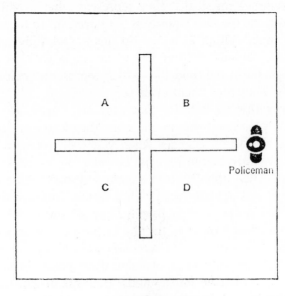

In the studies which Hughes conducted the policeman was placed initially as in the diagram so that he could see the areas marked B and D, while the areas A and C were hidden from him by the wall.

The child was then introduced to the task very carefully, in ways that were designed to give him every chance of understanding the situation fully and grasping what was being asked of him. First, Hughes put the boy doll in section A and asked if the policeman could see the boy there. The question was repeated for sections B, C and D in turn. Next the policeman was placed on the opposite side, facing the wall that divides A from C, and the child was asked to 'hide the doll so that the policeman can't see him'. If the child made any mistakes at these preliminary stages, his error was pointed out to him, and the question was repeated until the correct answer was given. But very few mistakes were made.

Then the test proper began. And now the task was made more complex. Another policeman was produced and the two were positioned thus:

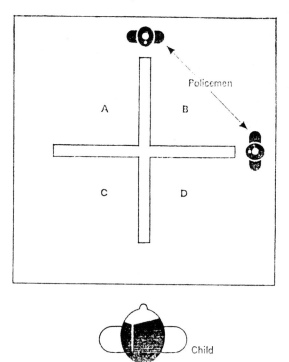

The child was told to hide the boy from both policemen, a result which could only be achieved by the consideration and co-ordination of two different points of view. This was repeated three times, so that each time a different section was left as the only hiding place.

The results were dramatic. When thirty children between the ages of three-and-a-half and five years were given this task, 90 per cent of their responses were correct. And even the ten youngest children, whose average age was only three years nine months, achieved a success rate of 88 per cent.

Hughes then went on the further trials, using more complex arrangements of walls, with as many as five or six sections, and introducing a third policeman. The three-year-olds had more trouble with this, but they still got over 60 per cent of the trials correct. The four-year-olds could still succeed at the 90-per-cent level.

It seems to be impossible to reconcile these findings with Piaget's claim that children under the age of seven are very bad at appreciating the point of view of some other person in the literal sense of being unable to figure out what that other person can see. However, though Hughes' findings cannot be reconciled with Piaget's *claim*, some way must be found of reconciling them with Piaget's *findings* — for these are not suspect. Research by other investigators has fully confirmed that, if children are given the Piaget 'mountains' task, they do indeed have extreme difficulty with it — but not, it now seems, for the reason Piaget suggests. For what reason, then?

One must obviously consider the differences between the two tasks — and these are many. One difference which Hughes noted is that the 'policemen' task, while it certainly involves the co-ordination of points of view, merely requires the child to figure out whether an object will be visible and does not require him to deal with left — right reversals and so on. That is, he must decide *what* can be seen but not exactly *how* it will appear. Now it is perfectly clear that the calculation of how something will look from a given position when the scene is fairly complex will give pause to many an adult. But this hardly seems to explain why young children, in tackling the 'mountains' task, so frequently choose their own point of view instead of a different, though wrong, one. When this fact is considered along with Hughes' findings, it is difficult to avoid the conclusion that the children who make 'egocentric' responses to the 'mountains' problem do not fully understand what they are supposed to do.[1]

By contrast it is quite evident that, in the 'policemen' problem, a situation has been found which *makes sense* to the child. Hughes was very careful about introducing the tasks in ways that would help the children to understand the nature of the problem, but in fact his precautions were largely unnecessary: the children seemed to grasp the situation at once. We have then to ask why this was so easy for them.

---

[1] In another study, Hughes used a simplified version of the mountains task and found that it was possible, by taking great care over the way in which the problem was introduced, to get a high proportion of correct responses from pre-school children. So this lends further support to the view that Piaget's subjects did not understand.

Notice that we cannot appeal to direct actual experience: few, if any, of these children had even tried to hide from a policeman. But we *can* appeal to the generalization of experience: they know what it is to try to hide. Also they know what it is to be naughty and to want to evade the consequences. So they can easily conceive that a boy might want to hide from a policeman if he had been a bad boy; for in this case it would be the job of the policeman to catch him and the consequences of being caught would be undersirable.

The point is that the *motives* and *intentions* of the characters are entirely comprehensible, even to a child of three. The task requires the child to act in ways which are in line with certain very basic human purposes and interactions (escape and pursuit) — it makes *human sense*. Thus it is not at all hard to convey to the child what he is supposed to do: he apprehends it instantly. It then turns out that neither is it hard for him to do it. In other words, in this context he shows none of the difficulty in 'decentring' which Piaget ascribes to him.

Reference

PIAGET, J. and INHELDER, B. (1963) *The Child's Conception of Space*, London, Routledge and Kegan Paul.

Stages of Concept Formation

(From Vygotsky, L.S., 1962, *Thought and Language*, MIT, pp. 58–69).

Spontaneous concepts, those that are learned in play and investigative behaviour, develop through everyday activity. Vygotsky distinguishes these from true concepts which he considers are rarely developed before adolescence. He argues that language is particularly important in the formation of true concepts which takes place in a social world. (He places far more emphasis than Piaget on the social environment and on language as a social activity.)

The extract below describes work carried out in the USSR on concept formation and how language acts to structure the process. It demonstrates how the provision of the verbal labels, given by language users, serves to focus attention on relevant attributes. Vygotsky describes stages of concept formation, and of particular importance is the pseudo-concept which precedes a true concept. It is readily mistaken for a true concept, as illustrated in school when the correct use of a definition can mask for the teacher the flimsy foundations of the child's understanding. Discussion and problem-posing questions are ways in which the true concept can be distinguished from the pseudo-concept.

Concept formation is the result of a complex activity in which all the basic intellectual functions take part. The process cannot, however, be reduced to association, attention, imagery, inference, or determining tendencies. They are all indispensable, but they are insufficient without the use of the sign, or word, as the means by which we direct our mental operations, control their course, and channel them toward the solution of the problem confronting us.

The presence of a problem that demands the formation of concepts cannot in itself be considered the cause of the process, although the tasks with which society faces the youth as he enters the cultural, professional, and civic world of adults undoubtedly are an important factor in the emergence of conceptual thinking. If the environment presents no such tasks to the adolescent, makes no new demands on him, and does not stimulate his intellect by providing a sequence of new goals, his thinking fails to reach the highest stages, or reaches them with great delay.

The cultural task per se, however, does not explain the developmental mechanism itself that results in concept formation. The investigator must aim to understand the intrinsic bonds between the external tasks and the developmental dynamics, and view concept formation as a function of the adolescent's total social and cultural growth, which affects not only the contents but also the method of his thinking. The new significative use of the word, its use *as a means of concept formation*, is the immediate psychological cause of the radical change in the intellectual process that occurs on the threshold of adolescence.

No new elementary function, essentially different from those already present, appears at this age, but all the existing functions are incorporated into a new structure, form a new synthesis, become parts of a new complex whole; the laws governing this whole also determine the destiny of each individual part. Learning to direct one's own mental processes with the aid of words or signs is an integral part of the process of concept formation. The ability to regulate one's actions by using auxiliary means reaches its full development only in adolescence.

IV

Our investigation brought out that the ascent to concept formation is made in three basic phases, each divided in turn into several stages. In this and in the following six sections, we shall describe these phases and their subdivisions as they appear when studied by the method of 'double stimulation'.

The young child takes the first step toward concept formation when he puts together a number of objects in an *unorganized congeries*, or 'heap', in order to solve a problem that we adults would normally solve by forming a new concept. The heap, consisting of disparate objects grouped together without any basis reveals a diffuse, undirected extension of the meaning of the sign (artificial word) to inherently unrelated objects linked by chance in the child's perception.

At that stage, word meaning denotes nothing more to the child than a *vague syncretic conglomeration of individual objects* that have somehow or other coalesced into an image in his mind. Because of its syncretic origin, that image is highly unstable.

In perception, in thinking, and in acting, the child tends to merge the most diverse elements into one unarticulated image on the strength of some chance impression. Claparède gave the name 'syncretism' to this well-known trait of child thought. Blonski called it the 'incoherent coherence' of child thinking. We have described the phenomenon elsewhere as the result of a tendency to compensate for the paucity of well-apprehended objective relations by an overabundance of subjective connections and to mistake these subjective bonds for real bonds between things. These syncretic relationships, and the heaps of objects assembled under one word meaning, also reflect objective bonds in so far as the latter coincide with the relations between the child's perceptions or impressions. Many words, therefore, have in part the same meaning to the child and the adult, especially words referring to concrete objects in the child's habitual surroundings. The child's and the adult's meanings of a word often 'meet', as it were, in the same concrete object, and this suffices to ensure mutual understanding.

The first phase of concept formation, which we have just outlined, subsumes three distinct stages. We were able to observe them in detail within the framework of the experimental study.

The first stage in the formation of syncretic heaps that represent to the child the meaning of a given artificial word is a manifestation of the *trial-and-error* stage in the development of thinking. The group is created at random, and each object added is a mere guess or trial; it is replaced by another object when the guess is proven wrong, i.e., when the experimenter turns the object and shows that it has a different name.

During the next stage, the composition of the group is determined largely by the spatial position of the experimental objects, i.e., by a purely syncretic *organization of the child's visual field*. The syncretic image or group is formed as a result of the single elements' contiguity in space or in time, or of their being brought into some other more complex relationship by the child's immediate perception.

During the third stage of the first phase of concept formation, the syncretic image rests in a more complex base: It is composed of *elements taken from different groups or heaps that have already been formed by the child in the ways described above.* These newly combined elements have no intrinsic bonds with one another, so that the new formation has the same 'incoherent coherent' as the first heaps. The sole difference is that in trying to give meaning to a new word the child now goes through a two-step operation, but this more elaborate operation remains syncretic and results in no more order than the simple assembling of heaps.

V

The second major phase on the way to concept formation comprises many variations of a type of thinking that we shall call *thinking in complexes*. In a complex, individual objects are united in the child's mind not only by his subjective impressions but also by *bonds actually existing between these objects.* This is a new achievement, an ascent to a much higher level.

When the child moves up to that level, he has partly outgrown his egocentrism. He no longer mistakes connections between his own impressions for connections between things — a decisive step away from syncretism toward objective thinking. Thought in complexes is already coherent and objective thinking, although it does not reflect objective relationships in the same way as conceptual thinking.

Remains of complex thinking persist in the language of adults. Family names are perhaps the best example of this. Any family name, 'Petrov', let us say, subsumes individuals in a manner closely resembling that of the child's complexes. The child at that stage of development thinks in family names, as it were; the universe of individual objects becomes organized for him by being grouped into separate, mutually related 'families'.

In a complex, the bonds between its components are *concrete and factual* rather than abstract and logical, just as we do not classify a person as belonging to the Petrov family because of any logical relationship between him and other bearers of the name. The question is settled for us by facts.

The factual bonds underlying complexes are discovered through direct experience. A complex therefore is first and foremost a concrete grouping of objects connected by factual bonds. Since a complex is not formed on the plane of abstract logical thinking, the bonds that create it, as well as the bonds it helps to create, lack logical unity; they may be of many different kinds. *Any factually present* connection may lead to the inclusion of a given element into a complex. That is the main difference between a complex and a concept. While a concept groups objects according to one attribute, the bonds relating the elements of a complex to the whole and to one another may be as diverse as the contacts and relationships of the elements are in reality.

In our investigation we observed five basic types of complexes, which succeed one another during this stage of development.

We call the first type of complex the *associative type*. It may be based on any bond the child notices between the sample object and some other blocks. In our experiment, the sample object, the one first given to the subject with its name visible, forms the nucleus of the group to be built. In building an associative complex, the child may add one block to the nuclear object because it is of the same color, another because it is similar to the nucleus in shape or in size, or in any other attribute that happens to strike him. Any bond between the nucleus and another object suffices to make the child include that object in the group and to designate it by the common 'family name'. The bond between the nucleus and the other object need not be a common trait, such as the same color or shape; a similarity, or a contrast, or proximity in space may also establish the bond.

To the child at that stage the word ceases to be the 'proper name' of an individual object; it becomes the family name of a group of objects related to one another in many kinds of ways, just as the relationships in human families are many and different.

VI

Complex thinking of the second type consists in combining objects or the concrete impressions they make on the child into groups that most closely resemble *collections*. Objects are placed together on the basis of some one trait in which they differ and consequently complement one another.

In our experiments the child would pick out objects differing from the sample in color, or in form, or in size, or in some other characteristic. He did not pick them at random; he chose them because they contrasted with and complemented the one attribute of the sample which he took to be the basis of grouping. The result was a collection of the colors or forms present in the experimental material, e.g. a group of blocks each of a different color.

Association by contrast, rather than by similarity, guides the child in compiling a collection. This form of thinking, however, is often combined with the associative form proper, described earlier, producing a collection based on mixed principles. The child fails to adhere throughout the process to the principle he originally accepted as the basis of collecting. He slips into the consideration of a different trait, so that the resulting group becomes a mixed collection, e.g., of both colors and shapes.

This long, persistent stage in the development of child thinking is rooted in his practical experience, in which collections of complementary things often form a set or a whole. Experience teaches the child certain forms of functional grouping: cup, saucer, and spoon; a place setting of knife, fork, spoon, and plate; the set of clothes he wears. All these are models of natural collection complexes. Even adults, when speaking of dishes or clothes, usually have in mind sets of concrete objects rather than generalized concepts.

To recapitulate, the syncretic image leading to the formation of 'heaps' is based on vague subjective bonds mistaken for actual bonds between objects; the associative complex, on similarities or other perceptually compelling ties between things; the collection complex, on relationships between objects observed in practical experience. We might say that the collection complex is a *grouping of objects on the basis of their participation in the same practical operation* — of their functional cooperation.

VII

After the collection stage of thinking in complexes, we must place the *chain complex* — a dynamic, consecutive joining of individual links into a single chain, with meaning carried over from one link to the next. For instance, if the experimental sample is a yellow triangle, the child might pick out a few triangular blocks until has attention is caught by, let us say, the blue color of a block he has just added; he switches to selecting blue blocks of any shape — angular, circular, semicircular. This in turn is sufficient to change the criterion again; oblivious of color, the child begins to choose rounded blocks. The decisive attribute keeps changing during the entire process. There is no consistency in the type of the bonds or in the manner in which a link of the chain is joined with the one that precedes and the one that follows it. The original sample has no central significance. Each link, once included in a chain complex, is as important as the first and may become the magnet for a series of other objects.

The chain formation strikingly demonstrates the perceptually concrete, factual nature of complex thinking. An object included because of one of its attributes enters the complex not just as the carrier of that one trait but as an individual, with *all* its attributes. The single trait is not abstracted by the child from the rest and is not given a special role, as in a concept. In complexes, the hierarchical organization is absent: All attributes are functionally equal. The sample may be disregarded altogether when a bond is formed between two other objects; these objects may have nothing in common with some of the other elements either, and yet be parts of the same chain on the strength of sharing an attribute with still another of its elements.

Therefore, the chain complex may be considered the *purest form of thinking in complexes*. Unlike the associative complex, whose elements are, after all, interconnected through one element — the nucleus of the complex — the chain complex has no nucleus; there are relations between single elements, but nothing more.

A complex does not rise above its elements as does a concept; it merges with the concrete objects that compose it. This fusion of the general and the particular, of the complex and its elements, this psychic amalgam, as Werner called it, is the distinctive characteristic of all complex thinking and of the chain complex in particular.

VIII

Because the chain complex is factually inseparable from the group of concrete objects that form it, it often acquires a vague and floating quality. The type and nature of the bonds may change from link to link almost imperceptibly. Often a remote similarity is enough to create a bond. Attributes are sometimes considered similar, not because of genuine likeness, but because of a dim impression that they have something in common. This leads to the fourth type of complex observed in our experiments. It might be called the diffuse complex.

The *diffuse complex* is marked by the fluidity of the very attribute that unites its single elements. Perceptually concrete groups of objects or images are formed by means of diffuse, indeterminate bonds. To go with a yellow triangle, for example, a child would in our experiments pick out trapezoids as well as triangles, because they made him think of triangles with their tops cut off. Trapezoids would lead to squares, squares to hexagons, hexagons to semicircles, and finally to circles. Color as the basis of selection is equally floating and changeable. Yellow objects are apt to be followed by green ones; then green may change to blue, and blue to black.

Complexes resulting from this kind of thinking are so indefinite as to be in fact limitless. Like a Biblical tribe that longed to multiply until it became countless like the stars in the sky or the sands of the sea, a diffuse complex in the child's mind is a kind of family that has limitless powers to expand by adding more and more individuals to the original group.

The child's generalizations in the nonpractical and nonperceptual areas of his thinking, which cannot be easily verified through perception or practical action, are the real-life parallel of the diffuse complexes observed in the experiments. It is well known that the child is capable of surprising transitions, of startling associations and generalizations, when his thought ventures beyond the boundaries of the small tangible world of his experience. Outside it he often constructs limitless complexes amazing in the universality of the bonds they encompass.

These limitless complexes, however, are built on the same principles as the circumscribed concrete complexes. In both, the child stays within the limits of concrete bonds between things, but in so far as the first kind of complex comprises objects outside the sphere of his practical cognition, these bonds are naturally based on dim, unreal, unstable attributes.

IX

To complete the picture of complex thinking, we must describe one more type of complex — the bridge, as it were, between complexes and the final, highest stage in the development of concept formation.

We call this type of complex the *pseudo-concept* because the generalization formed in the child's mind, although phenotypically resembling the adult concept, is psychologically very different from the concept proper; in its essence, it is still a complex.

In the experimental setting, the child produces a pseudo-concept every time he surrounds a sample with objects that could just as well have been assembled on the basis of an abstract concept. For instance, when the sample is a yellow triangle and the child picks out all the triangles in the experimental material, he could have been guided by the general idea or concept of a triangle. Experimental analysis shows, however, that in reality the child is guided by the concrete, visible likeness and has formed only an associative complex limited to a certain kind of perceptual bond. Although the results are identical, the process by which they are reached is not at all the same as in conceptual thinking.

We must consider this type of complex in some detail. It plays a predominant role in the child's real-life thinking, and it is important as a transitional link between thinking in complexes and true concept formation.

X

Pseudo-concepts predominate over all other complexes in the pre-school child's thinking for the simple reason that in real life *complexes corresponding to word meanings are not spontaneously developed by the child: The lines along which a complex develops are predetermined by the meaning a given word already has in the language of adults.*

In our experiments, the child, freed from the directing influence of familiar words, was able to develop word meanings and form complexes according to his own preferences. Only through the experiment can we gauge the kind and extent of his spontaneous activity in mastering the language of adults. The child's own activity in forming generalizations is by no means quenched, though it is usually hidden from view and driven into complicated channels by the influences of adult speech.

The language of the environment, with its stable, permanent meanings, points the way that the child's generalizations will take. But, constrained as it is, the child's thinking proceeds along this preordained path in the manner peculiar to his level of intellectual development. The adult cannot pass on to the child his mode of thinking. He merely supplies the ready-made meaning of a word, around which the child forms a complex — with all the structural, functional, and genetic peculiarities of thinking in complexes, even if the product of his thinking is in fact identical in its content with a generalization that could have been formed by conceptual thinking. The outward similarity between the pseudo-concept and the real concept, which makes it very difficult to 'unmask' this kind of complex, is a major obstacle in the genetic analysis of thought.

The functional equivalence of complex and concept, the coincidence, in practice, of many word meanings for the adult and the three-year-old child, the possibility of mutual understanding, and the apparent similarity of their thought processes have led to the false assumption that all the forms of adult intellectual activity are already present in embryo in child thinking and that no drastic change occurs at the age of puberty. It is easy to understand the origin of that misconception. The child learns very early a large number of words that mean the same to him and to the adult. The mutual understanding of adult and child creates the illusion that the end point in the development of word meaning coincides with the starting point, that the concept is provided ready-made from the beginning, and that no development takes place.

The child's acquisition of the language of adults accounts, in fact, for the consonance of his complexes with their concepts — in other words, for the emergence of concept complexes, or pseudo-concepts. Our experiments, in which the child's thinking is not hemmed in by word meanings, demonstrate that if it were not for the prevalence of pseudo-concepts the child's complexes would develop along different lines from adult concepts, and verbal communication between children and adults would be impossible.

The pseudo-concept serves as the connecting link between thinking in complexes and thinking in concepts. It is dual in nature: a complex already carrying the germinating seed of a concept. Verbal intercourse with adults thus becomes a powerful factor in the development of the child's concepts. The transition from thinking in complexes to thinking in concepts passes unnoticed by the child because his pseudo-concepts already coincide in content with the adult's concepts. Thus the child begins to operate with concepts, to practice conceptual thinking, before he is clearly aware of the nature of these operations. This peculiar genetic situation is not limited to the attainment of concepts; it is the rule rather than an exception in the intellectual development of the child.

Representational Systems and Intellectual Development

(From Bruner, J., 1974, *Beyond the Information Given*, Allen and Unwin, pp. 316–20.)

Bruner is a cognitive psychologist who has made major contributions to the study of intellectual development, to curriculum development (through his work on the social studies curriculum: *Man: A Course of Study*), and to early childhood education through his directorship of the Oxford Preschool Research Project. This extract illustrates his work on the study of cognitive growth. Here, he distinguishes three modes of representation: 'enactive representation, iconic representation, and symbolic representation — knowing something through doing it, through a picture or image of it, and through some such symbolic means as language.' He conceives of cognitive development, not as a series of stages (as does Piaget, pp. 250–252), but as the successive mastery of the three modes, along with the ability to translate one into the others. He indicates how in young children the enactive and iconic modes predominate, but how the symbolic mode becomes increasingly important as children get older.

A useful concept for conceiving of the growth of intellect is the idea of representation. There is no need here for a long discussion of representation; only a few of the features of the concept need concern us. In effect, representation or a system of representation is a set of rules in terms of which one conserves one's encounters with events. A representation of the world or of some segment of one's experience has several interesting features. For one thing, it is in some medium. We may represent some events by the actions they require, by some form of picture, or in words or other symbols. There are many subvarieties within each of these three media — the enactive, the iconic, or the symbolic. A representation of an event is selective. In constructing a model of something, we do not include everything about it. The principle of selectivity is usually determined by the ends to which a representation is put — what we are going to do with what has been retained in this ordered way. Representations, by virtue of their summary nature, are rulebound in the sense that each representation is not an arbitrary or random sampling of what it stands for. That is to say, a representation of a spatially extended event uses a spatial notation that is common to a larger set of extended events. Much of spontaneous learning consists of inducing more general rules for more economical or more effective ways of representing similar events. And much of this learning consists of a kind of translation of one representational system into another, as when we become capable not only of following a given path habitually, but of representing it by an image in our mind's eye.

There are three kinds of representational systems that are operative during the growth of human intellect and whose interaction is central to growth. All of them are amenable to specification in fairly precise terms, all can be shown to be affected and shaped by linkage with tool or instrumental systems, all of them are within important limits affected by cultural conditioning and by man's evolution. They are, as already indicated, enactive representation, iconic representation, and symbolic representation — knowing something through doing it, through a picture or image of it, and through some such symbolic means as language. With respect to a particular knot, we learn the act of tying it; when we know the knot, we know it by some habitual act we have mastered and can repeat. The habit by which the knot is organized is serially organized, governed by some schema that holds its successive segments together, and is in some important sense related to other habitual acts that facilitate or interfere with its learning and execution. What is crucial is that the representation is expressed in the medium of action with many features constrained by the nature of action, for example, its sequential and irreversible nature.

An image of a knot carried in your mind or on a page is not the same thing as the knot being tied, although the image can provide a schema around which action can be sequentially organized. An image is a selective, simultaneous, and often highly stylized analogue of an event experienced. Yet it is not arbitrary in its manner of referring to events as is a word. You can recognize an image of something, once having seen the something in question. You cannot recognize the appropriate word by knowing only the event it signifies. Linguistic signification is, in the main, arbitrary and depends upon the mastery of a symbolic code. A linguistic description, therefore, involves knowing not only the referents of words, but the rules for forming and transforming utterances. These rules, like the rules of image formation and habitual action, are distinctive to the medium of language.

Growth involves not a series of stages, but rather a successive mastering of three forms of representation along with their partial translation each into the others. The child in the early months of life literally defines events by the actions they evoke. Piaget's brilliant descriptions of the six- and seven-month-old child are readily replicated. The child has great difficulty at this age separating a percept and an act. To restore an object lost from view, he will perform an act appropriate to it. In time, perception becomes autonomous or relatively autonomous from action, and the child now has two semi-independent systems for representing things and a task of translation to master — to bring action and appearance into some correspondence.[1]

Symbolic representation is clearly the most mysterious of the three. Present evidence suggests that much of human syntax — rules of stunning power — is learned in the two or three years between the ages of two and four or five. There must be a huge innate component in this learning, in this unlocking of a syntactic component. It is not only mastered very swiftly and effortlessly, but first acquired in certain universal forms not to be found in the diverse adult speech communities into which children enter, so that pure imitation is hardly the relevant answer. Nor does syntactic competence bear much relation to the child's capacities on the semantic level. The child can say it correctly long before he can use his words and sentences in a fashion realistically appropriate to the situation. Only slowly does he learn to relate the language he speaks to his thoughts about things, to order his representation of the world by the syntactical logic inherent in his speech. As he makes progress in that direction, again there is the task of translating from one mode of representation to another, of resolving the conflicts and contradictions that characterize the difference between how one does it, how it looks, and how one says it.

How does the idea of representation measure up to our four criteria? The formal properties of a representational system are, I believe, amenable to close and precise description, notably the languages in terms of which symbolic and iconic representations are effected. The description of action patterns remains obscure, though concepts of backput (Drever, 1962), the *TOTE* unit (Miller, Galanter, and Pribram, 1960), and reafference (Held, 1965) help to clear up our understanding of action patterns as modes of representing events. It is also plain that the notion of representation does not, so to speak, stop at the human skin. The technologies that a culture provides through language, myths and explanations, metrical and reckoning systems, tools, and its disciplines of knowledge, all reinforce, amplify, and enrich human representational capacities. With respect to a biological and evolutionary perspective, let me only comment that modern ethnological conceptions are centrally concerned with representation in such mechanisms as releasers and imprinting, much of it deriving from the originating idea of the *Umwelt* first proposed by von Uexküll. Finally, if education is not concerned with instilling skill and zest for representing one's experience and knowledge in some balance between rich particularity and economical generality, then I am not sure what else it is about.

[1] See Bruner *et al.* (1966) for a fuller account of the process whereby a world of imagery comes first to be abstracted from action and there comes to be coordinated with it in a fashion that permits her order integration of sensorimotor behavior.

Experiments

An experiment by Olson was carried out with the aid of a simple piece of apparatus: a rectangular board of five columns and five rows of small light bulbs. Each bulb, upon being pressed by the child, either lights up in brilliant scarlet red or remains unlit, depending upon whether the bulb is part of a pattern or not. The child's task is to discover, by pressing as few bulbs as possible, which one of several patterns presented to him are hidden in the bulb board. Only one bulb can be pressed at a time. Figure 1 shows the board with two alternative patterns. The child must press to determine which of the two is on the board.

Children are introduced to the task by being shown the correspondence between a single model and the board and then tested for their comprehension of the task. Different patterns, varying in difficulty and in number of alternatives, are presented to the child, his task always being the same: to press the bulbs that will tell him which alternative pattern lights up on the board. For ease and brevity, we consider now the pair of alternatives on the board in Figure 1:. a *T* and a top horizontal bar.

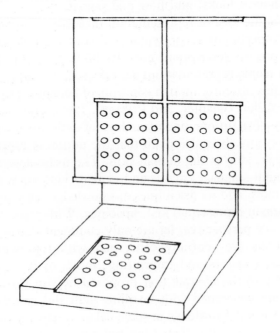

Figure 1. Apparatus used in the Olson experiment

The best way to describe the general course of development in the handling of this task is in terms of the strategies characteristic of the three-year-old, the five-year-old, and the eight-year-old. Their performance characterizes major turning points in development. The three-year-old is, in effect, searching the board for bulbs that will light up — his conception of positive instances. His search is not random. Likely he will start at an edge and, having pressed a bulb, the chances are that he will press one of its immediate neighbors. To put it figuratively in the interest of brevity, he is hoping that a perceptual pattern will spring from the board and often he must be restrained from pressing more than a single bulb at a time. His actions, he hopes, will produce the figure that can then be recognized as corresponding to one of the two before him. Needless to say, three-year-olds rarely succeed.

By age five, it is quite different. Now the child is quite capable of carrying an image representation to the task. But the procedure is striking in one special feature. No matter how many alternatives are presented, the five-year-old will try out one at a time, testing it and eliminating or accepting it, the latter often on insufficent evidence. Each test of an alternative model is of that model and does not use priorly encountered information. In the task of discriminating the *T* from the top horizontal line, a five-year-old, for example, will check the five bulbs across the top and announce it is the horizontal bar. If you then urge him on to check whether it might possibly be the *T*, he will check the vertical as well. But if these should prove not to light, it is almost certain that the child will simply go back to checking the horizontal one again. Confirmation seems to involve direct test of a hypothesis presently in force about a particular image, or perhaps it is better to say direct test of an image.

What is striking about the eight-year-old is that he seems to be able to deal with information properly defined rather than simply in terms of single images. He can deal simultaneously with the patterns before him by dealing with their inclusion, exclusion, and overlap, in order to isolate distinctive features. The older child characteristically takes much longer to decide which bulb to press, though by age nine the choice time begins to speed up again as the child becomes master of the task of using symbolic operations as a basis for dealing simultaneously with many alternative images.

What are we to make of this shift from an active search strategy, to a pattern-matching strategy, and finally to an information-selection strategy? What does this tell us of the growth of representation? The initial search strategy shows a strong carry-over of an early interdependence of action and percept, as if the child were trying to create a response-produced stimulus, to get it all out there by his acts so that it may be discriminated. By the fifth year, the child's choice of bulbs to be pressed is controlled by the patterns before him — but one pattern at a time — and he is not able to embed the alternatives into the hierarchical structure that is the essence of symbolic representation. Only when the apparatus of symbolism can be applied to the task can the set of alternative images be fused into what can be described as an information space, characterized by distinctive features.

References

BRUNER, J.S.; OLIVER, R.R.; and GREENFIELD, P.M. *et al.* (1966) *Studies in Cognitive Growth*, New York, Wiley.
DREVER, J. (1962) 'Perception and action', *Bulletin of the British Psychological Society*, 45, 1.
HELD, R. (1965) 'Plasticity in sensory-motor systems', *Scientific American*, 213, 5, pp. 84–94.
MILLER, G.A.; GALANTER, E.; and PRIBRAM, K.H. (1960) *Plans and the Structure of Behaviour*, New York, Holt.

Language and Learning

(From DES, 1975, *A Language for Life* (the Bullock Report), London, HMSO, pp. 47–50.)

The passage reproduced below is taken from the report of the Bullock Committee, set up to enquire into the teaching of reading and other uses of English. The report produced a wealth of observations and recommendations regarding policy and practice in the teaching of English, but its authors considered it necessary to provide this theoretical examination of the relationship between language and learning as the foundation for their findings. In focusing on language, one of Bruner's three modes of representation (pp. 271–276), the extract examines the relationship between language and inner representation, language and thought, and language and discovery. Without detailing its sources, it draws on the findings of very extensive work in linguistics and in the psychology of language.

Language and Learning

Man interposes a network of words between the world and himself, and thereby becomes the master of the world.

Georges Gusdorf

4.1 It is perfectly obvious that asking and telling play a persistent role in the day to day behaviour of human beings, and that without the exchange of information in words we should not be able to achieve a fraction of our customary activities. Add to this that we write and read letters, listen to radio and television, read newspapers and look things up in books, and it will be evident that verbalised information plays a crucial role in our affairs. This, however, if current theories are to be believed, is no more than the tip of the iceberg. It is the role that language plays in *generating* knowledge and *producing new forms* of behaviour that typifies human existence and distinguishes it from that of all other creatures.

4.2 These current theories stem from a powerful movement of ideas developed over the past fifty years, according to which man's individual, social and cultural achievements can be rightly understood only if we take into account the fact that he is essentially a *symbol-using animal*. By this account what makes us typically human is the fact that we symbolise, or represent to ourselves, the objects, people and events that make up our environment, and do so cumulatively, thus creating an inner representation of the world as we have encountered it. The accumulated representation is on the one hand a storehouse of past experience and on the other a body of expectations regarding what may yet happen to us. In this way we construct for ourselves a past and a future, a retrospect and a prospect; all our significant actions are performed within this extended field or framework, and no conscious act, however trivial, is uninfluenced by it. We interpret what we perceive at any given moment by relating it to our body of past experiences, and respond to it in the light of that interpretation. No doubt the processes of representation and storing are selective. Some things we are unable to interpret and their meaning is lost to us; some we may interpret but fail to store, and much that has been stored is certainly beyond the reach of deliberate recall. (Experiment has shown, however, that this does not necessarily mean we cannot be influenced by such things in interpreting fresh experiences.)

4.3   Language is one of a number of ways in which we represent the world to ourselves, and if its workings are to be seen in perspective it is necessary first to look briefly at one of the other ways. The most obvious example of an 'inner representation' is probably the visual memory we carry away of some object we have looked at and can no longer see. It is this memory which enables us, in confronting a new scene on a later occasion, to recognise an acquaintance among a crowd of strangers. We could hardly expect however, that the person recognised will look *exactly* as he did on that first occasion. It must be that our memory enables us to generalise beyond the situations on which it is based, or we should fail to recognise an old friend wearing a new expression. By generalising from our visual memories, in fact, we may make a good deal of sense of something we have never set eyes upon before. Thus, from much looking at many faces we come to recognise that a stranger is middle-aged rather than young, male rather than female, European rather than Oriental — not to mention the prior recognition that it is a human face that confronts us and not the face of a cat or an ape.

4.4   One of the keys to an understanding of language lies in realising that it is the prime means by which we construct *generalised* representations. At its simplest level of operation, a word that names an object is for a young child a filing-pin upon which he stores successive experiences of the objects themselves. As his experience grows, he uses the word to refer to an increasing range of objects, and applies it more and more consistently in the ways the adults do about him. He becomes increasingly aware of the characteristics of the category of objects named by the word. Thus he is employing language to assist him in generalising from visual (and indeed all other) modes of representing his experience. He does not, of course, do this without assistance. He may invent some words and apply them to categories of his own creation, but the vast majority of the words he uses will be taken over from the speech of the adults around him; and the objects these words refer to will be principally those to which the adults refer in using them. To sum up, then, we have to generalise from particular representations of past experiences in order to apply them to new ones, and language helps us to do this by providing a ready means of classifying these experiences. The important thing to remember is that as long as every event is experienced as unique and different from all other events we cannot set up expectations regarding the future. It is by recognising recurrences that we learn from our experience.

4.5   This brief account began at the simplest level of operation of language, with what *a word* can do. But of course, language is more than a mere inventory of words; it also includes highly complex rules for combining words into continuous speech or writing. An obvious example of such rules is the relation of the subject of a sentence to the predicate or the relation of a verb to its object. In addition to a vast array of grammatical rules, there are also lexical and semantic relationships built into language. The term 'flower', for example, is part of a hierarchy of terms: it subsumes the categories named by 'buttercup' and 'daisy' and is itself subsumed under other categories such as 'plant'. A speaker profits from the constraints upon his language behaviour, because they are the rules of the 'language game' that make communication possible. Having taken a word into his speech vocabulary, a child learns by degrees to use it for more purposes, for more complex purposes, and for purposes approximating more and more to adult uses. A similar process operates with respect to the rules governing language. For example, a child will first use the words 'buttercup', 'daisy', 'flower', and 'plant' without regard for their values in this hierarchy; later, however, when he is able to use the hierarchical distinctions, he will have acquired a very useful strategy of thinking, as any player of the 'Twenty Questions' game will recognise. Some psychologists go so far as to claim that the language rules gradually 'internalised' in this way 'become the basic structures of thinking', indeed, that 'a child's intellectual growth is contingent on his mastering the social means of thought, that is, language.'[2] For other psychologists, this would be too close an identification of thought with language. However, there is no need to enter this controversy, since it is enough to state what would be generally agreed: (a) that higher processes of thinking are normally achieved by the interaction of a child's language behaviour with his other mental and perceptual powers; and (b) that language behaviour represents the aspect of his thought processes most accessible to outside influences, including that of the teacher.

4.6   The plausibility of this claim has been greatly strengthened in recent years by the work of Chomsky and his associates in attempting to discover structural features to be found in all languages. If all languages embody some rules in common and those common rules are seen to be closely related to universal modes of human reasoning, then clearly the link between language and thinking is one that must be acknowledged. The simple fact would appear to be that people of all races have developed languages as their means of organising their experience of the world; and in doing so they have acquired, in common, characteristics specific to the human race. As a child gains mastery of his particular mother-tongue he learns by degrees to apply its organising power to his own experience, and as a result his mental processes take on new forms. So complete is the transformation that it is impossible for us to reverse the process and conceive of our situation in the way we saw it as inarticulate infants.

4.7   The famliar facts with which each of us goes armed to meet new experiences are in origin statements about the world, and we require language to make those statements. However, it would be perfectly possible to state here that the page the reader has before him is green in colour, and that is patently *not* a fact. Language used in that way is the language of hypothesis, the formulation of possibilities. It is crucial in the sense that *what is* can be said to exist in its own right, open to contemplation, whereas *what might be* takes a form in which it may be contemplated only when it is in some way represented or symbolised. It may be said that all behaviour is experimental: that, for example, as we walk from one part of a building to another, we test out the hypothesis that an aperture is indeed open and not protected by a plate glass door. And there may be occasions when the hypothesis is abruptly disproved. It would be very rash, however, to claim that in such a situation language had any direct role to play. It is when our behaviour moves into more problematic situations that the need arises for a hypothesis to be elaborated, to take on the form of a statement of the possibilities, and here we must use language. The effort to formulate a hypothesis, to put into words some possibility we have envisaged, results in a 'spelling out' to which we may then return, in the light of further experience and in search of further possibilities. By a kind of spiral, the formulation itself becomes a source from which we draw further questions, fresh hypotheses. The statement we have made becomes an object of our own contemplation and a spur to further thinking. It is probably true to say that the higher thought processes become possible to the child or adolescent who in this way learns to turn his linguistic activities back upon his own formulations.

4.8   If such claims are to seem feasible, two things must be remembered. One is that language provides us with a generalised representation of experience, and generalising has the effect of reducing the multiplicity of experience to a more manageable form. The other is that the complex rules governing the combination of elements when we speak or write impose order upon the experiences we succeed in putting into words. There are implications here for two familiar enough forms of classroom activity. In group discussion the spoken contribution of each member may be worked upon by speaker and listeners alike, and in the immediacy of face-to-face speech they make corporate enquiry a powerful mode of learning. Secondly, in the practice of writing the child left alone with his evolving utterance is engaged in generating knowledge for himself, particularly when the writing is frequent, brief, and strenuous rather than occasional and at length. At the same time he is developing mental operations which will afterwards be of service to him in writing, speaking, reading, listening or thinking.

4.9 It is a confusion of everyday thought that we tend to regard 'knowledge' as something that exists independently of someone who knows. 'What is known' must in fact be brought to life afresh within every 'knower' by his own efforts. To bring knowledge into being is a formulating process, and language is its ordinary means, whether in speaking or writing or the inner monologue of thought. Once it is understood that talking and writing are means to learning, those more obvious truths that we learn also from other people by listening and reading will take on a fuller meaning and fall into a proper perspective. Nothing has done more to confuse current educational debate than the simplistic notion that 'being told' is the polar opposite of 'finding out for oneself'. In order to accept what is offered when we are told something, we have to have somewhere to put it; and having somewhere to put it means that the framework of past knowledge and experience into which it must fit is adequate as a means of interpreting and apprehending it. Something approximating to 'finding out for ourselves' needs therefore to take place if we are to be successfully told. The development of this individual context for a new piece of information, the forging of the links that give it meaning, is a task that we customarily tackle by talking to other people.

4.10 In the Committee's view there are certain important inferences to be drawn from a study of the relationship between language and learning:

(i) all genuine learning involves discovery, and it is as ridiculous to suppose that teaching begins and ends with 'instruction' as it is to suppose that 'learning by discovery' means leaving children to their own resources;

(ii) language has a heuristic function; that is to say a child can learn by talking and writing as certainly as he can by listening and reading;

(iii)   to exploit the process of discovery through language in all its uses is the surest means of enabling a child to master his mother tongue.

References

1 See, for example, LURIA, A.R. and VINOGRADOVA, O.S. (1958) 'The Dynamics of Semantic Systems, *British Journal of Psychology*, 50.
2 VYGOTSKY, L.S. (1962) *Thought and Language*, Massachusetts Institute of Technology Press.

Reception and Discovery Learning

(From Ausubel, D. *et al.* (1978) *Educational Psychology. A Cognitive View*, 2nd ed., Holt, Rinehart and, Winston, pp. 24–77, 28–79.)

The view that children discover knowledge has its justification in observations of spontaneous learning through play and activity. Piaget's conclusions that logical thought and intelligence develop from actions upon the objects and events in everyday life, combined with studies of trial and error learning, have led to the argument that schools should use discovery methods. In discussion of appropriate methods of learning, discovery has usually been contrasted with rote learning; a 'bolting on' of ready-made concepts and information. Ausubel shows in this extract that discovery and rote learning are not on the same continuum, and that it is inaccurate to assume that material presented verbally is necessarily rote in nature. Concepts presented ready-made may be meaningfully incorporated into existing cognitive structures, or they can be rote and meaningless, depending on what is already understood by the learner, and how new learning is presented. The teacher's task is to present information in a meaningful way, which links closely with existing understanding. In this way, positive transfer from old to new learning may take place, and therefore is more readily available for application.

Reception versus Discovery Learning

In reception learning (rote or meaningful) the entire content of what is to be learned is presented to the learner in final form. The learning task does not involve any independent discovery on the student's part. The learner is required only to internalize or incorporate the material (a list of nonsense syllables or paired adjectives; a poem or geometrical theorem) that is presented so that it is available or reproducible at some future date. In the case of meaningful reception learning, the potentially meaningful task or material is comprehended or made meaningful in the process of internalization. In the case of rote reception learning, the learning task either is not potentially meaningful or is not made meaningful in the process of internalization.

Much of the confusion in discussions of school learning arises from the failure to recognize that rote and meaningful learning are not completely dichotomous. Although they are *qualitatively* discontinuous in terms of the psychological processes underlying *each* and therefore cannot be placed at opposite poles of the same continuum, there are transitional types of learning that share some of the properties of both rote and meaningful learning (for example, representational learning or learning the names of objects, events, and concepts). Further, both types of learning can take place concomitantly in the same learning task. This same qualification also holds true for the distinction between reception and discovery learning. In somewhat simplified terms, these relationships are shown in diagrammatic form in Figure 1, in which these two dimensions of learning are viewed as orthogonal to each other.

The essential feature of discovery learning, whether concept formation or rote problem solving, is that the principal content of what is to be learned is not given but must be discovered by the learner before it can be meaningfully incorporated into the student's cognitive structure. The distinctive and prior learning task, in other words, is to discover something — which of two maze alleys leads to the goal, the precise nature of the relationship between two variables, the common attributes of a number of diverse instances, and so forth. The first phase of discovery learning involves a process quite different from that of reception learning. The learner must rearrange information, integrate it with existing cognitive structure, and reorganize or transform the integrated combination in such a way as to generate a desired end-product or discover a missing means-end relationship. After discovery learning itself is completed, the discovered content is made meaningful in much the same way that presented content is made meaningful in reception learning.

Reception and discovery learning are thus two quite different kinds of processes. It will be shown later that most classroom instruction is organized along the lines of reception learning.... Verbal reception learning is not necessarily rote in character. Much ideational material (concepts, generalizations) can be internalized and retained meaningfully without prior problem-solving experience. And at no stage of development does the learner have to discover principles independently in order to be able to understand and use them meaningfully.

It is important to note at this point that reception and discovery learning also differ with respect to their respective principal roles in intellectual development and functioning (Ausubel, 1961). For the most part, large bodies of subject matter are acquired through reception learning, whereas the everyday problems of living are solved through discovery learning. Nevertheless, some overlap of function obviously exists. Knowledge acquired through reception learning is also used in everyday problem solving, and discovery learning is commonly used in the classroom both to apply, extend, clarify, integrate, and evaluate subject-matter knowledge and to test comprehension. In laboratory situations, discovery learning provides insight into scientific method and also leads to the contrived rediscovery of known propositions. When employed by gifted

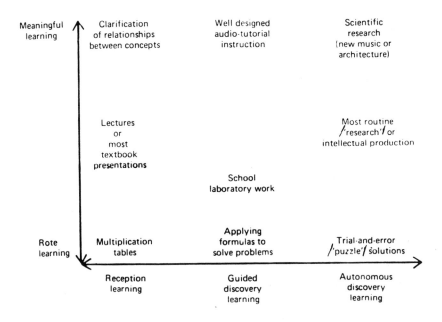

Figure 1.   *Reception learning and discovery learning are on a separate continuum from rote learning and meaningful learning*

persons it may generate significant new knowledge. In the more typical classroom situation, however, the discovery of original propositions through problem-solving activity is not a conspicuous feature in the acquisition of new concepts or information. As far as the formal education of the individual is concerned, the educational agency largely transmits ready-made concepts, classifications, and propositions. In any case, discovery methods of teaching hardly constitute an efficient *primary* means of transmitting the *content* of an academic discipline.

One can justifiably argue that the school is also concerned with developing the student's ability to use acquired knowledge in solving particular problems systematically, independently, and critically in various fields of inquiry. But this function of the school, although constituting a legitimate objective of education in its own right, is less central than its related transmission-of-knowledge function. This is true in terms of the amount of time that can be reasonably allotted to this function, in terms of the objectives of education in a democratic society and in terms of what can be reasonably expected from most students.

From the standpoint of psychological process, meaningful discovery learning is obviously more complex than meaningful reception learning. It involves an antecedent problem-solving stage before meaning emerges and can be internalized (Ausubel, 1961). Generally speaking, however, reception learning, although phenomenologically simpler than discovery learning, paradoxically emerges later developmentally and, particularly in its more advanced and pure verbal forms, implies a higher level of cognitive maturity. Greater intellectual maturity in this case makes possible a simpler and more efficient mode of cognitive functioning in the acquisition of knowledge.

Thus concepts and propositions are typically acquired during the post-infancy, preschool, and early elementary-school years. This comes about as a result of inductive processing of verbal and nonverbal concrete-empirical experience — typically through autonomous problem solving or discovery. The young child, for example, acquires the concept of a chair by abstracting the common features of the concept from multiple incidental encounters with chairs of many different sizes, shapes, and colors, and then generalizing these attributes. Reception learning, on the other hand, although also occurring early, does not become a prominent feature of intellectual functioning until the child is cognitively mature enough to comprehend verbally presented concepts and propositions in the absence of concrete, empirical experience — until, for example, he or she can comprehend the meaning of 'democracy' or 'acceleration' from their dictionary definitions. In other words, inductive concept *formation* based on non-verbal, concrete, empirical problem-solving experience exemplifies early developmental phases of information processing. Concept *assimilation* through meaningful verbal reception learning exemplifies later stages.

Meaningful versus Rote Learning

Although the distinction between reception and discovery learning discussed above has absolutely nothing to do with the rote-meaningful dimension of the learning process, the two dimensions of learning were commonly confused. This confusion is partly responsible for the widespread but unwarranted twin beliefs that reception learning is invariably rote and that discovery learning is inherently and necessarily meaningful. Both assumptions, of course, reflect the long-standing belief in many educational circles that the only knowledge one *really* possesses and understands is knowledge that one discovers by oneself. Actually, each distinction (rote versus meaningful and reception versus discovery learning) constitutes an entirely independent dimension of learning. Hence a much more defensible proposition is that *both* reception *and* discovery learning can be *either* rote *or* meaningful depending on the conditions under which learning occurs (Ausubel, 1961). The relationships between rote and meaningful learning, as well as their orthogonal relationship to the reception-discovery dimension are shown diagrammatically in Figure 1.

In both instances meaningful learning takes place if the learning task can be related in nonarbitrary, substantive (nonverbatim) fashion to what the learner already knows, and if the learner adopts a corresponding learning set to do so. Rote learning, on the other hand, occurs if the learning task consists of purely arbitrary associations, as in paired-associate, puzzle-box, maze, or serial learning, if the learner lacks the relevant prior knowledge necessary for making the learning task potentially meaningful, and also (regardless of how much potential meaning the task has) if the learner adopts a set merely to internalise it in an arbitrary, verbatim fashion (that is, as an arbitrary series of words). . . . It is true that much potentially meaningful knowledge taught by verbal exposition results in rotely learned verbalisms. This rote outcome, however, is not inherent in the expository method, but rather in such abuses of this method as fail to satisfy the criteria of meaningful verbal learning (Ausubel, 1961).

There is much greater reluctance, on the other hand, to acknowledge that the conditions of meaningful learning just mentioned also apply to problem-solving methods. Performing laboratory experiments in cookbook fashion without understanding the underlying substantive and methodological principles involved confers little appreciation of scientific method. Neither does 'discovering' correct answers to problems in mathematics and science, without really understanding what one is doing, add to knowledge or problem-solving ability. Students accomplish this latter feat merely by rote memorising 'type problems' and mechanical procedures for manipulating algebraic symbols. Nevertheless, it must be recognised that laboratory work and problem-solving are not genuinely meaningful experiences unless they meet two conditions. First, they must be built on a foundation of clearly understood concepts and principles; second, the constituent operations must themselves be meaningful.

Reference

AUSUBEL, D. (1961) 'In defense of verbal learning', *Education Theory*, 11, pp. 15–25.

Play and Intellectual Development

(From Tamburrini, J., 1974, 'Play and intellectual development', *Paedaogica Europaea*, 9, 1, pp. 51–3, 54, 57–8.)

It is characteristic of living creatures that they explore their environment. In the healthy young of many species, this is manifested in play. There is, however, no general agreement as to the role of play in intellectual development or as to the most appropriate way to maximize its impact. This extract summarizes two very influential views on the role of play. Piaget suggests that play serves three important functions in cognitive development:

1 it reflects a child's 'schemes' ('the psychological organisations of an individual's past actions and experiences through which he selectively anticipates and filters events');
2 it helps to consolidate the skills, actions and meanings a child has acquired;
3 it results in incidental learning, for example, of the properties of materials and of the reactions of others.

Vygotsky emphasizes the role of play in the development of imagination through its liberation of the child from situational constraints. The extract relates these views specifically to nursery education but the implications drawn for teacher intervention in play and for the provision of materials are equally applicable to play situations in infant or first schools.

For several decades there has been general acceptance among educators that play in early childhood has important educative functions. But there is by no means general agreement concerning the precise nature of the role of play in intellectual development, and differences can be found in educational practices and prescriptions which reflect sometimes a lack of clarity and sometimes a controversy.

Some nursery school teachers adopt a comparatively bland and passive role, intervening in children's play activities only to resolve social conflict, to offer comfort when things go wrong, and to provide materials children need. In contrast, other teachers adopt a highly active role in which they see play as richly exploitable for mathematics and language teaching. They intervene frequently and consistently in children's play activities requiring them, for example, to count the cups and saucers in their dramatic, familial play, or to measure the constructions they have built from blocks.

Paradoxically both kinds of teacher may underestimate the role of play in cognition.

Among teachers of the first kind are many who have been influenced, directly or indirectly, by the psychoanalytic tradition. As Almy (1966, p. 6) points out, 'a symptom of (their) preoccupation with the emotional is apparent lack of involvement in the intellectual life of the child'. These teachers may pay lip-service to a notion that play is related to intellectual development, but an inability to explicate the relationship in precise terms is indicated by their practices: they seem to show a lack of awareness of the diagnostic information concerning a child's level of cognition revealed by his play; they do not provoke problems in the context of play by judicious questioning of children; and they are unlikely to pay sufficient attention to the sorts of potential that particular materials may have for problem-solving activities and conceptual development.

Teachers of the second kind undervalue the role of play in intellectual development in a different way. Unlike teachers of the first kind they provoke problems in the context of children's play activities, but the way that they do so involves prejudgment. They may ignore the problems with which a child is concerned in his play, so that the problems they provoke may well be extrinsic rather than intrinsic to a child's preoccupations. They are likely to value highly structured play materials which embody a specific problem or are meant to teach a particular concept more than less structured materials which can be used in a variety of ways. The former kind of teacher, by contrast, is likely to favour materials which lend themselves to a diversity of play activities.

Parallel with these differences among teachers are differences among theoreticians in their conceptions of the role of play in cognition. According to Biber (1959), for example, a teacher should not structure a child's play. Reality and logic, she believes, are only secondary to play whose main function she conceives of as an outlet for emotional concerns. By contrast, Olson (1970, pp. 158–171) has devised a highly structured educational toy to teach the concept of diagonality. Generalizing from research into the effects of this toy on the learning of the concept, Olson suggests that an educational toy should be unambiguous in the sense that it should lead to a construction embodying the concept the children are expected to learn and that it should provide constant informational feedback. The one thing an educational toy should do automatically, according to Olson, is to inform the child if he is using it in an appropriate way. What is appropriate is, of course, predetermined by the adult.

Before any conclusions can be reached as to whether Biber's and Olson's positions are complementary or incompatible two issues need to be clarified. Firstly, as Almy points out, a distinction needs to be made between spontaneous play and play structured by the adult. 'Progress can only be made when a clearer differentiation is made between two forms of play, both holding legitimate places in the nursery school curriculum, but each having certain specific characteristics. The first form of play, the one so highly valued by the nursery educator, is activity that is self-initiated by the child. It is lacking in structure other than that given it by his interests and by his imagination. The second form is adult-prescribed activity, initiated and directed by the nature of the equipment' (Almy, 1966, p. 3). Secondly, it should be recognized that there is not one single relationship between play and cognition but several. Any attempt to describe play in unidimensional terms is bound to lead to spurious controversies. The exchange between Sutton-Smith (1971) and Piaget (1971) is an example of a controversy which to some extent dissolves when it is recognized that each emphasizes different but related functions of play in intellectual development. . . .

Piaget (1951) conceptualizes play in terms of 'assimilation' and 'accommodation', the invariant, twin functions which account for intellectual development. Central to Piaget's concept of assimilation is the notion of 'schemes', the psychological organizations of an individual's past actions and experiences through which he selectively anticipates and filters events. Thus schemes (and post-operational concepts) constitute systems of meanings which determine what an individual pays attention to and how he interprets that to which he has selectively attended. Assimilation takes place when an individual interprets an aspect of external reality in terms of one of his existing systems of meanings or when he acts on an aspect of external reality in terms of one of his existing action patterns. Accommodation occurs when an individual modifies or elaborates a meaning or a pattern of action to tally with a segment of external reality. Intelligent adaptation takes place when assimilation and accommodation are in equilibrium. Play, however, 'manifests the peculiarity of a primacy of assimilation over accommodation which permits it to transform reality in its own manner without submitting that transformation to the criterion of objective fact' (Piaget, 1971, p. 338). This is not to say that there is no accommodation in play, for assimilation is never pure.

There are three ways in which accommodative elements occur in play. Firstly, accommodation is involved in the imitative components of symbolic play: when a child pretends to be a bus driver and imitates what he conceives to be the characteristic actions of bus drivers, he adapts his actions to reality. Imitation, according to Piaget, represents the opposite pole to play — there is a primacy of accommodation over assimilation. Secondly, symbolic play evokes absent objects and events through images. But imagery, according to Piaget, is interiorized imitation and, therefore, again involves a primacy of accommodation over assimilation. Thus, when a child upturns a cardboard box to sit in and pretends it is a bus and he the bus driver, he evokes the situation through images or interiorized imitation as well as through overt or gestural imitation. Thirdly, and most important-ly for the educator, in the course of his play a child is likely to meet obstacles which require that he modifies his actions in some way. Other children with whom he plays will not always be willing to adjust to his desires or demands: his playmates may not wish continually to play the part of passengers while he plays the part of the bus driver. Material objects do not always meet his intentions: the cardboard box may not take his weight. To carry through the intentions that are part of his play a child must, perforce, accommodate to such aspects of external reality. This is incidental learning in play.

From the point of view of the educator there are three important interrelationships between play and intellectual development implicit in Piaget's conceptualization of play. Firstly, play reflects a child's schemes. A sensory-motor scheme or a symbolic meaning system only becomes ludic when it is firmly established: 'when the child has overcome the difficulties inherent in the corresponding "serious" action, the (ludic) assimilation is more concentrated on his own activity' (Piaget, 1951, p. 162). Secondly, play has the important function of consolidating the skills, actions and meanings a child has acquired. Through exercise it prevents the atrophy of schemes and enables the child to relive his past experiences. Since in early childhood experimental and logical thought has yet to be constructed and reality cannot therefore be assimilated to it, assimilation of reality to the ego (play) is a necessary transition. It is necessary not simply to fill a time gap but for the exercise and consolidation of existing schemes: 'for the child assimilation of reality to the ego is a vital condition for continuity and development' (*ibid.*, p. 166). The implication is that without facilities for play a child's acquisition of concepts is likely to be founded on a narrow and inadequate base. Thirdly, there is incidental learning in play, referred to above, as a child accommodates to obstacles in the play context....

... Vygotsky (1966) argues that all play involves the creation of an imaginary situation, and that this is one of its two most significant criterial attributes. The second important characteristic of play is that it is rule-bound. Games with rules are essentially games involving an imaginary situation, he suggests. To play chess, for example, is to create an imaginary situation. And what is usually called 'symbolic' play involves rules, not rules formulated in advance, but rules stemming from the imaginary situation, for if a child engages in home-play she must obey the rules of maternal behaviour or of a baby's behaviour depending on whether she pretends to be a mother or a baby. Thus, 'just as...every imaginary situation contains rules in a concealed form...the reverse (is true) that every game with rules contains an imaginary situation in concealed form'

(Vygotsky, 1966, p. 10). Play is of great importance, Vygotsky suggests, in liberating the child from situational constraints. The very young child is bound by situational constraints in that things dictate to him what he must do: a table is to be eaten from, a chair to be sat on. But in play a child may impose his own meanings on material objects: the table may be sat under because it represents a house, a chair may be eaten from because it represents a table. Thus, 'in play activity thought is separated from objects, and action arises from ideas rather than from things.... Action according to rules begins to be determined by ideas and not by objects themselves', (*ibid.*, p. 12). When a child pretends that a piece of stick is a horse he crosses a critical threshold in his psychological development, for the stick 'becomes a pivot for severing the meaning of horse from a real horse, one of the basic psychological structures determining the child's relationship to reality' (*ibid.*).

The implication of Vygotsky's thesis is that play has a leading role in the development of imagination. Adult imagination involves the organization and reorganization of meanings in the absence of concrete referents: thought is severed from the object. Play is a transitional stage in this direction: when the child creates an imaginary situation meanings are severed from situational constraints, but he cannot yet completely sever thought from objects. He needs things to act as pivots: 'in order to imagine a horse, he needs to define his actions by means of using the horse in the stick as a pivot' (*ibid.*). However, in adult imagination there are also constraints. The organization and reorganization of meanings in thought are constrained by the public criterial rules of the relevant context. Vygotsky's thesis implies a continuity between childhood play and adult imagination in that both are rule-bound. Support for this notion of continuity comes from Vygotsky's analysis of the development of childhood play in terms of the development of rules. 'Towards the end of development in play what had originally been embryonic now has a distinct form, finally emerging as purpose and rules' (*ibid.*, p. 17)....

... Although the state of theory and research into play in early childhood requires that one should be tentative in formulating precise interrelationships between play and intellectual development, certain broad implications have emerged which are of significance for education.

Clearly questions of whether a teacher should or should not intervene in children's play activities, and of whether nursery school provision should be in terms of unstructured play facilities or of activities virtually prescribed by the adult through highly structured materials, are much too polarized. Instead educationally significant questions would be concerned with what sort of learning is facilitated by specific sorts of teacher intervention and with what aspects of development are best served by unstructured play on the one hand, and by highly structured materials on the other hand.

Piaget's and Vygotsky's formulations would suggest two sorts of intervention by nursery school teachers in relation to children's play. Firstly, play, since it reflects a child's schemes, would seem to provide valuable diagnostic information for a teacher which should preamble the provision of appropriate material. Secondly, incidental learning which can occur in the play context would be enhanced by the provocative intervention of a teacher with judicious comments and questions. This is a more complex role than that conceived by the too simplistic question of whether nursery school teachers should or should not intervene in children's play.

Incidental learning within the play context is facilitated by appropriate materials as well as by judicious verbal intervention by a teacher. Materials which have a built-in diversity so that they can be structured and organized in many ways would seem to be particularly fruitful for incidental learning incidents. For when children initiate spontaneous play activities they generate intentions and hence problems within the play context. It would seem that such self-generated problems are more likely to provide incidental learning situations than problems extrinsically posed by the adult through highly structured materials. As Olson's work indicates highly structured materials are likely to be ignored by children for whom the extrinsic problem they present is too advanced. And when, on the other hand, they are played with by children who can solve the problem the very tightness of their structure may preclude a diversity of activities and may therefore result in poorly elaborated play. This is not to suggest that highly structured materials should not be included in nursery school provision, but rather they are better conceived of as fulfilling specific purposes for particular children to whom the extrinsic problem they embody is well matched.

If Vygotsky is correct in conceiving an important function of play to be the first severing of meanings from situational constraints, the provision of materials which can be organized in a variety of ways would have an additional value. Sears (1966) compares the value of an old automobile versus that of a small pedal car as nursery school equipment. He favours the latter, for in it the child has to change speed and direction to avoid obstacles, whereas with the old automobile he tends simply to make engine-like noises and steering motions with his hands. Sears' preference is justified if one thinks in terms of incidental learning in the play context, for there is certainly more accommodative potential in the pedal car. However, Vygotsky's conceptualization of play would suggest other comparisons. Nursery school children frequently build make-believe cars from large blocks. They are apt to sit in these too and make engine-like noises and steering motions. But they also build other structures out of large blocks. In other words, blocks can be used in a variety of ways that allow a child to 'sever the meaning from the obj ct'. Nursery school provision should include both sorts of material.

References

ALMY, M. (1966) 'Spontaneous play: An avenue for intellectual development', *Bulletin of the Institute of Child Study*, 28, 2.

BIBER, B. (1954) 'What play means to your child,' *Childcraft*.

OLSON, D.R. (1970) *Cognitive Development: The Child's Acquisition of Diagonality*, New York, Academic Press.

PIAGET, J. (1951) *Play, Dreams and Imitation in Childhood*, London, Routledge and Kegan Paul.

PIAGET, J. (1971) 'Response to Brian Sutton-Smith', in HERRON, R.E. and SUTTON-SMITH, B. (Eds) *Child's Play*, New York, Wiley, pp. 337–40.

SEARS, R. (1966) 'Process pleasure', in BRUNER, J. (Ed.), *Learning about Learning*, Washington, U.S. Bureau of Research, pp. 44–7.

SUTTON-SMITH, B. (1971) 'Piaget on play: A critique', and 'A reply to Piaget: A play theory of copy', in HERRON, R.E. and SUTTON-SMITH, B. (Eds), *Child's Play*, New York, Wiley, pp. 326–43.

VYGOTSKY, L.S. (1966) 'Play and its role in the mental development of the child', *Voprosy Psikhologii*, 12, 6 (from a stenographic record of a lecture delivered in 1933).

Identification and Imitation

(From Schaffer, H., 1968, 'Identification', in Lunzer, E. and Morris, J., *Development in Human Learning*, Granada Publishing, pp. 55–61.)

Psychologists are interested in how society impinges on the growing child and how it shapes and canalizes his or her behaviour in some directions rather than others. Psychologists of education have a particular interest in the role of schools, especially teachers and a child's fellow-pupils, in this process. The extract below illustrates the 'social learning' perspective briefly referred to in the introduction to this section of the source book. Central to this perspective are the process of identification and the part played by imitation and modelling. It is argued that although parents have the most decisive influence on a child's identification, other individuals (such as teachers) and groups (such as the peer group, pp. 302–305) can, and do, serve as models. Two particular areas are examined in some detail: sex-typing, and the development of conscience.

Having formed a strong bond to certain selected individuals, the child will inevitably wish to conform to their standards of behaviour and avoid their disapproval of inappropriate conduct. He does so by becoming like them — by incorporating their standards and thus identifying with them.

The task of socialization is at first almost entirely in the hands of the child's family. This is the primary social group in which he is introduced to the mores of society and which helps him to acquire the basic skills necessary to cope with the environment. In so far as social learning is a function of social contagion, i.e. the extent to which the individual comes into contact with others, the family is likely to provide the most powerful formative influence on personality development, for in the early years, at the time of maximum susceptibility, the child will be in almost continuous contact with family members. On an overt level, their influence manifests itself in the child's tendency to imitate their ways of behaviour and consequently to become more and more like them in speech, dress, eating habits and other personal characteristics. Habits of imitation can, in fact, be learned if the child is suitably rewarded for doing so (Miller and Dollard, 1941). However, imitation is not merely conditioned by overtly given rewards and instructions but depends on the total parent — child relationship and the powerful, though often subtle, feelings which a child develops towards those on whom he is emotionally dependent. The whole process that leads the child to think, feel and act as though the characteristics of another person were his own is called identification. The person with whom the child identifies is known as the model, and identification may thus also be regarded as the wish to be the model. Two qualifications must, however, be added: in the first place, a child need not necessarily identify with the whole model but may do so with only certain of its parts or attributes, and in the second place this tendency can be a wholly unconscious process.

Most of the difficulties of studying identification arise from this latter point. Freud, to whom much of the credit must be given for drawing attention to this process, was mainly concerned with it as a defence mechanism, i.e. as a way of dealing with the anxiety which the child experiences as a result of the feelings of hostility that parental frustrations engender. Afraid of losing the parents' affection as a result of these hostile feelings, the child solves the conflict by repressing his aggression and instead adopts the safer course of himself, as it were, becoming the aggressor through incorporating the parents' characteristics. The Freudian theory thus views identification as being mainly based on the child's negative feelings towards his parents and in this way differs from the learning theory account, which proposes instead that the child's wish to be the parent arises from his past experiences of feelings of gratification and pleasure associated with the presence of the parent, as a result of which he adopts his characteristics in order, so to speak, to supply his own rewards.

Whichever view is the correct one, the process is clearly a very important one in making the child into an acceptable member of society. Most of the research dealing with it has investigated it in relation to two areas: sex-typing and the development of conscience.

From a very early age on boys and girls are expected to behave differently. Already at three and four years of age children have formed definite and sex-appropriate preferences when asked to choose from such toys as guns, dolls, kitchen utensils and soldiers (Hartup and Zook, 1960), and the strength of these sex-linked preferences tends to increase with age. To some extent learning the appropriate role is due to direct training procedures employed by the parents, but there is evidence suggesting that it is also a result of identification with the same-sex parent. The little boy is expected to be 'like daddy' and to engage in masculine activity like hammering in nails and kicking footballs, while the little girl is similarly encouraged to imitate her mother's interests in cooking, knitting, etc. Society thus guides the child towards the appropriate model and gives him or her the opportunity to form the relevant identification with it. This process involves, of course, not merely the imitation of certain interests and hobbies but also the incorporation of more basic personality characteristics. Aggression, for instance, is regarded as being a mainly masculine trait and therefore fostered in boys by contact with their father. In one investigation

(Sears, 1951) pre-school boys whose fathers were away on military service were found to have developed less aggression than boys whose fathers were at home. No such difference was found between father-present and father-absent girls of the same age.

Many attempts have been made to ascertain those characteristics in a child's family environment which foster strong sex-identifications. There is general agreement that the quality of the relationship with the parent is the most decisive factor in this respect. In a study of five-year-old boys (Mussen and Distler, 1959) a test was administered to measure strength of masculine identification. The scores were then compared with the boys' perception of their fathers (as obtained from the endings which the children supplied to incomplete stories), and it was found that boys with high male identifications tended to see their fathers as warmer and more affectionate than boys with low male identifications. Similar evidence has come from another study (Payne and Mussen, 1956), this time on adolescent boys and using 'test similarity' as a criterion of father-identification: again the strength of identification and the perception of the father as warm, helpful and kind were related. The same finding also applies to girls, for those with high femininity scores on sex-role tests have been found to have warmer relationships with their mothers than girls with low scores. It is thus the rewarding, positive qualities of the parents that promote identification rather than their negative, fear-arousing characteristics.

Another parental quality which encourages the child to model himself on the parent can be described as the latter's 'power'. In the study of five-year-olds quoted above the boys with high male identifications described the father not only as warm but also as strong, powerful and competent: clearly all qualities which aroused the child's incentive to be like the father. Similarly, the parent's interest in the child and the amount of time spent with him promoted identification, suggesting that it is primarily those variables which describe the parents' salience in the child's experience that affect this process.

A child's parents will usually, of course, exercise the most decisive influence on the nature of his identifications. They are, however, by no means the only individuals who will serve as models, and indeed identifications may subsequently be formed with groups and institutions as well. In the case of sex-identification, a study by Koch (1956) shows the importance of family members other than parents. Girls who have older brothers, it was found, tend to be more 'tomboyish' than girls with older sisters, and likewise boys with older sisters have a somewhat higher proportion of feminine traits than boys with older brothers.

Whether sex-linked behaviour is, in fact, solely a function of social learning, as so many writers seem to assume, or whether constitutional factors do not also play a part, remains as yet an unsolved problem.

Certainly anthropological material concerning the very different conceptions of sex-roles found in other societies indicates that behaviour regarded by us as natural' may turn out to be a product of socialization rather than inheritance. Yet in the area of sex-linked behaviour above all the assumption of the '*tabula rasa*' child ought to be avoided until more data have been gathered to enable us to make more precise statements regarding aetiology than we can make at present.

The other main area in which the process of identification has been studied is the development of conscience. The learning of moral standards and prohibitions starts early in life in relation to such mundane things as feeding, elimination and aggression, and it is here rather than on the lofty plane of morality and ethics that the foundations of conscience are laid. At first 'right' and 'wrong' are, from the child's point of view, purely arbitrary notions that are imposed on him by external agents. Sooner or later, however, he learns that these agents will follow 'right' actions with praise and 'wrong' actions with punishment and withdrawal of love. In order to avoid the latter consequences he begins to incorporate the rules of behaviour expected of him, so that his conduct is no longer exclusively governed by sanctions employed by other people but becomes increasingly regulated by the feeling of guilt which he experiences after all transgressions. Thus, in the adequately socialized child, the tendency to model his behaviour after that of his parents results in the incorporation of adult moral standards and the capacity for self-punishment.

The progression from external to internal regulation of behaviour takes a long time and may, in some individuals, never be completed. Again, a satisfactory relationship with the parents appears to be an essential prerequisite for such a development, for children with a highly developed conscience have mostly been found to have warmer, more accepting parents than children of the same age with less well developed consciences. A further influence, however, has also been isolated, namely the actual technique which parents employ in order to impose conformity. In general, withdrawal of love has been found far more effective in producing a strong conscience than physical punishment, deprivation of privileges, or the giving of tangible rewards (Sears, Maccoby and Levin, 1957). However, this relationship only holds in those cases where the parents are also generally warm and affectionate towards the child, for otherwise, presumably, there would be less love to take away and the child would not be as affected by the threatened loss as a child who has a rather more affectionate relationship with his parents. Thus the children most advanced in conscience development appear to be those whose parents are relatively warm towards them but who make their love contingent on the child's willingness to conform to their demands.

Once again one must remember, however, that parents are not the only models a child encounters. Influences outside the home also play their part in shaping conscience: a conclusion borne out by an interesting finding on boys with criminal fathers (McCord and McCord, 1958). This investigation showed that such boys are less likely to become criminals themselves if accepted by their fathers than if rejected by them. Where the parent model is found by the child to be opposed to society's norms, parents' acceptance may actually operate against identification.

Just in what way identification is to be differentiated from imitation is still an open issue. Some writers distinguish between these terms on the basis of the degree of specificity of the behaviour pattern which is learned; others consider that identification presupposes the existence of an attachment to the model, whereas this is not a necessary precondition in the case of imitation; and still others believe that imitation is a process that requires the model's presence at the time, whereas identification refers to the performance of the model's behaviour in the latter's absence. However, one recent body of research stemming from the work of Bandura and Walters (1963) has proceeded from the assumption that the two terms refer in fact to the same set of behavioural phenomena and to the same learning process, and that no useful purpose is served by making any distinction between them. Both terms, according to these writers, apply to the manner in which patterns of social behaviour are acquired through a process that may most suitably be labelled as *observational learning*. Whereas previous theories had stressed the need for rewards to be made available if imitation is to occur, these investigators have shown that, through simple exposure to a model and the opportunity to observe him perform certain activities, children will acquire new responses that match those of the model and which can, moreover, be reproduced not only at the time but also be replicated at a later date. Thus, in a typical experiment (Bandura, Ross and Ross, 1963), nursery school children watched a model behaving aggressively in a play situation by showing, for instance a number of unusual hostile responses towards a large inflated rubber doll. When the children were subsequently allowed to play in the same situation it was found that they showed precisely matching responses and tended to behave far more aggressively than children who had not previously been exposed to a model. Moreover, there was no difference in the extent of imitation between children who had observed a real-life model and children who had observed a filmed model, suggesting not only that exposure to aggression can heighten and also shape the nature of children's aggressive reactions, but also that this influence can be exerted by means of pictorial as well as real-life stimulation.

From experiments such as these Bandura (1962) concludes that social behaviour is typically acquired by means of imitation, that this may take place merely on the basis of 'sensory contiguity' (i.e. the opportunity to observe and attend to the activities of others), and that such learning usually involves the imitation of large segments of behaviour or whole sequences of activities rather than proceeding through the slow, gradual acquisition of isolated responses, each of which must be differentially reinforced by a suitable programme of rewards and punishment. However, imitation is by no means conceived of as a purely passive process, as exposure of an individual to a set of stimuli is no guarantee that he will attend to and learn the relevant cues. It is, however, a virtue of this conceptual approach that it is possible, through a variety of laboratory experiments (cf. Bandura, 1965) to isolate the conditions under which imitating does occur and thus to specify both the environmental and the subject factors which make for optimal susceptibility to the influence of social models. In this way those adult — child similarities of behaviour, which have given rise to the concept of identification in psychodynamic theories, can be studied empirically and traced back to their developmental origins.

There can be little doubt that identification is an extremely complex process and that it is as yet little understood despite the growing amount of research into it. This is partly because of the rather crude techniques that have been used to investigate it: for instance, parental identifications have been measured by the relative amounts of handling of father-dolls and mother-dolls in structured doll-play situation yet the validity of this technique remains unknown. Similarly in research on moral development the choice of criteria for conscience, such as the type of endings which a child supplies to uncompleted stories, is not based on any established association with actual behaviour. Nevertheless, this area does represent an earnest attempt to find out how society impinges on the growing child and the manner in which it shapes and canalizes his behaviour. At present our theories about identification may be rather more impressive than their empirical underpinnings, but at least they serve to draw attention to some of the more subtle forms of interaction between the child and his social environment and to the wide range of variables which may influence any one behavioural activity.

References

BANDURA, A. (1962) 'Social learning through imitation', in JONES, M.R. (Ed.) *Nebraska Symposium of Motivation*, Lincoln, University of Nebraska Press.

BANDURA, A. (1965) 'Behavioural modification through modelling procedures', in KRADNER, L. and ULLMANN, L.P. (Eds) *Research in Behaviour Modification*, New York, Holt, Rinehart and Winston.

BANDURA, A. and WALTERS, R.H. (1963) *Social Learning and Personality Development*, New York, Holt, Rinehart and Winston.

BANDURA, A.; ROSS, D.; and ROSS, S.A. (1963) 'Imitation of film-mediated aggressive models', *J. Abnorm. Soc. Psychol.*, 66, pp. 3–11.

HARTUP, W.W. and ZOOK, E.A. (1960) 'Sex-role preferences in three and four-year-old children', *J. Consult. Psychol.*, 24, pp. 420–6.

KOCH, H. (1956) 'Attitudes of young children towards their peers as related to certain characteristics of their siblings', *Psychol. Monogr.*, 70, 19.

McCORD, J. and McCORD, W. (1958) 'The effect of parental role model in criminality', *J. Soc. Issues*, 14, pp. 66–75.

MILLER, N.E. and DOLLARD, J. (1941) *Social Learning and Imitation*, New Haven, Yale University Press.

MUSSEN, P. and DISTLER, L. (1959) 'Masculinity, identification and father — son relationships', *J. Abnorm. Soc. Psychol.*, 59, pp. 350–6.

PAYNE, D.E. and MUSSEN, P. (1965) 'Parent — child relations and father identification among adolescent boys', *J. Abnorm. Soc. Psychol.*, 52, pp. 358–62.

SEARS, P.S. (1951) 'Doll play aggression in normal young children: Influence of sex, age, sibling status, and father's absence', *Psychol. Monogr.*, 65, 323.

SEARS, R.R.; MACCOBY, E.E.; and LEVIN, H. (1957) *Patterns of Child Rearing*, New York, Harper and Row.

Learning and the Peer Group

(From Rubin, Z., 1980, *Children's Friendships*, Fontana, pp. 93–7, 106–7.)

The importance of the peer group in the growing up process is explored in this extract from *Children's Friendships*. Children are beings in a social world, and friendship groups often characterized by rules, rituals and initiation ceremonies, provide a context for learning about self and developmental concerns. Developmental tasks, culturally mediated, are likely to form the substance of many same-sex groups in the later primary school years. Becoming a sexual being is of increasing importance as puberty approaches, and with it attitudes towards the other sex, adult relationships and self are formed. At younger ages the developmental concern is more with learning culturally accepted standards of behaviour in such areas as toileting, and the beginnings of cooperative behaviour in games. Flexible teaching approaches, where friendships rather than ability groups are used, have potential for harnessing the importance of the peer group for school learning.

In the early school years children often become especially interested in forming 'official' groups. A commonly observed pattern is for a group of eight- or nine-year-olds to form a club — typically admitting only boys or only girls — invest a tremendous amount of energy into deciding on officers and their official titles, find nothing to do after that, and then disband. For my own part, I was a charter member of a club for seven-year-olds called the Penguins whose two major activities were acquiring extensive information about penguins and standing outside in the freezing weather without a coat for as long as we could. Like most other groups of this sort, the Penguins did not last very long. But in the making and unmaking of such groups, children are conducting what may be informative experiments in social organization. Through such experiences, children develop increasingly sophisticated understandings of groups, from an early conception of a group as merely a collection of people in one place to a later conception of a group as a collective organization in which individuals are united by common interests and goals.

Children's groups characteristically take on their greatest importance in late childhood — the years between about nine and twelve. At a time when children must leave the safety of the family, to become more autonomous persons, a group of friends can play a valuable supportive role, especially in the domains of sexual and emotional development. Despite the psychoanalytic notion that childhood is a period of sexual latency — the calm before the storm of puberty — sexual concerns are likely to be prominently revealed in groups of nine- to twelve-year-olds. American boys, for example, are likely to participate in 'bull sessions' devoted to the exchange of sexual information. According to Gary Fine, 'These sessions are filled with loud (almost hysterical) giggly laughter, insults, and bravado,' all of which may testify to the underlying significance of the topics being discussed. Although group discussions may arouse anxiety, they may also provide needed reassurance and support as children deal with the concerns of growing up.

At the same time, children's groups pose the central issue of inclusion and exclusion. Even among toddlers in the kibbutz, group membership is closely linked to the exclusion of nonmembers. On the kibbutz carousel, for example, the children always make room for members of their own group but do not let members of other groups join them. In nursery school, ...inclusion and exclusion are constant themes of social life. It is through the continuing negotiation of who is 'in' and who is 'out' that children establish and maintain group boundaries. When Josh, Tony, and Caleb want to play spaceship, they usually shout to one another and discourage any other children from joining in. A revealing exception comes on a day that Tony is absent from school and another boy, Eddie, is allowed on board:

When I inquire into the matter, Josh (Captain Kirk) tells me that Eddie is Spock, adding that 'He's on my crew'.

'But I thought Tony was Spock,' I protest.

Josh looks at me disdainfully and then explains the obvious: 'Tony's not here today.'

'Well, how about when Tony gets back?'

Josh glances at Eddie and replies, 'Then *he's* not playing.'

Eddie was not admitted to regular membership in the space group because he had relatively little in common with Josh, Tony, and Caleb. Eddie was slower-moving and slower-talking than the other three boys and had trouble keeping up with their often frenetic pace. In addition, because of his shoulder-length hair, Eddie appeared 'girlish' to the other boys. These differences contributed to his exclusion from the space group. For if pairs of friends tend to be similar to one another, similarity of attributes and skills typically plays an even larger role in determining the membership of cliques and groups.

The membership of a group may take shape in several different ways. Sometimes an individual child with valued skills plays a central role, with others entering the group by gaining the leader's approval. In other cases the group begins with an existing pair of friends, who then proceed to include others in their activities. Josh and Tony became friends early in the year and only later took Caleb, a slightly younger and smaller boy, into their group as a sort of junior member. In still other instances the group is based primarily on joint participation in a particular activity.

Whether the activity is playing in a band or building sand-castles, children will be included only if they have the skills and interests that enable them to take part. All of these processes of group formation are likely to produce a relatively homogeneous membership. Just as in groups of adolescents and adults, moreover, there are strong pressures to exclude the 'deviant' child, whether the difference is with respect to appearance, skills, or temperament. In many school settings, race is another basis of group membership. 'They [other black girls] get mad because you've made a white friend,' a black twelve-year-old reports. 'They say that blacks are supposed to have black friends and whites are supposed to have white friends.' Indeed, the link between group solidarity and similarity is so prevalent as to approach the status of a universal law of social behaviour.

Groups also have the effect of *making* their members — or prospective members — similar to one another. There is usually strong pressure on children to conform to the expectations and standards of their groups, both because of concern about being accepted and because of the assumption that 'if everyone in my group is doing it, it must be right'. The influence of group membership on children's behaviour is especially striking in the kibbutz. Even in the youngest kibbutz groups, the children themselves play an important role in enforcing standards of behaviour. When one of the children has a toileting accident, for example, the others all look at him and shout, 'Haggai did a BM, Haggai did a BM! Not on the floor, Haggai, not on the floor!' Similarly, when one child has hit another and made him cry, all the other group members come up and hit the first child. 'How many times do I have to tell you not to hit other children?' one of them adds. Such peer influence proves to be extremely effective in regulating the children's behaviour.

The degree to which children conform to group norms and beliefs appears to increase during the years of childhood, often reaching its peak at about the age of twelve. . . .

Why do boy's and girls' friendships differ in these ways? Douvan and Adelson try to explain the difference in terms of a psychoanalytically derived view that boys have a greater need to band together and rebel against paternal authority. Other behavioural scientists have speculated — albeit without solid evidence — that there are biologically based predispositions for males to bond in groups and for females to be concerned with intimate, nurturant relationships. But the different patterns of friendship seem to be best understood as outcomes of early learning experiences. Part of this learning may come from the different games and sports that boys and girls play. Janet Lever observes that girls' games (such as playing house or jumping rope) are likely to involve close contact with a single, well-liked person, whereas boys' games (such as baseball or football) are more likely to be played in larger groups and to call for cooperation even with teammates who may not be well-liked personally.

Whether sex-typed games and sports are viewed as causing the differences or as reflections of already existing differences, it is clear that boys and girls grow up with somewhat different models of social relations. In their intimate friendships, girls develop their aptitude for nurturance and emotional expressiveness, social skills that are most relevant to close personal and family relationships. In their larger groups, boys learn to operate within systems of rules and to get along even with people they don't especially like, social skills that are most relevant to modern organizational life. Each sex learns something of importance, but at the same time each sex is deprived of opportunities to learn other important skills. I suspect, for example, that the social learning of childhood is responsible in large measure for the special difficulty that men often have in forming intimate friendships. My own view is that it would be valuable for both boys and girls to have more positively sanctioned exposure to the games, sports, and social patterns that are typically associated with the other sex, as a means of encouraging the fuller development of individual children's potential for rewarding social relationships.

The Teacher's Influence on Moral Behaviour

(From Wright, D., 1971, *The Psychology of Moral Behaviour*, Harmondsworth, Penguin, pp. 239–44.)

Becoming a moral being is an important part of a child's development. The culture and its values are mediated through parents, extended family, teachers, the media, and as the child grows older, through the peer group, which plays an increasingly important role in influencing behaviour, dress and values (pp. 302–305). Wright draws this out in an integration of theories of moral development but places his emphasis on the influence of school and class teacher. He suggests that the role of the teacher needs to be broadened beyond academic classroom concerns into the pastoral and social domain if the teacher is to influence moral behaviour. In the primary school, and certainly in the infant department, there is less division between academic and pastoral care than in the secondary school. The greater contact between teacher and children in the primary school may allow for more direct experience of the teacher's attitudes and values than in the secondary school, when additionally peer groups increase in importance. Wright points out that children extract the essence of the classroom climate, that they understand the implicit meaning or intention rather than only what is explicitly stated.

Though there is at present little evidence to show that the school has much impact upon the child's moral development, we can at least say something about the way its influence is mediated. If we wanted to know the nature of the moral education going on in any school our best strategy would be to seek answers to five questions: What is the nature of the relationships between staff and pupils? What actions are rewarded or positively reinforced? What actions are punished or negatively reinforced? What is the nature of the example set by staff? What kind of talking goes on in relation to morality?

The importance of staff-pupil relationships is obvious. If they are characterized by mutual hostility or indifference, the school may be actually encouraging antisocial behaviour. If their most salient features are power and control on the part of the teacher and fear and submission on the part of the pupils, then what the pupils will be learning is discretion and the avoidance of being found out, but not self-control. The more internalized moralities of the conscientious and autonomous characters depend upon relationships of mutual liking and democratic equality.

The relationship between teacher and pupil considerably influences the effectiveness of the teacher as a source of reinforcement and example. Here the important thing is how this reinforcement and example are actually seen by the pupil, and this may not coincide with what the teachers intend. It is obviously possible for a school to encourage obsequious time-serving, lying, snobbery and conceit, and to discourage truthfulness and integrity, without the staff having any clear idea of the fact.

School punishment is unlikely to lead to increased self-control in the child unless he has sufficient affection for the teacher to be partly on his side (though it will make him more careful about being found out); and if this affection exists the teacher's disappointment and disapproval are likely to be sanction enough. Of all sanctions corporal punishment is the least effective in increasing moral restraint in the offender, and it may have certain negative effects. If the teacher is mainly concerned with deterring others, however, there may be some point in such punishment. The evidence suggests that others can be vicariously conditioned by seeing an offender punished. Of course if in their view the punishment is unjust, or if there is in the school an unspoken norm which defines the staff as the enemy, then the effect will be very different.

Punishment of offenders is probably the least important factor, especially since many punishable offences at school have only tenuous moral implications. Much more important is the example set by the teacher. Obviously he will be a respectable citizen and not a criminal. But he faces a certain occupational hazard (which others face, though usually to a lesser extent). Through his authority he can control the child's response to his own behaviour. It is possible for a teacher to be rude to a child in ways in which he would not dare to be to an adult — his authority protects him from the social feedback which would otherwise inhibit him. A teacher can imperceptibly slide into the habit of more or less continually setting an example of bad manners, injustice, bullying, or even mild sadism, without knowing it, for the children have been trained to inhibit the responses which would bring home to the teacher the real nature of his conduct. I am not suggesting of course that this often happens. The important point is that because of the role he occupies in the classroom the teacher is unlikely to be fully aware of the nature of the example he is setting.

Moral education at its most conscious and deliberate takes the form of talk. Several different kinds can be distinguished. Exhortation and preaching are probably the least effective. It all depends upon whether the teacher is accepted as a natural leader by his pupils, as distinct from the occupant of a social role; that is, it depends upon whether he has any influence in shaping the norms that exist among the pupils themselves. A particular danger associated with the roles of parent and teacher is what has been called 'identification with the superego'. In his anxiety to help the moral development of his pupils the teacher may find himself recommending standards that are higher than the ones he actually lives by, and this will be seen as hypocrisy by the more perceptive of young people he teaches. The commonest form that moral education takes is discussion. This can range from, in effect, moral philosophy at one end to discussion of social problems like drugs and venereal disease at the other. The aim is primarily to inform and to encourage responsible judgement. Finally the school can provide opportunities for children to work through their own moral problems with the help of a sympathetic adult. In this situation the teacher's role has really become that of the counsellor. It seems probable that it is this kind of 'moral talk' which will have the greatest impact upon the child's behaviour.

Finally we should look carefully at the kind of self-concept our education develops in children...when people's self-esteem is reduced their moral controls are weakened. This raises the interesting question of the extent to which the damage done to self-esteem by academic failure in the classroom has repercussions in the child's moral life outside it. Schools commonly hold up two identities before the child, the positive one (the 'good boy') which includes politeness to staff, hard work, cheerfulness, obedience, cooperation, and so on, and the negative one (the 'bad boy') made up of the opposites of these. It sometimes seems that children who fail to qualify for the positive identity, however much they try, end up by opting wholeheartedly for the negative one — if they cannot have fame in a competition in which the odds seem weighted against them they will have notoriety instead. Children only have an incentive to live up to the high opinion of their teachers if these teachers have a high opinion of them. Distrust is no cure for untrustworthiness — it merely increases it. Likewise being unsympathetic to children who lack sympathy for others is not likely to make them more sympathetic.

All this is in a way obvious. What it boils down to is that the first step for anyone who has to take responsibility for the moral education of children should be to examine the morality of his own actions towards them. Children become moral by living in a community in which honesty and generosity are valued, which is just and which therefore supports and encourages protest against injustice which may occur within it, and so on. What is not so obvious is that we have to decide not simply whether we are going to throw the resources of the school community into making children moral, but what kind of character we wish to see emerging at the end. The discussion of character in the previous chapter illustrates some of the main options before the educator. Whether he likes it or not he will be tending to produce one such character rather than another. It is true that genetic predisposition and family background may leave so deep an imprint on character that the influence of school is superficial, even negligible, by comparison. But it is also the influence which is most under our control and we are obliged to use it as responsibly as we can.

Presumably schools are never actually intended to encourage the amoral character. But they may do so inadvertently, especially if moral development is not thought to be their concern. Sometimes, perhaps because of dissension among the staff and the stress of coping with impossibly difficult children, the school's morale can sink so low that on balance its moral influence is more harmful than good, so that, for example, flattery is always rewarded and expedience invariably takes precedence over justice. The conformist character would tend to be fostered by a school in which children are herded together in large groups all the time and where opportunity to form individual friendships is minimal. If the staff are distant and ineffective, and follow a *laissez-faire* policy, the child ends up by being influenced mainly by peer groups in which the influence of adults is totally absent. It is not difficult to picture the kind of school which encourages the authoritarian character. The staff are remote and powerful people. In the child's eyes the principal virtue is obedience to authority. Hierarchy runs all through the school, with great emphasis upon the powers and privileges of older pupils and staff. The main lesson the child learns is that as you gain power so the rules become more adjusted to suit your pleasure and convenience, and they increasingly enable you to make use of others. Relationships of mutual respect are rare and tend to be restricted to those at the bottom of the hierarchy. English schools do not seem to be designed to produce the collectivist character though certain movements within them which stress the grouping of children for work purposes and the deliberate use of the group to change the individual might be said to be a small step in this direction. The conscientious character will tend to be the product of small schools, with small classes, where there is a lot of staff-pupil contact of a warm and friendly kind, and where high standards are set and the staff present a unanimous front over what these standards are.

The view taken here is of course that the character most worthy of cultivation is the altruistic-autonomous. Though developmentally speaking this must be an achievement of adulthood, school life may facilitate its emergence. The kind of school most likely to encourage it is one in which pupils and staff come from varied backgrounds and where there is plenty of opportunity for individual relationships to flourish, both among pupils and between pupils and staff. Relationships of this kind provide the child with an experience of the interhuman, of trust and creative personal exchange, which makes the point of moral principles seem obvious, and they form the context in which he can talk out his own moral problems and experience giving them shape and meaning (as distinct from discussing more abstract and hypothetical moral issues in a group or class situation). What he needs to find in the staff is unanimity over the importance of commitment to basic moral principles coupled with diversity of judgement over their application. Democratic moments between staff and pupils are common. What the child learns is that moral issues are of the greatest importance, that they are controversial, and that they can only be settled by reasoning and the appeal to common values and never by the exercise of authority and power. And he also learns that, though he has no alternative but to live by his own standards, these standards are relative and partial, and always in need of revision.

What I have said amounts to the claim that the really valuable part of moral education occurs outside the orthodox teacher role, when the teacher is for the moment 'off duty', or in his role as unofficial counsellor. Of course school organization and all the chores that teachers are burdened with make this kind of private and individual contact difficult — but not impossible, for some teachers manage a lot of it. Its very rarity can make it that much more significant and memorable for the child. Teachers have also to shake loose from constrictive professional roles which inhibit them from being personal, and which compel them to present to the child a united, safe and usually conservative front on the really important things like values, moral rules, religion and social problems. There is evidence that teachers are not seen as fully human, by adolescents anyway (see Wright, 1962). If teachers are to exert a wider influence than just an academic one then they must be able to meet their pupils outside their normal role. There is a simple belief which underlies the whole discussion, namely, if we are to take moral education seriously, and even more if we take the autonomous character as the ideal to be pursued, then it is no use supposing that moral education is something that can be tacked on to the existing curriculum as an extra; on the contrary, all aspects of school life must be looked at in its light, and it must enter centrally into our concept of what a school is.

Reference

WRIGHT, D. (1962) 'A comparative study of the adolescent's concepts of his parents and teachers', *Educational Review*, 14, pp. 226–32.

Coping with Anxiety and Stress

(From Wolff, S., 1981, *Children Under Stress*, Harmondsworth, Penguin, pp. 11–13.)

Wolff is concerned with children responding with normal processes to potentially troublesome events and experiences. She makes the point that children deal with experiences with the cognitive structures available to them at the time. A new-baby born at the time the child starts full-time school may be a greater source of stress than that same baby born a year later. After a year in school, the child has normally dealt with being separated from the parent during the day, and has re-established feelings of security. Wolff does not deal with the question of individual differences in temperament which may make one child experience more adversely than another the identical event at the same time. She does point out that early experiences may have long-lasting effects, and unsatisfactory relationships from the child's point of view may adversely affect later abilities to trust adults or to respond to events without aggression. The teacher who knows his or her class well as individuals will adopt different tactics according to how the child's needs are perceived.

With rare exceptions, problem children are no different from other children. They react with normal psychological mechanisms to their life experiences. All children in the course of growing up encounter minor stresses: accidents and illnesses, the birth of a new baby, a move of house and school, the inevitable demands for increasing maturity and self-control. Most children at some time react to these stresses with temporary behaviour disorders, such as nightmares, bedwetting, temper tantrums or excessive fears. Parents usually know almost intuitively what these symptoms mean and they respond by lessening the pressures on the child. Serious difficulties arise only when the stresses are overwhelming or when the adults are too preoccupied to attend to the child's signals of distress. Skilled psychological help is then necessary, although the reactions of the child are 'normal' in the sense that any child under these conditions would react similarly.

There are two indications that psychological appraisal and skilled help are needed for a child. The first is the occurrence of a critical life situation. The second is severe or persistent disturbance of behaviour. A crisis such as admission to hospital, bereavement or the break-up of a family is generally recognized as stressful. Most people are concerned about the possible effects on children of such events, and evidence is accumulating that expert help at these times can prevent psychological disturbances in later life.

In known situations of crisis children's disturbed behaviour is often overshadowed by the events themselves. Some outward signs of distress are expected and when they occur they are as a rule tolerated and understood. Many children, however, are identified as in need of special help not because of the life situation in which they are caught but because of the behaviour disturbances they display. For example, children who draw attention to themselves because they steal repeatedly or because they soil themselves are children suffering from unrecognized, hidden stress and this is often aggravated by the adverse responses which their difficult behaviour elicits from other people.

Whether a situation is stressful for a child varies with the developmental level he has reached. The disappearance of his mother into hospital, for instance, is not noticed by a baby under three months because he is not yet aware of people and objects as distinct from himself. After seven months of age there is clear evidence that a baby misses his mother. But the nature of the anxieties aroused by her departure and the ways in which the child copes with his upset differ according to his maturity. At eighteen months he may think his mother has gone forever because he cannot imagine a future and his understanding of language is too poor for him to be consoled by explanations and reassurances. At four, when the child is egocentric and regards himself as the originator of everything that happens around him, and when he views all bad events as, magically, caused by some failure on his part, he may explain his mother's illness as due to his own misdeeds. To understand the impact of adverse events and circumstances on children, we need to know how at different stages of their development they perceive and think about the world, that is, we must know something about their *intellectual development.*

The child's intellectual level determines how he experiences his environment. His *social and emotional development* has to do with what he experiences. This, of course, is determined in large measure by the culture in which he grows up. Parental attitudes and child-rearing practices are part of this culture and so are the provisions made for children in the wider world. Social and emotional development also occurs in recognized stages. These are, however, less universal than the stages of intellectual growth, and their characteristics as outlined by psychoanalysts hold with any certainty only for children in our Western culture. A major contribution of the psychoanalysts has been to show that at each stage of social and emotional development the child begins to be concerned with particular aspects of his relationship with the people in his environment; that each stage presents its own problems to be solved; that different sources of anxiety exist at different stages; and that with increasing maturity the child's responses to excessive stress undergo progressive changes.

A second and equally important psychoanalytic contribution is Erikson's proposition (1965) that each stage of childhood can set a unique and permanent stamp on future personality. The experiences of childhood are not lost. When they are favourable the individual reaches maturity with his potentialities for human relationships, for work and for happiness unimpaired. He responds to his environment in a realistic way and he can adapt to changing circumstances. When childhood experiences are overwhelmingly stressful, arrest of personality occurs and a pattern of repetitive maladaptive behaviour may be set in train, which like an ill fate prevents the individual from ever achieving his full potentialities in adult life. A child, for example, who was deserted by her mother in childhood may be unable to master this event satisfactorily at the time. It often happens that such a person continues even in adult life to seek for a loving mother and in so doing makes inordinate and inappropriate demands on other people such as her husband, or even her employer. When these other people realize they cannot meet the demands made upon them, they turn away, once more abandoning the crippled individual just as her mother had abandoned her in the past. Help for children under stress fulfils a double purpose: the relief of present anxieties and the prevention of personality defects in later life.

Adverse events are harmful for children when they arouse more anxiety than the child can cope with. A knowledge of intellectual and emotional development helps us to understand the impact and the consequences of such events. But circumstances can be harmful for children not through commission but through omission: they can deprive the child of essential learning experiences. Children separated from their mothers and reared in children's homes during their first three years of life may be permanently handicapped in their emotional relationships with other people. Children from culturally deprived homes often do not achieve their full educational potential in later life. Just as physical growth is stunted by nutritional deficiency in childhood, so personality growth also is impaired if the environment does not satisfy the child's psychological needs.

Reference

ERIKSON, E. (1965) *Childhood and Society*, Harmondsworth, Penguin.

Understanding Classroom Learning: An Ecological Approach

(From Desforges, C. *et al*. (1984) 'Understanding the quality of pupil learning experience', in Entwistle, N. (Ed.), *New Directions in Educational Psychology I: Learning and Teaching*, Lewes, Falmer Press.

In recent years psychologists have become interested in how children actually learn in classrooms and in the implications of this research for teaching. This extract arises out of work at Lancaster University into the processes by which tasks are allocated to children in classrooms and the degree to which these tasks are matched to advance children's learning. The authors use a transcript from a primary classroom to illustrate two important features of classroom learning:

1   children do not merely receive tasks from teachers but interpret them; and
2   teachers are rarely in a position to appreciate the processes by which children adapt to classroom tasks.

To underline the complexities, the authors introduce an ecological model. This shows that children influence and interpret the tasks given in the classroom and that they acquire 'interpretative competence', that is, the capacity to discern what the teacher wants. The authors conclude by drawing out some speculative implications of the ecological model for attempts to improve the quality of learning experiences offered in classrooms.

Several recent studies have raised concern about the quality of the learning experiences provided for pupils in schools (Anderson, 1981; HMI, 1978, 1982). Specifically, it appears that many of the tasks given to pupils are not well matched to their attainments. In some areas of the curriculum HMI found that over two-thirds of the work given to children was not appropriate to fostering their learning. Anderson (1981) showed that for many children, inappropriate tasks were an enduring fact of classroom life. In particular, tasks which were too difficult were assigned frequently to low achieving children. Unfortunately it is one thing to recognise a problem and quite another to know what to do about it. . . .

Psychologists especially have been more than forthcoming in offering teachers prescriptions on how to design ideal learning environments. It is now very widely recognised that such advice has had very little impact on the practice of teaching (Atkinson, 1976; Ausubel and Robinson, 1969; Farnham-Diggory, 1976; Glaser *et al.*, 1977). There are no doubt many reasons for this lack of impact. Some arise out of the manner in which those who have studied teaching and learning have oversimplified the lives of classroom participants (Bronfenbrenner, 1976). Until recently, research on learning has ignored the processes of teaching, and research on teaching has neglected the processes of learning.

Consequently some of the advice to teachers emanating from research was consistent only with theories of cognition and therefore did not attend to the constraints on the teacher.

The approach from theories of cognition has been adopted by Bruner (1964), Ausubel (1968) and Posner (1978), for example. It is also manifest in most of the attempts to generate pedagogic implications from Piaget's theory (Duckworth, 1979; Schwebel and Raph, 1974). Typically ignored here are the teacher's limited resources of materials and time and the attention she must pay to the social and emotional needs of her pupils. Typically overestimated is the teacher's autonomy of action in respect of the choice of aims, teaching materials, timetable organisation and the selection of priorities. The impracticality of this approach has long been asserted (Sullivan, 1967, for example) and is now accepted as an issue to be taken seriously in the development of pedagogy (Ginsburg, 1981; Kuhn, 1979).

Conversely some of the advice was consistent only with theories of teaching and set aside the problems and potential of the learner.…

It is becoming increasingly clear that classrooms are much more complex learning environments than has previously been admitted by researchers (and possibly by teachers) and that if efforts are to be made to improve the quality of learning experience provided for pupils, then attempts must first be made to understand the connections between the processes of teaching and learning as they operate, and interact, in real classrooms.

Some of the complexity of classroom teaching and learning is illustrated in the following account and analysis of a seven year old girl's efforts to work through a number assignment allocated by her teacher.

The girl, Helen, is of average ability for her top infant class and she is one of 28 children being taught by a very experienced teacher of infants. The events were recorded as part of a routine observation of the classroom during a major research study on the quality of pupil learning experience in primary schools (Bennett and Desforges, in preparation).

The teacher had placed a number of workcards in Helen's book. Helen collected her book and then the following took place:
9.25 a.m. In Helen's book the teacher had written '1.4.81. money' under which Helen wrote:

> I have 9p
> I buy a box of crayons for
> I have   change

9.30 a.m. Helen looked at a price list.

9.40 a.m. The teacher asked Helen what she was looking for and concluded that Helen has mis-read 'crayons' and had been trying to locate the cost of chocolate instead.

9.42 a.m. The teacher showed Helen the price list she should have been looking at. Helen studied it and eventually found the price of crayons.

9.44 a.m. She began counting out amounts in half pence pieces but did not have enough of them for her purposes. She then got a box of cardboard money and counted out 9p in half pence pieces. After laying these out on her desk Helen counted out 11p in half pence pieces. She counted all the half pence and wrote 15p in the space for recording the change.

9.49 a.m. Helen's next card was as follows:

> I have 19p
> I buy a car for _____
> I buy a rocket for _____
> I spend _____
> I have _____ change.

Having read the card, Helen searched the pictures on the price list for the cost of the items.

9.53 a.m. She established that a car cost 10p but failed to find the cost of a rocket.

9.55 a.m. Eventually Helen found that a rocket cost 7p. She began counting half pence pieces and then announced, 'I've lost count now.'

9.57 a.m. Helen had 19 pence worth of half pence pieces on her desk.

9.59 a.m. She collected 10p and put it on her desk. She then apparently went in search of more coins but changed her mind and returned to her desk without any. She counted out 17p in half pence pieces.

10.02 a.m. Helen counted all the half pence pieces on her desk and wrote down $18\frac{1}{2}$p.

10.03 a.m. She returned all the coins to their box and went to the teacher's desk.

10.04 a.m. The teacher marked Helen's work and asked her what 'change' meant. The work in Helen's book looked like this:

> I have 9p
> I buy a box of crayons for $6\frac{1}{2}$p
> I have 15p change
> I have 19p
> I buy a car for 10p

I buy a rocket for 7p
I spend 1½p
I have 18½p change

On the basis of the above record it seems that this task is very much too difficult for Helen. She appears to be struggling with some of the reading necessary to the task. She does not appear to know when to subtract in respect of these money problems. She does not appear to know about the denomination value of coins and indulges in a strange preoccupation with half-penny pieces. This in turn leads her into performance difficulties. She fails to keep track of her counting behaviour in the face of the sheer quantity of half pence coins. Finally she does not appear to know what the word 'change' means.

Helen appears to be so far out of touch with this task that we are bound to ask why she was given it in the first place. Why was the teacher so late in discovering that Helen did not know what the work 'change' meant? How had the teacher failed to notice all of Helen's other problems?

Before observing Helen the research worker had asked the teacher why she had allocated this task to her. The teacher had said that she wanted to familiarise Helen with half pence in simple shopping sums. All the children had been working with money for some time. The teacher pointed out that half pence had been introduced two days earlier in accordance with the very detailed school mathematics scheme.

In the light of this information the teacher's behaviour becomes much more comprehensible. That is not to say it was justifiable. However it is at least clear that the teacher was moving Helen through the maths scheme.

When Helen had completed her work for the teacher, the research worker interviewed her in an attempt to understand her problems with the task.... [On the basis of this interview, the task did not appear to be wildly beyond Helen.] Why then, did she have such problems with it? Why did she make it so much more difficult than the teacher intended by attempting to do it in half pence only? And why did the teacher not recognise her difficulties?

We have to infer answers to these questions. Helen had done money sums over the previous two days. Every sum had focussed on half pence and their conversion to pence. Every sum had been done using half pence only. On the day of the shopping sums the teacher had given Helen no specific instructions. The nature of the task was assumed. Helen knew what to do when she found the cards in her book i.e. she assumed that they had to be worked in half pence. The performance problems caused by handling such large quantities could have caused her to regress in the execution of familiar, simple skills. Such regression is well known. On her own initiative Helen presumably got little but confusion out of this task.

The teacher's behaviour can be understood if it is recalled that Helen took her work to the teacher's desk. The teacher did not see Helen in action on these sums. She did not see the processes by which Helen got into her mess. She saw only the product. Given that, the teacher's insight was impressive in identifying Helen's difficulty with the word 'change'. Nonetheless she was of no help to the child on this task. Clearly, even if the teacher had monitored Helen's on-task performance closely and had thereby dealt with her confusion as it emerged, it is likely that she would have missed another problem somewhere in the class. A teacher cannot be everywhere at once.

The above is an account of only one classroom event. A great deal of supplementary evidence was necessary even to begin to comprehend the actions of the participants. It is dangerous to make generalisations from a unique event. However, whilst this event was unique, it had many features in common with hundreds of other events observed in the course of the research project referred to earlier. It was selected for illustrative purposes because its features exemplify a pattern which is not at all unusual in the classrooms observed.

In this respect, two critical features must be stressed. First, the child does not merely receive the task given by the teacher. Children do not act as a tape recorder for the teacher's instructions. They interpret and frequently adapt the tasks assigned. . . .

The second common and critical feature is that teachers are rarely cognisant of the processes by which children adapt to and process tasks. They work with the products of children's efforts rather than the processes. This must not be interpreted as the consequences of lazy teaching habits. With limited resources at her disposal (especially the resource of time) and 30 children to work with, the teacher too must adapt to her classroom in a way which apparently gives her maximum return on effort.

In terms of the actual quality of learning as experienced by pupils, the evidence suggests that this return on effort is significantly less than ideal.

Understanding the Quality of Learning Experience

If the above argument is accepted it is clear that repeating the old familiar advice to teachers about good management, increasing time on task, developing carefully structured schemes and the like is going to have the effect it always had; that is, no effect at all. Helen was working in a well managed classroom; she spent a large amount of time on her task and she was moving through a detailed and respected number scheme.

In order, for example, to improve the quality of Helen's learning experience, it seems essential first of all to lay bare the adaptive and inventive processes of classroom teaching and learning. Once these are comprehended there may be some prospect of manipulating them to the advantage of all concerned.

In an effort to do this, some educational researchers have moved away from correlational studies of learning and teaching and adopted an ecological approach to understanding classroom life. Since this approach shows some promise, its essential features are outlined below.

Ecology is the study of how organisms shape and adapt to their environment. The essential characteristic of the ecological framework is that, '... individuals and their environment are seen to be engaged in a process of progressive mutual accommodation' (Cohen, 1980). In order to understand these adaptations it is necessary to describe the main features of the environment and the resources of the inhabitants.

The most detailed attempt to do this in respect of classrooms has been made by Walter Doyle (1979a, 1979b, 1980). Doyle characterises classrooms as complex information systems with three important general properties. First, there is an abundance of information sources (books, exercises, verbal and non verbal behaviour) any one or combination of which may assume instructional significance. Secondly, these sources are not consistently reliable as instructional cues. Thus, despite the amount of information available, that monitored for a given task may be inadequate. Finally, the classroom is considered to be a mass-processing system. Many people take part and many interests and purposes are served. Many stimuli are generated at any given moment and the simultaneous occurrence of events leaves little time for participants to reflect. This confers an immediacy on experience and decisions. It also limits the degree to which the quality of information can match the needs of a particular pupil.

The complex information environment of the classroom is inhabited by teachers and pupils all of whom are considered to have severe limitations on their capacity to deal effectively with the abundance of information. They cannot attend to many things at once....

The limitations on attentional capacity are such that selections must be made from potentially available sources of information. Strategies must be developed to optimise these selections in order to increase the predictability of classroom life. To this end it is necessary to make many actions routine. The advantage of making actions automatic is that it reduces the load on information processing capacity or focal attention. This frees more attention for monitoring the environment....

In Doyle's view, the notion of the classroom as a complex and abundant information environment to which people with limited capacities for dealing with information must adapt, represents the context in which classroom learning must be understood. In this respect the crucial aspect of the environment which links teachers and pupils is considered to be the tasks which teachers present for pupils to process. Pupils endeavour to accomplish tasks in a process which Doyle describes as, 'an exchange of performance for grades' i.e. the pupil tries to deliver what the teacher is predicted to reward. In order to adapt to the environment the pupil must indulge in those activities which make clear to him which performances will deliver the good grades. It must be emphasised that in this model the learner is not the passive recipient of the teacher's instructions. On the contrary, students are seen as to some extent determining the level of demand which teachers make on them. In other words they 'set the rate for the job' to some degree.

From the researcher's point of view, understanding learning entails discovering how the student influences, and subsequently interprets, the task structure and ultimately delivers the required performance in exchange for the expected rewards. From the pupil's adaptive point of view, the assessment structure operating in the classroom offers him the clearest specification of what he must do to be 'successful'. That is to say, those behaviours which the teacher rewards are the behaviours to strive for. Doyle suggests that 'Answers a teacher accepts and rewards define the real tasks in the classroom.' Thus if a teacher emphasised 'quality of organisation' as a property to strive for in essay writing, but rewards essay *length*, then the adaptive response from pupils would be to deliver long essays in order to collect the predicted rewards.

The problem for the pupil in his struggle to adapt is to acquire 'interpretive competence', that is the capacity to discern what the teacher wants. This is not easy to attain because both tasks and rewards may be complexly and ambiguously defined in classrooms. For example, a teacher was recently observed to talk to a class of six year old children for 45 minutes about the countries of origin of the produce commonly found in fruit shops. This monologue was illustrated using a tiny map of the world and extensive reference was made to many foreign countries. She finished by asking the children to 'write me an exciting story about the fruit we eat'. The children had to decide what she meant by this! They were helped in part by the fact that they had heard the instruction before in respect of other contents. In fact the children wrote very little. They took great pains to copy the date from the board. (The teacher did not ask them to do this. It was presumably taken for granted as part of the task specification.) They formed their letters with great care and used rubbers copiously to correct any slips of presentation. Whilst this went on the teacher moved about the class commending 'neat work' and 'tidy work' and chiding children for 'dirty fingers' and 'messy work'. No further mention was made of 'exciting' content or of 'stories'. It seemed that the children knew perfectly well what the teacher meant when she asked for an 'exciting story about fruit' even though in this case, the overt task definition (i.e. the teacher's instructions) stood in sharp contrast (although not necessarily in contradiction) to the reward structure.

Once they have discerned what teachers want there is some evidence that pupils offer resistance to curriculum change (Davis and McKnight, 1976). They show a marked lack of interest and an increase in disruptive behaviour when new demands are made on them. This is especially the case when the manner in which to fulfil the demands is difficult to discern (as is the case in problem-solving approaches to learning for example). Doyle (1980) suggests that pupils learn how to respond to one form of task specification — an achievement which brings predictability to their classroom lives — and resist having to discover a new specification and how to fulfil it.

The ramifications of this model in terms of the problems teachers might have in providing appropriate explanations of task demands for a large group of individuals, and those that the pupil might have in identifying and/or controlling a teacher's task demands are provocative. It must be stressed, however, that Doyle's model is not an account of how classroom learning comes about, but an account of what, in ecological terms, pupils come to believe is expected to be learned. Thus, for example, the pupil who does manage to acquire the interpretive competence to learn that, overt remarks notwithstanding, his teacher reinforces long essays, still has to learn how to write a long essay. Doyle provides no account of how pupils might learn either 'interpretive competence' or the skills necessary to convey such competence into reward earning performances.

In order to account for school learning it seems clear that the processes of both task allocation and task working must be monitored in classrooms. However, this in itself would be insufficient. It seems additionally necessary to ascertain the cognitive demands which tasks place on children, the manner in which children meet, avoid, or adapt these demands, and the impact that these experiences have on the child's cognitive progress.

Improving the Quality of Learning Experience

Attempts to improve the quality of learning experience must involve altering the learning environment and/or the capacities of the participants by, for example, providing new materials or new skills. These alterations would shift the ecological balance of the classroom. This in turn would produce corresponding changes in adaptation. The relationship between innovation and outcome at the level of classroom learning might, in this light, be expected to be complex. It might nonetheless be predictable in ecological terms.

Thus some apparently major shifts (for example, adopting a new scheme or giving the teacher more subject expertise) might be expected to have little or no effect, since they leave the classroom behaviours and reward structures relatively untouched. On the other hand apparently minor alterations in teaching behaviour might be expected to demand major readaptations on the part of pupils. For example, if a teacher adopted a policy of occasional but detailed interviews with each child in which the child's capacity but detailed interviews with each child in which the child's capacity to reveal his thinking processes was rewarded (as opposed to his capacity to fill a page neatly), children might be expected to develop ways of meeting this new demand. It would not be possible, or necessary, to interview all children on all tasks: it would be sufficient that the child expected to get such an interview — and that occasionally he did.

Such an apparently minor change requires great skill and planning in its execution and interpretation. Done clumsily, the interview turns into an interrogation focussing on the child's weaknesses. Children might then adapt by staying away from school. But interviews based on developing specific competencies could help the teacher better to understand the pupil's difficulties and the child to learn that schooling rewards the development of personal understanding and not simply the reproduction of 'correct answers'.

These points are somewhat speculative. The major point to be emphasised is that an ecological approach to understanding classroom life can be used to design and predict the outcomes of innovations aimed at improving the quality of pupils' learning. It also provides a caution about the dangers of over-simple analysis and interpretation.

References

ANDERSON, L.M. (1981) 'Student responses to seatwork: Implication for the study of students' cognitive processing', paper presented to A.E.R.A. (Los Angeles).

ATKINSON, R.C. (1976) 'Adaptive instructional systems: Some attempts to optimise the learning process, in KLAHR, D. (Ed.) *Cognition and Instruction*, Hillsdale, N.J., Lawrence Erlbaum Associates.

AUSUBEL, D.P. (1968) *Educational Psychology: A Cognitive View*, New York, Holt, Rinehart and Winston.

AUSUBEL, D.P. and ROBINSON, F.G. (1969) *School Learning: An Introduction to Educational Psychology*, New York, Holt, Rinehart and Winston.

BRONFENBRENNER, U. (1976) 'The experimental ecology of education, *Teachers College Record*, 78, 2, pp. 157–204.

BRUNER, J. (1964) 'The course of cognitive growth'. *American Psychologist*, 19, pp. 1–15.

COHEN, M. (1980) 'Policy implications of an ecological theory of teaching: Towards an understanding of outcomes', in BLUMENFELD, P.C. *et al.* (Eds), *Ecological Theory of Teaching*, Research report ETT 80–85, San Francisco, Calif., Far West Laboratory.

DAVIS, R.B. and McKNIGHT, C. (1976) 'Conceptual, heuristic and algorithmic approaches in mathematics teaching', *Journal of Children's Mathematical Behaviour*, 1, pp. 271–86.

DOYLE, W. (1979a) 'Classroom tasks and student abilities' in PETERSON, P.L. and

WALBERG, H.J. (Eds), *Research on Teaching: Concepts, Findings and Implications*, Berkeley, Calif., McCutchan.

DOYLE, W. (1979b) 'Making managerial decisions in classrooms', in DUKE, D.L. (Ed.), *Classroom Management*, Chicago, Ill., University of Chicago.

DOYLE, W. (1980) *Student Mediating Responses in Teacher Effectiveness*, Denton, Tex, North Texas State University.

DUCKWORTH, E. (1979) 'Either we're too early and they can't learn it or we're too late and they know it already: The dilemma of "applying Piaget",' *Harvard Educational Review*, 49, 3, pp. 297–312.

FARNHAM-DIGGORY, S. (1976) 'Toward a theory of instructional growth', in KLAHR, D. (Ed.), *Cognition and Instruction*, Hillsdale, N.J., Lawrence Erlbaum Associates.

GINSBURG, H.P. (1981) 'Piaget and education: The contributions and limits of genetic epistemology'. in SIGEL, I.E.; BRODZINSKY, D.M.; and GOLINKOFF, P.M. (Eds), *New Directions in Piagetian Theory and Practice*, Hillsdale, N.J., Lawrence Erlbaum Associates.

GLASER, R.; PELLEGRINO, J.W.; and LESGOLD, A.M. (1977) 'Some directions for a cognitive psychology of instruction', in LESGOLD, A.M. *et al.* (Eds), *Cognitive Psychology and Instruction*, New York, Plenum Press.

HMI (1978) *Primary Education in England: A Survey by HM Inspectors of Schools*, London, HMSO.

HMI (1982) *The New Teacher in School* HMI Matters for Discussion No. 15, London, Department of Education and Science.

KUHN, D. (1979) 'The application of Piaget's theory of cognitive development to education', *Harvard Educational Review*, 49, 3, pp. 340–60.

POSNER, G.J. (1978) *Cognitive Science: Implications for Curriculum Research and Development*, paper presented to the AERA, Toronto, March 1978.

SCHWEBEL, M. and RAPH, J. (1974) *Piaget in the Classroom*, London, Routledge and Kegan Paul.

SULLIVAN, E. (1967) 'Piaget and the school curriculum', *Bulletin of the Ontario Institute for Studies in Education.*

Practical Implications of Plowden's View of Learning

(From CAC, 1967, *Children and Their Primary Schools* (The Plowden Report), London, HMSO, paras 533, 535, 538, 540–2.)

The following extracts from the Plowden Report demonstrate how views of children's cognitive development can be applied to the organization of learning in the primary school. The importance of talk with other children and adults as a means of learning is a central feature. Within the context of shared activities through a 'centre of interest' or class topic, sources for communication are created. The teacher has an active role in establishing the context. Providing suitable materials, being flexible with the use of time, and acting as leader to the children, are active aspects of the teacher's organization. These, matched with the teacher's knowledge of individual children and an understanding of child development, are considered by Plowden to be fundamental in education. It was not by chance that the Plowden Report opened with the statement, 'At the heart of the educational process lies the child.'

533.   Learning is a continuous process from birth. The teacher's task is to provide an environment and opportunities which are sufficiently challenging for children and yet not so difficult as to be outside their reach. There has to be the right mixture of the familiar and the novel, the right match to the stage of learning the child has reached. If the material is too familiar or the learning skills too easy, children will become inattentive and bored. If too great maturity is demanded of them, they fall back on half remembered formulae and become concerned only to give the reply the teacher wants. Children can think and form concepts, so long as they work at their own level, and are not made to feel that they are failures.

534.   Teachers must rely both on their general knowledge of child development and on detailed observation of individual children for matching their demands to children's stages of development....

535.   At every stage of learning children need rich and varied materials and situations, though the pace at which they should be introduced may vary according to the children. If children are limited in materials, they tend to solve problems in isolation and fail to see their relevance to other similar situations. This stands out particularly clearly in young children's learning of mathematics. Similarly, children need to accumulate much experience of human behaviour before they can develop moral concepts. If teachers or parents are inconsistent in their attitudes or contradict by their

behaviour what they preach, it becomes difficult for children to develop stable and mature concepts. Verbal explanation, in advance of understanding based on experience, may be an obstacle to learning, and children's knowledge of the right words may conceal from teachers their lack of understanding. Yet it is inevitable that children will pick up words which outstrip their understanding. Discussion with other children and with adults is one of the principal ways in which children check their concepts against those of others and build up an objective view of reality. There is every justification for the conversation which is a characteristic feature of the contemporary primary school. One of the most important responsibilities of teachers is to help children to see order and pattern in experience, and to extend their ideas by analogies and by the provision of suitable vocabulary. Rigid division of the curriculum into subjects tends to interrupt children's trains of thought and of interest and to hinder them from realising the common elements in problem solving. These are among the many reasons why some work, at least, should cut across subject divisions at all stages in the primary school. . . .

538.   The extent to which subject matter ought to be classified and the headings under which the classification is made will vary with the age of the children, with the demands made by the structure of the subject matter which is being studied, and with the circumstances of the school. Any practice which predetermines the pattern and imposes it upon all is to be condemned. Some teachers find it helpful in maintaining a balance in individual and class work to think in terms of broad areas of the curriculum such as language, science and mathematics, environmental study and the expressive arts. No pattern can be perfect since many subjects fall into one category or another according to the aspect which is being studied. For young children, the broadest of divisions is suitable. For children from 9 to 12, more subject divisions can be expected, though experience in secondary schools has shown that teaching of rigidly defined subjects, often by specialist teachers, is far from suitable for the oldest children who will be in the middle schools. This is one of our reasons for suggesting a change in the age of transfer to secondary education. . . .

540.   The idea of flexibility has found expression in a number of practices, all of them designed to make good use of the interest and curiosity of children, to minimise the notion of subject matter being rigidly compartmental, and to allow the teacher to adopt a consultative, guiding, stimulating role rather than a purely didactic one. The oldest of these methods is the 'project'. Some topic, such as 'transport' is chosen, ideally by the children, but frequently by the teacher. The topic cuts across the boundaries of subjects and is treated as its nature requires without reference to

subjects as such. At its best the method leads to the use of books of reference, to individual work and to active participation in learning. Unfortunately it is no guarantee of this and the appearance of text books of projects, which achieved at one time considerable popularity, is proof of how completely a good idea can be misunderstood.

541. A variation on the project, originally associated with the infant school but often better suited to older children, is 'the centre of interest'. It begins with a topic which is of such inherent interest and variety as to make it possible and reasonable to make much of the work of the class revolve round it for a period of a week, a month or a term or even longer. Experience has shown that it is artificial to try to link most of the work of a class to one centre of interest. It has become more common to have several interests — topic is now the usual word — going at once. Much of the work may be individual, falling under broad subject headings. One topic for the time being can involve both group and class interest, and may splinter off into all kinds of individual work.

542. When a class of seven year olds notice the birds that come to the bird table outside the classroom window, they may decide, after discussion with their teacher, to make their own aviary. They will set to with a will, and paint the birds in flight, make models of them in clay or papier maché, write stories and poems about them and look up reference books to find out more about their habits. Children are not assimilating inert ideas but are wholly involved in thinking, feeling and doing. The slow and the bright share a common experience and each takes from it what he can at his own level. There is no attempt to put reading and writing into separate compartments; both serve a wider purpose, and artificial barriers do not fragment the learning experience. A top junior class became interested in the problem of measuring the area of an awkwardly shaped field at the back of the school. The problem stimulated much learning about surveying and triangles. From surveying, interest passed to navigation; for the more difficult aspects of the work, co-operation between members of staff as well as pupils was needed. For one boy, the work on navigation took the form of a story of encounters of pirate ships and men-of-war, and involved a great deal of calculation, history, geography and English. Integration is not only a question of allowing time for interests which do not fit under subject headings; it is as much a matter of seeing the different dimensions of subject work and of using the forms of observation and communication which are most suitable to a given sequence of learning.

Author Index

Subject Index

access
to education, 166–9
accountability, 45, 49–50, 209–19
anxiety, 311–13
arts, 73–7
assessment
of mathematics teaching, 90–2
of teachers, 48–9
Assessment of Performance Unit (APU), 20, 215
attainment
and social class, 170–8
Austin, Mr, 45–50
autonomy, 119–20, 128, 134–8, 139–45, 148, 158–9, 212–15, 309

behaviourism, 245–6, 295–301
Britain, *passim*

child-centred approach, 14, 16, 18, 20, 42, 51, 53–4, 57–9, 63, 108, 111–12, 113, 123–6, 127–33, 141, 164, 225–8, 232–6
child development, 118–19, 245–326
cognitive development
see intellectual development
community education, 93–7, 187–92
comprehensive education, 16–17
concept formation, 262–70
see also child development; intellectual development
curriculum, 10, 14, 25–7, 29, 38, 45, 50, 51–4, 57–9, 84, 90–1, 101, 104–6, 109, 112, 117, 120–1, 128, 132, 134, 135, 139–45, 156, 187, 200–5, 206, 271, 314, 325

Department of Education and Science

(DES), 9, 20, 216, 217
developmental tradition, 3, 5–6, 62
disadvantaged areas
see Educational Priority Areas programmes; inner cities
discovery learning, 283–7

ecology
and classroom learning, 314–23
education
for life, 98–103
management, 209–19
see also primary education
Education Acts (1870), 12
(1902), 11
(1918), 11
(1944), 1, 3–4, 9, 15, 30, 34–6, 61, 80, 209, 210
(1964), 9
educational conservatism, 62, 78–86, 107, 134–8
Educational Priority Area programmes, 93–7, 184–6
elementary education, 1, 3–4, 8, 9–11, 12, 15, 20, 22–3, 31, 62, 104–6
Ellis, Mr, 45–50
environment
and children's learning, 246, 247, 253
equality
and education, 187–92
see also social class and education
examinations
at 11+, 8, 16, 17–18, 22–3, 47–8, 155, 166, 172

first schools, 9
further education, 34, 35, 37, 61

THE STUDY OF PRIMARY EDUCATION: A SOURCE BOOK
VOLUME 2: CURRICULUM AND TEACHING
PROBABLE CONTENTS

(iii) Aims

Who decides?
(From White, J., (1979), 'Aims and curricula: do heads and teachers have the right to decide?', *Primary Education Review*, 7)

Primary teachers' aims
(From (a) Ashton, P., (1978), 'What are primary teachers' aims?', in Richards, C., (ed.), *Education 3-13 1973-77*, Nafferton)

   (b) Ashton, P., (1981), 'Primary teachers' amiss 1969-77', in Simon, B. and Willcocks, J., (eds.), *Research and Practice in the Primary Classroom*, RKP)

(iv) Curriculum Issues

The Primary Curriculum: perennial questions and general issues
(From Richards, C., (1981), 'The primary curriculum: perennial questions and current issues', *Primary Education Review*, 12)

Continuity — goals and policies
(Dean, J., (1980), 'Continuity', in Richards, C. (ed.), *Primary Education: Issues for the Eighties*, A. and C. Black)

Within-school Continuity
(From Benyon, L., (1981), 'Curriculum continuity', *Education 3-13*, 9:2)

Continuity and Liaison: primary-secondary practices
(From Findlay, F., unpublished manuscript)

Continuity from Pre-school to Infant School
(From Cleave, S., (1982), 'Continuity from pre-school to infant school', *Educational Research*, 24.3)

Continuity and Progression
(From DES, (1983), *Science in Primary Schools*, HMSO)

Curriculum Consistency
(From Richards, C., (1982), 'Curriculum consistency', in Richards, C. (ed.), *New Directions in Primary Education*, The Falmer Press)

The Range of the Primary Curriculum
(From DES, (1978), *Primary Education in England*, HMSO)

The Problem of Match
(From DES, (1978), *Primary Education in England*, HMSO)

The Role of Assessment in Matching
(From Harlen, W., (1982), 'The role of assessment in "matching"', *Primary Education Review*, 13)

(v) Assessment, evaluation and accountability

Testing and assessment
(From Thomas, N., (1982), 'Testing and assessment', *Primary Education Review*, 13)

Assessment of Pupil Performance: an example from mathematics
(From APU, (1980), *Mathematical Development*, HMSO)

Who's afraid of evaluation?
(From MacDonald, B., (1976), 'Who's afraid of evaluation?', *Education 3-13*, 4:2)

An Accountability Model for Progressive Education
(From Elliott, J., (1979), 'Accountability, progressive education and school-based evaluation', *Education 3-13*, 7:1)

Approaches to accountability at school level
(From Becher, T. et al., (1981), *Policies for Educational Accountability*, Heinemann)
An American perspective on the evaluation of the primary curriculum
(From Eisner, E., (1974), *English Primary Schools: some observations and assessment*,
   National Association for the Education of Young Children)

(vi)   Developing the Curriculum
Curriculum policy-making
(From Garland, R., (1982), 'Curriculum policy-making in primary schools' in
   Richards, C., (ed.), *New Directions in Primary Education*, The Falmer Press)
Developing Policies for the Whole Curriculum
(From Garland, R., (1981), 'Developing policies for the whole curriculum', *School
   Organization*, 1:1)
School-based Curriculum Development
(From Richards, C., (1980), 'Brief reflections on INSET', *British Journal of
   Inservice Education*, 6:2)
How do teachers plan?
(From McCutcheon, G., (1980), 'How do elementary teachers plan? The nature of
   planning and influence on it', *The Elementary School Journal*)

(vii)   Other Aspects
Principles for record-keeping
(From Clift, P. et al., (1981), *Record-Keeping in Primary Schools*, Macmillan)
Influences on Primary School Teaching
(From Taylor, P. and Reid, W., (1973), 'Influence and Change in the Primary
   School', *Education 3-13*, 1:11)
Curricular Integration or Differentiation?
(From Dearden, R., (1976), *Problems in Primary Education*, Routledge and Kegan
   Paul)
Learning how to Learn
(From Dearden, R., (1976), *Problems in Primary Education*, Routledge and Kegan
   Paul)
Discovery Methods
(From Bantock, G., (1969), 'Discovery Methods', in Cox C. and Dyson A., (eds.),
   Black Paper Two, Critical Quarterly Society)
The Realities of Classroom Life
(From Jackson, P., (1968), *Life in Classrooms*, Holt-Reinhart and Winston)
The Hidden Curriculum in the Infants' School
(From Roberts, T., (1979), 'The hidden curriculum in the infants school', *Durham
   and Newcastle Research Review*, VIII, 47)
Messages conveyed by physical forms
(From Evans, K., (1979), 'The physical form of the school', *British Journal of
   Educational Studies*, XXVII, 1)
Aspects of the 'paracurriculum' in three primary schools
(From Cooper, I., (1982), 'The maintenance of order and use of space in primary
   school buildings', *British Journal of Sociology of Education*, 3:3)
Learning at Home and At School

(From Atkin, J. and Goode, J., (1982), 'Learning at home and at school', *Education 3-13*, 10:1)

Parents and the Curriculum

(From Hewison J. and Tizard J., (1981), 'Parental involvement and reading attainment', *British Journal of Educational Psychology*, 50, 2)

Sex-role differentiation and the hidden curriculum.

(From Clarricontes, K., (1983), 'Some aspects of the hidden curriculum and interaction in the classroom', *Primary Education Review)*

II TEACHING

Teaching styles

(From Bennett, S. et al., (1976), *Teaching Styles and Pupil Progress*, Open Books)

Exploratory and didactic teaching

(From DES, (1978), *Primary Education in England*, HMSO)

Teaching styles — an alternative typology

(From Galton, M., (1979), 'Strategies and tactics in junior school classrooms' in Richards, C., (ed.), *New Directions in Primary Education*, The Falmer Press)

Dilemmas of Schooling and Formal/Informal Teaching

(From Berlak, A. and H., (1981), *Dilemmas of Schooling*, Methuen)

A Comparison of Progressive and Non-Progressive Methods

(From Antony, W., (1979), 'Progressive learning theories' in Bernbaum, G., (ed.), *Schooling in Decline*, Methuen)

Teaching Styles and Pupils' Progress

(From Bennett, S. et al., (1976), *Teaching Styles and Pupil Progress*, Open Books)

Teaching Styles and Pupils' Progress: a re-analysis

(From Aitken, M. et al., (1981), 'Teaching styles and pupil progress: a re-analysis', *British Journal of Educational Psychology*, 51:2)

Teaching Styles and Children's Progress: results from ORACLE

(From Galton, M. and Simon, B., (eds.), (1980), *Progress and Performance in the Primary Classroom*, Routledge and Kegan Paul)

Formal or Informal Teaching: which is the more effective?

(From Gray, J. and Satterley, D., (1981), 'Formal or informal? A re-assessment of the British evidence', *British Journal of Educational Psychology*, 51:2)

Inside Primary Classrooms: a view from ORACLE

(From Simon, B., (1980), 'Inside the primary classroom', *Forum*, 22:3)

Children's Behaviour in Junior School Classrooms

(From Roydell, D., (1975), 'Pupil behaviour in junior classrooms', *British Journal of Educational Psychology*, 45:2)

Children's Early Intellectual Investigations: an observational study

(From Armstrong, M., (1980), *Closely Observed Children*, Readers and Writers Co-operative)

Open Plan Schools: results of an observational study

(From Bennett, S., et al., (1980), 'Open plan primary schools: findings and implications of a national inquiry', *Education 3-13*, 8:1)

The Effects of Streaming in the Primary School

(From Barker-Lunn, J., (1970), *Streaming in the Primary School*, NFER)

Organisational Policies of Junior Schools

(From Barker-Lunn, J., (1982), 'Junior schools and their organisational policies', *Educational Research*, 24:4)

Tasks and Social Relationships in Classrooms

(From Bossert, S., (1979), *Tasks and Social Relationships in Classrooms*, Cambridge University Press)

Towards a Revitalised Pedagogue

(From Simon, B., (1981), 'Why no pedagogy in England?', in Simon, B. and Taylor, W., (eds.), *Education in the Eighties: the central issues*, Batsford)

Teachers: their purposes and uncertainties

(From Lortie, D., (1975), *Schoolteacher*, University of Chicago Press)

III ROLES

Power and Decision-Making in the Primary School

(From Coulson, A., (1978), 'Power and decision-making in the primary school', in Richards, C., (ed.), *Power and the Curriculum*, Nafferton)

The Role of the Primary Head

(From Coulson, A., (1976), 'The role of the primary head' in Peters, R., (ed.), *The Role of the Head*, Routledge and Kegan Paul)

An Effective Headteacher

(From Waters, D., (1979), *Management and Headship in the Primary School*, Ward Lock)

The Role of the Deputy Head

(From Coulson, A. and Cox, M., (1975), 'What do deputies do?', *Education 3-13*, 3:2)

The Role of the Post-Holder and School-Based Curriculum Development

(From Campbell, J., previously unpublished paper)

Class and Specialist Teaching

(From DES, (1978), *Primary Education in England*, HMSO)

The Primary School and Its Supporting Services

(From Fitzherbert, K., (1980), 'Strategies for prevention' in Craft, M., et al. (eds.), *Linking Home and School*, Harper and Row)

Proposals for Parental Participation

(From Central Advisory Council for Education (England), 1967, *Children and their Primary Schools*, HMSO)

Family-School Relations

(From Taylor, W., (1980), 'Family, school and society', in Craft, M. et al. (eds.), *Linking Home and School*, Harper and Row)

Parental Attitudes, Right and Power

(From Becher, T., et al., (1981), *Policies for Educational Accountability*, Heinemann)

Parental Involvement in Primary Schools

(From Clift, P., (1981), 'Parental involvement in primary schools', *Primary Education Review*, 10)

Parental Participation and the Pursuit of Equity

(From Sallis, J., (1981), 'Pennies from Heaven', *Primary Education Review*, 10)

The Community School

(From Halsey, A., (ed.), (1972), *Educational Priority*, volume one, HMSO)

Parent-Community-School Relationships

(From Golby, M., (1981), 'The Primary curriculum', *Aspects of Education*, 26)